Others in Japanese Agriculture

JAPANESE SOCIETY SERIES
General Editor: Yoshio Sugimoto

Lives of Young Koreans in Japan
Yasunori Fukuoka

Globalization and Social Change in Contemporary Japan
J.S. Eades, Tom Gill and Harumi Befu

Coming Out in Japan: The Story of Satoru and Ryuta
Satoru Ito and Ryuta Yanase

Japan and Its Others:
Globalization, Difference and the Critique of Modernity
John Clammer

Hegemony of Homogeneity: An Anthropological Analysis of Nihonjinron
Harumi Befu

Foreign Migrants in Contemporary Japan
Hiroshi Komai

A Social History of Science and Technology in Contemporary Japan, Volume 1
Shigeru Nakayama

Farewell to Nippon: Japanese Lifestyle Migrants in Australia
Machiko Sato

The Peripheral Centre:
Essays on Japanese History and Civilization
Johann P. Arnason

A Genealogy of 'Japanese' Self-images
Eiji Oguma

Class Structure in Contemporary Japan
Kenji Hashimoto

An Ecological View of History
Tadao Umesao

Nationalism and Gender
Chizuko Ueno

Native Anthropology: The Japanese Challenge to Western Academic Hegemony
Takami Kuwayama

Youth Deviance in Japan: Class Reproduction of Non-Conformity
Robert Stuart Yoder

Japanese Companies: Theories and Realities
Masami Nomura and Yoshihiko Kamii

From Salvation to Spirituality: Popular Religious Movements in Modern Japan
Susumu Shimazono

The 'Big Bang' in Japanese Higher Education:
The 2004 Reforms and the Dynamics of Change
J.S. Eades, Roger Goodman and Yumiko Hada

Japanese Politics: An Introduction
Takashi Inoguchi

A Social History of Science and Technology in Contemporary Japan, Volume 2
Shigeru Nakayama

Gender and Japanese Management
Kimiko Kimoto

Philosophy of Agricultural Science: A Japanese Perspective
Osamu Soda

A Social History of Science and Technology in Contemporary Japan, Volume 3
Shigeru Nakayama and Kunio Goto

Japan's Underclass: Day Laborers and the Homeless
Hideo Aoki

A Social History of Science and Technology in Contemporary Japan, Volume 4
Shigeru Nakayama and Hitoshi Yoshioka

Scams and Sweeteners: A Sociology of Fraud
Masahiro Ogino

Toyota's Assembly Line: A View from the Factory Floor
Ryoji Ihara

Village Life in Modern Japan: An Environmental Perspective
Akira Furukawa

Social Welfare in Japan: Principles and Applications
Kojun Furukawa

Escape from Work: Freelancing Youth and the Challenge to Corporate Japan
Reiko Kosugi

Japan's Whaling: The Politics of Culture in Historical Perspective
Hiroyuki Watanabe

Gender Gymnastics: Performing and Consuming Japan's Takarazuka Revue
Leonie R. Stickland

Poverty and Social Welfare in Japan
Masami Iwata and Akihiko Nishizawa

The Modern Japanese Family: Its Rise and Fall
Chizuko Ueno

Widows of Japan: An Anthropological Perspective
Deborah McDowell Aoki

In Pursuit of the Seikatsusha:
A Genealogy of the Autonomous Citizen in Japan
Masako Amano

Demographic Change and Inequality in Japan
Sawako Shirahase

The Origins of Japanese Credentialism
Ikuo Amano

Pop Culture and the Everyday in Japan: Sociological Perspectives
Katsuya Minamida and Izumi Tsuji

Japanese Perceptions of Foreigners
Shunsuke Tanabe

Migrant Workers in Contemporary Japan:
An Institutional Perspective on Transnational Employment
Kiyoto Tanno

The Boundaries of 'the Japanese', Volume 1:
Okinawa 1868–1972 – Inclusion and Exclusion
Eiji Oguma

International Migrants in Japan: Contributions in an Era of Population Decline
Yoshitaka Ishikawa

Globalizing Japan: Striving to Engage the World
Ross Mouer

Beyond Fukushima: Toward a Post-Nuclear Society
Koichi Hasegawa

Japan's Ultra-Right
Naoto Higuchi

The Boundaries of 'the Japanese', Volume 2:
Korea, Taiwan and the Ainu 1868–1945
Eiji Oguma

Creating Subaltern Counterpublics: Korean Women
in Japan and Their Struggle for Night School
Akwi Seo

Aftermath: Fukushima and 3.11 Earthquake
Yutaka Tsujinaka and Hiroaki Inatsugu

Learning English in Japan
Takunori Terasawa

Social Stratification and Inequality Series

Inequality amid Affluence: Social Stratification in Japan
Junsuke Hara and Kazuo Seiyama

Intentional Social Change: A Rational Choice Theory
Yoshimichi Sato

Constructing Civil Society in Japan: Voices of Environmental Movements
Koichi Hasegawa

Deciphering Stratification and Inequality: Japan and Beyond
Yoshimichi Sato

Social Justice in Japan: Concepts, Theories and Paradigms
Ken-ichi Ohbuchi

Gender and Career in Japan
Atsuko Suzuki

Status and Stratification: Cultural Forms in East and Southeast Asia
Mutsuhiko Shima

Globalization, Minorities and Civil Society:
Perspectives from Asian and Western Cities
Koichi Hasegawa and Naoki Yoshihara

Fluidity of Place: Globalization and the Transformation of Urban Space
Naoki Yoshihara

Japan's New Inequality:
Intersection of Employment Reforms and Welfare Arrangements
Yoshimichi Sato and Jun Imai

Minorities and Diversity
Kunihiro Kimura

Inequality, Discrimination and Conflict in Japan:
Ways to Social Justice and Cooperation
Ken-ichi Ohbuchi and Junko Asai

Social Exclusion: Perspectives from France and Japan
Marc Humbert and Yoshimichi Sato

Global Migration and Ethnic Communities:
Studies of Asia and South America
Naoki Yoshihara

Stratification in Cultural Contexts: Cases from East and Southeast Asia
Toshiaki Kimura

Modernity and Identity in Asia Series

Globalization, Culture and Inequality in Asia
Timothy S. Scrase, Todd Miles, Joseph Holden and Scott Baum

Looking for Money:
Capitalism and Modernity in an Orang Asli Village
Alberto Gomes

Governance and Democracy in Asia
Takashi Inoguchi and Matthew Carlson

Liberalism: Its Achievements and Failures
Kazuo Seiyama

Health Inequalities in Japan: An Empirical Study of Older People
Katsunori Kondo

Others in Japanese Agriculture
Koreans, Evacuees and Migrants 1920–1950

Kenichi YASUOKA

Translated by
Teresa Castelvetere
Edited by
Karl Smith

Kyoto University Press
Kyoto

Trans Pacific Press
Melbourne

First published in Japanese by Kyoto University Press in 2014 as *Tasha tachi no nōgyō-shi: Zainichi chōsenjin, sokaisha, kaitaku nōmin, kaigai ijū.*

This English edition published in 2018 jointly by:

Kyoto University Press
69 Yoshida Konoe-cho
Sakyo-ku, Kyoto 606-8315, Japan
Telephone: +81-75-761-6182
Fax: +81-75-761-6190
Email: sales@kyoto-up.or.jp
Web: http://www.kyoto-up.or.jp

Trans Pacific Press
PO Box 164, Balwyn North
Victoria 3104, Australia
Telephone: +61-(0)3-9859-1112
Fax: +61-(0)3-8611-7989
Email: tpp.mail@gmail.com
Web: http://www.transpacificpress.com

© Kyoto University Press and Trans Pacific Press 2018.

Designed and set by Sarah Tuke, Melbourne, Australia.

Distributors

Australia and New Zealand
James Bennett Pty Ltd
Locked Bag 537
Frenchs Forest NSW 2086
Australia
Telephone: +61-(0)2-8988-5000
Fax: +61-(0)2-8988-5031
Email: info@bennett.com.au
Web: www.bennett.com.au

USA and Canada
International Specialized Book Services (ISBS)
920 NE 58th Avenue, Suite 300
Portland, Oregon 97213-3786
USA
Telephone: 1-800-944-6190
Fax: 1-503-280-8832
Email: orders@isbs.com
Web: http://www.isbs.com

Asia and the Pacific (except Japan)
Kinokuniya Company Ltd.
Head office:
3-7-10 Shimomeguro
Meguro-ku
Tokyo 153-8504
Japan
Telephone: +81-(0)3-6910-0531
Fax: +81-(0)3-6420-1362
Email: bkimp@kinokuniya.co.jp
Web: www.kinokuniya.co.jp
Asia-Pacific office:
Kinokuniya Book Stores of Singapore Pte., Ltd.
391B Orchard Road #13-06/07/08
Ngee Ann City Tower B
Singapore 238874
Telephone: +65-6276-5558
Fax: +65-6276-5570
Email: SSO@kinokuniya.co.jp

All rights reserved. No reproduction of any part of this book may take place without the written permission of Trans Pacific Press.

ISBN 978-1-925608-97-7 (hardback)

ISBN 978-1-925608-16-8 (paperback)

Front cover photo: Adapted from Photo 2.4 of this book on page 127.
Spine photo: Adapted from Photo 1.3 of this book on page 47.

Contents

Figures	viii
Tables	ix
Photos	xi
Acknowledgements	xii
Introduction	1
1 The ethnic problem in Japan's farming villages	18
2 Evacuation, return to farming and postwar settlement	90
3 Farmers' lived experience of borders from Manchuria to postwar settlement	142
4 Japanese expatriate 'others': Postwar land reform and migration	192
5 Putting down roots: Postwar administration of overseas agricultural emigration and farmers	224
Conclusion	254
Notes	268
Glossary	322
Bibliography	326
Name Index	351
Subject Index	353

Figures

1.1:	Proportion of Koreans in 'farmhand' numbers (1930)	35
1.2a:	Numbers of days off from work by a Japanese worker (Genji) in 1928	42
1.2b:	Numbers of days off from work by a Korean worker (Haruyama) in 1928	43
3.1:	Changes in government agencies related to settlement and emigration	154
C.1:	People movements and connections to land in the prewar and imperial periods	260
C.2:	Composition of postwar people movements	262

Tables

1.1:	Changes in the number of Korean farmers	20
1.2.1:	Korean population in Manchuria by occupation (end of June 1935)	28
1.2.2:	Korean population on the Japanese homeland by occupation (1930)	29
1.3:	Proportion of Koreans in the 'farmhand' population (1930)	32
1.4:	Employment period and working hours	40
1.5:	Number of Koreans employed in agriculture	56
1.6:	Korean farmer households, numbers and land area by prefecture and city (1943)	58
1.7:	Number of Koreans residing in Kyoto Prefecture	66
1.8:	Number of Koreans residing in urban areas and rural districts	66
1.9:	Occupations of Koreans in Kyoto Prefecture	67
1.10:	Number of households and size of farms run by Koreans residing in Kyoto Prefecture and engaged in agriculture, 1941–1943	68
1.11:	Distribution of Koreans engaged in agriculture in Kyoto Prefecture (September 1943)	69
1.12:	Koreans related to agriculture in Uji Police Office records Household survey by size of operations	70
1.13:	Distribution of Korean households in Uji Police Office records (September 1944)	70
1.14:	Size of holdings of Korean farmers in Terada Village (October 1944)	75
1.15:	People engaged in agriculture by hamlet, Terada Village	77
1.16:	Number of postwar Korean farmers (1946, 1955–1991)	86
2.1:	Evacuation progress (1945)	91

2.2:	Results of Agricultural Land Development Corporation Works (National)	108
2.3:	Employment situation for evacuees (3 villages on the outskirts of Tokyo), May 31 1945	112
2.4:	Number of wartime and postwar settler households in Kyoto Prefecture (end of 1952)	133
2.5:	Personal histories of postwar land reclamation settlers in Kyoto Prefecture (end of 1952)	133
3.1:	War victims, repatriates and demobilized soldiers in Kyoto Prefecture (1946)	160
3.2:	Welfare and Livelihood Stability Fund recipients (Kyoto: 1950)	161
3.3:	Place from which returned, household composition and permanent domicile of returnees living in the Takanogawa Dormitory	162
3.4:	Background of settlers in the Haradani settlement	183
5.1:	Number of Japanese postwar government-assisted overseas emigrants (1952–1991)	225
5.2:	Number of postwar farm households (1944–1968)	230
5.3:	International comparison of hourly average wages (manufacturing)	232
5.4:	Wage disparities between Japanese agriculture and industry	232
5.5:	Number of school graduates employed in agriculture (1950–1960)	233

Photos

1.1: Mori Hatsuya 'Naichi zaijū hantōjin mondai (The problems of Koreans living on the homeland)', Graduation thesis 1945.   21
1.2: Korean backboard (left) and conventional Japanese backboard (right)   34
1.3: National Farmers' Union (Zennō), Osaka Youth Division, Oretachi no nyūsu (Our News)   47
1.4: Application for Approval to Change the Cultivators of the Land 1947   80
2.1: Kishi Yamaji in his youth   96
2.2: Kishi Yamaji's Diary   118
2.3: Family photo in the house at the rear of Goma Elementary School   123
2.4: On their reclaimed land in Gomagō   127
3.1: Kyoto Railway Station circa 1935   147
3.2: Haradani Settlers' Monument   187
4.1: Conference of Absentee Landlords advertisement   205

Acknowledgements

This book is based on a partially modified translation of my original Japanese-language work published in 2014 by Kyoto University Press.

I completed my doctoral dissertation at Kyoto University in 2011, which was refereed by Professors Noda Kimio, Suehara Tatsurō and Mizuno Naoki. I am greatly indebted to Professor Noda for his supervision. The Japan Society for the Promotion of Science (JSPS) enabled me to spend the academic years of 2010–2012 at Osaka University and Dōshisha University. Professor Tomiyama Ichirō at Dōshisha kindly accepted me as a post-doctoral fellow. From 2013 to 2015, I continued my work as a researcher at the Iida City Institute of Historical Research in Nagano Prefecture, the only facility in Japan managed by a local government for local historical studies, where I learned much from Director Yoshida Nobuyuki, his staff and local residents there.

Since October 2015, I have worked as a faculty member of the Japanese Studies Course of the Graduate School of Letters at Osaka University. I am grateful to my colleagues, in particular, Professors Sugihara Tōru, Kitahara Megumi, Hirata Yumi, Unoda Shōya and Kitamura Tsuyoshi. During this project, Iijima Mariko, Matsuda Hiroko, Tokunaga Yū, Adachi Yoshihiro, Yasuko Hassall Kobayashi and Mariko Tamanoi provided helpful comments. Graduate students, Cho Seajin and So Yuna also provided me with excellent assistance. Thanks are due also to Professors Wendy Matsumura and Katsuya Hirano who offered extremely helpful advice and comments.

The translation and publication of this book was supported by a Grant-in-Aid for Publication of Scientific Research Results (Grant Number 16HP6006), provided by the Japan Society for the Promotion of Science, to which I express my sincere appreciation. Without this valuable support, my work would not find its way overseas. This book may prove to be hard to read, because I initially wrote it in Japanese historical research context. It is my hope that

Acknowledgements *xiii*

this publication is a medium for future dialogue between different academic traditions. I wish to express my gratitude to the staff of Trans Pacific Press for translating, editing and bringing this difficult book to print in a limited space of time.

Finally, I would like to thank my family – my mother and father and Mai, my partner – for their unfailing support throughout my research. While growing up, our three children, Akari, Tomo and Ren, taught me a great deal.

Yasuoka Kenichi
December 2017

Introduction

> The peasant question is the basis, the quintessence, of the national question.
>
> J. V. Stalin, 'Concerning the National Question in Yugoslavia'

Posing the question of 'others'

Rural villages as sites where migration and settlement intersect

Revolutionary changes have occurred in human migration in Asia in the latter half of the 19th century. The large volume of human movement was caused by many factors, including wars between states and political violence that rapidly escalated the disruptiveness of these movements; uneven economic development; the expansion of colonial rule; and the instability of the natural environment. Such large-scale human migration has assumed an unavoidable significance today for those of us trying to grasp a historical understanding of different regions.[1] Japan is, of course, no exception to these changes.

This book uses connections between people and the land to re-examine the processes through which modern Japanese society underwent extensive changes, with a particular focus on the Asia-Pacific War and the postwar period. In order to clarify the various forms assumed by these connections, I elucidate the connections between migration on the one hand, and agriculture and rural villages on the other. Migration, as used here, refers to human actions of border crossing in response to social conflict. Borders demarcating the territories of modern nation-states are representative, but not exclusive, examples of this. Ordinary people encounter borders drawn between cities and villages within a nation-state. The meanings invested in these borders differ depending on the ethnicity, occupation and gender of the people who confront them. Certainly, governing authorities often use violence at decisive stages to establish borders. Yet, at the same time, people's lives often traverse these borders; existing borders become unstable and new borders are drawn. Borders separate, but they are also places where different people meet. We must also recognize that sometimes people are thrown into foreign places not because they are relocated, but because the border itself moves due to the disappearance of the 'state' that once governed them. In other words, even though people who live under the jurisdiction of a nation-state stay put, borders move for reasons that have nothing to do with them.

Modern migration can be understood from two perspectives. On the one hand, there is state intervention. Modern states consider people who are under their rule as a mobile 'population' and thus as the target of their intervention.[2] On the other hand, for individuals, migration is also, in one way or another, a *voluntary proactive action* aimed at escaping a crisis close at hand in search of improved living conditions or mere survival[3] (excluding forced migrations brought about by direct violence, such as human trafficking and forced migration). The sphere of activity has remarkably expanded for people in the modern world, who are forced to sell their own labor power in an expanded and integrated market. Migration lies between the voluntary and the involuntary. Arguably, the vertical relations between states and peoples – which are mediated by the market in each respective period – are etched in the process.

Of course, migration is impacted by many factors other than relations between the state and the people. It is also conditioned by relations between the people who are moving and the inhabitants of both the places from which and towards which they move. Furthermore, the (perceived) differences between these people are deeply etched in this process. When we trace migration, we find that groups represented as a people cannot immediately be assumed to be homogenous; they are always internally diverse and contain multilayered tensions. It is therefore essential to focus on the specific nature of the relationships between migration and settlement rather than analyzing them from the perspective of slogans like 'From Settlement to Migration.' Even if the conflict inside these horizontal relationships is sometimes extremely violent, they often prove to be the starting point for attempts to find solidarity among people with diverse backgrounds and for attempts to shape new relationships. The social domain comprising this kind of duality and ambiguity must be clearly distinguished from the (vertical) relations between people and the state.

It is not sufficient, however, simply to draw distinctions. In practice, differences between people are either vertically ranked in a hierarchy or organized horizontally alongside each other as a form of variegation, depending largely on the state.[4] The figures for prewar emigration from Japan, for example, show that out of the approximately 3.40 million expatriates with no military record, as many as 2.89 million (85%) lived in former colonies or China. We therefore cannot avoid examining the ways that the state impacted these people's migration experiences.[5]

Regions become the 'sites' of these various vertical and horizontal relationships. Regions are an inevitable setting for dealing with multiple migrations and their intersections. The word 'region' here is used in the sense of people's spheres of activity and life worlds rather than a specific set of physical boundaries (because people's lives have multiple backgrounds, their spheres of activity and life worlds are also multi-layered). Similarly, when we consider people's lives in the regions, it is practically impossible to avoid studying agriculture. Historical research on migration has gained popularity in recent years, but the activity of 'agriculture' has not been given adequate treatment in this research. Meanwhile, long-standing critical historical studies which have focused on regions have also failed to recognize the cross-border nature of human mobility.[6]

For the vast majority of people living in Asia, both before and during industrialization, everyday life and 'agriculture' have been profoundly linked. This is still the case today. Agriculture offers ample opportunities for pursuing supplementary types of self-support despite the fact that the development of the market economy changed the ways people lived and worked together. Therefore, agriculture retains a social significance that is far more important than is indicated by measures of its contribution to the national economy (GDP). This book attempts to understand the lives of people who migrate and those who settle from the perspective of agriculture not only because this perspective allows us to grasp the multiple relations of people's movement but also because it pushes us to examine the universal significance of agriculture.

This book focuses on the periods during and immediately after the Asia-Pacific War. Throughout the Asia-Pacific War, Japan executed a policy of total warfare, bringing to bear its extreme dual nature. On the one hand, everything in Japanese society, including people and nature, was mobilized as 'resources'. On the other hand, things whose mobilization would have been either impossible or inefficient were excluded from the state's mobilization efforts. During and after the war, borders fluctuated in an unprecedented fashion. Actions by various nation-states fundamentally changed the framework of 'self and other'. In this book, I will trace the ways of life of Korean farmers who were, in effect, foreign laborers in this period; evacuees who moved out of the cities; 'Manchurian' settler-farmers who returned to postwar Japan; overseas emigrants who were designated as absentee landlords; and farmers who lived in Japan's postwar farming villages. I will simultaneously reconstruct these periods.

All of the groups listed above came from various backgrounds but they all occupied minority positions in farming areas. This book makes use of the category of 'others' in order to understand these different minorities connected with agriculture. The term 'others', in its most basic sense, denotes people who are not 'us'. This immediately raises the question: To whom did 'us' (= 'self') refer in modern Japan? In this respect, agriculture has supplied us with an experiential basis for a 'we'-consciousness, with its roots in the connections between people and nature. This is the basis for the regular invocation of agriculture when a modern nation-state seeks to naturalize the institutional realities of the 'nation'; in short, agriculture is invariably invoked when the nation tries to make its people imagine a shared descent. The consciousness of 'self' in Japan has been continuously shaped through its deep links with agricultural practices. This idea can be seen in the slogan 'Agriculture is the source of the nation'. Agriculture is a catchword that has shaped the bedrock of national identity. This has considerably influenced individuals' self-perceptions. *Nōhonshugi* (the idea that agriculture should form the basis of Japan's economic and social life) was a Japanese philosophical expression of this sort of wisdom. Imperial Japan, ignoring the facts of militarism and industrialization, embraced an official ideology of *nōhonshugi* and promoted it until the end. For example, we find the following in *Kokutai no Hongi* (Fundamentals of Our National Polity).

> Our people's affection for the homeland and their inclination to become one with her is exceedingly strong, and this is shown by the manner in which those engaged in farming blend and conform to the changes of the seasons.[7]

Here the relationship between the state and the people is likened to a relationship between people and nature with the mediation of agriculture. Japanese nationalism, which had made *nōhonshugi* – formularized as wisdom in this way – an indispensable component of itself, represented the state as a direct extension of the family and the village. Simultaneously, patriotism came to be equated with love of birthplace, which was in turn equated with love of the environment (we can see the strength of connections to the land – the connections of self-awareness with being in one place – by recalling how powerfully the word *yosomono*, or 'stranger', which also connects places and people in a different way – can exclude people).

Consequently, in this book, the treatment of minorities connected with agriculture as 'others' does not start from an essentialist prescription of anyone in particular; rather, it is an attempt to uncover the 'self' in modern Japan by focusing on and elucidating those sites where divisions between 'self' and 'other' waver and are reorganized in the relationships among people. I endeavor to present an image of village society as it changes from taking in 'others' – who represent new differences generated by war and colonial rule – as well as the development of the market. Put another way, I depict how people who had once been members of a 'self' came to be separated out as 'others'. Yoon Geoncha argued that 'self-awareness' is only possible in relationships with 'others' and is the source of imaginative power. He maintained that perceiving the existence of 'others' is indispensable for an awareness of history.[8] During the more than twenty years that have passed since then, there have been a large number of studies examining 'others', but one wonders about the extent to which these have objectified 'others' while ignoring questions of the nature of 'self'. It is undesirable, if not impossible, to discuss the otherness of people in a group without re-questioning the relationship between 'other' and 'self'. This question sets the stage for the formulation of the central theme of the present project. More importantly, I take the position that the nature of the hierarchy that links 'others' and 'self' reflects the character of a period, and that this can be an important clue to understanding the historical past. Using a fresh historical research perspective, I aim to present materials to inform debates over the normative question of coexistence with others.

Those marginalized by studies of 'Japanese' agriculture

The people featured in this book have lived extremely marginalized lives, even for Japanese farmers. This study abundantly references cities, which is quite unusual in histories of agriculture. Cities constitute significant borders in the lives of these men and women. These people have been marginalized not only in their everyday lives, but they have also been practically or completely overlooked in agricultural research and rural studies. In this sense, they should be regarded as having been twice marginalized.

However, their marginality in academic investigation is not because they were not worthy of consideration; rather, it was largely due to the inability of the methodological frameworks of scholarship to deal with their presence. Accordingly, I seek to redress this problem. At the same time, in order to make my research approach clear, I will refer to the history of scholarship from two angles: (1) research on 'Japanese' agricultural history and (2) periodization. Furthermore, I will refer to the relevant research separately in each chapter because its individual arguments are often wide-ranging.

Migrants and villages in modern society

Historically, there have been various trends in scholarship which takes agriculture, farming villages and farmers as its subjects. Most begin from the premise that farmers are 'traditional' and 'native'. Because of this, studies that focus on new arrivals in agriculture and farming villages are uncommon. In this work, I have explored farming villages as places that are constructed by those who settle in them. I have also presented the various currents in socio-economic history research, which focuses on the history of modern agriculture and provides the foundation of my research. As my goal is to articulate the history of relationships, I hope to make a contribution to this area of research.

Marxism has had a decisive impact upon the research framework for examining agricultural problems in Japanese historical studies.

Japanese Marxism has also long regarded villages and small farmers as 'destined to perish'. This research framework had its intellectual and political beginnings in the late 1920s, and has sprouted numerous trends since. Yet, as a whole, they commonly used 'typological methodology' as their 'weapon for criticism'. This methodology connects individual cases with 'stages' on the basis of Marxist 'stage theory'. Here decisive questions were formulated within a broad Marxist framework. How did the pre-modern mode of agricultural production ('feudal' or 'traditional') change into a 'modern', 'capitalistic' mode of production? Alternatively, how much has not changed? In asking these questions, an enormous amount of effort has been expended on ascertaining how particular Japanese cases have fitted or not into these various 'stages'.

Furthermore, this approach identified a form of dominance known as the 'landlord system' as the basis of modern Japanese capitalism. Based on this presumption, the 'landlord system' assumed a central position in defining historical stages. When postwar Japanese historiography began alongside the forceful prescriptive power of Marxism, historical research focused on identifying discontinuities in these stages – discontinuities that would 'inevitably' lead to the demise of capitalism. That is, there was a strong sense of a pending revolutionary change from the present to the future.

While Lenin (for example, in *To the Rural Poor* and *The Development of Capitalism in Russia*) had a powerful influence on this approach, there was a great investment in theoretically identifying the protagonists of the social revolution. In this regard, the class of poor peasants who had become redundant through the capitalist development of agriculture was seen as an important force, based on the assumption that they would be allied with the working class.[9] Consequently, the assumption that the peasant class would dissolve has provided the core methodological focus. Villages were seen as slowing down this fragmentation process and were considered to be 'distortions' in the modern period; from the start, there has been practically no positive position regarding the autonomy and stability of small farmers.

These assumptions started to change in the late 1960s. Subsequently, both the volume and quality of research into the history of agriculture and farming villages in Japan increased rapidly. For example, new horizons were opened up by Teruoka Shūzō and Nishida Yoshiaki through their re-discovery of the prewar research of Tanaka Sadamu (thesis of the advancement of owner and tenant-farmers)[10] and Kurihara Hakuju (thesis of the standardization of middle-scale farmers).[11] These researchers moved away from analyzing the position of the 'poor peasants' within the relations of production, in which they were supposed to be the bearers of the social revolution. Instead, they shifted their central focus to the issue of production management. They once again made advances in the productivity of small farmers the heart of analyses. Rather than calling this a move from politics to economics, we should say that it was a move towards economics coming to be understood as political.

Following this change of emphasis in analysis in the 1970s, subsequent research focused on the 'village' (*mura*). This was a landmark shift which continues to be influential today. Specifically, Saitō Hitoshi's ground-breaking 'autonomous villages thesis' argued that the organization of farmers in tenant-farmer disputes was an expression of a cooperative mechanism for supporting small farmers that was based on traditional village society.[12] From the latter half of the 1960s, there was vigorous discussion about 'community' in various areas, particularly within the government. Considerable attention was paid to the role of villages as the main protagonists in implementing new policies aimed at reducing the acreage allocated to agriculture while improving rice productivity. Against this backdrop, there was high regard for the autonomy and efficiency which villages had developed since early modern times. Villages also assumed a prominent position in the rapidly growing Japanese economy. More recent research trends show a decisive tendency to understand the processes of economic development in modern Japan in terms of the cooperative relations of the village.[13]

Following this, the time span of such historical investigations has been expanded. There have been attempts to explore commonalities within the abundant studies of agrarian society (for example, rural sociology and folklore studies), which has become the new normative framework for such research. However, an examination of recent and contemporary agrarian studies reveals a pressing need for a new framework. The prevailing framework of analysis is based on an image of farmers as static and fixed, and an image of villages that are confined within a set area; portrayals which diverge from the empirical facts. Even in the field of rural studies, with limited exceptions, there has been little interest in migration; and, even in the exceptions, the studies tend to characterize farmers as settled and unchanging. These studies, seen from today's perspective, can be criticized for ignoring the presence of 'others' in agricultural history during processes in which the persistently primitive and native 'self' changes appearance.

We have finally realized that we cannot ignore important social connections which are produced through the interactions and exchanges between a new influx of people and those already in a place.[14] Intersections between the histories of agriculture and emigration are also becoming focal points in migration studies. We see this when Sakaguchi Mitsuhiro proposes investigating the modern history of the 'village' by tracing the history of emigration.[15]

Theories of 'imperial history' and comparative history

Another point of debate concerns arguments about areas beyond the Japanese 'homeland', particularly in the colonies. In advancing my arguments, I rely heavily on studies in the socio-economic history of agriculture. One of the most important theoretical achievements in this field is the formulation of regional typology. Agricultural problems are largely constrained by conditions of natural and social geography. Consequently, it is only possible to link empirical research in individual regions to a holistic understanding by positioning each study within a regional typological structure. Critical historical studies in postwar Japan have preserved this very important orientation towards a holistic understanding.

However, it is also necessary to point out a contrary pattern that emerged from the 1960s to the 1980s. During this period, individual studies focusing on agricultural villages were refined (amidst the influence of social history and with the accumulation of increasingly sophisticated arguments) in pursuit of a more holistic understanding. At the same time, regional typological analysis tended to lose sight of the whole of Japan as an empire (and its zones of dominance) and to fail to keep in sight 'domestic' Japanese agriculture as a whole.[16]

We would do well to recall what prominent agricultural economist, Ōtsuki Masao stated during the war about agricultural problems in imperial Japan.

The history of agriculture in Japan in the Showa period [1926–1989] is a history of intricate relations between agriculture in overseas territories and that on the homeland, and, to put it plainly, it was a history of relations of rivalry. In fact, we can say that this is the fundamental origin of the agricultural problems that surfaced here and there in these years.[17]

Through its focus on people, this book takes another critical look at the intense changes that took place in Japanese villages in terms of their mutual relationships as *imperial villages*.

This approach also resonates with research trends since the 1990s to foreground an East Asian regional perspective. One influential and important current that has surfaced involves attempts to use a comparative methodology to expand the scope of analyses in keeping with the reality of empire in the Asian region. While this current did not explicitly overlap with efforts towards writing 'imperial history' in the field of 'Japanese' history, it concurred with them.[18]

If we look at the themes of symposia held by the Japanese Association of Agricultural History simply by listing the most conspicuously related items, we find particular themes have been tackled again and again: 'A comparative historical examination of postwar agrarian reform' (1996); 'Japan in Asia (I): For new developments in agricultural history' (1998); 'Japan in Asia (II): The organization of irrigation and village society' (1999); and 'The formation, development and reorganization of supply and demand structures for Japan's reliance on foreign grains' (2001).

In this context, Noda Kimio (ed.), 2003, *Senji Taiseiki (Sengo Nihon no shokuryō, nōgyō, nōson 1)* (The wartime regime period (Food supply, agriculture and villages in postwar Japan I)) (Nōrin Tōkei Kyōkai) offers a synthesis of themes in the 1990s. Socio-economic historical research examining the wartime agricultural problem found a new base in Noda's collection. The research presented here relies heavily on the empirical evidence that Noda provides. If I were to summarize the contents of this book in the terms of the research that Noda presents, I would say the book pursues answers to the question: how are we to go back and deal with the effects of 'empire' within regional history? Komagome Takeshi has already engaged in new efforts to reflect on studies of 'imperial history', an approach which has been criticized on the grounds that it ultimately preserves a Japan-centric perspective.[19] The challenge here is to take on the accumulated studies of 'imperial history' thoughtfully, while seriously reflecting on his criticisms of them in order to advance existing research. I wish to pry open regional history by drawing near to the micro-domains of Japan, as part of Asia. In so doing, I find it possible to broadly grasp the particularities and universalities of Japan and to lay a basis for re-examining the concept of the 'modern' which while being the name given to a historical period is simultaneously a value. Additionally, in order to re-visit all of this in terms of empire, I will not focus solely on relations with Asia but will also address relations with the Americas.

Redefinition of postwar and periodization

Periodization is a topic of fascination for historians. I will articulate the relationship between debates over periodization and this book's focus on a particular period. I will also elucidate the relationship between periodization debates and the problem consciousness that underpins my research. Here I will set out my own thinking concerning arguments about the total war system, which has in the past few decades raised important questions regarding period-classification.

The question of how we are to understand imperial Japan during the Asia-Pacific War, its defeat in August 1945, and the postwar period continues to be a broadly social issue that goes far beyond the research framework of historical scholarship. The breadth and significance of this historical period demands an analytical approach that goes far beyond the Marxist stage theory outlined earlier. In recent years, there has been a large accumulation of empirical work in many areas of historical scholarship concerning wartime and postwar 'Japanese' society. Examined as a whole, studies concerned with the center of empire have been progressing spectacularly. However, empirical studies examining the people in the regions, situated as part of a whole, during these periods have declined.

According to Mori Takemaro, there is a discernible tendency for postwar Japanese historical scholarship to consistently underrate the extent of the changes that occurred in the immediate postwar period (revolution, transformation, or reform?).[20] The theory of the 'total war system' had a significant impact on historical scholarship in the 1990s. Today, such arguments have become so commonplace that they can be found even in the work of scholars such as

Amemiya Shōichi, who produces historical overviews aimed at the general public. Seeing the fall of the Tōjō Cabinet in July of 1944 as a decisive turning point, Amemiya's analysis of the so-called postwar reforms distinguishes between those that were imposed by the occupation and those that resulted from a continuation of internal reforms that started during the war, and argues that defeat brought about no social change.[21] At the same time, other analysts, some of whom disagree with Amemiya on various issues, also constructed a similar myth, drawing from widespread mass media comments obsessed with the date of 15 August as a decisive breaking point. As a consequence, the arguments seeking to overturn the prevailing view have won wide support and have formed a common understanding among scholars.[22]

I am disturbed by the fact that colonial rule and war victims are given so little attention in arguments about the total war system, which emphasize continuity between the wartime and postwar periods. There will, of course, always be something that has to be excluded in order to limit the scope of a research project, and specialization ought to be respected. Nevertheless, I cannot overcome my discomfort at arguments which talk about the wartime period while rendering the victims almost an abstraction. The general tendency is that research concentrates on institutions, trends of the central government, or its planning, all of which serve to keep the relationships between the people themselves at a distance from discussions about periodization.

There are reasons why personal feelings form the basis of war-related periodization, which have concentrated around the time after the fall of the Tōjō Cabinet and have been strongly linked with the sweeping sacrifices made in the final stage of the war. Fujita Shōzō has criticized research methods that mechanically distinguish between personal feelings and knowledge. He said that 'picking out one point from the flow of what an individual is feeling, and making a fixed image of this is what constitutes the fundamental form of a concrete feeling (*jikkan*)'; and 'therefore, concrete feelings themselves contain an element of abstraction, and are not something in opposition to abstraction.'[23] In order to approach people's feelings of discontinuity in terms of their historical consciousness, it is necessary to elucidate their personal experiences and discuss how the process of abstraction unfolded.[24]

There remain, however, considerable areas of neglect within the empirical research that forms the basis for discussing continuity and discontinuity. Particularly weak is the year-long period from July 1944 until the surrender in August 1945. In the period following the fall of the Tōjō Cabinet, occasioned by the fall of Saipan, war damage and forced mobilizations within the Japanese archipelago were severe, and the contradictions in the total war system became clear. Research on the wide-ranging war victims in this period, however, is highly individual, idiosyncratic, and insufficiently based in a broad awareness of the period. Ōkado Masakatsu et al., for example, have criticized the total war system theory for over-emphasizing equalization among different classes, genders, and ethnic groups and failing to grasp the significant differentiation that occurred at the time. They proposed that the wartime period be analyzed within the context of interrelations between differentiation and equalization.[25] Of course, we must be aware that there is always an interrelation between differentiation and equalization in all periods. Ōkado et al.'s criticism, however, seems to simply present an eclectic solution which undervalues the differentiation brought about by death, the ultimate form of loss. I agree that, in the final phase of the war, there were rising demands for a 'radical' equalization among people, but this certainly was not a result of the total war system having constructed an equal society; rather, it was a response to the extremely large disparity between the prevailing ideology and lived-experience. This book will concentrate its efforts on clarifying the differences brought about through the execution of war.

A similar endeavor can be found in research that assumes that the individuality of this period is etched in the behavior of the people who lived in the spatio-temporal zones of the wartime and postwar periods. This is particularly the case in works that emphasize the postwar democratization, such as: Kitagawa Kenzō who has taken youth groups, The Association of Bereaved Families, and war widows as his subjects;[26] and Akazawa Shirō, who focused on the postwar history of the Yasukuni Shrine.[27] There are countless other activities that still remain hidden today. One of the themes of this book is exhuming people's efforts that have been buried in the frameworks used by previous research and that later generations have judged negatively as having merely 'mushroomed all over the place' or being 'ephemeral' in nature. By gauging the nature of people's logic and their mutual relations, this book attempts to formulate the framework for interpreting the surrounding periods and to scrutinize its points of divergence from and conformity with reality.[28]

Methods and organization: Nation-state theory and 'others'

This book follows in the footsteps of other critical studies, but I would like to add another point about the methodology of 'others'. As Seyla Benhabib writes, 'Every nation has its others, within and without.'[29] This approach makes the 'nation' a particular subject of inquiry. More particularly, this approach investigates what a 'nation' excludes and the way in which it addresses heterogeneity.

It is not possible to ignore the impact of nation-state theory on the development of historical research in Japan since the 1990s. It criticized the framework of previous historical research for its focus on individual countries, which had a logic of exclusion. The conventional approach proved to be implicitly restrictive in the sense that only Japanese 'nationals' were defined as 'Japanese'. Nation-state theory was highly influential, even on those who had fiercely attacked the oppressiveness of the state. According to the new perspective, the 'nation' that was supposedly in opposition to the state is also oppressive. This is a powerful critique of prevailing discourses about a 'racially homogenous nation.' It stimulated research about people who live inside the violence of assimilation and dissimilation, including *Zainichi* Koreans, 'Okinawans' and the Ainu – who were forcibly incorporated into the periphery of the Japanese 'nation', albeit in respectively different forms.

Despite these important theoretical developments, it is undeniable that research has not taken up analysis of the processes of subjectivization as a nation – the way in which the so-called 'ethnically homogenous' 'Japanese' (to put it bluntly, people who believe that they are 'normal Japanese') have fostered the notion of being members of a 'nation' in their daily interactions with this imagery. The concept of nation is invariably imagined as an internally homogenous entity, but the constituents that are bundled together as nation are always and in many ways heterogeneous. A nation is invariably in a state of flux. Consequently, whilst the concept of 'nation' is an institutional framework that is intrinsically exclusive, we must carefully examine how this concept is imagined in each time period and by each agent; it is a 'floating signifier' that points to things that are inconstant.

(Consider, for example, the brief period after 1989 when, in the countries of Eastern Europe, the word 'market' took on not only an economic meaning, but many other things too, including the end of bureaucratic control and civil freedoms.)[30] In this book, I assume the analytical framework provided by nation-state theory, with repeated emphasis on the exclusionary dimension. The problems of modern exclusion highlighted by nation-state theory have not been resolved; they should continue to be questioned. At the same time, I also refer to trends among people who are wholly invested in being members of a 'nation' as well as those who discretely attempt, while being part of a 'nation', to distance themselves from the meaning conferred by this term. This is one of the methodologies used in this book. I will advance the discussion in each chapter on the basis of individual themes, and then attempt a synthesis in the Conclusion.

Each chapter of this book is organized on the basis of the nature of how each experience came about. With the exception of Chapter 5, which focuses on the postwar period, the book focuses on the events of 1945. This is one of the methodologies of this book. Contemporary society – which remains incapable of reaching agreement about the war – is looking to historical research for answers. This book is a multifaceted attempt to clarify this time as a 'starting point'. Each chapter is independent of the others, with clear cross-referencing in the text. I have also attempted to clearly indicate connections with other contexts.

Using various documents, the primary aim of this book is to draw near to the true condition of the people who, through migration, either arrived in farming villages on the Japanese 'homeland' or were separated from them. It is practically impossible to deal independently with the members of social groups formed through specific migrations. As mentioned, the history of migrants is always a history of relationships. The history of Korean agricultural laborers is, at the same time, the history of the Japanese landlords who employ them; the independence of evacuees cannot be analyzed by ignoring relations with the existing inhabitants of farming villages; and the experiences of repatriates in their birthplaces and in urban society were indispensable to their re-formation into groups.

In order to deal with this multiplicity of relationships, I have actively used every type of source in the course of my research. This could be seen as the result of my own personal problem consciousness, in which macro historical patterns can be observed inside many microscopic matters, but this research style also derives from the fact that no one comprehensive group of documents exists that corresponds to the entirety of this book. I have used all possible sources as much as I could: starting naturally with administration documents from the national level and from towns and villages, newspapers, the accounts of farm families, individuals' diaries, and even pamphlets. Of course, not all of the documents about people who migrated have survived. At the same time, I tried to consistently direct my interest at multi-faceted descriptions of politics at various levels of society. Throughout the book there are references to activities that are expressed as social movements. This is because both the 'equivalence' and hierarchy of various groups are largely constructed via activities that seek to form connections and sever these connections.[31]

A methodology that relies on these sorts of 'fragments' is vulnerable to criticism. Some readers might find fault with the vagueness of the concepts that the study uses. I deliberately remain in this domain, though, because where everything is vague, there is more room for miscellaneous fragments to be contextualized. I have chosen this methodology because, at present, I sense theoretical possibilities in uncovering these fragments as much as possible, describing them thoroughly and then sending them back to the drawing board for theoretical processing.

In this book, I have focused on the region of Western Japan with Kyoto at its center but, in cases where I have deemed it necessary to paint a broader picture, I also comment on other regions. The following is an outline of the book's layout.

Chapter 1 deals with Koreans in farming villages on the Japanese 'homeland'. Koreans, who ceased being 'foreigners' at the time of the 1910 'annexation' of Korea, began appearing on the Japanese 'homeland' as agricultural laborers in the 1920s, becoming tenant-farmers along the way. By the final stages of the war, migration into farming villages rapidly accelerated, but in the postwar period the majority of these migrants returned home. This chapter nevertheless highlights the processes through which some migrants settled in the villages after the agrarian reforms.

Chapter 1 deals with a relatively long period of time, compared to Chapters 2 to 4, which focus on the final stages of the war and the period of postwar reform. In Chapter 2, I use a diary left behind by an individual writer, Kishi Yamaji, to look at the people who, in the final stages of the war, evacuated the cities and engaged in what the government euphemistically called 'a return to farming'. Kishi had a unique personal background: in April 1945, he used his personal connections to evacuate the capital, Tokyo for rural Kyoto; he commenced farming; and, in the postwar period – as a settler-farmer – he became a leading figure in the settler-farmers' movement.

In Chapter 3, I deal with the process by which the settler-farmers, who had gone to 'Manchukuo' (the Japanese puppet state in Manchuria) as agrarian emigrants before the war and who had returned to Japan after the war, were re-settled in various regions of the newly reconfirmed domestic 'Japan'. In addition to investigating the policy background underlying the re-settlement of the large number of returnee settler-farmers, I am also interested in two further questions: what was their status in postwar Japan, and what demands did they make on the nation?

Chapter 4 looks at the treatment of Japanese emigrants who owned land in Japan and were classified as absentee landlords under postwar agrarian reforms. I am particularly interested in the process by which their lands were purchased. While previous research on agrarian reform has focused on landlord-tenant relations, the aim of this chapter is to shine light on the transnational dimension of these reforms.

The central focus of Chapter 5 is overseas agricultural emigration policy during the 1950s. By examining the processes of prewar and postwar emigration, we can once again address the issue of individuals and groups. In doing this, I will be sketching the policies linking Manchuria settlers to postwar settlers and agricultural emigrants. I also analyze the postwar *bunson imin* (branch village) policy, which divided villages, deeming some households to be 'appropriate' and others 'surplus'. The latter were encouraged to emigrate and establish branch villages overseas. The central question for me in this context is why – despite these pressures – people did not emigrate. This type of questioning, I think, can get us closer to understanding the nature of the 'self' in postwar Japan.

The Conclusion connects the various migration processes that have been tracked in the foregoing chapters and attempts to show the underlying changes over the time periods in question. I reconsider the implications of the assertion that migration is not an individual matter, but one based in relationships. Through this approach I am able to draw conclusions about the differences between prewar and postwar Japan that have not been revealed by previous research.

1 The ethnic problem in Japan's farming villages

'But, mum, if you leave here, will there be anywhere for you to go?'
'Yeah, I could go to the farmer in Tanabe, they're about to harvest their rice. He says I can stay there until the barley sowing is over.'
'So, you're going there?'
'Yeah, it's not great that I'll only just be surviving.'

Jeong Seunbak, *Tondagawa* (Tonda River)

Links between agriculture and ethnic groups

Koreans and 'contradictions' in Japanese agriculture

In early October 1942, a number of concerned parties met at the Marunouchi Hotel in Tokyo for the 'Conference on the establishment of a new agricultural organization'. The meeting had been requested by the Agricultural Administration Bureau of the Ministry of Agriculture and Forestry, which was preparing its draft budget for the next fiscal year. Ishiguro Tadaatsu, a former Agriculture Minister, made the following comments to the participants about a recent sudden increase in the return of tenant land to land-owners:

> there has been talk for a while now about a strong inclination to restore land held by tenants because of the wage gap between agriculture and other industries, but meanwhile the tendency for *hantōjin*[1] to encroach on this land has been remarkable. How to avoid this is also a major racial issue. The *hantōjin* are largely working hard in an attempt to improve their socioeconomic standing in Japan, but what we do about this is a major issue confronting the farming villages that are the foundation of our nation. These sorts of things cannot normally be said openly, but I urge you to express your thoughts candidly in this venue.[2]

Ishiguro was still a central figure in these matters. Although he had resigned from the top post in the agricultural administration, he was Chairman of the Patriotic Agricultural Association at the time of the conference. What was this wartime 'Korean farmer problem' about which he had been harboring a sense of crisis all this time? What were these 'racial' groups of which he spoke? In this chapter, I will address these questions by explaining the following. What are the connections between the modern Japanese state's policy toward foreigners and agriculture? How did the Koreans who came to the Japanese 'homeland' establish themselves in farming villages (the Japanese colonization of Korea led to a surge in their numbers after 1920)? How did the ways in which they were present in these villages change in the postwar period, following defeat and liberation? How did the state deal with all of these issues? Clarifying these issues requires rethinking the image of Japanese agriculture and farming villages. To date, Japanese farming has been discussed on the basis of an axiomatic premise in which Japanese farmers are 'Japanese people'. While reviewing works on agricultural history, my aim will be to shed some light on wartime and postwar changes from the perspective of assumptions about the Japanese nation and agriculture.

Apart from prewar surveys and studies, there is no historical research of Japanese agriculture on the 'homeland' (Japan, excluding the colonies) from the perspective of Korean farmers, who were an ethnic minority.

Little research has examined *Zainichi* Koreans' connections with farming villages and agriculture. This includes research on wartime mobilization, such as studies of the mobilization from Korea of labor for the 'homeland' in the form of the Korea Agricultural Patriotic Service Youth Corps;[3] Tsukasaki Masayuki's examination of mobilization by the 'Self-support Corps' and 'Agricultural Work Corps' under military conscription;[4] and Ōkubo Yuri's investigation into Koreans working on the wartime expansion of agricultural land.[5] Takano Akio looked at the connections between Korean and Japanese farmers in the 1920s and 1930s in villages on the outskirts of the urban periphery and the people who undertook the lowest grade urban jobs, such as human waste management.[6] Apart from these works, though, there has not been any research about the Korean people who lived in farming villages and were directly engaged in agricultural production.

Table 1.1: Changes in the number of Korean farmers

	Employed in agriculture	Employed in forestry	Total	% of employed people
1920[a]	1,006	281	1,287	3.7
1930[b]	16,820	3,238	20,058	7.7
1940[c]	15,820	11,756	27,576	5.3

Source: Compiled by author using the 'National Census' for the respective year.
Notes: [a] From the '1920 National Census'. Refers to the numbers for whom this was the 'principal occupation'. [b] From the '1930 National Census'. 'Farming businesses'. Also includes totals for people engaged in animal husbandry and sericulture. [c] From the '1940 National Census Tables'.

Despite the paucity of research, there was a consistent increase in the number of Koreans engaged in agriculture in the Japanese homeland before the war (Table 1.1). They worked in agriculture and constituted a large proportion of the working population. We need to be clear from the outset that the fact of Koreans becoming farmers cannot be ignored. While the number of people in a group is not directly related to its social importance, in terms of numbers alone, the presence of Korean farmers was significant.[7]

This chapter also focuses on the postwar period of repatriation and the process by which Koreans established themselves in Japanese farming villages. There is an enormous body of work about *Zainichi* Koreans during this period. If we follow Suzuki Kumi's categorization of historical research, we find the following currents: 1) the Japanese government; 2) GHQ policy analysis; 3) activities by *Zainichi* Korean associations; 4) responses by the prefectures; 5) and the repatriation of laborers. Suzuki describes the local conditions at two Japanese ports from which Koreans were both dispatched and repatriated.[8] Following Suzuki's categorization, this chapter is a study of processes at the village level, but from the dual perspectives of repatriation to Korea and becoming established in Japan.

The sources for this include: pamphlets and survey reports published by the administration; the newspapers of various groups; and prefecture and village-level administrative documents. I will also refer to individuals' notes and autobiographies; in particular, Mori Hatsuya, *Naichi Zaijū Hantōjin Mondai: Nōkō Tenkan Keikō to no Kanren ni tsuite* (The problem of Koreans living on

Photograph 1.1: Mori Hatsuya 'Naichi zaijū hantōjin mondai (The problems of Korean living on the homeland)', Graduation thesis 1945 (held in the library of the Division of Natural Resource Economics in the Graduate School of Agriculture, Kyoto University).

the homeland: Links with changing agricultural trends). [9] Mori's work focused on one of my examples – Terada Village in the Kuze District of Kyoto Prefecture during the war. My objective in this chapter is to illuminate the conditions under which new contradictions emerged in Japan's farming villages, and the significance of these developments.

Foreign agricultural laborers in the modern world

Japanese colonial rule over Korea was the obvious precondition for Korean farmers establishing themselves in Japanese agriculture. Locating their actions within the context of the rise of capitalism in Asia, however, we can develop a more accurate sense of how to position this phenomenon.

The origins of Korean farmers in the 'homeland' can be traced to the middle of the 19th century, as various Asian countries 'opened' their economies to the global market. Modernization transformed relations between the state and its people, and led to agrarian reforms in several countries. Mass movements of people and capital soon followed, assuming a wide variety of forms.

There was not a uniform pattern to the development of human migration in Asia. In the case of China, it took two forms. First was a response to labor shortages in the Americas following the abolition of slavery. After the US government passed the Chinese Exclusion Act of 1882, Chinese emigration shifted destinations from the United States to Southeast Asia. Second was the migration of Han people to Manchuria, in China's northeast, an area to which migration had previously been prohibited. In Japan's case, emigration to fulfill market demands for labor had begun in the early Meiji era, but government policy had generally discouraged emigration except to colonize Hokkaido. At the same time, Japan managed to absorb a large portion of its surplus labor force, particularly young women, into its domestic spinning industry, boosting productivity and becoming the largest silk producer in the world.[10] In the case of Korea, there were largely 'scattered' forms of migration which continued in an interrupted fashion from the Joseon period's (1392–1897) restrictions on migration until Japanese colonial rule.

It is important to note that the connection between migration and agriculture is not limited to Asia or Japan but was observed throughout the world at the time of the formation of nation-states. Germany, for example, experienced a sudden increase in migrant agricultural laborers, largely from Poland, a situation that arose simultaneously with the sudden increase in emigration to the US, the absorption of its workforce into the industrial sector, the importation of cheap grains via international markets, and the critical labor shortage brought about by the capitalist development of its agrarian sector. After 1885, Prussian deportation had been implemented. Under the Colonization Law of 1886 (*Ansiedlungsgesetzgebung*), Polish landowners were forced to sell their land and the domestic colonization (*Innere Kolonisation*) of German farmers and laborers began. These were the conditions in which, in 1890, the German Social Policy Association (*Verein für Sozialpolitik*) made the problem of agricultural labor the theme of its convention, and the young sociologist, Max Weber, presented his analysis of the agricultural labor system in the Eastern Elbe region. Weber raised the question, 'To which ethnic group does the agricultural proletariat belong?' His discussion of 'the Slavification of the eastern areas of the country as a crisis for the German nation-state' indicates that this was an important issue at the time.[11]

In the United States, the system of indentured agricultural servants began to decline after Bacon's Rebellion in the 17th century. From the end of the 17th century to the mid-19th century, slavery was extensively practiced.[12] With the abolition of slavery, the connections between people and land were once again cast as an ethnic problem. With the gold rush in the west (1848), and the construction of the Transcontinental Railroad (completed 1869) the sudden increase in the numbers of foreign laborers taking advantage of developments in agriculture (fruits and cereals) became a problem. The sudden increase in the number of Japanese laborers after Chinese immigration was banned in 1882 fed into theories of 'scientific racism'. The 1920 census was the first time that the proportion of land ownership by ethnic group was recorded.[13] The immigrants and land issue, which encompassed land owned by Japanese migrant agricultural laborers, peaked between the California State Alien Land Law of 1913 and revisions to the Immigration Act 1924. This became an important social problem on the west coast of the United States. Filipinos and Mexicans arrived in increasingly large numbers to meet the demand for agricultural laborers following the prohibition of further Japanese immigration.[14]

In Germany and the United States, issues of foreign agricultural laborers were explicitly discussed in terms of a social 'crisis'. There were considerable differences between Europe and Asia in the complexity of the extensive migrations of people. In Europe, these migrations had begun before the concept of an 'ethnic group' assumed its modern meaning, while in Asia, the extensive mixing of peoples began after the new conception was well-established. Furthermore, in European countries, people flowed into the agricultural sectors because industrial laborers were organized and the power of unions restricted the employment of low wage laborers. A major difference in the Japanese case is that workers were only permitted to organize under extremely oppressive conditions and there was great demand for low wage labor in the urban industrial sector. Let us now look at actual cases in Japan and Asia throughout this period.

Absence of Chinese agricultural laborers in Japan

While this chapter primarily focuses on Korean agricultural laborers in the period from Japanese imperialism to postwar Japan, any discussion of foreign laborers must consider the issue of laborers from the largest Asian country: China (Chinese working as *oyatoi gaikokujin* (hired foreigners) in the agricultural sector are not included).[15] What was the reaction of the Japanese authorities when they temporarily permitted a 'different ethnic group' to connect to the land through the medium of 'labor'?

Of considerable importance to the so-called problem of foreign laborers is the 1899 decision 'Matters relating to residence and work by foreigners possessing freedom of residence based on treaty-like customary practice' (Imperial Ordinance 352). This decision coincided with the appearance of mixed residence. It made administrative approval a requirement for 'laborers' seeking residency. The director of prefectural government offices was given responsibility for laborers' residency applications. 'Laborers' in this edict excluded those engaged in household duties and waiting tables. The intended targets were 'laborers' in '*agriculture*, fishing, mining, civil engineering and construction, manufacturing, transportation, rickshaw pulling, stevedoring, and other odd jobs' (emphasis added). A further directive issued simultaneously by the Home Minister instructed officials that they must be vigilant in the case of 'laborers from China'; they must not allow these laborers to engage in anything other than odd jobs; and, even then, for the time being, permission was to be granted only with the Home Minister's approval.[16]

We can see the practical application of these prescriptions in official documents of the time. For example, in July 1916, a letter was sent from the Governor of Okayama Prefecture to the Home Minister seeking official approval for a 26-year-old Chinese man in Kōjo Village who sought work as an agricultural laborer. The letter explains that the young man is of docile disposition and will work honestly, and that he is not likely to be a bad influence on his fellow laborers. The response of the Police Affairs Bureau in the Ministry of Home Affairs was that it would be difficult to classify agricultural labor as an 'odd job'. Accordingly, the Police Affairs Bureau immediately drafted instructions stating that, if they were to grant approval in this instance, 'this case would inevitably induce others to travel to Japan for this purpose in future' and that 'this case would be given sufficient consideration in future. Please note that this decision must be accepted'.[17]

As this (draft) response suggests, the Japanese authorities applied different standards to different groups of agricultural migrants at that time. On the one hand, they allowed agricultural emigration – particularly to North America – and urged the United States government to allow Japanese to own land there. On the other hand, they officially permitted foreigners to establish themselves in farming villages in Japan while consistently suggesting that, 'full consideration will be given to their situation in the future'. In practice, however, Japanese authorities refused to recognize agricultural labor as falling within the scope of official policy.[18] This approach led to the complete exclusion of Chinese from the agricultural sector. (In reality, this specific request for approval suggests that the young man was already working on a farm.)[19] As a consequence of these restrictions, the 'issues of foreign laborers' in the agricultural sector on the Japanese 'mainland' became a matter specifically of Korean farmers.

Colonial rule and Koreans in Japanese farming villages

Changes in Japanese farming villages: post-WWI

Koreans appeared as agricultural laborers on the Japanese 'homeland' in the 1920s. This process was a complex outcome of two changes – namely, the transformation of Japanese agriculture and the transformation of Korean agriculture (as a result of Japanese colonial rule).

Let us begin with a simple account of the state of Japanese agriculture. The First World War had considerable impact on Japanese agriculture. Climbing wages in the industrial sector led to climbing wages in the agricultural zones on the urban periphery, forcing substantial changes in agricultural operations that relied on hired labor. During this period, the urban population was growing rapidly and new lifestyles emerged as demand for labor rose in the urban areas. Simultaneously, rural youth – including those who had until then provided the labor that tided over farming villages during the peak labor demands of farming seasons – flowed into the cities.[20]

Meanwhile, this period, known as 'the stage of collective tenant disputes', saw a sudden increase in tenant disputes in villages and a transformation of existing village landlord-tenant relations. The prevailing view is that medium-sized farmers – primarily in western Japan where there had been innovations in agricultural technology – who ran family cooperatives and who did not depend on hired labor, were focusing their activities on advances in productivity. From the end of the 19th century, farmers attempted to ensure their survival by adding the production of silk, vegetables and fruit as crops such as cotton, sweet potato and indigo declined because of competition from international markets.[21]

Emphasizing changes at the center while ignoring those taking place in the peripheries has the consequence of moving us further away from a holistic understanding even as our analysis becomes increasingly refined. In contemporary Japan, the image of agricultural laborers is predominantly one of day laborers. A century ago, however, the term referred to an extensive array of employment conditions, including: day laborers; seasonal laborers; and laborers hired by the year (*sakuotoko* (male farmhand), *sakuonna* (female farmhand)). These terms will be used as appropriate in the following discussion.

The scale of operation of Japanese agriculture has consistently declined in modern times. The number of laborers hired by the year, who once constituted the regular agricultural labor force, fell away as they were replaced with a family labor force – typical practices of small-scale farmers (*shōnō*). According to Nakamura Satoru, following a peak at the end of the 17th century, numbers continued to decline, with about one million remaining around the end of the 19th century.[22] And yet, the young children of tenant-farmers and small land-holders were hardly ever sent out to be farm hands.[23] The children of farming families could widely be seen babysitting and engaged in domestic activities until they were of conscription age. They were the so-called *toshiyatoi* (laborers hired by the year, or servants). According to Ōtsuki Masao, 'laborers hired by the year' were rarely seen in the Tōhoku region and had practically vanished from the Kansai region by the start of the First World War.[24] Around the same time, monthly wages for laborers hired by the year in Kizu, in the southern part of Kyoto Prefecture, went from 35 yen in 1913 to a peak of 80 yen in 1919, but dropped back slightly to 70 yen in 1920 (still double the 1913 wage).[25]

Furthermore, it is generally accepted that the numbers of other types of agricultural laborers also declined from this time. Also, the prevailing view is that, as Japanese agriculture developed, there was also a reduction in the numbers of farmers at the top and the bottom of rural stratification. In the midst of all this, 'laborers hired by the year' were seen as 'something outdated' that disappeared with the development of capitalism. However, what I want to argue is that although these supposedly outmoded practices disappeared from the lives and perspectives of the Japanese people, they did not cease to exist, but were instead performed by people from the colonies.

Korean agriculture, colonial administration and migration

The international context is essential to understanding what happened in colonial Korea at this time. The First World War was an important factor leading up to the Russian revolution. Japan, alongside other countries, embarked on 'The Siberian Intervention', an interventionist war against the revolutionary government. Anticipating that this military adventure would stimulate an increasing demand for food, rice merchants predicted an increased market price of rice and restricted sales in all areas. The growing discontent that followed developed into the 'Rice Riots', which became the archetype of urban disturbances in modern Japan.

Busy attempting to use the 'annexation' of Korea as a foothold for acquiring even more territory on the continent, the Japanese government used the military to suppress these riots, which posed a serious threat to its own survival. But its food policy nevertheless acquired sudden urgency, and it commenced full-scale efforts to turn its colonies into a food source. It was successful in Taiwan, where a newly developed breed of rice, *Hōraimai*, enhanced production. The *Sanmai Zōshoku Keikaku* (program to increase rice production) was also implemented in Korea.[26]

The Korean program was also successful in increasing yields of rice. But this rice was strictly intended for the mainland rice markets, leading to a 'famine export' in Korean villages. Each year, by spring, Korean villagers were starving, with some people reduced to eating grass. An exodus from the villages began. Although some of them migrated to Korean cities, huge numbers crossed the national borders into Manchuria, in northeast China. They came to be known as '*Zaiman Chōsenjin* (Koreans resident in Manchuria)'.[27]

In the late 19th century, large numbers of people in Asia left their birthplaces, undertaking arduous journeys.[28] It is common that large influxes of people stimulate secondary migratory flows of people

Table 1.2.1: Korean population in Manchuria by occupation (end of June 1935)

Occupation	Number of people
Agriculture	494,398
Stock farming	61
Fishing	41
Rice milling	1,398
Consumer finance	197
Pawn shop operator	419
Works contractor	686
Photographer	276
Retailer	10,769
Pharmacists	764
Commerce	10,826
Hotel business	2,329
Grocery store	3,642
Restaurants	3,325
Hairdressing	386
Bank employees	2,316
Officials	3,158
Teachers	1,866
Doctors	602
Notaries	142
Day laborers	33,115
Laundries	4
Other occupations	18,886
Unemployed	9,066
Non-workers	205,886
Total	804,556

Source: Compiled by author using Zai Man Nihon Taishikan, 1935, pp. 27–28.

whose goal is to take advantage of the markets created by the initial flow. The increased demand for grains to feed these masses served as a major pull factor.[29] Further stimulated by the push factor of starvation and colonial domination, large numbers of Koreans migrated into neighboring Manchuria.

The overwhelming majority of Koreans living in Manchuria were engaged in agriculture (61.4%, see Table 1.2.1). In contrast,

Table 1.2.2: Korean population on the Japanese homeland by occupation (1930)

Occupation	Number of people
Agriculture	20,058
Fisheries	1,444
Mining	16,304
Manufacturing	137,075
Commerce	26,848
Transportation	20,986
Self-employed	1,474
Domestic servants	3,368
Other work	31,372
Unemployed	159,011
Total	417,940

Source: Compiled by author using '1925 National Census'.
Note: The discrepancies in the total are consistent with the originals.

4.7% of Koreans on the Japanese mainland in 1930 were employed in agriculture (if we exclude the unemployed, the figure was 7.7% of all Koreans who were employed in Japan at the time (258,929 people); a significant proportion).[30] We can see that there are distinct differences in the manner in which Koreans established themselves in each place (see Table 1.2.2). There is no doubt that the nature of the composition of the migrant labor force, how it went about putting down roots in the areas to which it relocated, and the history of the migrants are all important. Regulation of the composition of migrant labor varied from place to place, depending upon both natural and social conditions in the host society (available land area and demand for food, for example).

From the middle of the 19th century, Manchuria was already the site of competing interests on the part of various countries. Following the 'annexation' of Korea by Japan, Koreans living in Manchuria were generally seen by Chinese people to be 'agents' of Japanese imperialism. Their presence was charged with political nuances, and they were kept under ever stricter surveillance. The issue of Koreans living in Manchuria continued to be a major theme, as is seen in a string of agreements. For example, the 1909 Gando Convention[31] was an agreement between China and Japan which determined the border between China and colonial Korea; the 'Treaty Regarding Southern Manchuria and Mongolia in the North-eastern Area' (1915) enforced recognition of the leaseholds of Koreans in Manchuria; and the 'Mitsuya Agreement' (1925) agreed that Chinese authorities would act to control so-called 'Korean malcontents'.[32]

The rising tensions culminated in the May 1930 Gando Uprising and the Wanpaoshan Incident, which originated in attempts by Chinese locals to destroy waterways used by Korean farmers living in Manchuria. Reports and false rumors about the Wanpaoshan Incident fueled uprisings in colonized Korea in 1931, particularly revenge attacks and atrocities against Chinese people. These sorts of events reveal the extreme importance of the connections between people and land throughout the various parts of Asia.[33]

Similarly, imperial Japan's 'national policy' of Manchuria settler migration should not be seen only from the perspective of the political issue of surplus population and military aims. It also had profound social and political meaning, which included 'planting' the 'Yamato race' in these areas through 'possession' of land. Unless we recognize this as 'racial expansionism', we will fail to appreciate the full significance of this policy.[34]

Intersecting transformations: Korean agricultural laborers

The intersection of transformations in 1920s Japanese agriculture with those in Korean agriculture led to changes in some regions of the Japanese mainland. For our purposes, one of the most significant of these was the appearance of Koreans as agricultural laborers, particularly *sakuotoko* (male farmhands). The 1920s had seen considerable increases in the numbers of Koreans living on the Japanese mainland. According to the census, there was more than a tenfold increase in only a decade, from 40,000 in 1920 to 420,000 in 1930.

There had been a small number of Koreans who migrated to Japan before annexation, and it is likely that some were working illegally in agriculture at that time, but I have not yet seen any documents to confirm this. Newspaper articles, though, attest to the presence of Koreans working as agricultural laborers in fruit orchards from immediately after annexation.[35]

A 1915 survey of Korean occupations, conducted by the Police Affairs Bureau in the Ministry of Home Affairs, confirms that, although extremely few, Koreans were engaged in agriculture at that time. They also appear in the statistics of a 'Fact-finding Survey of Farming Villages' in a 'Report of the Shiga Prefecture Agricultural Association' as 'Numbers of Korean day laborers'. This entry indicates that they had become an identifiable stratum.[36] We can also confirm from a 'Report of the Yamaguchi Prefecture Agricultural Association' that 'The matter of Korean day laborers' was an agenda item at a 1924 gathering of heads of agricultural associations, but the details are unclear.[37] If we look at 'The problem of Korean laborers', published by the Investigation Division in the Social Department of Osaka City that same year, it concludes that Korean laborers are inefficient as farm workers and that they have been 'a disappointment'.[38] Through these types of documents a picture begins to emerge of steadily increasing connections between Koreans and agriculture.

In 1920, there appear to have been a mere 1,287 Koreans engaged in agriculture throughout the whole of Japan.[39] By 1930, this had climbed to around 20,000 people, or 7.7% of all occupational categories for *Zainichi* Koreans. The increase in employment of Koreans in agriculture exceeded their increase in employment as a whole.

Male and female farmhands (roughly: hired by the year) make up a considerable part of these numbers: 8,661 (8,571 males and 90 females) (however, if we add all of the figures from separate statistics by administrative area, we get a slightly higher number of males: 8,598).[40] In sum, between 1920 and 1930 there was a progressive entrenchment of Korean agricultural laborers, particularly 'laborers hired by the year'.

Nationally, the total number of 'male and female farmhands' fell from around 385,000 in 1920 to around 247,000 in 1930. Koreans made up a mere 3.5% of these figures. There were significant regional differences, however. For example, there were few Koreans in the Tohoku region, where there were large numbers of laborers hired by the year. At the same time, there were large numbers of Koreans in western Japan, which experienced a rapid decline in numbers of laborers hired by the year. Hence, we need to at least

Table 1.3: *Proportion of Koreans in the 'farmhand' population (1930)*

Prefecture	Total population	Koreans	%
Hokkaido	16,633	1,256	7.6
Aomori	5,310	2	0.0
Iwate	2,885	7	0.2
Miyagi	13,285	7	0.0
Akita	13,269	1	0.0
Yamagata	15,595	1	0.0
Fukushima	7,475	12	0.0
Ibaraki	5,440	61	1.1
Tochigi	6,120	8	0.1
Gunma	5,446	17	0.3
Saitama	10,012	13	0.1
Chiba	4,573	50	1.0
Tokyo	6,269	27	0.4
Kanagawa	3,475	61	1.8
Niigata	9,700	35	0.4
Toyama	611	12	2.0
Ishikawa	384	38	9.9
Fukui	201	39	19.4
Yamanashi	2,376	240	10.1
Nagano	3,595	368	10.2
Gifu	1,406	224	15.9
Shizuoka	2,923	177	6.1
Aichi	780	219	28.1
Mie	765	96	12.5
Shiga	236	49	20.8
Kyoto	978	265	27.1
Osaka	1,762	508	28.8
Hyogo	1,855	223	12.0
Nara	1,172	472	40.3

Wakayama	992	289	29.1
Tottori	477	92	19.3
Shimane	1,015	65	6.4
Okayama	1,594	351	22.0
Hiroshima	1,246	177	14.2
Yamaguchi	2,002	638	31.9
Tokushima	1,112	27	2.4
Kagawa	1,151	24	2.1
Ehime	2,412	41	1.7
Kochi	1,619	31	1.9
Fukuoka	4,241	1,069	25.2
Saga	1,996	481	24.1
Nagasaki	2,412	87	3.6
Kumamoto	8,313	414	5.0
Oita	2,225	260	11.9
Miyazaki	5,495	27	5.0
Kagoshima	5,972	37	0.6
Okinawa	4,643	–	0.0
Total	193,448	8,598	4.4

Source: Compiled using '1930 National Census Report, Prefectures Volume'.

attempt to determine the situation in each prefecture. Furthermore, many Japanese who are hired by the year are young girls employed mainly for household chores such as child-care and laundry. Very few Korean women were employed for such tasks. The data for Koreans hired by the year do not distinguish between 'male and female farmhands'. It is particularly 'male farmhands' upon whom we are focused.

Koreans made up 4.4% of 'male farmhands'. While they were practically non-existent in the Tohoku region, they were found in large numbers in areas stretching from the northern part of Kyushu, western Japan (with the Kinki region at its heart), up to Hokkaido. The figure of 40.3% for Nara Prefecture stands out. The fact that ethnic substitution was progressing to a considerable degree is

 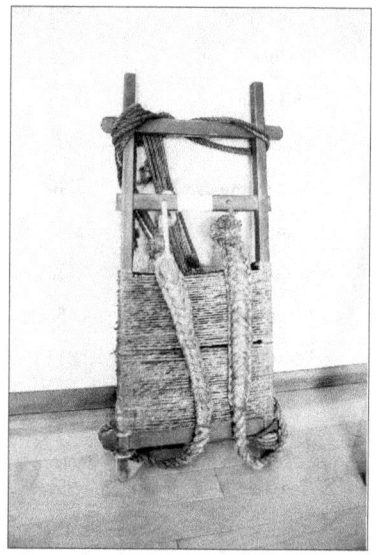

Photograph 1.2: Korean backboard (left) and conventional Japanese backboard (right) (Takamori Historical Museum, author's image)

confirmed by the figures in the Kinki region, Wakayama Prefecture (29.1%); Osaka Prefecture (28.8%), and Kyoto Prefecture (27.1%) (Table 1.3 and Figure 1.1).

This distribution reflects not only the large numbers of Koreans in these regions, but also the nature of agriculture and other opportunities for work there. Although we use the term farmers, the group that was able to make a living solely through agriculture was extremely small; we need to assume that they also engaged in alternative businesses alongside farming.[41] As we will discuss later, in northern Kyushu, there was a common pathway to agriculture from coal mining; and in Nara Prefecture, Wakayama Prefecture and the Chugoku region, the abundant forestry (mowing and charcoal making) work was agriculture-related.[42]

We must also consider the effect of the farming cycle, with its concentration of Korean labor employment to particular seasons, on the statistics we have been using. As a rule, the census and the Home Ministry Survey were conducted on the first of October and at the end of the year. But these are times when the fewest Koreans were

The ethnic problem in Japan's farming villages 35

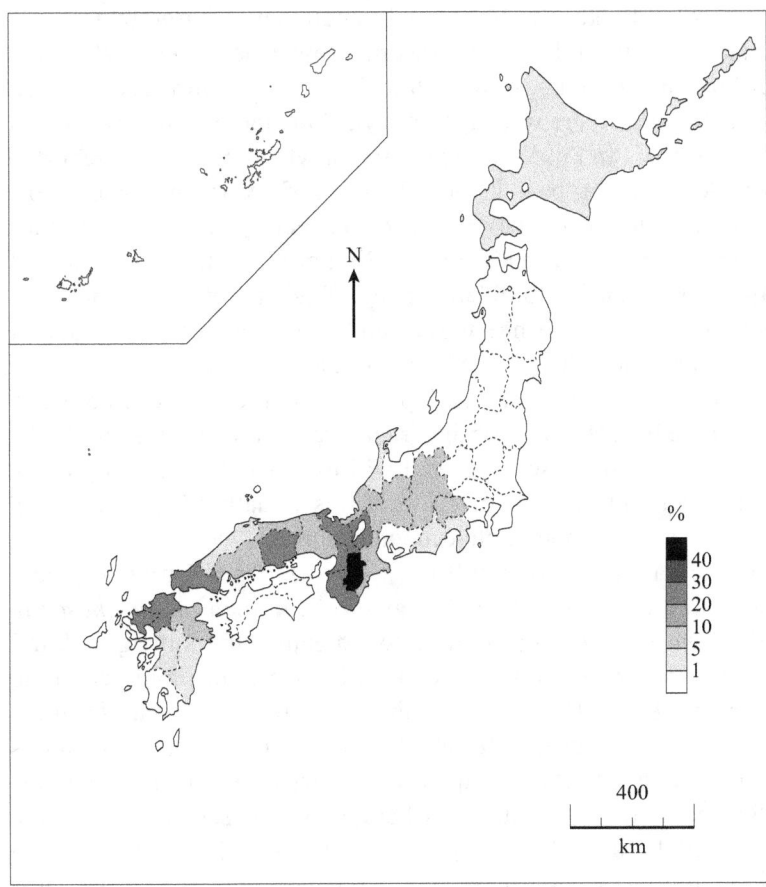

Figure 1.1: Proportion of Koreans in 'farmhand' numbers (1930)

Source: Compiled by the author using the '1930 National Census'.

employed. Many studies on the history of social policy have pointed out that large numbers of Koreans were employed in projects that were specifically aimed at reducing unemployment during winter, the slowest season for farmers. This suggests both that they moved seasonally between urban areas and farming villages and that the official data grossly misrepresented their importance to the agricultural sector.

Further evidence that a considerable number of Korean farmers were omitted from the statistics is a report by Tanaka Sadamu.

In 1943, Tanaka was contracted to conduct research by the East Asian Agricultural Research Institute. When he presented '*Sagaken Nōgyōron* (Discourse in agriculture in Saga Prefecture)', he observed that although there were apparently 5,000 laborers employed on an annual basis in Fukuoka Prefecture, only 400 households reported employing this type of laborer. This gap of several thousand people was presumably filled by Koreans (and people from isolated islands such as Ainoshima and Ōshima).[43] Similarly, a 1943 survey recorded 600 Korean agricultural laborers in Fukuoka Prefecture, but that is not nearly enough to meet the demand. This provides further support to my argument that we need to assume a figure many times higher.[44]

The following discussion looks at several examples in order to examine the state of Korean agricultural laborers in the late 1920s, in the midst of these changes. I will use two sources that provide insights into what this sort of work was actually like: *Nōka Keizai Chōsabo* (Farm household economic survey records), put together by the Faculty of Agriculture, Kyoto Imperial University, and Kawamura Wakaji's *Naichi Nōgyō Keiei ni Arawareru Chōsenjin Rōdōsha no Kenkyū* (Studies into Korean laborers in agricultural operations on the homeland).[45] The farm household economic survey, 1927–1933, has the limitation of being raw data from the original pilot surveys. Despite this, however, in addition to entries concerning the relationship between agricultural laborers and the finances of the individual households surveyed, several entries from the initial year of the survey also report on conditions in the village communities where the target farm households lived. Invaluable material is included in these descriptions, including a record of the conditions of the agricultural labor force. We can make two observations from these descriptions. First, laborers hired by the year virtually disappeared from all farming villages surveyed. Second, in those farming villages where laborers were still hired by the year they were largely immigrants from the colonies, as we saw in the census data above.

In one case, the record says of Ōta Village (Kyoto Prefecture), 'There are five or six Korean laborers hired by the year in the village, with practically no mainland Japanese, and the wages for Koreans are roughly 60% cheaper than those for mainland Japanese' (Survey Record 153). Again we see that Koreans provided a cheap labor force. Another entry about agricultural labor in the urban City of Kyoto confirms that there were also agricultural day laborers within the urban underclass. 'There are virtually no [Japanese] hired laborers; Koreans are usually employed [in this capacity]' (Survey Record 195).

Furthermore, we see many cases of Koreans establishing themselves in farming villages after working on construction sites. Construction camps (*hanba*) were generally put up only for the duration of the project and then taken down. This sometimes led to new relationships being formed. Features that stand out in the sources are: cases of residences in an agricultural village originally set-up as a railroad construction camp and works to reclaim arable land (Survey Record 155). Similar opportunities arose in 1927 for rebuilding projects following the Tango Earthquake (Survey Record 187: Goka Village).[46] We see a hybridization, as it were, of urban and farming village work.

The following case studies will illustrate the diverse avenues Koreans took into farming villages.

Case 1: Dealing with tenant-farmer disputes

In response to tenant-farmer disputes, landlords in Ajifu Village in Osaka Prefecture (present-day Settsu City) established the 'Hitotsuya Cooperative Farming Association' in 1920. The association included people directly managing rice fields of approximately 10 *chō* (9.9 ha), as well as Koreans hired as 'regular employees' (five Japanese and three Koreans). The tenant disputes in this village reportedly arose because improved transportation services to Osaka City led to a growing number of locals commuting as industrial laborers, and thus to a shortage of agricultural labor. In 1926, one option for farmers was to operate as a management improvement farm, receiving payments and guidance from Osaka Prefecture. Possibly because of this arrangement, wages for Korean 'regular employees' were considerably higher than in other regions (one yen, seventy *sen* per day in the busy farming season; and one yen, thirty *sen* in the slow season).[47] The possibility of 'regular employment' for Koreans leads me to conjecture that large numbers of Koreans were also employed temporarily as seasonal workers. This response to tenant disputes appears to be peculiar to the Kinki region, where such disputes were widespread.[48]

Case 2: Response to labor shortages on the family farm

The Farm Household Economic Survey conducted by the Ministry of Agriculture, Forestry and Fishery documents the employment of Koreans in Kyoto. It refers to a household named NK in Hōsono Village, in Survey Record 99. The family comprised two parents and a thirteen-year-old female student, who farmed 1 *chō* 8 *tan* (1.8 ha) of arable land. They faced a chronic shortage of labor and therefore employed two Koreans 'on a monthly basis'. The laborers received 15 yen per month (later reduced to 13 yen), quite a low wage for Kyoto Prefecture at that time.[49] There appears to have been a direct connection between the family and the Korean Peninsula. The records show that the household head sent a telegram to Gangwon-do in Korea on an 'employee matter' (17/5/1927). On 22 May, he went to Kyoto to meet him and hired him on a monthly basis. There are also records of him going to the post office to send the employees' monthly wages to his hometown (27/8/1927). The records also show the receipt of 'gratuities' from other farm households for the use of the Korean laborers to help with daily operations (15/5/1929), which suggests that the labor shortage was not limited to this particular farm household.

Case 3: Seasonally migrating agricultural laborers
It appears that few laborers were employed on a yearly basis in Ōkanmuri Village (Osaka Prefecture) because, although they were convenient in the short term, their labor efficiency was low. Accordingly, Koreans were employed to meet the peak demand for labor during the busy harvest season. I will quote the bookkeeper's analysis:

> Even in the suburban towns, quite a number of Korean laborers (such as construction and railway laborers) move into farming villages around November – because it is harvest time and because they dislike these other kinds of work. As a result of hardships in their previous lives they have a strong class consciousness and hostile spirit. Even though the majority possess an exceedingly low will to work and a gloomy nature, day laborers are more efficient than those hired by the year.

The wages for these harvest period laborers were 'usually 25 yen per month, 30 at the most', and they were given additional payments for meals, clothing, sleeping quarters and tobacco (Survey Record 235). This suggests that when there was demand for agricultural labor, Korean laborers preferred it to the harsh conditions on construction and railway projects. There is nothing surprising in this, considering that nearly all of the Korean laborers who came to Japan were from farming backgrounds.

Case 4: Entrepreneurial agricultural operations

There are many examples of actively seeking Korean labor for large-scale agricultural operations. This is perhaps the most typical pattern in the capitalist development of agriculture. A farm household from Kawanishi Village (Nara Prefecture) (Survey Record 309), which managed 9 *chō* (8.9 ha), employed three Japanese laborers hired by the year (two of these commuted from their own homes) and some Koreans hired by the year who lived with them. The commodity production of rice was their mainstay, but they were diversifying their operations to include fruit crops such as grapes and watermelons in order to capitalize on their proximity to an urban area. They had a management plan to convert some low-yielding sections of farmland into a mulberry plantation, selling the produce to neighboring sericulturalists. Through this process, they avoided the peak labor demand period and achieved an operation that was more compatible with hiring on an annual basis.

The source survey records describe Korean laborers as being hired by the year, but in fact, their situation was extremely fluid (see Table 1.4). They frequently quit their jobs. The proprietor would then go to Osaka, seeking mediation. He would be told that more laborers would be in Nara the following day. This suggests that the laborers' mediation network was an extensive and solid entity, but also indicates that there was a continuous and fluid supply of unemployed laborers who could immediately meet such demand.[50]

Their wages in the busy agricultural period were one yen per day and just short of 70 *sen* in the slow season. In the case of one 17-year-old Korean youth, the rate of pay was halved. Legal holidays were set at the first and fifteenth of the month and if any other rest days were taken wages would be docked accordingly. The total yearly wages for one Korean man, 'Haruyama' (every Korean employed as an agricultural laborer was given a Japanese name), who had worked all year, were 271 yen and 15 *sen*.

This operation also employed Japanese laborers on an annual basis. If we look at their wages, we see that Genji earned a total of 280 yen one year, an average of just over 23 yen per month. Considering that would get only three rest days per month, and ignoring the relative

Table 1.4: Employment period and working hours (1928–1929)

	March	April	May	June	July	August	September	October	November	December	January	February
Fukumatsu		——										
Tokumatsu		——————										
Yamamoto				————								
Haruyama		————————										
Okamoto					———							
Kaneyama				——								
Shimada				——								
Matsumoto						———						
Yamada								———				
Matsumura										————————		
Takichi	——————————————————————————————											
Genji	——————————————————————————————											
Working hours	1,655	1,480	1,622	1,920	1,564	1,099	902	1,077	993	915	925	905
Day hire work	245	102	166	505	737	662	243	281	652	312	42	21

Source: Compiled by author using Farm Household Economic Survey, no. 309, Kyoto Teikoku Daigaku Norin Keizaigaku Kenkyushitsu, 2006.
Note: Workers from Fukumatsu to Matsumura are Koreans, while Takichi and Genji are Japanese.

weight of the work, his conditions seems much the same if not worse than Haruyama's. It appears, though, that Genji took more days off due to village events and family obligations. Figures 1.2a and 1.2b provide data about the rest days taken by Japanese and Korean annual laborers respectively. They help to illustrate the differences in the rest days taken by Haruyama (the Korean) and Genji.

In 1928, Takichi, a Japanese laborer hired by the year, had 76.5 days off, while his Korean counterpart, Haruyama, had 45.8. Even though they are recorded under the same category of 'hired by the year' and received roughly the same total annual wages, there are significant differences in the two men's working patterns. Koreans were clearly working more for roughly the same income.

These sources do not indicate whether or not this differential treatment was an intentional labor management practice. An early 19th century study documents landlords' attitudes to labor management in this region. Tokunaga Mitsutoshi's research clearly shows that increasing labor efficiency was already a management concern as early as 1823. Yamamoto Kisaburō's *All the Yamamoto Farming Family's Shortcuts* (1823) points out that if employees are sent to cut grass on their own there is a notable decline in the 'quality' of labor as a result of loitering, afternoon naps and such things. The measures suggested to address this include imposing quotas on each worker and mixing some day laborers in among the others to stimulate competition.[51] This promotion of competition by mixing in people working under different employment conditions was commonly practiced by the landlords of this region. A similar strategy on plantations was to employ people from several different ethnic groups.

Also, as we see in the next case in northern Kyushu, labor shortages were a region-wide problem. In cases where laborers hired by the year were operationally essential,[52] another strategy was developed to meet this need: the agricultural trainee system.

Case 5: 'Agricultural trainee' system

The use of Korean laborers hired by the year also spread to the northern region of Kyushu. Details of the 'agricultural trainee system' which was developed in this region are primarily from the *Fukuoka Chihō Shokugyō Shōkai Jimusho* (Fukuoka area's Labor Exchange Office) 1928 publication, 'Conditions of Japanese and Koreans in Agriculture and Quarrying'.

42   Others in Japanese Agriculture

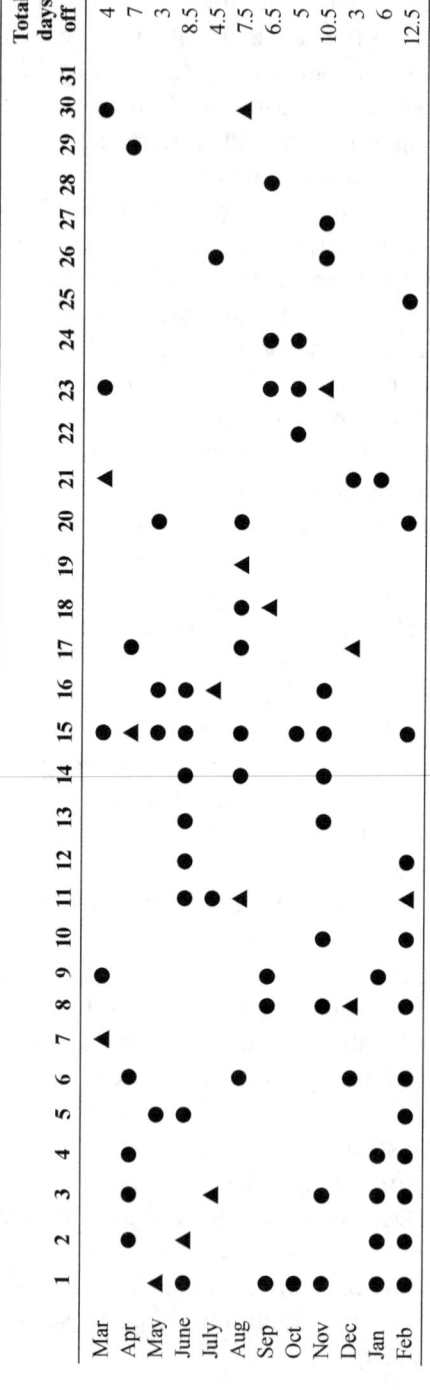

Figure 1.2a: Numbers of days off from work by a Japanese worker (Genji) in 1928

Source: Farm Household Economic Survey, no. 309, Kyoto Teikoku Daigaku Norin Keizaigaku Kenkyushitsu, 2006
Notes: ● = full day off; ▲ = half day off

The ethnic problem in Japan's farming villages 43

	1	2	3	4	5	6	7	8	9	10	11	12	13	14	15	16	17	18	19	20	21	22	23	24	25	26	27	28	29	30	31	Total days off
Mar	●						▲								●			▲			▲											35
Apr	●		▲																										▲			3
May	●				●										●																	3
June	●			▲											●																	2
July	●			●				▲							●								▲									55
Aug	●										▲								▲				▲							▲		35
Sep	●														●	▲		▲							▲							35
Oct	●			▲											●								▲									25
Nov	●					●	●			●				▲	●	●																7
Dec	●							●			▲				●							▲						▲				25
Jan	●	●	●												●	●																53
Feb	●	●													●																	45

Figure 1.2b: Numbers of days off from work by a Korean worker (Haruyama) in 1928

Source: Farm Household Economic Survey, no. 309, Kyoto Teikoku Daigaku Norin Keizaigaku Kenkyushitsu, 2006.
Notes: ● = full day off; ▲ = half day off

In the Kamoto District of Kumamoto Prefecture, only wealthy proprietors could afford to employ labor in the lean times following the First World War. Increases in the daily wages of 'laborers hired by the year' as well as those employed only during the peak seasons (May planting and September harvesting) led to extensive agriculture in this area.[53] Developments here differed from the Kinki region, where family management type farming was adopted relatively smoothly. In response to the steep wage rises for Japanese agricultural laborers, the Kamoto District Agricultural Association, in coordination with the office of the Governor-General of Korea, sought to employ Korean laborers on a yearly basis for farm work. An important factor here seems to have been that district farmers were able to employ Koreans working on construction projects and living in construction camps on the outskirts of urban areas as seasonal laborers during peak farming periods, which produced 'favorable operational results'.[54]

Koreans were employed under 'Annual Hire Employment Contracts' following negotiations between the Kamoto District Agricultural Association and the Social Division of the Internal Affairs Bureau in the Office of the Governor-General of Korea. Their wages of 60–100 yen per annum were significantly less than those paid to their Japanese counterparts – which were around two yen per day (including meals) for young men and one yen twenty *sen* for women. They were also considerably less than the wages for the other Korean agricultural laborers discussed thus far.[55] Even worse, these very meager wages were withheld, under the pretext of enforced savings which would be paid to them upon their return home. They received less than one yen per month of 'pocket money' that they were free to spend.[56]

Their employment conditions stated that, 'Korean applicants who were farmers and had the strong wish to leave could use their capital and yearly savings from their time on the mainland to buy farming and sericulture equipment upon their return to Korea to immediately start farming based on the management experiences learnt on farms in Kamoto District'. If we take this literally, we might conclude that their stay in Japanese farming villages was intended to be limited to the period of their employment, and that this employment was regarded as training aimed at producing 'key figures' for Korean agriculture.[57] When the farming villages' requests for extending the periods of employment were granted, it appears that the Governor-General's objective of training 'village mainstays' was compromised in favor of the agricultural associations' desires for a cheap and stable workforce. These contracts also stipulated that the workers' 'treatment shall be entirely as one of the family'. Comparisons of the actual treatment of these workers and their Japanese contemporaries would provide valuable insights.[58]

The main point here is to highlight a trend for farmers who depended on a hired workforce in the northern Kyushu region in the 1920s to employ Korean laborers as a cheap and stable workforce, and that the government was more than cooperative in facilitating their demands. When the newspapers reported on this trainee initiative, enquiries poured in from every part of the prefecture.[59]

Alongside these official programs for cheap Korean labor, we find indicators also of a black-market, as in the case of nine people who were arrested in Ōita Prefecture for the unauthorized recruitment, supervision and employment of Koreans on their own farms and others.[60] These ordinary farmers had extended their interests to become labor brokers. Further research into the labor processes of farming operations is required. For now, suffice to say that there is little doubt that large numbers of Koreans were employed as agricultural laborers in Japan's farming villages.

Furthermore, there are also cases, albeit exceptional, of Koreans organizing revolutionary movements to resist their marginalization and struggle for liberation.[61] Recognition of an ethnic aspect to the issue of agricultural laborers surely suggests scope for further examination of the contemporary 'left-wing' farmers' movement and its organization of agricultural laborers.

Systems in farming villages for procuring agricultural laborers gave rise to what could be called traditional forms of migratory labor. These included cases of bringing in groups from outside the village, a practice that had existed in diverse forms since before the modern period. It could be that links existed between these traditional forms of procuring a workforce and urban underclass laborers from the colonies – a group formed after the acquisition of colonial possessions – and, in some cases, local areas in the colonies.

The people who managed to establish themselves in Japanese farming villages in this pioneering way during this period went on to play central roles in the transformation of Korean farmers into tenant-farmers.

Japan's 'Grapes of Wrath': farmers and the 'ethnic problem'

The spread of Korean agricultural laborers was not generally regarded as a social problem in farming villages at the time. Some agricultural economists in the 1920s seem to have understood, as village registries became more widely known, that these documents contained entries about Korean agricultural laborers. It was not until the late 1930s, however, after the Sino–Japanese War was in full swing, that the presence of Koreans came to be more generally seen as an issue that should be investigated by the state.

This is not to say that no one had treated it as a 'social' issue. The farmers' struggle, with its aims of social revolution, recognized the presence of these subordinate laborers from the colonies. In the early 1930s, fruit and vegetable gardens had blossomed on the outskirts of the ever-expanding urban consumer markets, and it was obvious that the laborers were poorly paid. The severity of the situation varied widely from region to region, though and, consequently, there were regional differences in its problematization. Let us examine the case of Katashimo Village in Osaka Prefecture, where the production of grapevines was a burgeoning industry on the urban periphery.

According to 'On the Organization of Agricultural Laborers in Osaka', a report by the Farmers' Union (which repeatedly split over which path to be taken), grape pickers in Katashimo Village could be classified into poor farming families, unemployed and Koreans at a ratio of 6:3:1. The report's analysis was that, 'The Koreans' wages are approximately 40 or 50 *sen*, meaning that they are being exploited. Those with the ability to organize come from the poor farmers group, who are militant and demand land... [T]he unemployed and Koreans have no ability to organize, but they are asking for increased wages'.[62] Because grape picking is labor-intensive and restricted to a short season, it has engaged large numbers of foreign laborers in many countries.

Let us look at the issues raised by leaflets distributed in Osaka about *Zenkoku Nōmin Kumiai*, or *Zennō* (National Farmers' Union).

> Hurrah for the enhanced unity of Katashimo farmers! Wake up you proletarians working in the farming villages. The bosses call you (proletarians) '*Otokoshi* (derogatory expression) laborers'! You should stand up!

The ethnic problem in Japan's farming villages 47

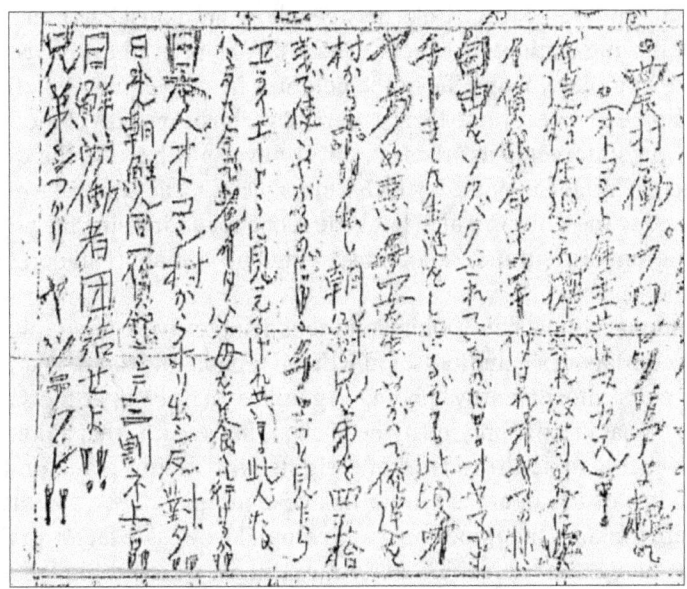

Photo 1.3: National Farmers' Union (Zennō), Osaka Youth Division, *Oretachi no nyūsu* (Our News) *(excerpt) (Hōsei University, The Ōhara Institute for Social Research Archives)*

There is no one more abused than us, made to work for a pittance and deprived of our liberty, like *oyama* [prostitutes]! Even *oyama* have a better life than us. Recently, the wicked officials have become cunning and are throwing us out of the village and using our Korean brothers and paying them 45 *sen*. It looks like a good deal! However, how can one care for one's elderly parents with such a pittance! Stand up against the removal of Japanese *Otokoshi* from the village! Pay Japanese and Koreans equal wages and give us all 30% raises! Japanese and Korean laborers unite! Brothers, stand and fight together! Organize demonstrations in other villages and fight against those bastards. No to the dismissals at the end of the year! Japanese and Korean laborers unite![63]

The author does not appear to have been well educated or trained as an organizer, but he concisely expresses the problems of agricultural laborers of the time. Above all, he clearly expresses his indignation

(Photograph 1.3). Strong links between the Communist Party and the far-left wing National Farmers' Union can be seen in the concerns of the exploited people from the colonies in this leaflet. An effort was made to reflect these local experiences in national revolutionary mission statements as 'theses', but it never got beyond the draft stage.[64] The slogan of the leftist Farmers' Union was *'Tochi o Nōmin e* (Land to the Tiller)', which left little scope for addressing the plight of migrant agricultural laborers seeking appropriate remuneration for their labor.

Other accounts have pointed out that disputes were breaking out between Japanese landlords and Korean tenants in Korea, and that a farmers' movement was being organized in Taiwan at the same time. What has not previously been clear, however, is that agitation for Korean agriculture workers' rights was taking place on the outskirts of urban areas on the Japanese mainland. We also have underestimated the importance of 'colonial rule' as a factor in this movement.[65] These revolutionary movements were prohibited and were brought to an end but, as will be discussed later, the important relationships that developed during this period carried over into the postwar period. There is scope for much further research into the social relationships surrounding the formation of nationalist Japanese (*Nihonshugi*) agrarian movements in the 1930s.

The Second Sino–Japanese War and Korean agricultural laborers

As the Sino–Japanese War escalated to total war in 1937, national administrators were faced with severe labor shortages. One of the possibilities that they canvassed was the mass introduction of Korean labor, under the provisions for wartime mobilization. The 1938 '*Nissi Jihenka Nōsan Gyoson Seisanryoku Jittai Chōsa Hōkoku* (Report of a Factual Investigation into Conditions in Rural Districts under the Second Sino–Japanese War)' by *Kikakuin Sangyōbu* (Industrial Division of the Cabinet Planning Board) is what would today be called a feasibility study. This survey was undertaken on the understanding that 'The issues of the mechanization of agriculture, Korean agricultural laborers, labor service and the regulation of agricultural labor migration are serious and urgent' problems. The thinking behind this report is evident at the beginning of the section dealing specifically with Korean agricultural laborers, which points out that Germany had managed to avoid total economic collapse during the First World War as a result of 7–800,000 foreign laborers.[66]

The labor shortage had already been recognized as a problem in Fukuoka Prefecture immediately after the Sino–Japanese War escalated. In September 1937, its 'ability to supply laborers' was around 32,900 but, by May 1938, it had fallen to around 8,500 people (a total of 235 of 296 towns and villages replied). When employment conditions, such as respondents' distance from places of employment, were taken into account, the potential for increasing the labor supply would have been 50% of the September 1938 and 40% of the 1937 figures.[67]

The participation of Koreans in agriculture increased in response. According to the Police Affairs Bureau in the Ministry of Home Affairs, statistically, there was a reduction in Koreans living in rural (farming) districts between June and December 1937.[68] However, the Industrial Division's report mentioned above points out that apart from owner-farmers, tenant-farmers and farmhands (farm employees) who were 'clearly engaged in agriculture', there was a 'considerable increase in the number' of people 'engaged in agricultural work in the busy harvest season, such as a variety of day laborers and second-hand dealers'. The report then says that 'we should, in fact, conclude that the use of Koreans increased considerably as a result of the influence of the war, at least during the busy harvest period'.[69] This, once again, suggests that there were more Koreans engaged in agriculture than we find in the statistics.

The Industrial Division report mentioned above was based on a survey of Onga District in Fukuoka Prefecture, where a young Korean had been taken in as an 'agricultural trainee' from a facility known as Shōwa House in Yamaguchi Prefecture. Someone affiliated with the Agricultural Association had informed the investigators that 'without Koreans, agriculture in Onga District will be wiped out'.[70] The report suggests that reliance on Japanese labor meant 'extreme difficulties and high wages', suggesting that the problem was not simply one of wages but also the overall quality of work.[71]

In Onga District the average size of cultivated holdings was particularly large. In Onga Village, where farm managers farmed more than 2 *chō* (1.9 ha), of the 180–220 laborers hired by the year, 45 were Koreans.[72] The trend in this village was:

On the homeland, young men in their prime leave home to work in or commute to factories and mines, and their wives are the one's primarily responsible for any agricultural work. Thus, the trend for having laborers hired by the year and temporary laborers is striking compared to other areas, and these annual and temporary laborers are increasingly being replaced by Korean laborers.[73]

As we have seen, in the Kamoto District of Kumamoto Prefecture (Case 5, above), the problem had primarily impacted middle-sized farms relying on employed labor. In this case, however, the problem was affecting family-managed farms. In general, as young women replaced men as the primary agricultural workforce, and as ever fewer laborers were hired by the year, increasing numbers of Koreans were hired to replace them. Furthermore, in the face of increasingly severe labor shortages, farmers displayed a clear preference for employment on an annual basis as a way of securing a reliable workforce, and Korean laborers were more likely to accept these conditions.

However, this survey failed to make any predictions about the future potential of mobilizing Koreans as an agricultural workforce under the wartime agricultural administration. Its summary makes no reference to importing more Korean laborers. It simply proposes moving towards an agricultural labor service, curtailing mobilization for factories, and increasing mechanization.[74] The administration attempted to facilitate the 'feminization' of the agricultural workforce by proposing village crèches and communal kitchens. All of this suggests that despite a clear understanding of the severity of the labor shortages, the authorities remained determined to control the number of Koreans in agriculture. We can see this in another case from this period, when the landlords in a region of Hyogo Prefecture repeatedly sought permission to recruit tenant-farmers directly from the Korean Peninsula, and the authorities repeatedly refused to give their approval.[75]

The mobilization of Koreans for forced labor, principally in the mining sector via the so-called 'recruitment' system, began the following year. It is important to note that the importation of an agricultural labor force was one of the options considered but ultimately rejected at this time.[76] Instead, Korean migration continued to be directed towards the northern part of Korea and the north-eastern part of China,[77] as the administration balanced policy requests from the entirety of imperial Japan, which was also attempting to deploy large numbers of Japanese agricultural emigrants. The restricted policy-based introduction of Korean agricultural laborers then carried over to the post-1941 'Agricultural Patriotic Service Youth Corps' system, whose role was limited to meeting demand for the peak farming periods. The next section examines the logic of an agricultural administration which evades the growing contribution of Korean labor in agriculture.

Koreans' transition to agriculture

Wartime agricultural policy and the Korean farmers' issue

The agricultural administration, which had been developed in the 1930s with the primary aim of overcoming the Depression, shifted its focus to prosecuting the second Sino–Japanese War. As production shifted completely towards heavy chemical and defense industries, Japan suffered severe labor shortages as well as a prolonged drought, which hit western Japan and Korea in 1939. Against this background, the agricultural administration turned its attention to practical problems such as 'measures to increase the production of food supplies', 'measures to deal with labor shortages' and 'agricultural land measures'. As the war front expanded, the impact of labor shortages extended beyond the usual labor areas and began to affect military strength. This prompted concerns about promoting and ensuring adequate population growth to meet the needs of the whole empire ('Plan for Establishing Population Measures', Cabinet decision 22/1/1941). To date, historical research on the 'Movement to Establish Imperial Farming Villages' has tended to focus primarily on measures to increase the output of food supplies and debates over the optimal size for agricultural production. We need to keep in mind that concerns about the population of the whole empire flowed into the agricultural sector as an ethnic problem.[78]

The policy outlined in 'The Matter of Establishing Imperial Farming Villages' – a cabinet decision taken in November 1942 – was to 'rely on the fundamental goals of the population and ethnic policies accompanying the building of a Greater East Asia'. As such it aimed at 'establishing imperial farming villages that are truly suitable as places for preserving and fostering agriculture and farmers of the empire'. The aim was to secure a proportion of the population of imperial farming villages as 'sources for fostering the Yamato race and also for strengthening self-sufficiency in food'.[79] I would also like to draw attention to the fact that in between the 'Plan for Establishing Population Measures' and 'The Matter of Establishing Imperial Farming Villages' the cabinet decision 'Policy Regarding the Use of Korean Laborers' was taken, on 13 February 1942. This decision marked the start of a policy of 'mediation by the bureaucracy' in the progressively expanding mobilization of Koreans as a means to address labor shortages on the mainland.[80] The cabinet decision containing this 'policy' led to repealing the 1934 'The Matter of Measures Regarding the Immigration of Koreans', which had suppressed Korean migration to the mainland. At the same time, as well as increasing food supplies, villages were explicitly tasked with being *the source of the nation*, i.e., the 'Yamato race'. At this point, the government's approach to the population problem had clearly changed.

Let us refer back to the quote in the first section of this chapter. As mentioned, Ishiguro was speaking at the 'Conference on the establishment of a new agricultural organization', which was held immediately before the cabinet decided 'The Matter of Establishing Imperial Farming Villages'. The former Minister of Agriculture, bureaucrats and other relevant parties were present at the conference. Ishiguro began by identifying two issues that needed consideration regarding the establishment of owner-farmers. The first was the likelihood that tenant-farmers would lose agricultural land due to the landlords' withdrawal of tenant lands. The other was the question of who would be in charge of this increased amount of available tenant land as it was returned to the landlords. Ishiguro's remarks, quoted at the beginning of this chapter, were made at this point in the discussion.[81]

Ishii Einosuke, Head of the Agricultural Administration Bureau responds in the following manner to Ishiguro's posing of these problems. (Note: like *hantōjin*, *senjin* is also a pejorative term for Koreans).

> The *hantōjin* problem is currently being secretly investigated, but this trend appears to be particularly striking in Ōita, Yamaguchi, Hiroshima, Fukuoka and Hokkaido... This trend must be checked by taking measures in the system, but as there is no reason to bring the matter of *senjin* to the fore, I think that we need to seek to avoid

this by spreading the net more widely. Thinking about this is still not complete, but one proposal that is being considered is the idea of requiring approval, when giving land to tenants, if the tenants are people other than current local cultivators. I think that something like a plan to prevent the abandonment of planted land should suffice. Labor could then be supplied for the portion of planted land that is abandoned by groups such as the Patriotic Agricultural Association.[82]

At the following year's conference, Ishiguro states even more clearly that, 'I have spoken about the flow of Koreans in the past, but this is an extremely delicate issue because *the use of this land has become connected with rule*' (emphasis added).[83] What is clear from these exchanges is that the agricultural administration was divided about Koreans becoming established in farming villages. Three points stand out. First, the Korean presence was seen as a major problem 'in ethnic terms'. Second, the authorities wanted to exclude Koreans from farming villages, but could not say so publicly, given the façade of the imperial slogan '*Naisen Ittai* (Japan and Korea as one body)',[84] and thus found ways of excluding them under another name through administrative procedures. And, third, the labor shortages this caused were to be covered up by various means, such as the activities of the Patriotic Agricultural Association. 'Securing the population of farming villages' was pursued with the exclusion of Korean farmers (the 'ethnic issue') as a hidden agenda. This agenda permeated the agricultural administration at that time.

This is clear from an exchange at this conference. When a participant asked: 'I think that maintaining both levels of food self-sufficiency and steady population levels are not necessarily compatible; so what would happen in cases where they are not?' Ishiguro replied, 'I would, ultimately, consider population levels to be paramount'.[85] Furthermore, because of the difficulty of achieving the target of 40% of the total population allocated solely for homeland farming villages, the policy aim, for the present, has been the maintenance of Japanese farmers as an ethnic group, using regions of 'Japan, Manchuria and Korea'. Importantly, Ishiguro – who had already foreseen that the war situation would deteriorate – was skeptical about whether or not emigrants would become bearers of that kind of ethnic base. In short, he thought that no matter how far one went one should defend to the last the character of homeland farming villages as the source of the nation.[86]

To foreshadow the conclusion of this section, contrary to these intentions on the part of the agricultural administrators, the number of Koreans who became tenant-farmers in farming villages in the final stages of the war increased.

From agricultural laborers to tenant-farmers

The appearance of Korean tenant-farmers in farming villages had been noted in the Agricultural Economics Society of Japan since 1938, but full-scale national surveys by the Agricultural Administration Bureau only began in 1942.[87] Ishiguro probably got his figures from these surveys. In this section, I will outline changing trends in Korean farmer numbers in the period leading up to the war, using Ministry of Home Affairs statistics. After that, I will examine wartime trends of Koreans converting to agriculture. For this, I will use the Agricultural Administration Bureau's assessment of national trends in 1943, '*Saikin ni okeru Naichi Zaijū Hantōjin no Nōkō e no Tenkan Keikō* (The recent trend for Koreans living in mainland Japan to convert to agriculture)'.

Let us look once again at employment trends in agriculture leading up to the final stage of the war. The Ministry of Home Affairs statistics presented in Table 1.5 differ significantly from the national census statistics due to different survey methods. The national census relies on survey respondents by region, while the Ministry of Home Affairs statistics use household data collected by police. The Ministry's data, which are based on the residents' self-assessments in a region, appear to be more accurate, and better suited to verifying trends because, unlike the census, the data is classified by class and available by specific years.

The employment workforce made up by farmers fell for a few years from 1930, possibly due to the effects of the global depression, but recovered from 1933. It is at this point that the trend towards the creation of tenant-farmers began. Then, with the full-scale eruption of the Sino–Japanese War in 1939, figures for tenants and farmhands reversed for the first time. A clear difference compared to previous Japanese agricultural laborers is that the transition from hired agricultural laborer to tenant-farmers occurred in the space of one generation. (Of course, transition to becoming tenants was not the sole path taken. Large numbers have flowed into other industries. In Fukuoka and Yamaguchi Prefectures, in particular, the war brought about an overall decline in the number of agricultural laborers.)[88] Even after this time, a conspicuous trend towards the creation of tenants remained.

The Ministry of Agriculture and Forestry survey conducted in 1943 is an excellent source, showing class divisions (such as owner-farmers and tenants), as well as the areas under cultivation.

For this survey, the Agricultural Administration Bureau relied on the government offices connected with tenants in each prefecture to collect data on five items:
1. the recent trend for Koreans living on the mainland to convert to farming
2. the numbers of Koreans and Korean households living in the prefecture
3. the number of resident Korean households connected with farming, the size of the relevant area, and the household's classification (owner-farmers, tenant-farmers, and people engaged in agricultural work)
4. the distribution, by region, of resident Koreans connected with farming
5. the responses of the relevant authorities to resident Koreans.

The survey results have been compiled into Table 1.6. The following points emerge from this data.

First, there was a sudden increase in tenant-farmers during the war. Following the 1920s, tenant-farmers in farming villages, initially small proprietors who owned their own house and general agricultural materials, accumulated assets over a long period despite the harsh conditions. Tenant-farmers had thus been able to establish themselves in farming villages, but as the war escalated, this process accelerated. Their numbers increased, from 12,456 in 1942, to 20,807 (a little over 8,000 households) in 1943.

The total area of land that they cultivated appears to have exceeded 6,000 *chō* (5,940 ha), but this is not entirely clear. Yet, they hardly ever became landowners. And of the 1,156 *chō* (1,146 ha) held by landowners, 1,082 *chō* (1,073 ha) (93.4%) were in Hokkaido.

Korean farmers had diverse experiences, but the administration had no overall understanding of them. In fact, officials in 24 prefectures reported no trend towards farming. These figures, however, are not very meaningful because of the lack of any unified basis for determining what constituted a trend towards farming. The determination was, in effect, entrusted to the arbitrary judgment

Table 1.5: Number of Koreans employed in agriculture (from a Ministry of Home Affairs survey)

Fiscal year	Agriculture-related areas[a]				Total number of employed people[b]	Overall total	Remarks
	Owner farmer	Tenant farmer	Farmhand	Total			
1915				110	3,877	4,075	End of December
1917				107	13,931	14,502	End of December
1920				357	30,302	31,720	End of December
1921				415	29,845	32,274	End of June
1925				1,697	112,516	136,709	End of June
1926				1,427	124,254	148,015	End of June
1927				2,317	132,658	165,286	End of June
1929				3,060	214,912	271,280	End of June
1930				1,725	213,064	287,705	End of June
1931				1,635	198,736	311,247	End of December
1932				3,345	241,581	390,543	End of December
1933				5,260	275,212	456,217	End of December
1934	45	2,811	6,436	9,292	305,635	537,695	End of December
1935	107	3,605	7,030	10,742	347,894	625,678	End of December
1936	121	4,212	6,491	10,824	376,586	690,501	End of December
1937	206	4,327	5,236	9,769	386,256	735,689	End of December
1938	209	4,766	5,760	10,735	414,867	799,878	End of December
1939	359	5,460	4,492	10,311	489,961	961,591	End of December

1940	413	7,298	5,474	13,185	613,363	1,190,444	End of December
1941	490	8,386	5,772	14,648	777,023	1,469,230	End of December
1942	706	12,456	5,368	18,530	864,591	1,625,054	End of December

Source: Compiled by author using Naimusho Keihokyoku, *Shakai Undō no Jōkyō*.
Notes: [a] Only numerical values shown for 'agriculture' entries. This is because the number 'people employed' in agriculture is not known. [b] Following 1934, the unemployed, prisoners, students and children were omitted from the overall total.

Table 1.6: Korean farmer households, numbers and land area by prefecture and city (1943)

	Owner farmers			Tenants			Agricultural laborers			Total number of people
	House-holds	People	Area (tan)	Households	People	Area (tan)	Households	People	Area (tan)	
Hokkaido	241	480	10,820	1,007	1,724	24,200	185	228		2,432
Aomori				6	8	21.63	1	2		10
Iwate				6	21	29.7				21
Miyagi					10			6		16
Akita							1	2		2
Yamagata				2	11					11
Fukushima	29		188.7			9.1			u/k	?
Ibaraki				208	571	773.7				571
Tochigi	1	6	23	13	36	78.7		5		47
Gunma				4	20	2	5	24		44
Saitama				30		148.9		9		9
Chiba	2		8.6	148		873.5				440
Tokyo				46	60	108.1		15		75
Kanagawa		7	15		175	200		24	95	206
Niigata				28	73	150	2	8		81
Toyama				6	13	46		5		18
Ishikawa				49	147	247	8	10	74	157
Fukui				218	685	1,492.80	62	248	u/k	933
Yamanashi					178					178
Nagano	1	2	1	90	357	503	30	83		442
Gifu	1	3	4	7	42	46	8	55	u/k	100
Shizuoka				97	273	309.71	36	93	547.7	366
Aichi	7	30	42	307	900	921		160		1,090

The ethnic problem in Japan's farming villages

Prefecture	C1	C2	C3	C4	C5	C6	C7	C8	C9	C10	C11
Mie	3	4			159	369	670.601	19	32		405
Shiga	4	16			112	191	534	23	29	117	220
Kyoto			9.2	17	514	2,277	1,722.90	116	188	846	2,481
Osaka[a]											
Hyogo	3	14		13	202	622	668.619	32	86	49	722
Nara	15	21		61.7	192	262	89.5	145	170	970.8	453
Wakayama	3	11		10.5	131	233	434.7	113	215	u/k	459
Tottori					15	19	u/k		16		35
Shimane	6	28		21.6	200	920	978.5	12	46	56.6	994
Okayama					136	148	641.318	163	178		326
Hiroshima	2			4.8	657		2,961.90		1,070		1,070
Yamaguchi	8	18		180	2,119	4,266	1,040		486		4,770
Tokushima					7	19	23		3		22
Kagawa	5					22			21		48
Ehime	4	12		25	51	191	186.2	18	47	274.8	250
Kochi	1	6		3	10	37	34.2	6	7		50
Fukuoka	49	65		64	728	1,225	942	473	601	u/k	1,891
Saga	1	2		6	273	825	2,132.51	64	144	368	971
Nagasaki	1	7		0.2	30	38	236		45		90
Kumamoto	3	8		9	106	546	783		24		578
Oita	3	6		9.8	768	3,110	4,338.70	275	753		3,869
Miyazaki					23	115	46	15	60		175
Kagoshima	2	6		23.225	17	67	55.6	5	5		78
Okinawa					1	1	5				1
Total	390	757		11,560	8,723	20,807	48,685	1,817	5,203	3,398.9	27,207

Source: Nōrinshō Nōseikyoku, 'Saikin ni okerunaichi zaihantōjin no nōkō e no tenkan keikō ni kansuru ken' (1943)

Notes: u/k = unknown; [a] no recorded data for Osaka Prefecture.

of regional officials concerned with tenant-farmers. In Okayama Prefecture, for example, 326 people were actually engaged in farming, and yet the survey officials reported that 'although there are some rural districts, we saw no existence of this', and hence, no measures were taken. In contrast, there were also situations such as that in Aomori Prefecture, where measures were drawn up based on the presence of a mere handful of households engaged in farming.

There were also diverse forms of farming and making a living. We can assume that in almost all cases farmers had other part-time work based on what we know about the employment process. In western Japan, which had been a vanguard in the transition to agriculture in the 1920s, cultivated landholdings fell within the farm category even though they were on average only slightly over 3 *tan* (0.3 ha). In contrast, in places such as Fukuoka Prefecture, for example, where the average area of cultivated landholdings was a little over one *tan*, the main source of income for these farms should be seen as mainly coming from other businesses, such as day laborers in construction work.

Based on the average scale of operations, there are some for which the term farmer seems appropriate. In the case of owner-farmers, these are: 44.8 *tan* (4.4 ha) (241 households) in Hokkaido; and 6.5 *tan* (0.6 ha) (29 households) in Fukushima Prefecture. The scale for tenant-farmers is: 24 *tan* (2.4 ha) (1,007 households) in Hokkaido; 7.8 *tan* (0.8 ha) (273 households) in Saga Prefecture; 6.8 *tan* (0.7 ha) (218 households) in Fukui Prefecture; and 5.6 *tan* (0.6 ha) (768 households) in Ōita Prefecture.

Let us now look at specific responses from different prefectural administrations. First, Kanagawa and Shimane Prefectures provided guidance for Koreans to become established in farming villages, but this was an exceptional case. The proactive guidance offered in Kanagawa Prefecture can be seen in the statement: 'Interested parties should contact the municipal agricultural association; there are no other special steps required apart from our mediation to enable their use of empty wasteland'. In Shimane Prefecture, Koreans were considered a better alternative to adopting extensive agricultural practices.

In contrast, the majority of regulatory responses can be characterized as negative regulatory posturing. Each area regulated different things and to varying degrees. The stages that they went through appear to be: exercise caution about granting tenancies; be wary of land ownership; and, be on guard if Koreans begin to develop their own village communities. In Aomori, there was a trend towards granting tenancies, but clear policies existed to prevent Koreans from becoming owner-farmers. In Hokkaido, setting up as owner-farmers was allowed, but forming ethnic village communities was not. We have also seen that the Hokkaido Prefectural Police authorities did not permit large-farm operators to hire laborers directly from Korea. In Hyogo Prefecture, the posture was: 'we are being vigilant concerning land ownership'. This wariness about land ownership can probably be taken as the baseline for these discriminatory practices. Even in Hiroshima Prefecture, with its large number of tenant-farmers, it appears that the matter was considered, but no action was necessary since there were only two households of land owners.

Authorities in other towns and villages also faced this problem. Yamaguchi Prefecture strove for 'roundabout prevention'. Shizuoka felt that 'This is not something about which we should necessarily be pleased as it is bypassing the relevant city, town and village authorities'. Kumamoto steered Koreans into important industries as directed by the prefectural Special Higher Police Unit.

Yamanashi and Saga adopted firm control measures, thoroughly preventing migration. Yamanashi Prefecture appears to have forbidden migration to farming villages:

> The current policy of the prefecture is that although Koreans can be employed in civil engineering and construction works, which require heavy labor, they are prohibited from employment in other industries. Consequently, their situation is invariably one in which it is not possible for them to migrate to farming villages and engage in agriculture.

There is no evidence that any of these policies were in response to actual 'problems'. The people in charge of each administrative area were likely to have been aware of the national data. They made individual decisions about how to deal with Koreans becoming farmers on their own criteria. The central government at the time could not – or did not – provide clear criteria for dealing with the 'ethnic issue'. This was a fundamental contradiction for the imperial government, which was caught between differentiation and assimilation as the empire was expanding to incorporate people of different ethnicities.

Possibly as a reflection of this conundrum, most prefectures 'had no particular response'. It is important to note, however, that with few exceptions, prefectural authorities did not want to see Korean farmers established in villages. Many people said that they felt like this because of 'imperial farming villages'. Under the government's policy to establish 'imperial farming villages' (1942), farming villages were to be the bases for population production – to supply the military and labor forces. This policy was grounded in the assumed superiority of farmers over city people, and was tinged with ethnic overtones. The exceptional complaints by officials in Mie Prefecture are noteworthy in this regard. They argued that accepting Korean tenants – people who work hard under unfavorable conditions – would adversely impact efforts to improve conditions for Japanese tenant-farmers.

Another important point emerges in a report from Fukui Prefecture, which states that tenant-farmer disputes had arisen after Korean farmers had become established there. According to this report, following the tenant-farmer disputes in early 1930, landlords set up Korean tenant-farmers on the lands that had been returned to them by the previous Japanese tenants. These sorts of opportunities were not confined to Fukui; they would have been seen in many areas. In Gifu Prefecture, for example, *Kyōwakai* (Concordia Society; a wartime organization for controlling Koreans in Japan) entered into a contract to farm 5 *chō* (4.9 ha) of land.

These surveys reveal clear trends towards a 'transition to farming' among Koreans, but this appears to have been a closely guarded secret. Possibly as a result of the Ministry of Agriculture and Forestry survey, the Ministry of Home Affairs also came to see Korean farmers as an extremely important problem. The two ministries clashed over the development of closely-related organizations in farming villages. The year after this survey, 1944, the Public Peace Division of the Police Affairs Bureau, Ministry of Home Affairs, concluded that the numbers of Koreans becoming tenants and owner-farmers could not be overlooked, asking: 'Should we yield to this change? This would be to invite a situation in which the majority of mainland Japanese tenant-farmers and agricultural laborers, who have temporarily had to leave farming villages in wartime, are replaced by these Koreans'.[89]

Studies of the wartime labor mobilization of Koreans observe that in 1944, particularly after September when conscription of workers began, and 'blatant and violent kidnapping [of conscripts] became generalized, resistance by Koreans intensified'.[90] It is important to recognize, however, that before conscription began, steps had been taken for Koreans who had already been mobilized to 'become settled'. The cabinet decision 'Matters Concerning Amendments to the Policy Regarding the Use of Korean Labor' was taken on 12 February 1944, based on a combined submission by the Ministry of Munitions, Ministry of Health and Welfare, and Ministry of Home Affairs, which allowed Korean laborers to send for their families. This was seen as recognition of 'the not insubstantial efficacy of promoting the establishment of Korean laborers, particularly the skilled laborers in their ranks, and increasing production'.[91] These three ministries remained cautious about Koreans, but by the final stages of the war, they began to accept Koreans 'becoming settled' in order to secure a workforce. Of course, 'becoming settled', as used here, was limited to laborers settling on restricted sites such as coalminers' camps; it certainly did not extend to accepting 'settlement' in the sense of putting down roots as ordinary citizens. As Koreans established farms and households, however, they also began to make connections of one sort or another, with others in the region.

Another characteristic of these changes was the accelerating pace of their occurrence. At the time that numbers of tenant-farmers associated with farming villages was rapidly increasing, the demands of the war were beginning to transform the autonomous character of villages. Kawano Shigetō, who conducted a survey of farming villages in Fukuoka Prefecture in 1940, observed that the amount of time required for Korean farmers to become established in villages was rapidly diminishing.

> It should be easy for us to appreciate just how big the hurdles are that they must face in a society where every aspect of production and life is replete with totally different customs. They are literal strangers, who receive no government assistance at all, and most of whom come on their own. Under these conditions, it has generally taken a considerable amount of time for the initial arrivals to become established. In one example, there was a five-year period between coming to the Japanese mainland and arrival in a village, and then another five years between having arrived in the village and becoming a tenant. However, once the path has been opened up for settlers, not surprisingly, for the next arrivals, five years become three and then

three become one. Consequently, in the past it was usual for Koreans to temporarily engage in construction work or being longshoremen until they could become tenant-farmers. But today, the trend is for Koreans to come to Japan and immediately become established as tenant-farmers.[92]

This increasing pace of change is observable across the board, and is highlighted in the following example from Kyoto Prefecture. (The pace of change is also an issue in other chapters of this book. For example, evacuation began suddenly and accelerated rapidly. There are also strong similarities in the case of repatriations, although in some sense that was a more drawn out process.) The war produced other significant social transformations in its final stages.

Koreans in Kyoto Prefecture and their transition to farming

As the war progressed, ever increasing numbers of farmers left their fields to become factory laborers.[93] In many of these cases, cultivation was simply abandoned and tenanted land returned to its owners. These developments can be directly attributed to the mobilization of military forces and to the resultant labor shortages, which created opportunities for factory work. In the previous section, we examined various proposals to use Korean laborers to ameliorate this situation. Although the proposals did not become policies, the farming villages – unable to wait for the state to resolve their labor problems – introduced various measures of their own to preserve agricultural land.

Koreans, some of whom had lived in farming villages since the 1920s, were peripheral to these measures. They became more entrenched in farming villages by hiring the land abandoned by tenants and returned to landlords. In effect, the war provided more opportunities for Koreans to become settled in farming villages. The Agricultural Administration Bureau surveys, mentioned previously, clearly indicate that from the early 1930s until 1943 there was a steady reduction in laborers and a corresponding increase in tenant-farmers. Of course, the official statistics are not entirely reliable; we must also be aware of discrepancies in the classification of small land-holders, tenants and laborers in the surveys from different periods.

Some land-holders – although not many – received rent from tenants, rather than relinquishing their lands as wasteland. Almost all of them, though, were conscious of their responsibilities for maintaining the village's agricultural land. Japanese landlords would not have imagined that they were creating future land problems by renting land to Koreans instead of Japanese. Contractually, they would have been on equal terms with Japanese tenants, but stood in a position of dominance in relation to Korean tenants who were ethnic 'others' in the village. Furthermore, such tenancies conflicted with the intentions of the agricultural authorities, for whom Koreans should be prevented from establishing themselves in homeland farming villages.

Let us look at a case study of Terada Village (Kuze District, Kyoto Prefecture), to develop a clearer understanding of the transformations that occurred in the final stages of the war and the early postwar period.

To understand the context for this case study, let us look at trends for Kyoto Prefecture as a whole. In 1944, a Special Higher Police Unit report observed that Koreans' employment in urban areas was moving from 'peace industries' to 'industries for the present [increasingly dire war] situation'. The latter had until then been the preserve of the Japanese workforce. This was followed by the analysis that:

> On the surface, there is a high propensity for increased feelings of unease as a result of matters such as the food situation, the conscription of Koreans and air defense measures. There is a trend towards gradually attempting to transfer [Koreans] to these areas, but their previous tendency to congregate in cities is changing completely and increasing numbers are returning to Korea or possibly dispersing into rural areas.[94]

Similar trends are pointed out in documents the following year, which state that, 'The majority of these Koreans live in the town of Miyazu in Maizuru City, which is their core region, and are employed in places such as civil engineering and construction workplaces, mines and in naval operations'.[95]

There was a substantial relocation of Koreans from urban to rural areas in Kyoto prefecture from 1942 to 1943. However, overall numbers of Koreans in the prefecture declined during this period (Tables 1.7 and 1.8). Until the war, large numbers of Koreans had been engaged in the textile industry, but the wartime curtailment of business operations closed most of these places of employment. Finding new places to work became a major issue for both the unemployed and for the authorities concerned with preserving public order (Table 1.9).

Table 1.7: Number of Koreans residing in Kyoto Prefecture

Year	Number of people
1918	322
1919	612
1921	1,255
1924	5,576
1926	8,279
1927	11,111
1928	12,723
1929	14,653
1930	16,911
1931	18,796
1932	28,596
1933	32,594
1934	33,693
1935	41,025
1936	44,293
1937	50,619
1938	53,446
1939	58,230
1940	67,698
1941	80,612
1942	77,796
1943	74,079

Documents: Military Social Welfare Department, Kyoto Prefecture
Source: Mori, 1945, p. 21

Table 1.8: Number of Koreans residing in urban areas and rural districts

	1942 (year end)	1943 (year end)	Increases and decreases
Urban areas	54,767	48,795	−5,972
Rural areas	23,029	25,284	2,255
Total	77,796	74,079	−3,717

Documents: Military Social Welfare Department, Kyoto Prefecture
Source: Mori, 1945, p. 21

Table 1.9: Occupations of Koreans in Kyoto Prefecture

	Males	Females	Total
Occupations			
Officials	15	0	15
Military	5	0	5
School teachers	5	1	6
Ministers and monks	5	1	6
Doctors and lawyers	12	0	12
Journalists	5	0	5
Clerks	88	27	115
Other	109	15	124
Subtotal	244	44	288
Agriculture			
Owner farmers	16	8	24
Tenants	322	269	591
Subtotal	338	277	615
Other			
Hospitality	66	49	115
Other employees	288	261	549
Secondary and tertiary students	1,619	150	1,769
Primary students and juveniles	6,034	5,439	11,473
Prisoners	46	1	47
Commerce	1,662	311	1,973
Laborers			
Mining	2,165	87	2,252
——— in-mine	932	0	932
——— out-of-mine	1,233	87	1,320
Textile industries	1,807	1,842	[a]3,649
Metal and machine industries	2,264	236	2,500
Artisan	1,570	96	1,666
Handyman	694	140	834
Chemical industries	502	134	636
Civil engineering and construction	13,921	162	14,083
Communications and transportation businesses	782	17	799
Longshoremen	704	0	704
General servants	636	204	840
Subtotal	22,781	2,682	25,463
Household heads	202	158	360
Dependents	8,667	20,996	29,163
Unknown	1,765	499	2,264
Total	43,712	30,367	74,079

Source: Mori, 1945, p. 24. Special Higher Police Unit, Kyoto Prefecture (end of December 1943)
Notes: [a] Decreased rapidly due to business curtailment. There were 7,312 people in 1941 (Mori, 1945, p. 25).

Table 1.10: Number of households and size of farms run by Koreans residing in Kyoto Prefecture and engaged in agriculture, 1941–1943 (Units: households and tan)

	1941		1942		1943	
	Households	Area of operation	Households	Area of operation	Households	Area of operation
< 5 tan						
Owner farmers	0	0	2	3.5	2	3.5
Land-owning tenants	0	0	1	3.5	1	3.5
Tenants	168	445.5	265	650.2	410	1,035.6
> 5 tan ~ Just < 1 chō						
Owner farmers	0	0	0	0	0	0
Land-owning tenants	4	28.4	4	28.4	4	29.4
Tenants	54	394.7	73	400.6	95	627.4
> 1 chō						
Owner farmers	0	0	0	0	0	0
Land-owning tenants	0	0	0	0	0	0
Tenants	4	45.3	9	105.3	6	72
Totals						
Owner farmers	0	0	2	3.5	2	3.5
Land-owning tenants	4	28.4	5	31.9	5	32.9
Tenants	226	885.5	347	1,156.1	511	1,735.0
Cumulative total	230	913.9	354	1,191.5	518	1,771.4

Documents: Special Higher Police Unit, Kyoto Prefecture, Survey.
Source: Mori, 1945, p. 32.
Note: Figures are for the end of September in the 1943 fiscal year.

Table 1.11: Distribution of Koreans engaged in agriculture in Kyoto Prefecture (September 1943) (Unit: tan)

	<5 tan			>5 tan <1 chō		>1 chō	Total
	Owner farmers	Land-owning tenants	Tenants	Land-owning tenants	Tenants	Tenants	
Mukōmachi			(25) 64.7		(7) 38.8		(32) 103.5
Uji			(51) 131.6		(7) 47.2		(58) 178.8
Ide			(1) 4		(5) 13.0		(6) 17.0
Kizu			(12) 24.1		(2) 10.0		(14) 34.1
Kameoka			(4) 7.5				(4) 7.5
Shizan			(48) 97.6		(23) 131.3		(71) 228.9
Sonobe			(15) 27.1		(1) 5.0	(3) 37.5	(19) 69.6
Fukuchiyama			(23) 16.1				(23) 16.1
Ayabe			(21) 28.4	(1) 6.4	(5) 37.2		(26) 56.5
Higashi Maizuru			(2) 5.0				(2) 5.0
Maizuru							
Miyazu	(1) 1.5		(81) 218.5		(16) 101.1		(97) 319.6
Mineyama			(22) 54.8	(1) 9.0	(8) 52.7	(1) 11.0	(31) 118.5
Amino		(1) 3.5	(38) 166.9	(2) 14.0	(14) 88.1		(52) 255.0
Kumihama			(26) 64.2		(4) 85.0	(1) 11.0	(31) 160.2
Shimogamo			(15) 35.3				(15) 35.3
Fushimi			(20) 69		(3) 18.0	(1) 12.5	(24) 99.5
Yamashina			(2) 9.5				(2) 9.5
Uzumasa	(1) 2.0		(4) 11.0				(4) 11.0
Total	(2) 3.5	(1) 3.5	(410) 1,035.3	(4) 29.4	(95) 627.4	(6) 72.0	(511) 1,734.7

Source: Mori, 1945, p. 34.
Note: Numbers in parentheses indicate number of households.

Table 1.12: *Koreans related to agriculture in Uji Police Office records Household survey by size of operations (Unit: households)*

	1941	1942	1943	1944
< 5 *tan*	15	38	51	60
> 5 *tan*	3	5	7	46
Just < 1 *chō*	0	0	0	13
> 1 *chō*	18	43	58	119

Documents: Uji Special Higher Police Department
Source: Mori, 1945, p. 32.

Table 1.13: *Distribution of Korean households in Uji Police Office records (September 1944)*

Terada	27
Makishima	22
Yodo	18
Higashi Uji	10
Ogura	9
Miyakonojō	9
Mimaki	8
Ōkubo	7
Others	9
Total	119

Documents: Uji Special Higher Police Department
Source: Mori, 1945, p. 34.

According to the Special Higher Police Unit, the main types of work available in rural districts were in mining (nickel ore and manganese ore) and for laborers on projects for wartime reclamation activities,[96] but my focus is on the 'transition to farming' trend, which developed at this time.

The number of Korean farmers rose dramatically across Kyoto Prefecture between 1941 and 1943 (Table 1.10). They were particularly numerous in Miyazu and Shuzan, where mining is popular, and in Uji (Table 1.11). In the Uji region, these numbers increased again in

1944 (Table 1.12). As will be discussed, this trend continued to expand right up until the end of the war in 1945.

Next, I will address two characteristics of farming at this time. The first is the idiosyncrasy of tenant-farming. The acquisition of property ownership rights by Korean farmers merits attention. However, the fact that, even in 1943, only two households had achieved this, and that their average holdings were 1.8 *tan* (0.2 ha), leads us to think that their farming was geared towards self-sufficiency. The second concerns the operations of the landed tenant-farmer and tenant-farmer class, which were quite different from those of Korean farmers. Landed tenant-farmers cultivated from over 5 *tan* (0.5 ha) to just less than 1 *chō* (0.9 ha), with an average of over 7 *tan*, while some tenant-farmers cultivated areas over 1 *chō* (0.9 ha) (Table 1.11). In Kyoto Prefecture, tenant-farming ranged from medium to large operations. These can be assumed to have been well-established farms but, as will be discussed in the case of Terada Village, the Koreans were tenants on land that Japanese had let go and which had poor fertility. Hence, we must be cautious about discussing the scale of operations on the basis of average holding size. However, the fact that in the midst of the movement to establish Japanese imperial farming villages Korean farmers managed to accumulate even this much land is of considerable social significance.

Let us now turn to our case study. In the Uji region, which had seen a sudden increase in farms over 5 *tan* (0.5 ha) between 1943 and 1945 (Table 1.12), there were large disparities between villages. Terada Village was where the highest number of Koreans had settled (Table 1.13). Terada Village is a typical example of Koreans in Kyoto Prefecture moving to rural districts and converting to the agricultural sector.

Korean farmers in the final stages of war

Circumstances of becoming established

Terada Village is situated in the southern part of Kyoto Prefecture, near the center of the Yamashiro Plain, and roughly halfway between the cities of Kyoto and Nara (today it is part of Jōyō City in Kyoto Prefecture). Its eastern portion is sandy and suited to cultivating sweet potatoes; the western part is flat and devoted largely to paddy fields. During the war, it had roughly 400 productive farm households,[97] 2,749 *tan* (273 ha) of rice fields (about 70% is tenanted land); and 700 *tan* (70 ha) of vegetable fields. Terada was a farming area and over half of its households were farming households.[98]

The southern region of Kyoto Prefecture is characterized as: being the heart of commercial agriculture; operating under a system of large landlords; the regional base of the Kyoto chapter of the Japan Farmers' Union; and a place where agrarian reforms have been thoroughly achieved.[99] Our case study comes from the leading agricultural area in the Kinki region.

The farmers' movement had been strong in this region since the Taisho Democracy, and the farmers' union[100] had been based here during the war. The Kyoto chapter of the National Farmers' Union formed the Kyoto Patriotic Farmers' Union Alliance[101] (Chairman: Tanaka Yoshio[102]), via the All-Japan Farmers' Union Kyoto Prefecture Federation. Terada Village was, however, the largest branch of the All-Japan Farmers' Union, as well as home to 262 of the Patriotic Farmers' Union's 647 members.[103] As there were in the order of 400 households running commercial farms, the movement covered a considerably wide area. The idea that there was a connection between the development of the farmers' movement and Korean farmers becoming established has already been suggested by examples from other areas, but I will leave it to future research to elucidate this process in Terada.

What were the circumstances that led to the Koreans' transition to farming in Terada Village? In 1928, a 'camp for housing laborers' for laying the railroad for the Nara Electric Railway was set up in the village. People from this camp who had worked on farms as day laborers during the peak farming season reportedly went on to become farm employees, and ultimately acquired the status of tenants. Four of the nineteen households of Korean farmers cultivating more than 3 *tan* (0.3 ha) were from this group, with a long history of residence in the village. These farmers appear to have assumed a leadership position vis-à-vis other Korean farmers.[104] Mori suggests that the mediation of these leading Korean farmers may have been instrumental in laborers finding new employment.[105] Unemployment in Kyoto spread following the wartime curtailment of business operations (the impact of which was particularly severe in the Nishijin silk fabrics industry, which employed substantial numbers of Korean laborers). Around this time, the use of Koreans to assist with farming activities on farms where *Kyōwakai* had enlisted farmers became widespread. Frequent reporting of this situation is likely to have generated an atmosphere in which landlords would accept the Koreans' mediation.[106] Particularly in the case of the *Kyōwakai* branch which had been installed in the Uji Police Station, there are reports that the police chief, a *Kyōwakai* member, was pouring his efforts into having Koreans use fallow land (*Kyoto*, 30/1/1943).[107] As discussed earlier, the core of the imperial agricultural administration opposed other ethnic groups establishing themselves in farming villages, but was aware that it could not openly express this view. This attitude was also present to some degree in local police administrations.

In Terada Village, it seems to have been 'mainly landlords who were farmers who requested Korean agricultural laborers'.[108] As in previous examples, if we single out the relevant portion, we see that,

> The landlords are largely landlords living in Terada Village, and they choose Koreans of good character who have been settled on their land in Terada Village as inhabitants for a long time. Thus, most of the people in the recent increase are either people with whom contracts have been concluded through the offices of these sorts of trusted people or indirectly through *Kyōwakai*. Otherwise, some people make contractual tenant agreements on the basis of lands contracted in the name of these sorts of trusted people.[109]

The newspaper article cited above (*Kyoto* 30/01/1943) enables us to confirm that there were also occasions in which *Kyōwakai* acted as a mediator for employment in agriculture.

Maintaining their operations reached an even more parlous state for the village landlords. When the village was surveyed in 1945, the situation had become one in which, 'we heard the most passionate attempts by landlords who owned these untilled lands to actively find Koreans in Terada Village and Tanabe Town'.[110] It was not the norm in Terada Village, but there was a continuing tendency for land-owning tenants to abandon land that they held as tenants, which thus became available as tenant holdings. This was an important route for becoming a tenant-farmer, particularly for Koreans, who lacked agricultural capital such as farming implements.[111]

Having discussed the demand for Korean workers, I will now consider the 'motives' of the Koreans. Mori raises two points in this regard. First, Koreans 'became tenants so as to secure the right to be registered as agricultural personnel who are exempt from being drafted'. Second was 'the desire to ensure food self-sufficiency that stemmed directly from their customary food practices, and which they felt increasingly strongly as a result of the tightening of food distribution controls'.[112] The latter explanation might simply be ethnic prejudice, but as we see from Table 1.14, while the majority of the planted area was wet-land rice, they also planted other crops, possibly producing foodstuffs that are important for the Korean diet. The desire to maintain traditional foods is common among migrants. The desire for self-sufficiency might have been influenced by the policy – from the '1941 Labor Mobilization Plan' – of not drawing on 'agricultural laborers' who cultivated more than 3 *tan* (0.3 ha) or who were engaged in agriculture for more than 90 days a year. The construction of Kyoto airport at the time provided employment opportunities to supplement the income of Koreans who were 'transitioning to farming'.[113]

Farming and ways of making a living

Korean farmers in Terada Village generally specialized in wet-rice cultivation. Most households cultivated 3–4 *tan* (0.3–0.4 ha) of land, but there were four households with more than 4 *tan* (0.4 ha) and one whose operations exceeded 1 *chō* (0.9 ha) (farm family number 9) (Table 1.14). They were 'generally fixed rate tenants, paying a maximum of 1 *koku* (137 kg) of rice per *tan* (0.1 ha) and a minimum of 4 *to* (54 kg) but usually 6–8 *to* (82–109 kg)', because their 'land was mainly depleted rice fields in poor condition or land that the cultivator was attempting to have assigned the difficult-to-get classification of land unfit for cultivation'.[114] These contracts were concluded 'verbally', and in some cases 'the contract period was not specified. Some went so far as to include cancellation clauses allowing tenants to be discharged to the military if they were conscripted'.[115]

Considerable disparities emerge when numbers of Korean men and women engaged in agriculture on farms are compared with village communities of Japanese people (Table 1.15). Across Kyoto Prefecture as a whole, the total number of landed and other Korean tenants was 338 males and 277 females (Table 1.9). In contrast, in established Japanese farming villages, the ratio of men to women is roughly 1:1. If we now compare this breakdown by gender to the

The ethnic problem in Japan's farming villages 75

Table 1.14: Size of holdings of Korean farmers in Terada Village (October 1944) (Units: tan*)*

Farm number	Total village area under cultivation	Village area by crops		
		Wet-land rice	Barley	Other
1	6	5.6	0.4	
2	4	3.7	0.3	
3	3.3	3	0.3	
4	3.5	3.2	0.3	
5	4	4		
6	3.5	3.5		
7	3	3		
8	3.1	2.8	0.3	
9	9.1	7.5	1.6	
10	3.5	3.5		
11	4.7	4.6	0.1	
12	5.3	5	0.3	
13	5.7	5.5		0.2
14	4.2	4.2		
15	3.4	3.1		0.3
16	4.2	3.8		0.4
17	4	4		
18	3	3		
19	3	3		
Total	80.5	76	3.6	0.9

Documents: Teradamura Agricultural Association records.
Source: Mori, 1945, p. 44.
Note: Barley figures include second crops and dry field crops. I have used my discretion to amend the transcribed figures. Farm numbers were only assigned to operations with an area > 3 *tan*.

518 Korean farmer households in Table 1.6 (September 1943), we see that 97 farm households had established family-farms (couple), while in 421 households only one member of the couple (either the male or female) was engaged in agriculture. It is possible that there are discrepancies in the data due to different time periods of collection or other reporting issues as we have seen above. Nevertheless, we can safely conclude that there were significant differences between

Korean agricultural operations and those of Japanese households, which are based on family cooperation.[116]

In order to understand these differences, we need to know how Korean farm families were mutually connected. According to Mori,

> under the guidance of the authorities, one hardly sees any prejudicial treatment but, at present, because of the necessities of language and social living, these farmers are not part of the hamlet-run union. With the police from the local police box as chairman, the Koreans are organized as one unit of *Kyōwakai* and exceptional Koreans are brought in as members to function in the same way as the hamlet-run union.[117]

Despite the continuing establishment of Koreans in the village, they were excluded from the hamlet (more specifically, from the union that it ran), which was the most localized part of the wartime administration (and the most distant from the center of power). We see that the farming operations of Koreans were coordinated through *Kyōwakai* for purposes of control and mobilization (Table 1.15).[118]

The Koreans established themselves as a group which was relatively independent from the existing hamlet, and conducted their agricultural operations through a traditional Korean agricultural labor exchange practice called *'Pumasi'*.[119] Up to 30% of the Korean women in the village continued wearing their traditional dress despite strict admonitions from *Kyōwakai* not to do so.[120] The Korean farmers of Terada Village preserved and reproduced their ethnic traditions in the course of their daily lives despite the assimilationist policies that denied their ethnicity. The imperialist slogan 'Japan and Korea as one body' demanded that they abandon their ethnic distinctions, while at the same time the agricultural authorities imposed ethnically discriminatory policies to prevent their integration in the village.

Population surveys of the village after the war reveal that large numbers of Koreans were living in Terada village. In January 1946, there were a total of 499 Korean residents: 322 men, including those living in camps for construction laborers, and 167 women. This is 11.4% of the total population, which at this time was 4,369 people, 2,121 men and 2,248 women.[121] Significantly, with the demobilization largely completed by that time, Koreans accounted for more than 15% of the male population, and of the 30–39-year-old men, 21% were Korean.

Table 1.15: People engaged in agriculture by hamlet, Terada Village

	Males		Females	Total
	Adults	Minors		
Ōminami	52	7	58	117
Kominami	75	7	88	170
Chūtō	46	15	64	125
Chūsei	52	5	65	122
Hokutōnohigashi	43	4	49	96
Hokutōnonishi	39	5	36	80
Hokusei	39	2	54	95
Inuijō	45	6	51	102
Mizushi	76	19	76	172
Kyōwakai	23	—	11	34
Total	490	70	552	1,112

Documents: Teradamura Agricultural Association records.
Source: Mori, 1945, p. 41.
Note: Restricted to people engaged in agriculture full time

Furthermore, Koreans shouldered the burden for 187.9 *tan* (18.8 ha) of the village's total tenant lands (10.7%).[122] In terms of tenant (rice field) land area, only two of Terada village's ten hamlets cultivated more land than the Koreans. It appears that the Korean farmers' productivity surpassed the existing hamlets, cementing considerable status with the landlords of Terada Village, where the landlord system was maintained until defeat.

Zainichi Koreans in postwar agriculture

Return of Japanese and repatriation of Koreans

The war transformed Japanese farming villages despite the intentions of agricultural administration officials. There are reports of neighborhood associations in some villages having been composed entirely of Korean farmers.[123] Defeat brought an end to this change vector. At present, we do not have any sources that directly show how 15 August 1945 (the day the Japanese nation learned of its defeat) was experienced in Terada Village. With the collapse of the economy and the imminent demobilization, the problems facing Japan's farming villages changed at a stroke from severe labor shortages to a surplus population. As returning to their native place became a possibility, Koreans were faced with a choice between returning and settling. In this section, I will attempt to develop an initial understanding of what this decision looked like in practice in Terada Village.

Repatriation services for Koreans in postwar Japan commenced in March 1946. There are, however, extremely few historical sources for the period of so-called 'independent repatriations' that preceded these. This is the case for Terada Village as well.

Two sources allow us to trace the migrations of Koreans in this period. One is the Survey of the Repatriation Aspirations of Koreans, carried out in March 1946, which shows that there were 236 *Zainichi* Koreans in villages at the time. Although the survey asked about employment, many people left this field blank; only two households specified agriculture as their employment.[124] During the period of independent repatriation, particularly in the two-month period after January 1946, 47% left the villages. It is unclear how many of them had established themselves in villages or had been engaged in agriculture.

Presumably there was stiff competition to acquire agricultural land at this time. As well as the return of demobilized people, Terada Village also had a large intake of returnees from the colonies. The authorities established a returnee reception center, the Jōnan Plant in the village (see Chapter 3). As mentioned above, many of the tenancy contracts may have contained 'cancellation for discharge from the military' clauses.

It is important to recognize that the end of the war was double-edged for Koreans. While representing liberation from colonial oppression, Japan's defeat also increased presentiments of violence. A Korean woman, Oh Gisun, who had lived in Shūzan in Kyoto Prefecture as a tenant-farmer, recalled that it had been necessary, even before the war, to be alert to the look in people's eyes, but after Japan's defeat she was not 'even able to go up a mountain with a sense of ease'. Soon after the news of Japan's surrender, rumors spread that 'here and there [fellow Koreans] had been killed'. And so, understanding that 'that kind of thing could happen to us here in the countryside' they moved to the cities.[125] Their concerns were grounded in previous experiences of ethnic prejudice, which peaked in the massacres of Koreans following the Great Kanto Earthquake (1923).

It is thus no surprise that their concern was widespread. The following description is from Osaka Prefecture administrative documents.

> It is forecast that around 5,000 non-Japanese have flowed into districts of the city where they form a group with people from other prefectures. *They are afraid of rumors of retribution and revenge on non-Japanese* living in areas where their numbers are insignificant *for having been black market traders or their employees since the inception of the black market.* Since these people are prohibited from moving into houses in the city, they are probably unregistered. (emphasis added)[126]

'[N]on-Japanese living in areas where their numbers are insignificant' surely includes farming villages. The point is that the sudden disappearance of Koreans from Terada Village cannot be wholly attributed to repatriation, but also includes an undeterminable number of cases of 'flight' to urban areas where there was presumably greater security in concentrated groups of Koreans.[127]

The second source is an 'Application for Approval to Change the Cultivators of the Land' addressed to the Chairman of the Agricultural Land Committee in 1947 (Photograph 1.4). The repatriation of Koreans and their departure from the village are recorded under the pretext of a change of tenancy. There were fifteen entries for agricultural land that changed hands as a result of five Korean tenant-farmers leaving the village.

There were also cases of Japanese returning from Korea, who settled in the village, taking over the farmland of Koreans who had left the village.[128] This was probably an unexpected coincidence, which even the people concerned had not envisaged. This one farming village provides a clear picture of the mass migration that followed the collapse of 'empire'. While the names of tenant-farmers were generally recorded in the former tenant's column of this source, there were also cases where there were no names, but simply the word 'Korean' (Table 1.4). As a result of the haste of repatriation and flight from the village, as well as the vagueness of the wartime tenancy relations, these Koreans appear in the records merely as 'people with no name'.

Following the 'Survey of the Repatriation Aspirations of Koreans', a policy of repatriation was implemented. At this time, Terada Village was directed to cooperate on repatriation tasks with the branch of the

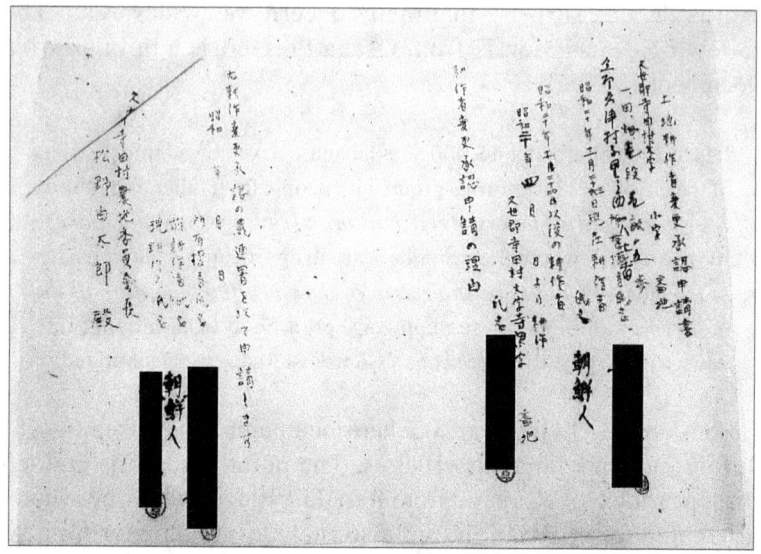

Photograph 1.4: Application for Approval to Change the Cultivators of the Land' 1947
Source: Nōchi nōgyō iinkai bunsho (Papers of the Committee for Farmland and Agriculture) (6038–2), held at the Historical Folk Museum of Jōyō City, photographed by the author. The previous cultivators are simply identified as Koreans.

League of Koreans Residing in Japan (*Zai-Nihon Chōsenjin Renmei*, hereafter *Chōren*), thus suggesting that a *Chōren* service counter had already been set up in the village.[129] However, the occupying force's GHQ had already issued a directive to the administration in Osaka to end its cooperation with *Chōren*,[130] and administrators in the Senzaki region had been directed to prohibit *Chōren*'s participation in repatriation activities.[131] It might be reasonable to expect that Terada Village would also have received a directive prohibiting *Chōren*'s participation in repatriation activities, but there is no indication of this in the village documents. There is, however, a later directive from the prefectural office to 'cooperate with the League [*Chōren*] in developing a plan for repatriating, and gathering, those wishing to return to Korea'. This suggests a time lag in the application of occupation policies in Uji district, which includes Terada Village.[132]

From June to August 1946, repatriation services were temporarily suspended due to the prevalence of cholera in southern Korea. When the threat had abated in September, 155 Koreans wanted to be repatriated (of the 2,271 living in the Uji region).[133] In other words, the number of Koreans wishing to be repatriated was negligible, and cooperation with *Chōren* is unlikely to have been problematic. A subsequent survey of the 'un-repatriated people' in Terada Village found a total of 187 still settled in the village.[134] The reason they gave for not repatriating was 'because of the insecurity of life resulting from difficulties based on the lack of domestic stability' in Korea. On 18 December, the policy of repatriating Koreans to south of the 38th parallel ended, and the postwar category *Zainichi* Koreans began.

Antagonism to becoming established

The process of agrarian reform was a decisive change in the lives of Korean tenants-after the war. An immeasurable factor in their new lives was the change in their status as Japanese citizens. Koreans, who had been imperial subjects were suddenly stripped of their Japanese citizenship and became foreigners. Let us review how this happened.

During colonial rule, Koreans were deemed to be subjects of the Japanese emperor and granted citizenship. After Japan's defeat and the collapse of the empire, their legal status became even more unstable. The Japanese government had recognized Koreans as Japanese people when it had suited them for control purposes. But once the Korean Peninsula had been granted sovereignty, the Japanese government disfranchised all Koreans, even those who had been long-term residents of Japan. Their Japanese nationality was not formally stripped, however, until the Peace Treaty came into effect in 1952. Between the surrender and the Peace Treaty they dwelt in an ambiguous grey-zone in which they were simultaneously Japanese nationals with Japanese citizenship, and subjected to the final imperial edict, the Alien Registration Ordinance (promulgated in 1947). There was considerable uncertainty about who was and who was not a Japanese national, and numerous problems emerged surrounding nationality and rights during the early postwar reforms. These problems were not confined to the area of agrarian reform with which I deal below.

Against this background, cases emerged, in Osaka and Niigata for example, of landlords selling agricultural land to people from the former colonies in order to escape the compulsory acquisition of land owned by absentee landlords, which formed part of the postwar agrarian reforms (see Chapter 5). These cases of what was called the 'foreigner problem' came to light in the initial stages of agrarian reform.[135] The emphasis of the Japanese government and occupation authorities on subjecting Koreans to agricultural land acquisitions in the same way as Japanese was intended to block these attempts by landlords to evade land acquisition. However, this ended up becoming entangled with the issue of agricultural land owned by Japanese living abroad, and led to delays in the process (see Chapter 4).

In February 1948, the Head of the Agricultural Administration Bureau, Yamazoe Risaku, issued a directive to the effect that the acquisition of agricultural land that belonged to foreigners and to Japanese living abroad be delayed until otherwise directed by GHQ.[136] This directive is seen as the beginning of 'disputes because of disarray in the handling of agricultural land and tenant lands belonging to Koreans'. On 26 March 1948, the Head of the Agricultural Administration Bureau issued another directive. This one postponed the acquisition of lands belonging to Koreans who had not declared an intention to obtain Japanese nationality. This indicates that there had been no differentiation on the basis of whether one was Japanese or not when it came to the purchase and transfer of agricultural land on which Koreans had been tenants.

This is roughly the same time as concerns that were raised about the role of Korean ethnic groups in agrarian reform. The minutes of the 10th Central Committee Meeting of *Chōren*, provides a record of the state of affairs around 1947. Kim Byeonso, who would later go on to publish *Haebang Shinmun* (Liberation News), which was very influential among *Zainichi* Koreans, asked Baek Mu, the committee chairman, about unemployed people in farming villages and whether agrarian reforms applied to '*Daisangokujin* (third country nationals)'. Baek Mu replied that he thought that there were no 'Korean farmers'.[137] Then, at the 13th Central Committee Meeting of *Chōren*, in January 1948, Kim Byeonso criticized the central committee for having failed to tackle the issue of agrarian reform despite having announced at the previous year's meeting that it would be investigated. He said that this reform was also relevant to Korean farmers, and raised the question of holding thorough negotiations concerning this issue.[138] The meeting also heard that 180 of 200 youths engaged in coal mines in Gifu Prefecture moved to reclaimed land near Lake Biwa, and were planning to set up a group farm. The central committee's decision, following a series of debates, was reported in the *Haebang Shinmun* as 'aiming to acquire land via the agrarian reforms, through the mediation of unemployed compatriots in the recruitment of owner-farmers that is being planned by regional government agencies in Tokyo and other areas'.[139] The 'disputes' concerning Korean land, recorded in the *Nōchi Kaikaku Tenmatsu Gaiyō* (Summary account of agrarian reform) discussed above, can be seen as a response to this sort of movement. Subsequently the 'Acquisition of Workplaces and Agricultural Land' was introduced as one measure towards securing livelihood rights. This was the theme of the slogans held aloft at the closing rally for the commemoration of the first anniversary of the Hanshin Educational Struggle in Osaka.[140]

At the time, the Kuze District *Chōren* branch, which covered Terada Village, was the largest branch in the rural districts of Kyoto Prefecture.[141] *Haebang Shinmun*'s coverage of *Chōren*'s Kuze Branch activities in relation to agricultural problems is piecemeal. One article reported on Korean farmers' struggles to 'acquire tenant land' in April. The paper also reports on actions supported by the Sasayama Branch of the Japan Farmers' Union and the Yamashiro Committee of the Japan Communist Party opposing the frequent repression of Koreans in this region.[142] Koreans living in farming villages in the postwar period cooperated with Japanese farmers' unions and political parties in their respective regions with a view to confirming the validity of their wartime tenancy contracts and acquiring land via the agrarian reforms. They also organized protests through their own organizations.[143]

In neighboring Shiga Prefecture, there are reports of the Head of the local Agricultural Land Bureau being forced to apologize after the Shiga Prefectural headquarters of *Chōren* objected to his declaration that it was improper to sell agricultural land to Korean tenants.[144] This report implies that regardless of directives from the central agricultural administration instructing officials to act impartially, power relations in local areas played a decisive role in the exercise of the right to purchase agricultural land.[145] In Takatsuki City, Osaka Prefecture, Korean farmers participated in the Japan Farmers' Union and engaged in struggles to obtain agricultural land and fertilizers.[146]

This can also be considered a form of opposition to the Japanese authorities who did not want Koreans to become established in village communities. In June 1946, the Head of the Uji District Office sent a directive to the Head of the Agricultural Land Committee of Terada Village titled, 'On the Matter of the Acquisition of Property by Foreigners'. Because this led to the promulgation of the 'Government Ordinance Regarding the Acquisition of Property by Foreigners' (Ordinance Number 51, 6 March 1949; hereafter 'Acquisition Ordinance'), the following directive was issued,

> With regard to recognizing rights concerning land or buildings and their transfer or disposal by any other means, the relevant permission and consent concerning the application of the Agricultural Land Adjustment Law and the Law Concerning Special Measures for the Establishment of Owner-farmers, et cetera, must be sought. Following this, the consent of Foreign Investment Committee must also be obtained.[147]

In short, the Law Concerning Special Measures for the Establishment of Owner-farmers of 1946, proclaimed that there could be no distinction between 'foreigner' and 'Japanese', so instead, the sale and transfer of land to 'foreigners' was prescribed by the Acquisition Ordinance.

Foreign Investment Committee was established to review the introduction of foreign capital into the private sector, which was both necessary for and a major concern during the reconstruction of the economy.[148] When drafts of the Acquisition Ordinance were initially reported in the newspapers, *Zainichi* Koreans involved in trade and commerce engaged in 'struggles opposing the application' of this to people from the former colonies. Their protests appear to have been heard, for when the ordinance was promulgated in March, it stated that 'people living in areas covered by this ordinance, who were in possession of Japanese citizenship on 2 September 1945 from that day on' would not be treated as 'foreigners'.[149]

This clearly meant that the 'Acquisition Ordinance' would not be applied to *Zainichi* Koreans. Yet documents from the Attorney-General's Office indicate that the way the Law Concerning Special Measures for the Establishment of Owner-farmers was to be applied in practice would include Koreans as subject to the ordinance.[150] Under conditions in which the ability of Koreans to establish themselves as farmers in villages was dependent upon power relationships, there was real potential for this directive to negatively impact upon them as the relevant authorities – either willfully or ignorantly – 'misread' this directive. The frequent 'doubts' expressed in the regions about the application of similar directives concerning the 'foreigner problem' provides support for this claim.[151]

We know that Koreans held voting rights on Agricultural Land Committees.[152] These rights had been an unforeseen response to an Agricultural Land Bureau query to the Attorney-General's Office, at the time of the re-election of Agricultural Committee members. The bureau had expressed a wish to adopt a policy of not recognizing the rights of foreigners, including Koreans, to be elected as Agricultural Committee members.[153] Koreans were continuously faced with this sort of instability, on various levels, throughout the postwar reforms.

Employment statistics for *Zainichi* Koreans are extremely scarce for the postwar period, making it difficult to track their movements. The following summary uses census and Ministry of Home Affairs statistics on foreigners living in Japan to fill out a picture of their situation (Table 1.16). These figures indicate that, excluding those who wanted to return to Korea, there were more than 13,000 Koreans engaged in agriculture. As we saw above, all of the Koreans in Terada Village wanted to return to Korea, so they are not included in these figures. When we include those who wanted to return, the number jumps to 25,600 Koreans engaged in agriculture in 1946.

The pattern that emerges is one of a significant number of Koreans continuing to engage in agriculture during the 1950s, following the agrarian reforms, followed by a sharp decline in numbers during and after the period of rapid economic growth. In the period of agrarian reform, Koreans appear to be quite numerous in agriculture as a proportion of employed people but, unlike urban areas, there were few regional areas where there was a concentrated Korean population.[154] With only one or just a few in a particular area, organization was difficult and they were frequently overlooked in studies and suveys. The failure to make their stories widely known continues to have considerable impact on the Japanese imagination today. It has enabled the perpetuation of the image of the 'Japanese people' as a nation supposedly defined by ancient and unvarying connections between a particular ethnic group and a particular land mediated by agriculture: 'Japan, the country'.

The progressive departure of Koreans from farming villages from the 1950s was a result of a significant decline in the opportunities that had enabled them to establish themselves in the first place.

Table 1.16: Number of postwar Korean farmers (1946, 1955–1991)

Year	Number of people
1946[a]	13,025
1955	13,165
1959	10,659
1964	8,282
1966	7,603
1969	5,333
1974	3,699
1985	1,871
1988	1,588
1989	1,441
1991	1,208

Source: Sōri-fu Tōkeikyoku, *Shōwa Nijūichinen Jinkō Chōsa Kekka Genpyō* (*Table of the Results of the 1946 Population Survey*); 1955 National Census (Hōmushō Nyūkoku Kanrikyoku *(Nyūkan Kyōkai from 1989), Zairyū Gaikokujn Tōkei* (*Resident Foreigners Statistics*). The entries for each year were compiled by the author from the figures for type of industry under 'Agriculture and Forestry'.
Note: [a] However, since the figures for 1946 do not include those people who hoped to return to Korea. The total number of Korean people living in Japan was 232,602.

Commercialised agriculture on the urban periphery, charcoal-making, and coalmining work all gave way to the rapid expansion of urban areas and the energy revolution (as oil and electricity replaced charcoal and coal). At the same time it became increasingly difficult to make a living in mountain villages.

Undoubdtedly, these processes of de-agriculturalization will be studied in detail in the future, but for now we must recognize the people who settled in Japan's farming villages and survived both the war and postwar changes.[155] Their settlement could also be read in terms of a general consistency in the wartime and postwar numbers of people, but there were sharp increases and sharp declines immediately before and after defeat. I would like to highlight how this is connected to future research.[156]

In the valley between 'self' and 'other' in imperial Japan

With the imposition of colonial rule by Japan, Korean society experienced significant upheaval, and the number of people coming and going between Japan and Korea increased. In Japanese farming villages, the commercialization of agriculture was already progressing rapidly as a result of land tax reform in 1873 and industrial development. At the same time, the development of both industry and the labor movement led to increasing wages to attract labor in the agricultural sector. Korean agricultural laborers hired by the year began to appear in the 1920s, primarily in western Japan, as a source of cheap labor. The discriminatory wage system that permitted the use of this cheap labor was accepted by the authorities to compensate for the management difficulties brought about by higher agricultural wages. As we have seen, there were other examples, in advanced regions, of devices such as an agricultural trainee system, developed in cooperation between agricultural associations and the government-general of Korea to keep wages low.

The employment type 'hired by the year' was a highly restrictive and servile form of employment that had long been in decline across Japan. These efforts to prop it up via the substitution of people from the colonies calls for re-examination, from a total 'empire' perspective, of what this meant for the modernization of Japanese agriculture. Such a perspective must take into consideration the fact that most of the Japanese who moved to the Korean colony and became landlords with the assistance of the Oriental Development Company were from the same regions that hired the majority of Korean laborers by the year.[157] We should also examine these developments in relation to the issue of agricultural laborers in other countries. In the United States and Germany, for example, the use of foreign agricultural laborers became social issues in the 19th century. Labor organization and the composition of cities are also relevant.

With the eruption of the Sino–Japanese War, the Industrial Division of the Cabinet Planning Board considered the mass introduction of Korean laborers. This was not adopted in connection with population deployment policies throughout the empire, but limited to the mobilization of labor for peak farming periods. The strategy behind this was twofold: an attempt to use Koreans as resources for controlling 'Manchuria'; and the state's desire to avoid connections being made between 'other ethnic groups' and Japanese farming villages.

By the 1940s, maintaining a 'mainland' agricultural population became a major issue, faced with the increasingly dire shortage of an agricultural workforce. Attention also needs to be paid to the conception and development, from 1943, of the 'Movement to Establish Imperial Farming Villages', an ethnic policy developed against the backdrop of a steep increase in the numbers of Koreans settling in villages. Nevertheless, the numbers of Koreans as farmers in villages continued to increase steadily in 1944 and 1945, despite the agricultural administrators' desires to exclude them. This can also be seen as a response to the considerable transformation of village autonomy wrought by wartime mobilization.

There was also a sharp increase in the numbers of Korean farmers who achieved a significant scale of operations. This occurred within the process of the 'return to farming' which was spurred on by business curtailments. The case of Kyoto Prefecture shows that Korean farmers, who preserved their ethnic traditions as part of their lives even under the control framework of *Kyōwakai*, played quite an important role in addressing the crisis in farming villages in the final stages of the war. This also means that Japanese farming villages, perceived as highly cohesive and relatively closed, experienced considerably different tendencies during the final stages of the war. At this point, the view from the heart of the empire – beginning with the agricultural administrators – was that the farming villages' response to the crisis was the real crisis. This so-called 'problem' of Korean farmers materialized as a new contradiction in imperial Japan during the final stages of the war. In addition to this concrete transformation, the vector of change is also important. The Japanese authorities – that is, the Ministry of Agriculture and Forestry and the Ministry of Home Affairs – 'panicked'. During the execution of total war, a radically new type of village appeared in imperial Japan.

However, these vectors of rural transformation were severed by defeat. Mobilization, repatriation and the food crisis changed the problem of farming villages, at a stroke, into a problem of surplus population, and agrarian reform policies developed in response to farmers' demands.[158] In the midst of all this, most Korean farmers chose to return to Korea, but those who elected to remain in the villages began to organize themselves, showing solidarity with Japanese farmers' movements and struggling to have the tenants' rights that they had achieved during the war recognized by the agrarian reform process. As the definition of who was a citizen wavered, the possibility of becoming settled remained unstable, dependent on local power relations. It is difficult to trace the movements of Korean farmers in the postwar period, but their lives in postwar Japanese villages continued to be prescribed in this manner.

Previous research has clearly shown that the retreat of the landlord system, which resulted from advances in small farmer management operations during the war, was the premise for postwar agrarian reforms. There is no doubt that the impact of occupation policies regarding agrarian reforms was an indispensable catalyst. It was, however, the potential of Japanese farmers, fostered over a long period of time, which made their realization possible.[159] However, we must recognize two *other historical prerequisites* for postwar agrarian reform. The first was the preservation of the landlord system throughout the war by Korean tenant-farmers – although there were regional variations to this. The other was the decline in ethnic disputes as Koreans returned home in vast numbers in the postwar period. Dealing with agrarian reform solely through an emphasis on continuity with the prewar system and the power of the occupation army has led to ignoring the history of colonial control by the state and the corresponding transformation of Japanese villages. Agrarian reform was one of the most important postwar reforms, introducing major change to Japanese society. It is not possible to understand agrarian reform without discussing the collapse of empire and colonial liberation, as well as the lives of the people who traversed these borders.

2 Evacuation, return to farming and postwar settlement

8 June, Taniguchi Zentarō died. Kishi also died.
They had been farming in Gomagō.
And so, now no witnesses remain.

>   Nakano Shigeharu '*Rokugatsu no Nikki kara*
>   (From June Diary)' (1974)

Evacuations immediately before defeat

Analyzing evacuation experiences

A Japanese popular dictionary, *Kōjien,* defines total war as 'fighting with all of one's might'. The idea behind 'total war' was an attempt to mobilize all people, as well as material resources, but what did this mean in practice? This chapter describes the conditions which prevailed during the final stages of Japan's total war by focusing on wartime migration – in particular *sokai* (evacuations) – away from the cities. I want to call the readers' attention to the militaristic nuance of this word 'evacuation'. How was it used during the war? The following is an advertising blurb, developed at the end of 1944, to be broadcast in places such as theaters as part of the 'Joint Campaign for Receiving Urban Evacuees' which was grappling with the issue in Nagano Prefecture.

> Forces march forward as impressive ranks of troops, and then encountering the enemy they immediately disperse and attack; by dispersing, they avoid unnecessary losses, putting into action their rehearsed maneuvers and proactively taking the fight to their enemy. Urban evacuation also means exactly the same thing; it has the same aims ... it is carried out as a preparatory measure, which leads to the type of powerful battle preparedness that follows.[1]

Table 2.1: Evacuation progress (1945)

	Pre-evacuation population	Evacuees	War victims	Total transferees
Tokyo	6,569,819	2,630,000	1,400,000	4,030,000
Yokohama	1,033,447	220,000	200,000	420,000
Kawasaki	380, 919	90,000	120,000	210,000
Yokosuka	298,132	50,000		50,000
Nagoya	1,348,061	580,000	270,000	850,000
Osaka	2,841,083	1,300,000	250,000	1,550,000
Kobe	918,101			400,000
Amagasaki	270,073		60,000	
Yawata	252,662	55,962		55,962
Kokura		184,230	38,395	38,395
Tobata	82,731	7,465		7,465
Wakamatsu	87,976	10,324		10,324
Moji	135,482	16,355		16,355
Total	14,402,716	4,998,501	2,240,000	7,698,501

Document: Ministry of Home Affairs
Source: Yamashita, 1948, p. 777.
Notes: Figures are as at 1 June 1945 except from Yawata to Moji are as at March. In the original table, there were distinct figures for evacuees and transferees in Kokura, but the author has consolidated these. This has also resulted in a change to the total number of transferees.

As we see in this excerpt, the term evacuation was a metaphor for creating an understanding of people's behavior as being military-like; it also had connotations of preparation for battle. This metaphor masks a considerable number of other things as well, but I will use it in the absence of a more suitable term.

In the final stages of the war, evacuations extended throughout Japanese society, encompassing both people and things. It must be stressed that these migrations were a large-scale phenomenon that occurred in an exceptionally intense manner over an extremely short period of time. In June 1945, just before the end of the war, the number of people evacuated from a total of 13 cities that had been designated as important under the 'Implementation outline for urban evacuation' of December 1943 – the Tokyo-Yokohama district, Kansai and northern Kyushu – reached approximately five million (see Table 2.1). Statistics also show that by August, this number exceeded 8.16 million.² If we also take war victims into account, then over half of the population in the major cities of Tokyo, Osaka and Nagoya left the places where they had lived up until that time. This is a much larger number than that of postwar civilian repatriates from *gaichi* (external territories). Furthermore, even allowing for the fact that evacuations were being implemented throughout this period over an ever-expanding area and scale from large to small and medium-sized cities, the migrations brought about by evacuation and war damage were on such an exceedingly large scale that they furnish rich possibilities for reimagining our idea of the people during wartime. While a system of total war aims to mobilize production and reproduction with a view to the national objective of victory, whether or not this mobilization structure was sustained right up until the end is important to how we view the changes from wartime to postwar.

Shimaki Kensaku, a writer who lived in Kamakura, wrote in his diary in September 1944:

> Thinking that it had been several days since I heard the voice of the old man in the neighboring house, who had been evacuated here two or three months ago, I learnt this morning that he had died… The rattle of death among the elderly in our neighborhood association has been conspicuous since last year. They were advanced in years, but it is hard to suppress the feeling that *people who would not have died had these been normal times seem to be dying.* When their resistance is at its lowest, something like wisdom is discernible in their eyes.³ (emphasis added)

These deaths are certainly not treated as 'deaths in action'. When we attempt to focus on daily life in wartime, we must take into consideration the significant number of these lives; of people who moved in an attempt to flee war damage, but who were ultimately obliterated. There is no doubt that evacuations initially arose from strategic needs, but we must consider the situation in which they found themselves, given the fact that the widespread evacuation that followed effectively 'created battlegrounds'. That is, their lives need to be seen in terms of maneuvers towards 'a decisive battle for the homeland'; in short, they were faced with decisions about life and death which were dictated by external factors. Evacuation research, in this sense, while primarily focused on an analysis of Asia and the final period of the Asia-Pacific War, is also quite separately an analysis of the condition of the people, who were perplexed by the wars that have recurred throughout the ages, and who have done what they could to survive these wars.

Similarly, evacuation tends largely to be imagined as having been migration 'from the cities to villages', but in reality, the vast numbers cited above did not all head to villages; rather, the majority of evacuees relocated to neighboring urban areas which had not been designated as evacuation areas. A survey of how many people had moved in with farming families between April 1945 and April 1946 recorded a total figure of 2.34 million men and women,[4] which includes demobilized military personnel. It is still not clear yet exactly how many people relocated during this period, but the case of a farm village in Nagano Prefecture indicates that the majority of evacuations occurred after April 1945.[5] But not all of these evacuees were accepted into farm villages.

Thus, not all evacuations were from city to farm village. Yet this impression has become deeply entrenched in the collective imagination of postwar Japanese society. The origins of this misconception lie squarely in wartime propaganda, which directly endorsed a 'return to farming', with an eye to increasing food production. The idea of the Japanese people 'returning' to farming was one of many wartime rhetorical devices used by the government. As discussed in chapter 1, the 'agriculture first' principle of the Japanese government deemed agricultural villages to be the foundation of the Japanese nation, a view that presumes that every Japanese was a farmer in the past and gives grounds to the expression, '*returning* to farming'. There is no doubt, however, that interactions with the other differed, depending on whether migration took place from urban to rural areas or between cities. Against the asymmetrical backgrounds of city versus farm village, city-to-village migration had the greater impact on both the migrants and village communities. In comparison, movements from large to small and medium-sized cities were only likely to be dealt with as the stories of individual families during the war. The particulars and social significance of such large-scale migrations are nonetheless still not adequately clear because the extremely short period of time and the rapidly deteriorating situation in which they occurred meant that administrators failed to keep track of them.

Furthermore, government policies were frequently being revised; and severe and repeated war damage imposed severe limitation on resources.[6]

In this chapter, I will use Kishi Yamaji's diary[7] of his experiences as an evacuee as a means to better understand these vast migrations. My methodology will be to weave together Kishi's individual wartime and postwar experiences with the changes that occurred in regional society.

Let us examine the efficacy of this method by considering the achievements and relevance of previous research. A substantial proportion of the research that has been conducted on wartime evacuations have been studies of the evacuation of school children. Drawing on this research, Kurokawa Midori focuses primarily on writings that reflect on school evacuations. She concludes that the mass relocations shook the boundaries between city and village. These encounters 'resulted in conflicts between people who were different and brought them to the fore'. (In this article Kurokawa also attempts to map out the spatial and class aspects of mass evacuation by examining the evacuation of disabled people, the colonies and occupied territories).[8]

As Kurokawa also points out, after the war large numbers of evacuees continued to stay in the places to which they had relocated, leading to 'cultural transmission'. On this point, Kitagawa Kenzō describes the influence of cultured evacuees on regional cultural movements after the war by focusing on the relationship between people like Kishida Kunio and Morita Sōhei, who had been evacuated to the Shimoina districts of Nagano Prefecture and who, from the immediate postwar period, had been engaged in cultural activities in *Seiwakai* (literally, Quiet conversation society), and in the youth association movement.[9] This chapter will attempt to reconstruct these experiences as they were lived by the people who moved to these areas.

As Kurokawa's research has shown, the evacuations significantly impacted the school children concerned. However, where whole families were evacuated, it was decisively the adults who had to cope with the various problems of daily life in wartime and worry about the responsibility of providing a livelihood for tomorrow. We cannot ignore these generational differences. While children's experiences of this period are very meaningful, in this chapter I will use Kishi's diary as a personal document to get close to the experience of adult evacuees. I will also focus on the fact that evacuees, as they attempted to adapt to conditions in the areas where they lived, were also protagonists who produced change in these places. Similarly, we will find that the social significance of the evacuation experience becomes clearer when we perceive evacuees from a perspective that takes into account postwar changes that afforded them extensive possibilities to pursue their personal interests and needs; in short, when they had secured a reasonable level of social freedom. I will therefore also focus on the relationship between the administration of evacuation and policies encouraging a return to farming, which has not been adequately addressed in research to date, and which I see as a key that links the wartime and postwar periods. It is here that we find the significance of this chapter's attempt to approach the event known as evacuation from the evacuees' perspective.

How have these mass migrations called evacuations been dealt with in research on the history of agriculture and villages? Agrarian reform is widely acknowledged as having had the greatest impact on postwar rural villages. It was pointed out that civilian repatriates, war victims and evacuees made up as much as 20% of the secretaries of municipal Agricultural Land Committees, which played an important role in the implementation of agrarian reform.[10] However, despite a vast amount of research on agrarian reform, there has not been any progress in research focusing on the people who migrated and played these important roles; the people who were *others* in farming villages. To date there have been practically no studies of the settler-farmer movements in the local community during the initial period after the war. This is also relevant to the next chapter: wartime evacuation and domestic settlement policies are very closely connected and are crucial to understanding the history leading up to postwar land reclamation policies.

Kishi Yamaji

Kishi Yamaji (real name: Itō Kōichi) was born in 1899 in the village of Naruto in Tokushima Prefecture (present-day Naruto City, Takashima). Kishi witnessed first-hand the Salt farm workers strike in his hometown and was influenced by the socialist movement. As a young man he developed a passion for writing. He entered a novel-writing contest for which the *Osaka Jiji Shinpō* newspaper offered a prize. Immediately after receiving an honorable mention in this

Photograph 2.1: Kishi Yamaji in his youth (supplied by Itō Jun)

competition, he left for Osaka, at the age of twenty. While working in Osaka as a journalist and editor he set his sights on literature. In 1926, he made his way to Tokyo where he won popular acclaim as a proletarian author for works such as *Gō sutoppu* (Go-Stop), *Dōshiai* (Comrade Kinship) and *Ninjutsu Buyūden* (A Heroic story of Ninja). He joined the Japan Proletarian Writers' League (hereafter, Writers' League) when it formed in 1929. He was an active participant in disputes concerning theory and practice, such as literary movements about the popularization of art. Kishi seems not to have been a member of the Communist Party before the war, but he was arrested on suspicion of having violated the Peace Preservation Law in 1932 and then again in 1934. On this latter occasion, he was found guilty and sentenced to prison for two years with a four-year suspension, and he was compelled to declare that he had 'converted'. In 1935, he launched *Bungaku annai* (A guide to literature) and worked as its editor, specifically seeking to introduce literature from overseas and the colonies, such as the work of Lu Xun.[11] He was also an active participant in *Jitsuroku bungaku* (Documentary literature), another magazine of this period which was launched in October

1935, and became one of its principal personalities (it was short-lived, ceasing publication in April 1936).[12] In 1937 he was charged with participating in a movement to rebuild the Communist party in Kansai, and was arrested for a third time. This time, faced with a sentence of one year in detention, he made a full conversion. Kishi became a popular author as his historical novel *Ishin zenya* (The Eve of Restoration) was serialized in the evening edition of the Yomiuri Newspaper during the Asia-Pacific War.[13]

We know a lot about Kishi Yamaji's prewar activities. This chapter focuses, however, on Kishi's activities in the final stages of the war. As wartime regulations tightened, it became virtually impossible to function as a writer and, in April 1945, sensing the inevitability of air raids on 'the homeland' once Saipan fell – and foreseeing a further deterioration of the war – Kishi and fellow proletarian author Taniguchi Zentarō (who was living in Kyoto) moved to Gomagō village in Kyoto Prefecture where they settled and engaged in agriculture. After the war, he became a key figure in the area. Using Gomagō as his base, He was active as a leader of literary movements and the agrarian settlement movements while also being an active member of the Kyoto Prefectural Agricultural Land Committee.

Before proceeding, though, it is worth noting that this monograph based on the experiences of an individual called Kishi Yamaji is likely to reflect the collective and social endeavors of a particular group of writers. Literary expression was heavily suppressed during the war, but writers began to organize again immediately afterwards. A typical example of this kind of movement is a convention in late 1945 to establish the New Japan Literary Society. In addition to raising issues such as writers' war responsibility, they also debated 'dispatching writers to the countryside'.[14] In the 'Inaugural Preparatory Issue' published in January 1946, the policy of dispatching writers from Tokyo became an appeal to writers who had already been evacuated to the countryside.[15] It should perhaps not be surprising that most writers who had evacuated remained in their new settlements immediately after the war. The writers who chose to stay were personally motivated to write and engage in literary exchanges with members of their local communities, but the people of the communities that had taken them in also sought opportunities for such exchanges with the writers. This can be seen in the writers' requests to their magazines for these activities to be reported upon, although there are few clear examples of such reports in the pages of *Shin Nihon Bungaku*.

However, this does not mean that there were no responses to these appeals. It is not possible to tell from reading Kishi's diary whether he knew about these appeals, but it is clear that for years after the war Kishi's activities were wholly concerned with responding to these sorts of appeals. Studies of these types of activities by other writers and cultured people are needed, as well as research on how widespread they were.[16]

The various types of diaries left by writers during the wartime and postwar upheaval, go far beyond the confines of literary studies. They are extremely important socio-historical sources.[17]

Writers' lives pre-evacuation: Success and failure

When we follow a single person's life it is because that individual held particular aspirations and to ask whether they acted in particular ways in pursuit of these aspirations, given the circumstances into which they have been thrown. The relationship between an individual and the whole emerges in the independent judgments and actions of the person concerned in response to the conditions of which they are aware. Personal factors such as the individual's state of health and relationship with their family are also, of course, a considerable influence on their decisions and actions. This approach will enable us to investigate points of intersection, and lack thereof, between Kishi's life as an individual and the lives of his contemporaries.

I will therefore begin by describing the circumstances in which Kishi found himself during the war, up until his evacuation. Excerpts from Kishi's diary will be quoted frequently in this chapter, but it is important to bear in mind that Kishi wrote his diary in an environment in which he might be arrested at any moment, and the diary might be used against him.

From the Writers' League to the 'imperial way principle'

Following his arrest and indictment in January 1934 on charges of having contravened the Peace Preservation Law, in order to avoid a prison sentence Kishi was compelled to denounce the communist party and declare that he would devote himself entirely to literary activities. He was sentenced to two years of penal servitude, with a four-year suspension.

In May, he published an article entitled 'The expansion of the Peace Preservation Law and the position of writers' in which he cited the section prohibiting 'propaganda activities' proposed in the bill to reform the Peace Preservation Law which was being discussed in the media at the time. He pointed out that the proposed changes would make it impossible for proletarian literature to continue engaging in activities that were currently legal. In addition, he declared, 'I will distance myself from the theory of proletarian literature'[18] and write literature from the 'perspective of the progressive internationalism that exists in our country, on the basis of the interests of the working class'.[19]

Although he avoided a prison sentence, his perception of himself as a left-wing 'writer' was no doubt shaken when at the trial, right before his eyes, a young man who had violated the same Peace Preservation Law received an eight-year prison sentence, and Kishi was then afraid that the young woman who had come to support the young man would 'recognize me as Kishi Yamaji'. 'I felt like my [suspended] sentence came at the expense of the hard-won efforts of that unknown young person's sweat and blood' (29/6/1934). During the fierce debates in the Writers' League before his arrest, Kishi had rarely displayed this sentimental side of himself. Note, however, that accepting responsibility for his 'crime' was part of the process of conversion.[20]

Before he was arrested, Kishi had already reached the conclusion that, in order to maintain the proletarian literature movement, support for the Writers' League should continue, but its activities ought to be 'dispersed'.[21] While he was in detention, however, the Writers' League had decided to dissolve itself as an organization. Kishi then threw himself into expanding his editorial activities with the magazines *Bungaku annai* and *Jitsuroku bungaku*, and continued exploring avenues for his literary expression. During this period, Kishi began using the term 'conversion writer', but he was still able to think of himself in terms of and make declarations about 'attempting to unite his literary efforts' with 'his proletarian stance and his commitment to working in the interests of *the majority of people*'.[22]

Kishi pursued a 'working class' stance to the extent that his magazine editing activities allowed. However, in 1936, seeing the 'left-wing publisher' *Nauka* being suppressed, he 'decided to take a step back in terms of magazine editorial policy, and ensure its lawfulness in every respect'. He anticipated that 'as the pages of the magazine lose their radical aspect so too will the support of readers decline, and we should be prepared for declining sales' (23/11/1936). And so it was that, as he had predicted, sales of the magazines worsened and Kishi's financial situation became so bad that 'there were not even any funds left to pay for sending off copy' (23/11/1936).

Then came the suppression of 1937, which had a decisive significance for Kishi. As part of the suppression of a movement to revive the Communist Party, which had been attempted from around the summer of 1936, both Kishi and Eguchi Kan were arrested and taken into custody on suspicion of having met with Miyaki Kikuo several times and having donated two yen (!) towards the movement.[23] Though not indicted, Kishi was placed in 'preliminary examination' for one year. Kishi's sentencing magistrate held that the work that they had been doing on *Bungaku Annai* was 'all part of a movement to rebuild communism' (4/5/1938). Kishi was forced to make a full 'conversion' in order to end his long period of detention and to avoid being prosecuted. Kishi made no reference whatsoever to this reconstruction movement in his subsequent writing, so we do not know whether he participated in it or what he thought about these activities, but this may be because he did not consider these matters to be relevant.[24] When Kishi was released on bail in 1938, he learned that Nakano Shigeharu and Miyamoto Yuriko had been banned from writing (12/1/1938). He also learned that Stalin's purges in the Soviet Union had now extended to people like Bukharin – 'elder statesmen who had founded the nation' – which left a 'dark impression' (3/3/1938). He was extremely interested in the 'Lyushkov Incident' in June 1938, the first case of defections by high-level officials from the Soviet Union. His diary entries convey a sense of how avidly he followed reports of these events.

Thinking at length about these various experiences, Kishi once again changed his position. In Kishi's words, his new stance was like taking the 'imperial way'. From this time on, through actions such as appearing in lectures with Noda Ritsuta, a friend from the 1920s who had already converted, Kishi gave the outward appearance of having undergone a total conversion. He wrote, self-mockingly, that the idea of interacting with the chief of police and the public prosecutor: 'having this sort of opportunity to associate in this way with these kinds of figures would not even have been the stuff of dreams a few years ago. I was awestruck by the extent to which reality had been distorted beyond human imagining' (19/9/1938).

Kishi did not spell out any systematic ideology for this 'imperial way', but we can faintly discern its outlines from his diary entry on 3 March 1939 when Britain declared war on Germany. Kishi asked himself what could serve as a basis for moving beyond the 'present-day bourgeoisie' *if not* international communism, which was discredited by Stalin's despotism, and decided that the answer 'could be sought in the imperial way'. This new ideology was only ever expressed in this negative manner. However, while he believed it was necessary for the imperial way to be distinguished from capitalism, he was unable to determine what 'power' might bring about the desired social transformation, and he continued to waver on this. It was clear to Kishi that the assistance associations that he saw around him were not up to the task. Conversion for Kishi appears to have been a matter of abandoning international communism rather than surrendering to the classes that aimed to defeat communism. Thus, he persevered with his criticism of capitalism. By bringing a different interpretation to the term 'imperial way' that had been imposed upon him, Kishi was narrowly able to hold onto an 'ideal' (3/9/1939). The *'majority of people'* upon whom Kishi had previously depended and who he had been trying to liberate were redefined from the proletarian class, which was assumed to be universal, to the *'majority of Japanese people'*.

Writers' lives in wartime: The success of historical novels

For Kishi, the literary turning point during the war came with the Yomiuri Newspaper's decision at the end of 1940 to serialize *Ishin Zenya*. Kishi reminisces about his five years of perseverance from the time of the advocacy of 'Documentary literature' following the dissolution of the Writers' League (2/11/1940).

> I also feel a sense of relief and peace of mind. Finally, in the fifth or sixth year of patient perseverance since I advocated documentary literature, with the arrival of a period such as the present one, which is constantly being called a new order, I can at last find spaces in which to publish my work on popular historical literature and earn some money. When working on literature, one's own thoughts and plans usually become common property, but it has taken at least five years of perseverance for this work to see the light of day.

Kishi's self-perception also began to change considerably due to the popular acclaim achieved by this serialization. He wrote story after story as his novels were serialized in numerous newspapers. He bought a villa in Karuizawa and hired large numbers of stenographers. The speed with which he had recovered from not even being able to pay freight costs a few years earlier is astonishing. It would, however, be wrong to think that he had no hesitations about this; in fact, it would be accurate to say that he had many doubts. Maruyama Yoshiji [25] – Kishi's close acquaintance from the days when together they had edited *Senki* (Battle Flag), the bulletin of the All Japan Federation of Proletarian Arts; with whom he had worked on editing *Bungaku Annai*; and who was active in the field of agrarian literature during wartime – strongly censured him at a banquet. Whilst Kishi parried the extremely intoxicated Maruyama's accusation that he was responsible for the defeat of the leftwing movement, it also gave him cause for self-reflection. He writes, 'Even when I say that the defeat was attributable to Japan's proletariat as a whole, is there not an element in this of compensating for the fact that "responsibility for the defeat" lies with me' (21/3/1941).

On 8 December 1941, when he heard reports of the declaration of war against the United States and Britain following the attack on Pearl Harbor, he made an entry in his diary that appears to have been addressed to himself. This entry can be read as Kishi writing as a precaution, having had a presentiment that he would be arrested.

> I have anticipated what has come to pass today since 1937, and there will not be better developments in Japanese society until we have realized the destiny that awaits us after today; this is because my thoughts have turned to not even wishing to live any longer and this conviction only grows stronger as the days go by.

A month later, in January 1942, along with Yoshikawa Eiji and others, he was invited to an expensive restaurant by Shōriki Matsutarō, owner of the Yomiuri Newspaper. Although Kishi records that they discussed the types of novels that they would write in response to the declaration of war between Japan and the US, at some stage he tore out and discarded the parts of the diary in which he had written his opinions. He doubtless decided that leaving a record of these would be unwise (10/1/1942). The period from 1941 until the first half of

1942 was when Kishi won popularity as a writer of the masses; a period in which he flourished as a writer.

The annihilation of writers' lives: Towards the final 'conversion'

However, the war thwarted Kishi's attempts to spur himself on to participate in the reality of life around him. The Yomiuri Newspaper's decision, in late September 1941, to reduce the length of the newspaper because of paper shortages, and the censorship of *Ishin Zenya* beginning in mid-September, prompted Kishi's decision to focus exclusively on writing books from that time on. In June 1942, the government proclaimed the Newspaper Industry Ordinance, which ordered the consolidation of all newspapers. Because this policy resulted in the unification of the Yomiuri and Hōchi Newspapers, Hōchi's serialization of Kishi's novel *Aohitokusa* (The commoner) – which had depicted wartime 'domestic' land settlement activities – was also terminated.

Although he continued writing various short pieces and critiques, as their serialization in newspapers came to an end, Kishi felt a growing desire to participate more directly in the war. As his livelihood grew precarious, social participation via literary works, the method to which he had aspired, began to change.

'I am a first-rate writer' (8/9/1942). With the success of *Ishin Zenya*, Kishi's perception of himself changed considerably. Around this time, Kishi was unsure about whether to volunteer as part of the navy news team, but since he was 'first rate' he decided that he would wait to be drafted rather than volunteering. However, his perception of himself was constantly shaken.

> I have lately been secretly worried about how 'my own' private life fits into the bigger, overall reality facing Japan. I have reflected on whether it is adequate. Partly so as to confer better literary motives to the autobiographical novel that I should leave behind; having survived, it would be loathsome to me to be referred to as a writer who simply lived until the end merely in Tokyo or within Japan during the Greater East Asia War. Although painful, participating directly in this war would be a splendid thing. I do not mind dying.
>
> Going from work to work; perhaps herein lies my escape. Checking the progress of the war daily, I have been unable to forget for even an instant that we are in the upheaval of a great war that engulfs the

whole world. How should I be living in this period that ought to make me afraid? Day after day, I feel that I am living a life of having been left behind, overlooked and on the wrong path. There is probably no one in the whole world who is able to accept excessively unreasonable realities.

Since 1937, I have been isolated in every sense (4/6/1943).

This progressive loss of publication spaces for writers was part of the total war mobilization. The May 1942 'Curtailment of Business Operations Ordinance' decreed the curtailment of business operations in the publishing world as well as small and medium-sized merchants. The following year, on 5 November 1943, the Information Board announced its 'Plan for the Curtailment of Publishing Businesses', and its decision to establish a headquarters for administering the curtailment of business within the Japan Publishing Association, an organization for publishing-related businesses. Then, on 25 February 1944, a cabinet decision adopted the 'Outline of Emergency Measures for the Decisive Battle', which had a decisive impact on Kishi and other writers. The following month, a general meeting of the Novels Section of the Japanese Literature Patriotic Association discussed 'problems such as interceding to find a change of occupation for unemployed writers' (27/3/1944). Some writers of popular literature commented in newspapers that this was 'an annihilation of writers' livelihoods'.[26] As a result, Kishi no longer received an income from his writing.

The form of participation in the war envisaged by Kishi at this stage bore an uncanny resemblance to what he had advocated during his proletarian writer period. Whereas in the Writers' League he had advocated a policy of writers organizing activities in farming villages and factories, now he wrote of 'the critical importance of "writers who have lost our means of earning a livelihood" as a result of the "massive curtailment of the publishing business" going into war plants and engaging in cultural and literary work for the benefit of factory workers' (25/12/1943). He also approached the Information Board and the Ministry of Education to propose a cultural policy that he had devised for establishing an 'Office for the Workings of the Mind' (12/4/1944). In sum, Kishi kept striving to participate in social matters via literature.

The final turning point for Kishi's wartime awareness was the fall of Saipan. What did this event which led to the resignation of the Tōjō Cabinet mean for Kishi as an individual writer? On 2 July, after hearing of the deteriorating state of the war, he was convinced that air raids over Tokyo were imminent. Then, as well as his prayers about these thoughts being 'madness', he spelt out his ideological conversion in writing.

> I cannot suppress my overflowing feelings toward the realities of war that lay stretched out before me, but from my position as a powerless solitary individual I have no means of putting these feelings into practice. If I think too deeply about it I simply end up tormenting myself in vain, and I shall probably finish up going mad.
>
> All day long today I thought about various things to do, exclusively about the problems in my own life. The results were akin to scooping up water from a large ocean to gain a few drops – these efforts were of no use at all regarding my comments above about the war; but, an idea that may just help me to get on with my life did emerge. Relocating far away from Tokyo, I would like to move to a place suitable to our children's secondary education and spend there about five years or so, lawfully obtaining extra rations. If Japan faces inevitable ruin, then wherever I am, whatever I do is futile.
>
> Right now, the navy has lost in its efforts to secure the mainland [Japan]. Unfortunately, the end of all thoughts of sticking by my Tokyo has arrived. In this period, the only thing that I can do is simply to move my life to the countryside. However, in implementing this small step of mine I almost do not notice that it contains all of the realities confronting Japan (2/7/1944).

This was Kishi's final conversion from the 'imperial way ideology' which was based on the standpoint of the 'majority' of the Japanese people. Hereafter, Kishi chooses to live solely to make his own living; this was his final wartime turning point.

Wartime evacuations and farming policies

The expansion of wartime settlement

Kishi said that the 'implementation' of his own evacuation 'contains all of the realities confronting Japan'. Although not in every area, there are aspects of the course pursued by Kishi – from evacuation and returning to farming to postwar settlement – that become feasible for the first time as a result of the overlapping of numerous policies of the wartime regime. I will now outline the wartime changes that made it possible for Kishi to take this action by looking at the evolution of evacuation and return to farming policies. I will also address the socioeconomic conditions of the region in which he resettled. This process was an important precursor to the postwar era. We see this, for example, in the fact that the Personnel Office of the Ministry of Agriculture and Commerce,[27] established in March 1945, and then the Arable Land Division of the Agricultural Administration Bureau, which will be the focus of this section, and the Head Office of Return to Farming were later amalgamated to form the postwar Reclamation Bureau.

As mentioned in the previous chapter, Japan's agricultural policy since the early 1930s had been targeted at overcoming economic depression, but once Japan entered its total war phase as the second Sino–Japanese War escalated, the policy turned towards the total mobilization of people and things with the aim of victory in the war. Under these policies, 'increasing food production', 'securing a labor force' and 'maintaining arable land' became the three principal objectives.[28]

Disregarding the feasibility of what it required, the mobilization prioritized military demands. As soon as mobilization began, signs of contradictions started to appear in all areas of society. The first contradictions with regard to arable land appeared in 1938 with the loss of 20,000 *chō* (19,834 ha) of arable land. This was compounded by the drought affecting Korea and western Japan in 1939, which led to a major decline in food production. In response, administrators from the Economics Divisions of Nagano, Yamanashi and Gunma prefectures began the development of cold highland areas in a number of districts[29] as a measure for revitalizing agricultural communities. At a stroke, increasing the food supply became a major national policy initiative. In April 1939, the 'Plan for Increasing Wartime Food Supply' was adopted, but it could not compensate for the continuing decline in production as a result of the destruction of agricultural land.

In March 1941, the Agricultural Land Development Law was enacted and implemented. A ten-year plan to achieve self-sufficiency in staple foods underpinned both laws. The plan, which was to be implemented by the Agricultural Land Development Corporation, was directed at clearing and improving agricultural land. The Corporation was tasked with opening up 100,000 *chō* (99,170 ha) of rice fields; 150,000 *chō* (148,755 ha) of land for other crops; 100,000 *chō* (99,170 ha) of large-scale drainage improvement works; and the construction of 50,000 homes for domestic immigrant farm owners.[30]

The Arable Land Division of the Agricultural Administration Bureau outlined these policies in the *Weekly Bulletin* in a manifesto titled 'Development of High Plains '.[31] It declared that these measures would provide 1,620,000 *chō* (1,606,554 ha) of flat terrain that could potentially be reclaimed on the Japanese 'homeland', and that developing these areas would build the defense of the nation. Mizoguchi Saburō was the Head of the Arable Land Division at the time, and was most likely responsible for drafting the 'Development of Highland' and for making this plan one of the key 'discourses on national land planning'. (Mizoguchi also wrote the Imperial Agricultural Association's 1940 *Conversations about National Land Planning: Manual for Farming Villages*.) When the postwar Reclamation Bureau was established, Mizoguchi continued to provide the central leadership.

Nonetheless, it proved practically impossible to achieve large-scale reclamation during the war; only about 15,000 *chō* (14,875 ha) of fields were reclaimed for crops. Hence the policy focus shifted towards land improvement for increasing production, which improved short-term results.[32] The large-scale reclamation program continued, however, and came to the fore once again in the final stages of the war and into the postwar period. Thus, the reclamation programs continued, yet the amount of arable land continued to decrease throughout Kyoto Prefecture. More specifically, almost 2,500 *chō* (2,479 ha) of arable land were lost during the period from August 1944 to February 1945.[33]

Changing occupations: Evacuation policy and returning to farming

Let us now turn our focus to the effects on people. The war had devastated the livelihoods of most people. Only by creating a new mechanism for controlling people's lives was the continuation of the war possible.[34] Price controls under National General Mobilization Law forced the majority of small and medium-sized merchants out of business. In parallel with the language of the battlefield, they were referred to as an 'army of the sick and wounded on the honorable home front'.[35] Total war mobilization led to commercial and industrial men and women considerably increasing the scale of wartime migrations. The return to farming policy, which was originally implemented as a measure to deal with people who had ceased working or changed

Table 2.2: Results of Agricultural Land Development Corporation Works (National)

	1941	1942	1943	1944	1945	Total
Reclaimed rice fields	983	740	781	487	997	3,988
Reclaimed plots	3,729	2,870	2,464	1,117	896	11,076

Source: Nōrin Daijn Kanbō Sōmuka, 1957, pp. 798–799.

occupation (hereafter: ceased working), later became intertwined with the evacuations of the cities which sought to minimize casualties from air raids. The lives of professional writers such as Kishi, who ceased working because of the restrictions on the use of paper, were part of this process.

The failure rate of small and medium-sized businesses had been increasing since immediately after the second Sino–Japanese War began in 1937, but it was not until 1940 that the cabinet reached a decision, 'On Small and Medium-sized Merchants', to address the issue of people who had ceased working. This was when the return to farming policy went into full swing. Placements in new jobs for these people were generally determined in the following manner:

1. munitions industry;
2. industries with capacity to expand productivity;
3. settlers in Manchuria (including pioneers of small and medium enterprises);
4. expanding migration into China and other areas in the South Seas;
5. expanding agricultural productivity (reclamation by government or private organizations and a return to farming'); and
6. construction works essential to national defense.[36]

It is clear from this list of possibilities for those changing occupation that a number of government ministries were involved in formulating them. The policies for a return to farming in the homeland took the form of pioneer teams made up of people changing occupation, which fell under the jurisdiction of the Ministry of Agriculture and Forestry.[37] They operated on the same principles as the policy for sending settler-farmers to develop Manchuria under the jurisdiction of the Ministry of Colonial Affairs.[38] These initiatives expanded further with the measures taken to deal with the spiraling increases in people changing occupation under the May 1942 curtailment of business operations, the August 1942 decision regarding 'Emergency Labor Measures', and the June 1943 'Curtailment of Industries for Increasing War Potential'. Strong controls were imposed on retailers and small and medium-sized businesses. As significant numbers of rice and fertilizer merchants were forced out of business, their reemployment became a continuous and serious social problem.

It is worth thinking of these developments in two stages. In the first stage, policies were aimed at one specific 'class' of people changing occupation. The second stage interlinked the evacuation of people with the return to farming, which incorporated a broader range of people. The increasing frequency of air raids and the preparations for 'defending the homeland' combined to accelerate the pace of evacuations of both production facilities and people.

The introduction of full-scale evacuation policies began in the latter half of 1943. On 8 February, in the Lower House Budget Committee of the 81st Imperial Diet, some Diet members asked whether the government was giving any consideration to evacuating cities, arguing that the present arrangements would 'counteract the ongoing situation' both from the perspective of air defense and that of people's spirit. The Home Minister, Yuzawa Michio, responded that 'there are no processes for dispersing people who are presently in cities to the countryside'.[39] At the time, the government's efforts to mount a city-based passive defense were limited to restricting any further factory construction. It was also around this time that there was talk of evacuating groups of schoolchildren from the cities, but this was seen as a wild idea and dismissed as a rumor by both intellectuals and ordinary townspeople.[40]

A mere six months later, on 21 September, however, the cabinet accepted a 'General Plan for Managing the National State of Affairs under the Current Situation'. This plan included a more specific 'Plan for Boosting Domestic Preparedness', which detailed the laws and regulations for the evacuation of the population. Furthermore, following a cabinet reshuffle in October, a decision was taken 'regarding the matter of evacuating factories and houses from the imperial capital and other large cities, and transferring people to the countryside'. Implementation of this evacuation was also included in revised air defense measures, which were announced in the middle of October. By the end of the year, air raid evacuation plans had been drawn up in every city. At around this time, the city of Hsinchu in Taiwan suffered an air raid. The newspapers, under directives from imperial headquarters, simply reported that 'losses on our side were insignificant', but on the 'homeland' the media had begun making frequent references to air raid precautions.[41]

Finally, on 21 December 1943, the cabinet adopted an 'An Implementation Outline for Urban Evacuation', which moved to 'implement the evacuation of the people, facilities and buildings so as to build strong air defenses in the imperial capital and other major cities'. Twelve major cities were designated (metropolitan Tokyo, Yokohama, Kawasaki, Osaka, Kobe, Amagasaki, Nagoya, Moji, Kokura, Tobata, Wakamatsu and Yawata).[42] Early in 1944, accounts of the evacuation began appearing in newspapers and magazines.[43] Measures for strengthening the air defense system and for the rapid and thorough implementation of evacuations were published in the February 'Outline of Emergency Measures for the Decisive Battle'. Then, in March, the 'Outline for the Acceleration of General Evacuation' was adopted by the cabinet. This prioritized the evacuation of buildings. The cabinet passed the 'Outline for Accelerating the Evacuation of Schoolchildren' in June, followed in November by the 'Outline for Implementing the Evacuation of the Elderly, Young and Expectant Mothers'. Measures were included to pay a relocation allowance to this last group, who were particular targets of the policy.[44]

The final turning point in evacuation policy was the combination of the evacuation and return to farming policies after March 1945. The rapid increase in the number of evacuations in this period targeted a broader range of groups, with the focus now turned to the labor force. Following the major air raids on Tokyo on 15 March, a 'Plan for Enforcing the Evacuation of Major Cities' was decided; and then food supply measures were added:

> Taking into account the changing outlook for the war situation from here on, the thoroughgoing evacuation of people and buildings from the major cities will be carried out speedily as part of the defense of the nation, under the rubric of food supply measures, thus promoting a posture of domestic self-sufficiency and readiness to fight.

It was also decided that 'leaving only the most essential machinery and people' in the cities, everyone else would be evacuated 'completely to the countryside, particularly to areas such as farming villages'.[45] Cities were treated as organs of the state; their status as living spaces for the people who had inhabited these spaces was largely extinguished. In a nation that had, until this point in time, suppressed all ideas and activities that might conflict with the private ownership of property, while thoroughly condemning 'individualism' and extolling the value of family and ethnos, suddenly it seemed as if all of those values had been lost.

On 30 March 1945, cabinet decided on an 'Outline of Emergency Measures Regarding the Employment of City Evacuees in Farming' in order to increase food production. This directed people to:

> comply with the demands of the evacuation of people from the major cities, receiving members of the evacuated population in an appropriate manner – building relations and providing the knowledge that they need to return to farming – making them into people who can contribute to increasing the food supply by positively instructing them on the steps involved in farming.

The plan set targets for an organized return to farming in Hokkaido, the Tohoku region and countryside areas to the west of the Kanto region on the Japan Sea side of the island, in time for the busiest period of farming in June. The targets were: 250,000 households (one million people), from the urban districts of Kanto and areas to its west; 50,000 households (200,000 people) from the city of Nagoya; and 150,000 households (600,000 people) from the Osaka–Kobe area. Although there is no record of the land areas involved and although these targets were never achieved, it is important to note that there had already been a plan in place for the return to farming and migration to these areas of 450,000 households (1.8 million people). Furthermore, there were also policies to offer as much land cleared by the Agricultural Land Development Corporation as possible to evacuees as well as land from the clearing of state-owned forests.[46] Separate policies were formulated concerning Hokkaido, which fell under the jurisdiction of the Ministry of Home Affairs. After the end of the farmers' busy season, the Head Office of Return to Farming was established in the Ministry of Agriculture and Commerce.[47]

Let us look at the extent to which the implementation of these mobilization proposals achieved the planned targets. Table 2.3 sets

Table 2.3: Employment situation for evacuees (3 villages on the outskirts of Tokyo), May 31 1945

	Students	Non-agricultural	Agriculture	No occupation
Mitamura, Saitama Prefecture	138	139	20	512[a]
Nakaison, Kanagawa Prefecture	n/a	38	61	402
Tamahoshō, Yamanashi Prefecture	n/a	9	38	306

Source: Ministry of Agriculture and Commerce Survey, Yamashita, 1948, p. 785.
Note: [a] Includes 'household' category.

out data about the employment of evacuees, obtained via a Ministry of Agriculture and Commerce survey. It is clear that although there were regional disparities in the rate of employment in agricultural and non-agricultural fields, the overwhelming majority of evacuees were unemployed. In fact, the idea that the mobilization would result in a return to farming was nothing more than a plan on paper; as the war progressed, things hardly ever went according to such plans. The rate of people movement far exceeded the government's expectations, with the number of evacuees having reached five million as at June 1945. Most of these people barely got by, merely enduring their state of 'unemployment' in farming villages far from the cities where they had been living. In addition to this forced unemployment, we should consider the forced migration of some 40,000 Chinese laborers to the hard labor sectors, an arrangement which was put in place from 1944. When we reflect on these two modes of enforcement, we must ask how we can coherently interpret the governance in this period.[48]

Nonetheless, although weak, a systematic foundation linking evacuation and a return to farming did take shape. Following this path, Kishi rented a plot of government-owned land that had been cleared and then sold to villagers by the Agricultural Land Development Corporation in Gomagō Village, Kyoto Prefecture.

Kishi Yamaji's evacuation

Let us return now to Kishi's urban life at the point when – having a presentiment that the war would end with the defeat of the Japanese military – he began thinking about evacuation. From around August 1944, matters had already reached 'a state in which, in this golden age of vegetables, vegetables are hardly available as rations for the people of the Tokyo area' (8/8/1944). Kishi had to travel from his home in Kichijōji to the environs of Shakujii to buy them every day. About this time, in September 1944, Kishi's eldest son was sent to Yamanashi Prefecture as part of an evacuation of groups of children. Kishi felt that the evacuation of his son had broken up his family. When taking food items to his son, Kishi was shocked by the dismal food situation that he witnessed and protested to the local authorities. The only real response he got, though, was from a local newspaper reporter who was present at the protest scene. He criticized Kishi, saying: 'I hear that school children from Tokyo can, if they ask, receive an extra eight *shaku* (144 cc) of rations on top of their standard entitlement of two *gō* and six *shaku* (0.468 liters). So I, frankly, find it offensive when you say that this is not enough' (20/9/1944). Kishi ultimately recalled his son from his place of evacuation.

Government propaganda sought to smooth the evacuation and return to farming with the slogan, 'the promotion of emotional harmony between cities and farming villages.'[49] As Kurokawa points out, however, the result was the exact opposite: city-dwellers and villagers were unavoidably confronted by the differences between their respective lifestyles. Rather than acknowledging the shared pain that they were all experiencing in a society in the advanced stages of collapse, the experience instead served to deepen conflict between city people and villagers. Of course, many of the residents of areas receiving evacuees were sympathetic and reached out to help. But the total lack of government assistance left the people to cope entirely on their own, making it almost inevitable that conflicts would deepen. Kishi sought the prefectural governor's intervention to evacuate to Yamanashi with no success, so he chose an evacuation destination in Kyoto, but this did not go entirely smoothly either.[50]

Kishi's thinking about evacuation wavered considerably between the end of 1944 and the New Year, as did that of many of the people living through this period. Quite a number of his acquaintances, who were writers and cultured people, had already taken the plunge and evacuated. Asahara Rokurō, an acquaintance who had evacuated saying 'I refuse to die by the side of the road', seems to have urged Kishi to action asking, 'What are you planning to do?' (1/1/1945).

At the beginning of February 1945, Kishi had 'lost five kilograms, my ribs are showing, and I have long, white hair' (2/2/1945). At the end of the month, he stopped off in Kyoto on his way back from a trip to Osaka, and began discussing going to the mountains of Kyoto Prefecture with Taniguchi Zentarō (27/2/1945). Kishi subsequently visited Kyoto several times, looking for a place where he could settle. Ultimately, through the good offices of Taniguchi, he ended up evacuating to Gomagō Village. A villager who worked at the Goma Railway Station had been distributed an allotment by the Agricultural Land Development Corporation, but 'being unable to manage it all, most had been left uncultivated'. Kishi rented part of a field from him, aiming to produce enough food for his family's needs (29/4/1945).

And so it was that Kishi evacuated to the village of Gomagō. Kishi moved his family into their new residence, a farmer's renovated hen house. Kishi writes a *tanka* (short poem) at this time in his notebook.

> Entering Tanba Province,
> Ascending via the Hozu,
> There is sadness,
> Regretting running away.[51]

For Kishi, who had sought social engagements, evacuation – just to live for the sake of one's own existence – was 'failure'; it was simply running away. This is one manifestation of the fact that, in the final stages of the war, even the material conditions that tie 'conversion' and 'mobilization' to the nation had broken down.

Rural society in the final period of the war

Let us now look at the village of Gomagō, the place where Kishi moved to. Reclaimed land in the village of Gomagō – an area made up of land running along the railway line from Gomagō Station on the Sanin Main Line to Shimoyama Station – spread across the administrative villages of Gomagō and Takahara, a total area of 200 *chō* (198 ha). The land was at an average elevation of 220 meters and was effectively flat, with a slope of 5 degrees; the average temperature was 16°C (60°F); and the soil had both acidic humus and a clay-like quality.[52] Both villages were at the southern edge of the cold snow belt district of Kyoto Prefecture.[53]

Gomagō is primarily characterized by its high proportion of forests and fields. It is a region of mountain villages, where farming families cultivate anywhere from 5 *tan* (0.5 ha) to just under 1 *chō* (0.9 ha) of land, as well as doing part-time work in prescribed forestry-related activities. Compared to other regions in the prefecture, the landlord system was not well-developed.[54] Gomagō had 479 farming households and a farming population of 2,496, but the proportion of subsistence farming families working less than 5 *tan* (0.5 ha) of land was less than 30%; a figure well below the national average of 42% (excluding Hokkaido).[55]

This district had long been meadow or pasture land, but with the growing use of chemical fertilizers by surrounding farmers, it became unusable. There had been suggestions of developing part of it as a park, but the wartime mayor and the Agricultural Land Development Corporation commenced public works leading to the reclamation of this land beginning from around the end of 1941.[56]

The reclamation of this land was promoted in February 1942, by the 'Ayabe Regional Branch of the Railway Apprenticeship Board'. At the same time, under the direction of the 'Nagoya Office of the Food Supply Corporation', 'teams of over 100 people are being dispatched daily from all towns and villages in the prefecture, and are engaged in reclamation activities'.[57] Students from Kyoto Imperial University also appear to have been mobilized for these reclamation works.[58] News of these works featured prominently at the time. From 22 July to 4 August 1942, the *Kyoto Newspaper* (*Kyoto* hereafter) carried eight special features under the heading 'Looking at the Agricultural Land Development Corporation in Gomagō Village in this prefecture'. According to the descriptions in *Tanba Ariran* (Tanba Arirang) – Kishi's account of his experience of settling in the area, which he turned into a novel – most of the laborers who worked for the contractors carrying out the corporation's basic public works business had been Koreans.[59] But there were no reports of these people in the newspapers.[60] In practice it had not been possible to mobilize enough local people because of a shortage of manpower. This is an example of literature highlighting the roles of people who had otherwise been rendered invisible by the media.

Settlers had constructed houses on some of the reclaimed land, and some of these houses were distributed among the local villagers, with the remainder being used to recruit new settlers; Gomagō received its first lot of settlers in 1943, the second in 1944, and by 1948 a total of 67 households had settled there.[61]

Many of the wartime settlers had to change occupations. As we have seen, the National General Mobilization Law forced many merchants and retailers out of business, leaving them to seek other means of making a living.[62] Before winding up their businesses, merchants from Gion and textile retailers from Nishijin had discussions with people in the Kyoto Chamber of Commerce and Industry, who had planned the reclamation of agricultural land and were in charge of Gomagō settlers (*Kyoto* 11/4/1943). The Chamber arranged an inspection tour of the reclaimed land for these business-people (*Kyoto* 24/4/1943). Kyoto industries, such as Nishijin fabrics, which were classified as luxury goods, were severely affected by the restrictions on business. The number of people who returned to farming in Kyoto because of wartime regulations had already reached 2,966 by 1941.[63] By 1944, the number of people, both male and female, who had become unemployed as a result of business closures had risen to 68,010; only 25,012 of these – a mere 36.8% – had made a 'complete change'. It must be assumed that the remainders were looking for employment.[64] Among those who had made the change were unskilled Korean laborers who used their local connections to return to farming (see Chapter 1). Japanese people were also organized into groups bound for Manchuria, such as the 'Heian Village Settlement Group' and the 'Kyoto Byōrei Village Reclamation Group' (see Chapter 3).[65] Hence, we must understand the reclamation of land in the 'homeland', including Gomagō, as but one part of a broader push for reclamation which included efforts in Manchuria, the southern areas of the Japanese empire, and Hokkaido. The ranks of settlers included people who had, for example, run dairy farms as family businesses in the city of Kyoto, and who now tried setting up business again in Gomagō. People with this type of experience made up the core group of settlers.

Kishi did not follow the established route to becoming a new settler. He settled by renting land that had originally been distributed to a villager. The wartime recollections of Shiogai Kanji, a long-serving mayor in this village with a relatively small number of subsistence farm families, indicate that the lives of farmers were comparatively stable. 'A decent farmer could deliver a good yield without too much hardship…in my village, only salaried employees and teachers ate the stalks of sweet potatoes'.[66] The efforts to increase the amount of arable land persisted across the nation. The reclamation policies which sought to achieve this, however, never captured the imagination of the people who already lived in the regions: the logic of nation and farming village were very far apart from one another.[67] It was in this gap that a route opened for evacuees like Kishi to rent land and become settlers.

Life after evacuation

From the day after his evacuation, Kishi immediately renewed his desire to 'realize a new literary work entitled "Report on Gomagō"' (29/4/1945). After having spent a month getting his house in order in Tokyo, Kishi settled down to farm work every day from May (29/5). He planted crops such as pumpkins, spring onions, melons, maize and tomatoes. His diary, which provided a polite running analysis of the war situation when he lived in Tokyo, had now become an agricultural journal (Photograph 2.2).

However, given the neglect of land in this region of highly acidic soils, harvests did not go as planned, no matter how much effort was expended. The war situation grew persistently worse. Large-scale air raids continued. Air raids over Osaka and Kobe caused even the skies over Gomagō to darken, more than 50 km away. Kishi continued with his agricultural work as he looked up at them from far away (1/6, 5/6). At the beginning of July, rations were cut once again, and the word 'starvation' began to appear in the diary (24/7). There were days when he reports feeling that he would collapse with hunger, yet he somehow managed to survive drinking hot water and tea (30/7).

Under these circumstances, Kishi began to view the people around him differently. Relations with Taniguchi, who had re-settled near Kishi, grew stormy (11/7), and we can see a deepening anger towards others. 'The farmers of Gomagō have the disposition of devils. Even if they manage to dig up some potatoes, foreseeing the future, they refuse to sell a single one, stockpiling them... Given this, was it a mistake to have struggled in the war?' (16/7).

Although he managed to keep going despite all of this, with assistance from the Agricultural Land Development Corporation employees and others, the important point in all of this is that evacuation from the city to the countryside hardly ever led to improved living conditions. Food shortages were extreme, and the much vaunted 'return to farming' utterly failed to increase the food

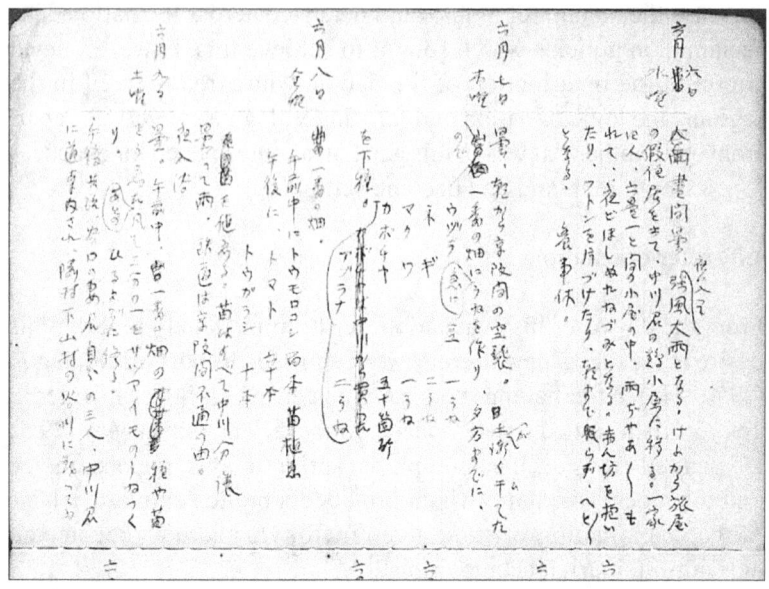

Photograph 2.2: Kishi Yamaji's Diary (Post-evacuation, early June, 1945)

supply. The fact that even Kishi, who ought to have been relatively well off, was in such straits provides some indication of how austere conditions were for other evacuees who had no connections.

A literary and Settler-farmers' Union movement

Beginnings of postwar reclamation

Land reclamation initiatives continued after the war. The systematic implementation of postwar land reclamation is typically spoken of as if it were a new stage but, really, the wartime reclamation initiatives were resurrected immediately after the war. In an interview with the Head of the Investigation Department of the General Affairs Bureau of the Nippon Steel Corporation and the Deputy Director of the Agricultural Land Development Corporation, from 2 September 1945, the latter reported that the Agricultural Land Development Corporation had a policy for 'the rapid reclamation of 3 million *chō* (2.98 million ha) of land nationally' 'in about a week from now', and that detailed planning for this was already underway. The Corporation sought Nippon Steel's assistance in developing a common policy, which would include employing people with experience in the Oriental Development Company, and the Manchurian and Taiwan Development Corporation. However, priority in selecting settlers was given to war victims and people who had worked in munitions factories and now had to find other occupations. Repatriates were not prioritized at this stage.[68] This was understandable given that a plan for Japanese who had established themselves in the colonies to remain where they were had already been decided on 31 August.

The process preceding the systematic postwar land reclamation was as follows. In October 1945, the Reclamation Bureau was created by merging the Personnel Office and the Head Office of Return to Farming with the Arable Land Division of the Agricultural Administration Bureau. According to Sasayama Shigetarō, Head of the Agricultural Administration Bureau under the Tōjō cabinet, in the early postwar period, opinion had been divided within his department over whether to pursue agrarian reform or land reclamation. Gradually the debate moved firmly towards a 'single-minded policy of reclamation'. Thus, on 9 November, the government passed a cabinet resolution on an 'Outline for the Implementation of Emergency Land Reclamation'.[69] This was a plan for realizing the reclamation of 1.55 million *chō* (1.54 million ha) of land and settling one million households in a five-year period by,

> responding rapidly to the demand for the creation of new farming villages that addressed the postwar food supply situation and demobilization; aiming for food subsistence via the implementation of large-scale clearing of new land and the reclamation of land from the sea as well as land improvement works while at the same time attempting to promote a return to farming by unemployed factory workers, soldiers and others.

In response to this national policy, on 18 December, Kyoto Prefecture adopted an 'Outline for Implementing Agriculture Countermeasures in Kyoto Prefecture', and, for the time being, settlers temporarily rented land from the Agricultural Land Development Corporation or Agricultural Associations, and attempted to set themselves up as owner-farmers.[70]

Although with different aims and on a different scale, through the appropriation of the domestic land reclamation policies of the Arable Land Division of the Administration Bureau and the return to farming policies of the Head Office of Return to Farming, wartime land reclamation was transformed, at a stroke, into postwar land reclamation. In this sense, postwar land reclamation was not a reform for solving the so-called social problems that persisted from the prewar period. Rather, it should be understood as a third development brought about by connecting the dismantling of the defense industry and repatriations following the war to a return to farming (see Chapter 3). Based on this policy, approximately 190,000 households (about 800,000 people) had become new settlers across Japan by 1955.[71]

Settlement in Gomagō and new ideals

Kishi did not personally hear the Emperor's speech announcing the acceptance of the Potsdam Declaration and Japan's unconditional surrender; he heard about it from others.

> I heard the reports of a midday broadcast by the Emperor in person, in the afternoon. It appears to have been an announcement of unconditional surrender. In the evening, the postman brought around the newspaper extra on his bicycle, and showed me the article on the Imperial Decree. Tears welled up as I read it. The idea of reading any other articles was loathsome. I didn't read them.

The next day he immediately set off with his eldest son to collect his clothes from relatives in Ibaraki, and on the 18th he went out to the fields to see to 'the pressing issue of potatoes'. Whatever people's mental state, life goes on. It was no doubt because Kishi recognized the gravity of the food shortages that, despite the austerities of life as an evacuee, he did not regard the end of the war as an opportunity to return to Tokyo. Two days after hearing that the war was over, Kishi met with the village head and discussed independently renting some village land (17/8/1945).

The end of the war brought a new round of people movements. September saw the beginning of the occupation by Allied Powers and changes in Kyoto's landscape. Large numbers of foreign soldiers were stationed in Kyoto, one of the primary occupation bases in western Japan. One day soon thereafter, Kishi was on his way to the offices of the Agricultural Land Development Corporation with Taniguchi when he was thrown some cigarettes and chewing gum from trains fully loaded with 'American soldiers' (9/9/1945). When, on 17 September, the Head of the prefectural Economics Department called all of the settlers together for a round-table discussion, Kishi took part (17/9/1945).

Around this time, Kishi purchased the household possessions of a Korean family who were leaving Gomagō.[72] From the outset of his evacuation, Kishi had had various interactions with Koreans. For example, he had been treating himself with ointment that he had obtained from a Korean neighbor (13/11/1945). The region was dotted with manganese ore, the mining of which was why large numbers of Koreans had settled in the village. The majority began to move out immediately after the war ended. As discussed in Chapter 1, a sense of 'panic' arose among Koreans living in farming villages.[73] In the process of their repatriation, they had to dispose of the property that they could not take with them, and Kishi acquired some of it. An important aspect of the changes that occurred between the prewar and postwar periods is that – as Koreans who had come to the village under the wartime mobilization returned to Korea – evacuees like Kishi who stayed behind became increasingly established in the village.[74]

One month after the emperor's surrender, Kishi records his new ideals about being in Gomagō. He had resolved on:

> engaging in agriculture, succeeding and then building a house, creating conditions in which it is possible to settle here without enduring the intolerable hardships that I am now enduring; I will invite my acquaintances from Tokyo and elsewhere, we must build a new village here that is based on the intelligentsia (13/9/1945).

When discussing Kishi's postwar activities, we can broadly establish three key areas. The first is the cultural movement, which also includes his activities as a writer and editor. The second is the Settler-farmers' Union movement, which we can further divide into two levels: his personal efforts, in Gomagō village, to put farming into practice and the All-Japan Settlers' League. The third area is his activities as a member of the Kyoto Prefecture Agricultural Land Committee. The following sections look at each of these initiatives in turn.

Cultural movement

Having set new goals, Kishi began working on one new initiative after another. Unsurprisingly, his initial emphasis seems to have been an extension of his prewar writing and editorial activities. While continuing to farm to provide his own food supply, Kishi also held talks with Japan Communist Party member, Makino Hiroyuki, as early as October 1945, and promoted the idea of launching a new magazine (25/10/1945). He found a sponsor in November, and by December he had hired an editorial department. And so it was that the magazine *Tōzai* (East–West) commenced publication in April 1946.

Nakano Shigeharu and Kurahara Korehito, with whom Kishi had previously worked, set up the New Japan Literary Association, while younger writers were involved in *Modern Literature*. Kishi also worked on writing novels while editing *Tōzai*. He continued discussing the Communist Party's literature department in Osaka with Makino, who worked with him on editing *Tōzai* (9/5/1946).

Kishi did not limit himself to these sorts of activities; he also established links with various cultural movements that had begun at that time in Kyoto. One example of this was his contribution to the magazine *Jiron* (founded January 1946), which proclaimed the 'promotion of democratic revolution' to be its mission.[75] In August 1946, Kishi gave a series of lectures for the Consumers' Union at the Gunze Silk Manufacturing Factory. While being invited by various unions to give lectures, he was also the literature teacher in the 'Kyoto Workers' Institute,' which was founded in July 1947. Labor unions, the city of Kyoto, and the prefecture of Kyoto had shared responsibility for this organization, but its management was principally in the hands of a workers' autonomous committee. The members of this management committee had various connections with prewar social and cultural movements.[76] Kishi does not seem to have expected that he would rejoin the party in the same manner as he had before the war, but his relations with the leftwing were rapidly restored in the early postwar period.

Settler-farmers' movement

Immediate postwar Gomagō

Kishi also devoted himself to the settler-farmers' movement.

Photograph 2.3: Family photo in the house at the rear of Goma Elementary School (From the left: Kyōji (Jun), Kishi, Yoshie and Takako)

Full-scale repatriation began from the spring of 1946, but there were also a large number of war victims whose livelihoods had been destroyed, as well as a vast number of people who had become unemployed when munitions production stopped. In the midst of these conditions, Kishi published an article entitled 'An invitation to fertile fields' (*Osaka Newspaper* 1/1/1946), which inspired the destitute.

In this article, Kishi stated: 'the country has collapsed, but my children can get hold of potatoes that their father has been able to grow. We must nurture the growth of the next era. I must not give up!' He then concludes with a somewhat more upbeat account of his situation than we find in his diary, saying:

> Is it not an ashamedly extravagant sort of life – two *kan* [about 7.5 kg] of potatoes each day! ... Just recently, the Agricultural Land Development Corporation has finally opened its own sawmill. This is in order to build houses for settlers. We still have plots of land for 40 settler households in this area. Of course, the labor required for cultivating land is not a life of ease without any hardship. If you decide that you have the stomach for being an owner-farmer of one *chō* of land and if you can work with strong determination and without delusions, then try it out and it will look after you.

A considerable number of people visited Gomagō after reading this article. Three days later, on 4 January, people from Fukuchiyama and Osaka visited his home after having read the article (4/1/1946). Tōzai's editorial department also received letters of enquiry (5/1/1946) as ten or so demobilized soldiers and war victims visited the area where Kishi lived. On 26 January, Kishi assembled these people together, offering 'consultations regarding whether or not to embark on the agricultural life with its autonomous and cooperative lives' (26/1/1946). It is unclear what Kishi intended by the term 'autonomous and cooperative lives' but, ultimately, three households of war victims from Osaka settled in Gomagō from among these people.

Like Kishi, considerable numbers of evacuees remained in places where they had settled during the war. Many of those who had changed occupations also chose to continue farming. In contrast, in urban area, some people who had been forced to change their occupation began seeking their reinstatement and organized a union immediately after the war ended.[77] Small and medium businesses which had been destroyed by the war would require tremendous effort to recover. Considering that it would be years before they could re-establish the sorts of businesses that they had once had, persisting with the new life established as an evacuee was a reasonable choice.

Settler-farmers' unions

On 21 March 1946, a ceremony for settlers was held at Gomagō Elementary School. In May Kishi started work on creating a settler-farmers' union. The organization of farmers' unions in Kyoto appears to have begun around the time of a rally held in November 1945 to hear speeches about the people's liberation. The first of these to be established was the Toba Farmers' Union in February 1946.[78] Other farmers' unions began to be established in early 1947, making the formation of unions quite an early postwar development.

Without examining the influences on the policies of contemporary farmers' union movements, such as *Nichinō* (Japan Farmers' Union), it is likely that their need to receive rations led them to accept the administration's guidance. Land reclamation and increasing agricultural productivity could not be achieved without rations of fertilizer and other agricultural materials, but their distribution was especially challenging in the chaos of the immediate postwar period. At this stage, the Settler-farmers' Unions and the prewar farmers' union movements, which played a central role in *Nichinō*, were qualitatively different.

The Gomagō Settler-farmers' Union was established on 19 May 1947, with one of the first wave settlers as its chairman. This was the first settler-farmers union in Kyoto Prefecture. But the chairman resigned two days later, due to a clash of interests between the first wave of evacuee-settlers, the earliest of whom already had two years of experience and all of whom owned some possessions, and the postwar settlers who had come into the area with absolutely nothing. This conflict was about whether fertilizer rations, under the postwar reclamation system, should be distributed to all, including the relatively more-established settlers, or should be limited to the most recent settlers, whose farming businesses were still insecure. The Farm Household Economic Survey, which looked specifically at reclaimed land in Gomagō, pointed out the problem posed for agricultural management by the unequal distribution of land between the first wave of settlers, who were given more than 2 *chō* (1.9 ha) of land, and later settlers, who received approximately 1 *chō* 5 *tan* (1.5 ha) which undoubtedly contributed to conflicts about rations.[79]

Kishi ended up playing a leadership role during the absence of a chairman. His diary entry for 11 June reads:

> In the morning, I went to the Division of Reclamation at the Kyoto Prefectural Office together with the other union officers and reported union business to the government officials. I also visited the Agricultural Land Division. I took possession of twenty lamps and ten pairs of rubber boots. There was a board meeting at the house of N's relatives in the neighborhood; an extraordinary general meeting to discuss the steps that need to be taken. It became clear that the youth are finally starting to stir. *Their manner – for example, holding the board meeting in a way that resembled how it is done in the prefecture – was practically totally due to the fervor of these youths for putting their training into democratic practice* [emphasis added].

Drawing on his prewar experience to lead the young settlers, Kishi built up the movement. His leadership in these sorts of conflicts is frequently seen after this period. Kishi's leadership skills were acknowledged by the person in charge of reclamation administration in Kyoto Prefecture at the time.[80]

When the Gomagō Settler-farmers' Union held an election of officials on 13 June, Kishi Yamaji was elected chairman of the union (by 13 of 20 votes). One of his elected deputies was Taniguchi Zentarō.[81] Under Kishi's leadership, the union strove for cooperation,[82] but there was fierce antagonism between Kishi and Taniguchi over the system of management. Kishi was ousted from the chair for a brief period and the two men broke-off their friendship.[83] Nonetheless, his installation as Chairman of the Gomagō Settler-farmers' Union, increased Kishi's participation in agricultural administration, and led to his appointment as Deputy Chairman of the prefectural Land Reclamation Society. He also played a role in the national settler-farmers' movement.[84] The area of Gomagō's reclaimed land was relatively small compared to other places in Kyoto Prefecture, but the prefecture's wartime policies of promoting Gomagō reclamation provided sound foundations for the connections that existed there.

The farming activities of the first evacuee-settlers in Gomagō would become central to production in the subsequent development of dairy farming in the area. On the basis of his experiences in the creation of their union, Kishi was influential in shaping their political focus. As settlers continued to pour into the prefecture in this period and local settler-farmers' unions continued to be organized, the Kyoto Prefecture Federation of Settler-farmers' Unions was established. Kishi was nominated, and later became, its first chairman.

Activities in the All-Japan Settlers' League
The organization of postwar settler-farmers had gotten underway in Osaka slightly before it did in Kyoto. The 'Osaka Settler-farmers' Cooperative' was established in January,[85] with its headquarters in the Arable Land Division of Osaka Prefecture.[86] Kishi's record of his settler-farmer period suggests that he received a written invitation from Osaka to attend the national meeting.[87]

In October 1946, a resolution was taken to establish the Japan Settler-farmers' League in Tsuchiura, Ibaraki Prefecture. At a general meeting on 20 March 1947, it changed its name to the All-Japan Settlers' League.[88] Kishi participated in the inaugural rally, held in the Central Labor Relations Meeting Hall in October, and became a central member of the standing committee as well as editor-in-chief of its magazine, *Settler-farmer News*.[89] The settlers'

Evacuation, return to farming and postwar settlement 127

Photograph 2.4: On their reclaimed land in Gomagō (Date taken unknown. Property of Itō Jun.) Top image: Taniguchi Zentarō front and Kishi Yamaji rear. Bottom image: Family photograph. (Information provided by Itō Jun)

groups positioned themselves as 'people who put democracy into practice' in their reclamation activities, which was the 'biggest postwar national policy' initiative, as well as in their plans to build new, autonomous, villages.

Two days after the inaugural rally, Kishi and other representatives of the Settler-farmers' League held negotiations on the rally's demands with people from the occupying force's Natural Resources Section. The head of the Land Reclamation Division of the Natural Resources Section, the Head of the Agricultural Economics Division, and the Head of the Agricultural Productivity Department were present. Kishi wrote in his diary that Sasayama, the head of Japan's Reclamation Bureau was also present, and said, 'Please do not say anything that would disadvantage the government; after all, you are all Japanese too, aren't you?'[90]

Kishi also came to play important roles in other national organizations concerned with settlement. For example, he records that, at a July 1947 meeting he was appointed to handle the seemingly intractable issue of the system for appointing a standing committee and deciding the articles of incorporation of the Preparatory Committee to establish the Japan Reclamation Association (8/7/1947). An individual writer, who had been in the depths of despair towards the end of the war, had – within the space of a mere two years – become a major player who was active at the very heart of one of postwar Japan's most important national policies: settlement policy.

Kyoto Prefectural Agricultural Land Commission

Kishi's appointment as Chairman of the Settler-farmers' Union led to him becoming a member of the Kyoto Prefecture Agricultural Land Committee, where he acted as in impartial committee member with responsibility for uncultivated land.[91] The challenges in this role included dealing with the objections of landlords concerning the release of their uncultivated land, and disputes about reclaimed land that had already been settled. Kishi applied himself to resolving the sorts of problems that follow settlement.

The problem of the Urairi settlement provides a case study through which we can trace historical sources of Kishi's activities in this area. Matters began with the settlement of 25 households (125 people) of war victims from Osaka on the uninhabited island of Tojima in Maizuru Bay. No-one in this group of settlers had any experience of agriculture. They included government clerks, returned soldiers and shopkeepers. Newspaper reports referred to this area as 'Osaka village' and described the settlers as being fired-up with expectations of 'demonstrating how to build an ideal village'.[92] However, reclamation immediately reached an impasse, and they were ultimately compelled to leave the area.[93] Kishi visited Urairi in April 1947 – along with Shimizu Kaoru from the Kyoto Prefecture, the Head of the Reclamation Department, a local council official and the Head of the Ministry of Finance's Branch Office. Following heated discussions, they decided to transfer all of the settlers to Gomagō (23/4/1947). The Urairi settlers were eventually transferred to the Shimoyama district, adjacent to Gomagō, but their hardships continued. *Osakafu Nōchi Kaikakushi* (History of Agrarian Reform in Osaka Prefecture) records its settlement results for 1946 as being the migration of 29 households to Gomagō,[94] but does not mention the forced relocation that followed the failure of the Urairi settlement which lay behind these resettlements.

Administrative ineptitude was not the sole factor at play; there was also the problem of relations with the inhabitants of the Shimoyama district. Kishi was wrestling with two cases of settlement problems at the same time: Urairi and Osadano. Osadano had been planned as a large-scale reclamation site in Kyoto Prefecture, but a quarrel broke out between the local inhabitants and the settlers during the second wave of settlers' training. This was land that had previously been forcibly requisitioned for military use. Thinking that the land would be sold to them following the withdrawal of the military, the locals reacted coldly towards the demobilized soldiers and war victims who settled there. There are reports that the locals began farming the land that was being used for training saying, 'This land has been handed down to us over the generations; do you think that we are about to let some nobodies from somewhere or other have it?'[95]

The settlers were not welcomed by the local farmers. They faced opposition from the landlord class when they acquired newly reclaimed land and from all of the villagers in cases in which common land, traditionally used for purposes such as collecting fuel and grass, had been reclaimed and allocated to new settlers. As discussed in Chapter 3, in one case, a plan to purchase uncultivated land to resettle a group of settler-farmers from Manchuria was opposed by all of the landlords in the Haradani district in Kyoto City. Kishi could see that the problem was not only the landlords; even senior members of the farmers' movement failed to understand the importance of opening up uncultivated land.[96]

Kishi influenced agrarian reform in the interests of settler-farmers, but his participation in agricultural committees brought the lives of small landlords to his attention. In an entry dated 30 June 1948, Kishi reflects on his participation in the prefectural Agricultural Land Committee using the expression, 'the tragedy of peaceful revolution'. On the whole, municipal agricultural land committees were managed on the initiative of tenant-farmers, particularly *Nichinō* members. However, it seems that Kishi's interests lay in hardships which saw no relief from these sorts of reforms. In his novel '*Sogan* (Petition)', the protagonist, who was a member of the Kyoto Prefecture Agricultural Land Committee, read a petition of a widowed landlord who had been dispossessed of her land. He felt compassion towards her, but he could not do anything for her.[97]

His work on the Prefectural Agricultural Committee came to an end at the close of 1948. On 3 October, having completed the purchase of 101% of the land it had sought, the Prefectural Agricultural Committee went out for sukiyaki as guests of the prefectural governor, in recognition of their services. At this event, at the request of an administrative official, Kishi approached the governor about releasing more money budgeted for reclamation (3/10/1948).

It had been possible to enforce the Compulsory Purchase of Land Act under the Agricultural Land Development Law, which had promoted prewar reclamation, but this had led to hardly any land reclamation. The fact that reclamation was almost completely achieved under the framework of postwar agrarian reform hints at just how important this reform was. It is also a reminder of the considerable difficulties inherent in the process of building relationships with the local inhabitants for the settler-farmers who came to live in the area against the backdrop of these powerful measures.

End of evacuation: Failure in the midst of reconstruction

In less than a year, beginning in late 1944, in 13 cities alone, it is estimated that at least eight million people – either by force or spontaneously – were torn away from the lives they had known until then as they responded to their rapidly deteriorating circumstances. This trend continued to accelerate until the end of the war, and continued briefly afterwards. Evacuation was a momentous event, making harsh demands of both those who moved and the inhabitants of the places to which they moved. Against some researchers who claim that even after these large-scale migrations the 'system' continued to be supported, I continue to question the merit of positing continuity between the wartime and postwar periods. That is, I continue to favor a discontinuity thesis.

The state dispersed the urban population in the interests of executing the war and striving for military efficiency. Meanwhile, as large numbers of people died in the increasingly frequent air raids, those who remained became more aware of the possibility that they too might be killed, and started to move out of the cities to escape the danger. Although some of these people were relocated under the directives of evacuation policies, we should recognize that there were important distinctions between them and those who moved of their own volition. These distinctions are often masked by the use of the Japanese term *sokai* (evacuation), which tends to evoke the policies that were formulated for the military's strategic purposes. Such masking hinders analysis of the variety of wartime experiences and sacrifices.

I was unable to find directly-related documents showing whether these voluntary evacuations exceeded the governments' expectations, but their response certainly did not reach the levels planned by the government. During the war, people acted with an awareness of the 'decisive battle for the homeland'. Although there are signs that there was at least some sort of plan to utilize the people who were moving, despite the various return to farming policies, the government was largely unable to include the masses of evacuees in productive activities. In this sense, the total war system, which sought to harness all of the people's energy and direct it towards prosecuting the war, instead collapsed in the war's final stages.

After the war, when faced with a choice of whether to stay in the places to which they had relocated or return to whence they had come, the majority of people chose to return. Kishi Yamaji also chose to return, finally. Further research is required to elucidate the great variety of motivations and decisions that people made at this time. What is important for present purposes is that people did not mindlessly choose the default option of returning to where they had called 'home', but rather, made conscious choices in response to the conditions of the immediate postwar period. We must recognize that even those choices that we view as if they were obvious were, in fact, chosen from among the complex of options available under the conditions that resulted from the defeat. My aim here is to begin to shed some light on the complexity of their decisions by studying Kishi's accounts of his experiences – even if his subsequent choice resulted in 'failure'.

Postwar reclamation in Kyoto Prefecture

I will now provide an overview of land reclamation activities in Kyoto Prefecture in the early postwar period. A target to reclaim 3,000 *chō* (2,975 ha) of land was set for Kyoto Prefecture, on the basis of emergency reclamation policies. However, as far as privately-owned uncultivated land was concerned, only 75% of the planned areas were actually released. With respect to the former military land, some was requisitioned by GHQ, but virtually all remaining areas were released beyond the initial expectation: while the release of 1,000 *chō* (991.7 ha) was the target figure, eventually 1,151 *chō* (1,141 ha) was released by the military for reclamation. By the end of 1952, 17 districts had received new groups of settlers and 1,784 *chō* (1,769 ha) had been reclaimed, although only 393 *chō* (389.7 ha) had been planted at this stage. By then, except for 17 settler groups, a total of 2,786 households of local farming families had obtained some reclaimed land, but here we focus primarily on the newest groups of settlers.[98]

In this chapter, I have attempted to demonstrate the continuation of wartime reclamation policies into the postwar period but, as is clear from Table 2.4, we see that in the case of Kyoto Prefecture the figures were 402 households of wartime settlers and 568 households of postwar settlers; thus, even the wartime proportion was quite high. The establishment rate was considerably lower for the wartime reclamations, with the majority of postwar settlers ultimately leaving farming.

Dairy and poultry farming were the core forms of agriculture. It is difficult to get a clear view of the living conditions from farmers during this period, but union figures indicate that almost 17% of farming households were receiving welfare, providing a good indication of the severity of their situation. Postwar settler-farmers continued to live in poverty.[99]

The personal circumstances of settlers presented in Table 2.5 do not say anything about the people who left farming before

Table 2.4: Number of wartime and postwar settler households in Kyoto Prefecture (end of 1952) (unit: households)

	Settler	Ex-farmer	Current	Establishment rate %
Group return to farming ventures	402	318	84	20.9
Post-emergency settlement ventures	568	271	297	52.3
Total	970	589	381	39.3

Source: Kyoto-fu Nōchibu Nōchi Kaitakuka, 1953, p. 12.
Note: An additional 337 households settled outside Kyoto Prefecture and 167 left agriculture, in the prewar and postwar periods.

Table 2.5: Personal histories of postwar land reclamation settlers in Kyoto Prefecture (end of 1952) (unit: households)

Changed occupation	110
Returnee settler farmers	72
Separated household	63
Demobilised	43
General returnees	34
War victims	16
Evacuees	6
Unemployed	4
Others	33
Total	381

Source: Kyoto-fu Nōchibu Nōchi Kaitakuka, 1953, p. 12.

this point in time. While the data suffers from these limitations, we can nevertheless see that those who changed occupations and settler-farmers repatriated from Manchuria constituted the vast majority of settlers. It is highly likely that evacuees were much more numerous in the early postwar period, but by 1952 they had all but disappeared, with a mere six households remaining. In this chapter, my primary focus has been on Kishi, an evacuee, and the Gomagō settlement area. As we have seen, the Gomagō settlement area was originally intended for the return to farming by people from Kyoto Prefecture who were changing occupation (war victims appear to have comprised the majority of the postwar settlers in this area). In Chapter 3, this study continues, focusing on another group: repatriated settler-farmers. Whereas the migration of Kishi and others like him was a response to the devastation of homeland cities, the migration of repatriates was determined by the collapse of the empire. The next chapter examines how these people attempted to connect with the new land.

Evacuees' homecoming

The 'Emergency Measures Controlling Movement into Urban Areas', which had restricted the migration of people into cities, were rescinded in March 1947, when people from the overseas territories were pouring into the country. Large numbers of evacuees could, at last, return to the cities and set about building new relationships.

On 1 January 1948, Kishi moved his family back to Tokyo, after a three-year absence. His intention was to devote himself to literature, but his diary reveals that he was in a state of anguish because life was still as austere as before and he was unable to do 'any real work' (12/11/1948) due to pressure to produce the sorts of 'texts that support daily life' (31/12/1948).

From around the middle of 1947, Kishi frequently recorded a desire to be able to invest more energy in producing literature:

> I would like to get away from this place, and gain some profitable time. (5/6/1947)

> I must struggle through the miscellaneous affairs of the reclamation issues and make a start on literature. (11/10)

> I think about removing myself from reclamation issues and immersing myself in literature. Even with reclamation issues, I only do what I can; unless Japan's national strength is restored, I am at a standstill and can do nothing about it. I have not reached the stage yet, around here, of thinking that I could stop what I am doing.

Even though his evacuation during the war had been a 'failure', he had sought to use the land that he had acquired there to make a start through the settler-farmers' movement. But his yearning to resume his participation in the literary movement remained strong, eventually spurring his return to Tokyo. Back in Tokyo, and pressed to write daily, Kishi also contributed to editing the collected works of Kobayashi Takiji, dug out his unfinished manuscripts, and was involved in assisting bereaved families.[100]

The 'Work Footwear Incident' and reclamation policy change

By October 1947, the rate of new settlements had fallen sharply, and the 'Outline for the Implementation of Settlement Operations' had been adopted to encourage local farming households to increase their planted acreage. During a visit to the Natural Resources Section, along with members of the standing committee of the All-Japan Settlers' League on 15 December, Kishi met with two officers from GHQ's Natural Resources Section. During this meeting, he got the impression that reclamation programs were no longer a priority for occupation policy. On 20 March 1948, together with members of the Japan Farmers' Union, the National Rural Youth Federation and the Agricultural Revival Council, he held a meeting in Settlers' Hall to discuss developing a movement for the purpose of breaking the deadlock in reclamation policy.

However, Kishi quickly became quite disillusioned with the settler-farmers' movement, following revelations of the Work Footwear Incident (1948). Leaders of the All-Japan Settlers' League were caught embezzling funds that they had received for distributing 30,000 pairs of work boots, which were rationed goods,[101] to the prefectures. The fallout included the secession from the union of the Hokkaido branch for a time, as well as the resignation of the chairman and deputy chairman.[102]

Kishi felt that he was unable to remain in the Settlers' League after these revelations of corruption. Thus, three days after the meeting in the Settlers' Hall, during another meeting to discuss organizing a nationwide general meeting about reclamation policies, Kishi resolved to quit (23/3/48). A sense of tragedy pervades a passage in the following day's diary entry: 'Is there a window somewhere, I wonder, to let in the light on life today in this country called Japan?' (24/3/48).

This sense of tragedy can be seen as reflecting the overall situation of farming villages at the time. While it is a fact that, immediately after the war, farm families profited by trading in the black market, this only continued for a short and limited time. For family farms with only limited opportunities for earning cash incomes, earnings from the black market were grossly inadequate to offset the impact of postwar inflation on family finances. Records of the Kyoto Branch of the Bank of Japan report that agricultural industries were barely keeping their operations afloat by trading in the black market and other sideline activities. It also reports that the substantial amount of savings in its accounts at the end of 1947 had been drastically reduced by May 1948.[103] These austere economic conditions continued until the mid-1950s, unabated even by the special procurement policies put in place by the occupation forces to combat the Korean War in the early 1950s.

Also in May 1948, a Natural Resources Section report, 'The Outlook for Japanese Agriculture', pointed out that the possibility of achieving reclamation policy objectives was slight. It concluded that 'under present conditions, plans for self-sufficiency in food supply will certainly end in failure' necessitating food imports.[104] This change in policy is reflected in the fact that 30,000 settler-farmer households left agriculture in this single year.[105] The Reclamation Bureau was dissolved the following year. Reclamation administration, which had accounted for 25% of the general agricultural budget in the 1946 financial year, was less than 6% in 1949.[106] Reclamation administration now faced a major turning point; a new era of land improvement was coming.

By this time, Kishi had already left Gomagō. The vast majority of evacuees returned whence they had come only a few years earlier. But this did not necessarily mean the end of their connections with the places where they had settled for those few years. In Kishi's case, although he severed ties with the central committee of the Settler-farmers' League, he continued to maintain very deep ties with Gomagō and the Federation of Kyoto Settler-farmers' Unions until 1950.

Ties with the settlement community

Although Kishi left the Settlers' League and quit the editorship of the *Settler-farmer News*, he maintained his ties with the Kyoto area. He frequently visited Kyoto, looked after the union's accounts, and provided advice about dispute tactics.[107] On 20 April 1948, the

Federation of Kyoto Settler-farmers' Unions was dissolved and a single Kyoto Settler-farmers' Union established. Soon thereafter, Kishi submitted a draft plan to establish a Kyoto Prefectural Settler-farmers' Cooperative at a meeting of the Committee for the Expansion of the Kyoto Prefectural Settler-farmers' Union.[108] On 5 September, the Committee appointed him as its representative for promoting a Preparatory Committee for the Establishment of Kyoto Prefectural Settler-farmers' Cooperative. As well as this sort of political participation, Kishi was also active on the business management side of things. For example, he held numerous discussions with an enterprise that was trying to introduce Angora rabbit breeding into settler farming. We find an entry in his diary for 11 October describing his reluctance to become head of the union. Nevertheless, he did so at a meeting of the Provisional Committee of the Kyoto Prefectural Settler-farmers' Union when he was asked to accept the role, because he was the sort of person who would not cause any bother.

Around the time that the trouble-filled operation of transferring the Urairi settlers to Shimoyama was completed and it was decided that they would receive prefectural support, Kishi visited a wintry Gomagō. The following entry appears in his diary on that day: 'As long as this village continues to exist here, it is a village that I have made. This was akin to the work of creating a novel' (22/12/48).

There are strong emotions here about a place where, ultimately, he was unable to stay. From 1948, Kishi's core activities moved to Tokyo, but on his occasional visits to Kyoto he still did some editorial work for the newspaper. Despite the increasingly anti-communist atmosphere at that time, the new 'Kyoto Prefecture Settlers' News' carried reports that, the Kyoto Prefecture Settler-farmers' Union, supported the Japan Communist Party because it was the only body developing reclamation policies.[109] In April 1950, the heads of Settler-farmers' Unions from each district in the prefecture held a meeting. During the afternoon session they listened to an invited speaker from the All-Kyoto Democratic Front Unification Conference, Ninagawa Torazō, before deciding which candidates would be endorsed in the gubernatorial election (13/4/50). Thus, the settlement of war victims became a political issue for the democratic front in Kyoto (see Chapter 3). Three days later, at the inaugural meeting to amalgamate the Settler-farmers' Union and the Settler-farmers' Cooperative, Kishi was asked if he would stay in his current position. He replied that he would not take up the office even if elected, and resigned as head of the union (16/4/50). This marks the end of Kishi's five years in the settler-farmers' movement in Kyoto Prefecture.[110]

An evacuee perspective: Kishi Yamaji's unfinished autobiography

Let's turn now to Kishi's personal reflections on the events of this period. From around the end of 1948, having decided that he was 'entering the final phase of my long literary activities' (8/12/48), Kishi began to refine his plans for an autobiographical novel. He began working on a manuscript entitled *Watashi no Bungakushi* (My literary history) in the late 1960s. A copy of this manuscript of more than 1,000 pages survives. Itō Jun has sorted through the sections up until the 1930s.[111] We learn from Itō that Kishi's plan when writing *Aru otoko no shishōgai* (The Private Life of a Certain Man) had been to write an autobiography that included his postwar settlement experiences. Kishi titled the settler-farmer period that we have been discussing in this chapter *Zetsubō Keikaku* (Project despair). As we consider Kishi's reminiscences about this time, it is important to bear in mind that we are talking about a 'story'.[112]

His notes on this work include an outline of his ideas. 'Date' in the passages quoted below is the protagonist's name. This is a name that Kishi frequently assigns to characters who are like him when he draws on his personal experiences as subject matter. His notes for the period immediately after the war include:

> A letter from a friend in Tokyo. Visits from a *Yomiuri* reporter and a *Shirakaba* (White Birch) reporter. At the same time as being unable to stand up and act because he is ashamed of himself – even though Date is urged to descend from the mountain – and having no faith in the literature of contemporary cultured people in a wounded Japan, or in the proletarian revolution.

When Date (Kishi) returns to Tokyo and sees the utter devastation of the city to which he has returned, he resolves to return again to his activities in the farming village. Kishi then describes his appointment as head of the Settler-farmers' Union using the words 'redoing things by participating in reality'. He was ready to come to grips with the fact that the war was over. This realization propelled

Kishi to a point where he finally stood ready to embark upon an action-oriented life once again, against his former decision that his own activities would be in the sphere of expression: literature and editing activities. In the margin at the outset of part three, there is a note about 'a democratic–cooperative farming village', from which we can see that Kishi understood the agricultural cooperative route that he had consistently sought in his union activities to be an issue of democracy.

Part three contains what appears to be a detailed description of events in 1948, when Kishi continued to be pressed with demands from Gomagō despite having retired from the Settler-farmers' Union. 'What were the realities that he saw? They were simply the picture presented by the Katayama and Ashida Cabinets, which were experiences of collapse'. 'How long before the people would rise up'? His criticisms of the settlers' movement were inexhaustible. The structural and economic constraints, as well as the figure who was continually conflicted and frustrated by long-standing abuses in the social movement all seem to lay heaped on top of the transformations of the postwar democratization process.

At the end of the manuscript for 'Project Despair', Kishi says 'these three years of my life were not at all a waste' because 'I was able to see the success of many settlers'. He closes with 'this stability was nothing other than waiting for the revolution. The above all arose from the midst of despair'. Kishi's long-awaited revolution never arrived, but his diary provides valuable insights into the lives of settlers during this period.

In this chapter, I have used Kishi Yamaji's surviving diary as a guide. Kishi's personal reflections on the processes of evacuation and returning home have helped to draw out the connections between evacuation and return to farming policies, and their evolution into postwar reclamation policies. Previous research has treated evacuation and postwar settlement as separate phenomena, but this study has been able to shed new light which shows a policy continuum upon which the wartime 'return to farming' policy was transformed into the postwar settlement policies.

Further research is needed to clarify how evacuation policies were implemented. We also need to compare the evacuation records across all geographical areas, including islands, coastal and upland areas. Various plans for evacuation acknowledged that there was not sufficient infrastructure for their implementation, but it is only with hindsight that we can see that evacuation did not lead to people putting down roots. We must also challenge the question of assumed universality of these evacuation plans by following the lives of individuals, for there is a particularly strong element of chance in their lives. Kishi's zigzag trajectory clearly reveals the significant instability in the social changes throughout the war and in the immediate postwar period. Despite the fact that Kishi found himself negotiating with GHQ officials and as the head of a national organization after the war, as soon as government policy permitted, he returned to Tokyo and set his sights once again on literature. From the perspective of the present study, which stresses continuities between the wartime and postwar periods, vast numbers of evacuees seem to have disappeared into a deep chasm between the two periods. And yet, individual people made personal decisions about how to deal with rapidly changing circumstances; they were not simply led around by the nose.

The social movements unleashed by the energy of people who had been liberated via the democratization processes in the early postwar period – even if 'ephemeral' – should be seen as a function of the idiosyncratic nature of this period. It is not possible to understand this period by ignoring the eruption of energy and the formation of a wide variety of groups by an extensive array of people. The importance of uncovering historical facts about individual experiences in the countryside continues to grow.

We have a clear image of Kishi from his diary, perpetually motivated to build the 'culture village' of his dreams while aiding postwar settler-farmers who were facing difficulties. Even as he suffered, he never relinquished hopes for the proletarian literature that the imperial government had forced him to suspend. He attempted to capitalize on his prewar experience and connections, organize people and teach them how to fight the administration. It was only because Kishi found himself on settlement land with few traditional fetters that he was able to take this stand. At the same time, it is clear that without the activism of Kishi and other cultured evacuees, the settlement of a small area of settlement land in the middle of Kyoto Prefecture could not have achieved the considerable influence that it did within the settler-farmers' movement of the early postwar era.

The settler-farmers' movement, which originated in Gomagō, was the site of sharp conflicts between Kishi and Taniguchi as well as other Japan Communist Party members. However, at the regional level, it was part of the extensive democratic movement that was developing in Kyoto. It also played a leadership role in the continued development of Gomagō Village: for example, in the continued operation of dairy farms by the wartime settlers who broke away from the postwar settlers when the union was established and the continuing growth of Wagyu beef production in the village.[113] These connections with the land were experienced by individual evacuees. We see an expression of this in Kishi's involvement in the launch in 1955 of the magazine Peasant literature. *Tanba Arirang*, Kishi's account of his experiences as an evacuee, was published in this magazine. In one passage, Kishi records the start of postwar settlement:

> With the start of state-run emergency settlement, 30-odd families of war victims and repatriates have temporarily been sent in to the former Agricultural Land Development Corporation's reclaimed land. They were only provisionally allotted some land; given no funds, no fertilizers, no tools, nothing at all. Most importantly, they had no houses to live in and had to sneak into farming meetings, tin huts, or a corner of school. They appeared on the cultivated land during the day with their strange appearance looking like tramps. Some even built lean-tos and lived in the mountains...The awful reality of repatriates and war victims suddenly hit me in the face.[114]

As in this depiction, though, most of the settlers were new 'others' who appeared in the villages at the end of the war. What would encounters with these 'others' lead to? Would they soon go away?

This chapter has examined postwar settlement from the perspective of 'homeland' policies. In the next chapter, we will re-examine it from the perspective of the collapsing empire.

3 Farmers' lived experience of borders from Manchuria to postwar settlement

> When our compatriot, who had returned home from the south, walked through the town of Uraga, children threw stones. 'Beggar, beggar!' they called. When I asked the children, 'Why beggars?' they were told 'He looks like a repatriate, so he is a beggar'.
>
> Yuasa Katsue, *Gaichi Hikiagesha* (Overseas repatriates)

Re-arguing 'spiritual demobilization of the people'

It has been said that a society's character is revealed in how it treats its most vulnerable citizens – those who have suffered crises and lost the source of their livelihoods – but also by the behavior of those who have been affected in these ways. In this chapter, I focus in particular on the processes by which Manchurian settler-farmers were repatriated into Japanese society immediately after the war.[1] I will focus on one aspect of the postwar unification of the people while simultaneously considering how memories and experiences of colonial rule carried over into postwar Japanese society.

In the previous chapter, we looked at Japan's expanding need to increase food supply in response to the 'crisis' brought about by the suspension of trade and the loss of colonies at the end of the war. The postwar emergency settlement, which pre-dated land reforms, was one of the important policies hammered out in response to this crisis. As discussed, the Reclamation Bureau was established within the Ministry of Agriculture and Forestry in October 1945, inheriting the domestic settlement policies that had been adopted during the war. Then, on 9 November, the cabinet decided upon an 'Outline for the Implementation of Emergency Land Reclamation'. Soon thereafter, large numbers of settler-farmers who had returned from Manchuria (repatriated settler-farmers) were re-settled in Japan. By the end of 1950, the vast majority of repatriations were completed, and of the 65,329 Manchurian settler-farmer households who had returned, 40%, or 26,499 households, had been resettled.[2] A substantial proportion of repatriated settler-farmers were not able to return to their 'hometowns', the places that had sent them off in the first place, and had to look to new areas. In short, for Manchurian settler-farmers, returning to their 'native country' did not mean returning to their 'hometown'.

These people who had borne the national policy of Manchurian settlement had been abandoned by their nation's military and were exposed to immense dangers. Yet, they were marginalized upon their return to Japan. The processes of repatriation and resettlement in accordance with national policy ran parallel to the processes through which ordinary Japanese citizens were coming to be known as 'the nation', under the new slogan, 'Building a New Japan'. The points at which these two processes intersect are where relationships between the nation-state and 'the people' can be seen most clearly. These intersection points also shed light on the myriad relationships that are found among the population. Hence, delving into the development of these parallel processes can be very illuminating.

We begin with a discussion of national policy and then examine the reception of repatriated settler-farmers in the postwar environment. This is followed by an outline of the general conditions of repatriates in the regions. I will also discuss the social movements of repatriates, and highlight their demands.[3] My focus in this chapter will be on urban areas for two reasons. First, because although the initial waves of settler-farmers sent to Manchuria were comprised mostly of farmers from agricultural villages, as time went on there were increasing numbers of people from urban areas who had to change occupations as various industries were shut down in order to divert their resources to the pursuit of total war. Second, many of the reception centers for repatriates were located in urban areas. It was not uncommon for repatriates to return to their places of origin but, finding no work there, having to return to a reception center. They were then moved on to re-settlement sites. Consequently, cities played an important role as transit points, and must be included in our analysis. In the next section, I will combine two different vectors – developments on the part of the state and regional repatriated settler-farmer movements – and discuss the ways in which imperial tours provided opportunities for repatriated settler-farmers' self-definitions, as the protagonists who would implement the new national settlement policy. The final section of this chapter traces a case of repatriated settler-farmers in Kyoto Prefecture.

In recent years, there has been an increasing amount of research about repatriated settler-farmers, following the publication of official documents. Various studies have examined the processes behind the establishment of related agencies and the formulation of policy. There has also been research into the very small social group known as repatriated settler-farmers, but these have rarely delved into the concrete policies behind individual case studies.[4] A series of studies by Michiba Chikanobu raises important points about how repatriation and postwar settlement are interconnected, putting into perspective Japan's period of rapid economic growth.[5] However, the importance of the Manchurian settlement and immediate postwar popular movements is unclear in Michiba's arguments. Both of these factors are essential to understanding the role of repatriates in postwar settlement. This chapter will also seek to untangle the intersection of these important historical factors.

However, it would be best to understand resettlement as having occurred under the policy guidance of bureaucrats. As the authors of these official policies neglected to analyze local conditions in the areas where they applied, it is not possible to clearly understand how these policies were 'agreed' upon. This chapter does not focus on the identity of those who formulated these policies or examine the mobilization process which carried over from the war. Its aim, rather, is to consider the specificity of the immediate postwar period and prospects for the people who lived through it.

Araragi Shinzō's *Historical Sociology of 'Manchurian Emigration* is a pioneering work focused on the Manchurian settler-farmers who were re-settled after the war. It investigates their journey from being sent to Manchuria until they established new villages in postwar Japan.[6] Araragi bases this research – which focuses on re-settlement in Kumamoto Prefecture – on unity among the settler-farmers. He stresses the importance of two factors: the shared experiences of Manchurian settlement and repatriation, and leadership within settler-farmer groups. Miyoshi Yutaka and Kitazaki Kōnosuke's studies make the same points (it is important, however, to take Itō Atsushi's critique of Miyoshi into account).[7] These works provide a sound foundation for understanding the experiences of settler-farmers in the postwar period. However, they focus on the experiences of particular groups of repatriated Manchurian settlers without adequately examining their relationships with the contemporary state and society. Their experiences and decisions ought to be discussed in terms of the circumstances in which they found themselves.

Aoki Takeshi, in contrast, is on the right track in his studies of resettlement in Shimoina District in Nagano Prefecture. Aoki investigates the processes through which repatriates were sent to postwar villages to be settler-farmers.[8] This is a valuable contribution to understanding their relationships with the local society. This chapter aims to contribute to the research by adding an urban perspective, which we still do not have for understanding the position of repatriated settler-farmers in Japanese society.

Kimura Kenji's research, a case study of the Senzaki region of Yamaguchi Prefecture, depicts repatriates in a dependent relationship. Kimura concludes that repatriates could not become established in the local society without the control and protection of the administration.[9] There is no doubt that repatriates were in a weak position in local society. This does not mean, however, that they were totally dependent. In this period, repatriates organized themselves; they criticized the local societies that excluded them and the administration which provided insufficient support; and, occasionally, they took matters into their own hands (for example, in squatting). Their organizations were connected to extensive and diverse popular democratization movements in the early postwar period. It is not possible to understand the experience of repatriation in this period without recognizing this point. Repatriation is important not simply because of the large numbers of repatriates, but also because of its impacts on the form of government, which makes it indispensable to an understanding of the period. Democratization also needs to be discussed in terms of the various forms of conflict within the new forms of government.

The social movements by repatriates are inseparable from the re-settlement of repatriated settler-farmers. The opportunity for a conversation with the emperor through imperial tours served to reinvigorate ideas of the 'nation', paving the way for the twin social vectors of policy and social movements to work together in directing repatriated settler-farmers towards re-settlement. Interest in Shimizu Ikutarō's pioneering work about the postwar imperial tours has recently been revived in the context of studies of the imperial system.[10] While I will discuss the imperial tours, my interest is not a political analysis of government power, but what the imperial tours meant for the people who experienced them.

This question, which is an underlying theme throughout this book, emerges from the intersections between studies of repatriation and postwar settlement, which multiplied in the 1990s and 2000s. We should, however, recall Maruyama Masao's 1951 statement about postwar settlement. Maruyama points out that the overall sense of duty was more fragile in postwar Japanese nationalism than it had been in the prewar imperial period. However, he makes the further point that the prewar national consciousness flowed down to the base of the social structure because of its relaxed focus on the central government. Maruyama called this 'the demobilization of national consciousness' and 'a spiritual demobilization'. Pointing to the settlement movement as an example of this, Maruyama says, 'the old nationalism had either died out or qualitatively changed. It would be more precise to say that it had vanished from the political surface only to be inlaid at the social base in an atomized form.'[11]

His use of 'social base' here refers to the family, the village and small local groups. It is therefore worth taking a microscopic look at how repatriates, who had lost their roots, lived in the midst of the vortex of the formation of a new postwar Japanese nationalism, and to think about how that effected national unity in postwar Japan.

My analysis in this chapter focuses primarily on the Kyoto region. Kyoto Prefecture did not send large numbers to Manchuria, and relatively few of the postwar repatriates settled in the prefecture. The land area allocated for such resettlement was correspondingly small relative to other places. Nevertheless, the patterns and conditions of resettlement can still be satisfactorily identified in this region. Our interest is in revealing the various relationships that shaped the resettlement experience, rather than a 'representative' sample of quantitative significance. Kyoto is of particular interest for research due to specific regional characteristics. The port of Maizuru in the north was one of the key repatriation ports, and Kyoto Railway Station became a center for repatriates.[12] Furthermore, Kyoto was unique among large cities in not being subjected to large-scale air raids, and thus escaping much of the devastation suffered by other cities. Hence, in the earliest postwar years, enormous numbers of repatriates flooded into it. Kyoto also stands out because of its relationship with the urban regional society that was well supported materially. The following discussion will bear these features in mind.

Farmers' lived experience of borders

Photograph 3.1: Kyoto Railway Station circa 1935
Note: This appears to be around 1935. It was a central hub for repatriates after the war. Kyoto Institute, Library and Archives.

The state's repatriated-settler farmer policy

Postwar settlement policy and Manchukuo bureaucrats

Chapter 2 provides a detailed account of the particulars of postwar settlement policy, but I will add a few brief points about it here. The Reclamation Bureau was established in the Ministry of Agriculture and Forestry on 26 October 1945.[13] On 9 November, it became responsible for the 'Outline for the Implementation of Emergency Land Reclamation'. This document set out the bureau's aims as,

> In response to demands for the construction of new villages under the postwar food situation and following demobilization, alongside attempting to achieve food self-sufficiency by implementing clearing, reclamation and land improvement projects, attempt also to promote the return to farming by factory workers who have lost their jobs, soldiers and others.

With a target of reclaiming 1.55 million *chō* (1.54 million ha) and establishing one million households of settlers in only five years, this plan was far more ambitious than the Manchurian settlement, which had aimed at settling one million households in 20 years.

People had already begun reclaiming land that had formerly been used by the military, immediately after defeat, and on the suggestion of the Personnel Office of the Ministry of Agriculture and Commerce, former military lands were progressively designated for agricultural development from September.[14]

Below, I set out the processes put in place to facilitate repatriated settler-farmers under postwar settlement policies. The Reclamation Bureau employed so many bureaucrats from the former Manchuria Colonization Bureau that one official remarked, 'Isn't this the return of the Manchuria Colonization Bureau?'[15] Sasayama Shigetarō, Head of the Reclamation Bureau, recalls that the central members of its Office for Increasing Reclamation were Waguri Hiroshi,[16] Tojima Yoshio, Tanigaki Senichi,[17] and Noda Tetsugorō. Of this group, at least Waguri, Tanigaki and Noda were bureaucrats who had been deeply involved in the Manchurian settlement.[18]

However, leadership in the early stages of resettling repatriates was by the Administration Bureau, Ministry of Foreign Affairs, which was set up on 26 August 1945. The Settlers' Division was established later. The bureaus in the Settlement Division of the Greater East Asia Ministry's Manchuria Secretariat that had been responsible for sending emigrants to Manchuria during the war were reorganized to oversee the repatriation of people to Japan.[19]

Behind the policy for the re-settlement of repatriates was a determination to make everyone who was fit for taking up agriculture as their occupation do so, based on the 'Relief Plan for Overseas Repatriates in Areas of Establishment' (25/4/1946). The Committee on Measures for Overseas Repatriates Taking up Agricultural Employment[20] was set up in the Ministry of Agriculture and Forestry for this purpose, with regular cross-sectional consultations within the bureau.

Subsequently, the Head of the Administration Bureau, Ministry of Foreign Affairs requested that all of the administrative officials involved in the emigration of farmers to Manchuria be assigned responsibility for providing relief. Furthermore, his instruction specified that preferential use be made of facilities in 'villages and places of people's birth (native village)'. Because state relief would not be sufficient, it also sought cooperation from all of the agencies that had previously been involved in sending emigrants.[21] There were also repeated calls for the prompt supply of relief, made in the name of the heads of the Administration Bureau, the Ministry of Foreign Affairs; the Social Bureau of the Welfare Department; and the Repatriation Bureau of Repatriate Relief Authority.[22]

There was, however, a realization that trying to repatriate people to their 'native villages' would quickly reach its limits. Let us consider the 'Manchurian Settlers' Remedial Treatment Plan (Draft)'[23] formulated in the Administration Bureau of the Ministry of Foreign Affairs. This draft plan outlined various 'objectives' for the treatment of repatriated settler-farmers.

> Taking into account their wretched condition of being totally exhausted and possessing nothing, as a result of the circumstances in which they were sent off and their long years of living as displaced persons in areas occupied by the Russians after defeat, the government and the people should unite to provide every measure to assist in their acceptance and to remake themselves. Alongside making use of their abundant experience as settlers and steering them primarily towards domestic emergency settlement ventures, bringing their propulsive power into play, guiding them, in particular, to become the nucleus of the construction of new agricultural villages.

This draft plan also includes 'Other Items of Remedial Treatment' which stipulates that 'the ex-leaders of settlement groups should be recruited as expeditiously as possible as employees of relief and settlement agencies. In the case of the settlement of former colonial-settlement units or companies of the Manchurian Youth Corps Brigade, their leaders should establish themselves as the groups' representatives'. Furthermore, it sets out a policy of absorbing into all of the different types of previously established settlement-related agencies, using this as a lever for the organization of settlers in general. In this way, bureaucrats concurrently engaged in systematic and organized domestic emergency settlement while promoting the self-reliance of repatriated settler-farmers.

In December 1946, the Ministry of Foreign Affairs' jurisdiction over the repatriated settler-farmers was transferred to the Ministry of Agriculture and Forestry. Ministry of Foreign Affairs records say that 'when it came to providing relief and mediating a change of occupation to agriculture for repatriated Manchurian settler-farmers, the guidelines for work in the section definitely followed the "Repatriated Manchurian Settlers' Remedial Treatment Plan"',[24] suggesting that the draft plan was effective.

Thus, while some key personnel transferred from the Settlers Division in the Ministry of Foreign Affairs to the Reclamation Bureau in the Ministry of Agriculture and Forestry, others were deployed throughout administrative agencies in Japan. The Remedial Treatment plan sets out that,

> In the case of paperwork related to Manchurian Settler-farmers, there is a need for central and regional agencies to come together and deal with the work that needs doing in close cooperation with one another. Therefore, we are deploying full-time support personnel to the regions in order to achieve this harmoniously and expeditiously.

We understand this to mean that full-time personnel were deployed to Agricultural Land Bureaus in some prefectures (including Tokyo, Aichi, Shimane, Iwate, Ōita, Yamaguchi, Gifu, Tottori and Nagano). In the case of Kyoto, several Greater East Asia Ministry bureaucrats were included in the list of prefectural Settlement Section chiefs.[25] This deployment corresponds to the deployment of people to Agricultural Associations by the Settlers' Relief Association, which we will look at in the following section. Both Waguri and Tanigaki, who worked in the Reclamation Bureau, moved to Agricultural Land Sections in local government.[26]

Establishing a nationwide association of concerned parties

Now, let us look at associations of repatriated settler-farmers which were established immediately after the Administration Bureau in the Ministry of Foreign Affairs. By the end of August 1945, immediately after defeat, the Manchukuo Repatriates' Relief Association was established and approved by the Ministry of Foreign Affairs, but its funds were immediately frozen and its activities curtailed.[27] The following March, it was reorganized as the Manchuria and Mongolia Compatriots' Relief Association. This was the first of the support associations for Manchurian repatriates.

Its relief activities were aimed at people returning from Manchukuo, including both civilians and government officials.

In contrast, Settlers' Relief Association provided support only to repatriated settler-farmers. The Manchuria and Mongolia Compatriots' Relief Association was reconstituted from the Manchurian Immigration Council, the prewar assistance agency in Japan for emigrants, and was approved by the Ministry of Foreign Affairs on 1 December 1945. Its chairman was Kodaira Gonichi. Other leadership positions were held by people who had participated closely in deploying Manchurian emigrants. Its managing directors, for example, were Ikoma Takatsune, Hashimoto Denzaemon and Morishige Tateo, all of whom were deeply involved in Manchurian settlement, an indication that points to the continuity of high-profile individuals in migration organizations. The prospectus for this association indicates that postwar settlement was an extension of Manchurian settlement, as we can see in the following passage.

> The people engaged in agriculture in Manchuria, will inevitably face various grave difficulties in accordance with the changing circumstances in international society following the end of the war. Thus, the task of helping them is an urgent one *in order to allow them to achieve their will*. (emphasis added)

Clearly, the association's activities were aimed at promoting the re-settlement of repatriated settlers, measures to facilitate and support repatriation, improving the state's treatment of repatriates, and backing the establishment of the Association for International Collaboration of Farmers; that is, mediating re-settlement.[28] The Manchurian Immigration Council had experienced an overall reduction in scale from its prewar days as an organization, but its personnel moved across to the National Agricultural Associations.[29]

The repatriated settler-farmers' association was created at the same time as the Settlers' Relief Association. Bureaucrats from the Administration Bureau of the Ministry of Foreign Affairs participated closely in the unification of the two. In August 1946, the National Settlers Self-support Association was established as the repatriated settlers' own association. It touted that 'rebuilding Japan will be our supreme parting gift to our shared will to die a glorious death'. Sō Mitsuhiko, who had served as head of the second Chifuri Settlement Group and then director of the Manchurian Development Corporation was appointed as its head. The mission statement of

the Self-support Association said that, 'the means for bringing about our own rehabilitation by our own efforts are to be found in domestic settlement', which would lead to rebuilding the fatherland. The mediation of settlement would be the core of its activities. The following were adopted as urgent motions at the first Meeting of Representatives of the Settlers' Self-support Association:[30]
1. We pledge to implement all settlement completely this year.
2. We insist that cultivatable land be opened up promptly.
3. Allow our representatives to participate as committee members of both settlers' and farmers' organizations.
4. Bring back un-repatriated settlers promptly.
5. Do not leave bereaved families without assistance.

They also aimed to cooperate with the All-Japan Settlers' League, which was a farmers' body run by settler-farmers, and to make it possible for members of the Self-support Association to be allowed to settle in areas where there were vacancies. The group also conducted various other activities, such as stationing a committee member permanently in the port of Maizuru in order to expedite the settlement of repatriated settler-farmers from districts in Siberia.[31]

The Relief Association, the Self-support Association and the Japan Reclamation Association all received support from the Reclamation Bureau, and prepared nation-wide re-settlement plans. These three bodies cooperated with each other, and between the end of November and early December 1946, they, 'mobilized the leaders of the former Manchuria settlement group and members of the former Manchurian Development Corporation; formed ten survey teams to look for land suitable for settlement; ... and conducted field surveys'. However, the wilderness of Konsen in Hokkaido was the only place left where large-scale re-settlement was possible, and hence a 'Committee for the Promotion of the Settlement of the Konsen District' was formed.[32] Nakamura Kōjirō guided settlement in this area. Nakamura was a former director of the Manchurian Development Corporation and head of the former Settlement Research Institute, as well as a founder and committee chairman of the Hokkaido Settlers' Self-support Association. This was the largest undertaking as an organized re-settlement plan, but it soon suffered an extensive reduction of scale due to lack of funds.[33] The important point, however, is that these leaders turned their efforts towards re-settlement based on smaller units across widespread regions.

Thus, the re-settlement of repatriated settler-farmers was overseen by bureaucrats who had been responsible for prewar emigration and people who had been connected with Manchurian settlement policies. Their efforts included organizing bodies of concerned parties, reorganizing relief bodies and formulating re-settlement policies (the 'Manchurian Settlers' Remedial Treatment Plan') as well as deploying individuals to related agencies that responded to these developments (the National Agricultural Association and all local government offices with responsibility for settlement). The large-scale re-settlement in the postwar period cannot be understood if we leave out these meticulous and wide-ranging top down preparations. Manchurian settlement was treated as an emergency, assuming the same urgency as wartime settlement under the slogan 'Building a New Japan' (changes in government agencies are shown in Figure 3.1). Meanwhile, as a result of the Under-Secretary's decision on an 'Outline for the Implementation of Settlement Operations' in October 1947, the focus of settlement policy shifted from new settlements towards increasing the area of planted land, and targeted the second and third (non-inheriting) sons in agricultural villages for settlement. The re-settlement of repatriated settler-farmers progressed simultaneously, with up to 90% of those awaiting new settlement in the 1948 financial year being repatriated settler-farmers.[34]

How did ordinary repatriated settler-farmers respond to these attempts by state and national leaders to organize their lives? How was the slogan 'Building a New Japan' received by repatriated settler-farmers in the regions? I will consider these issues in the following section through a focus on regional repatriates' movements.

Postwar local society and repatriates

The repatriate problem in local society

War victims squatting in elementary schools
The problem of repatriates in the regions was a politically important issue that was inseparable from the severe strains present in postwar Japan. To understand the severity and scope of the problem, let us begin by looking at cases in which the repatriate movements intensified local issues. At six o'clock in the morning on 20 August 1946, 403 repatriates (126 households) who were being housed in

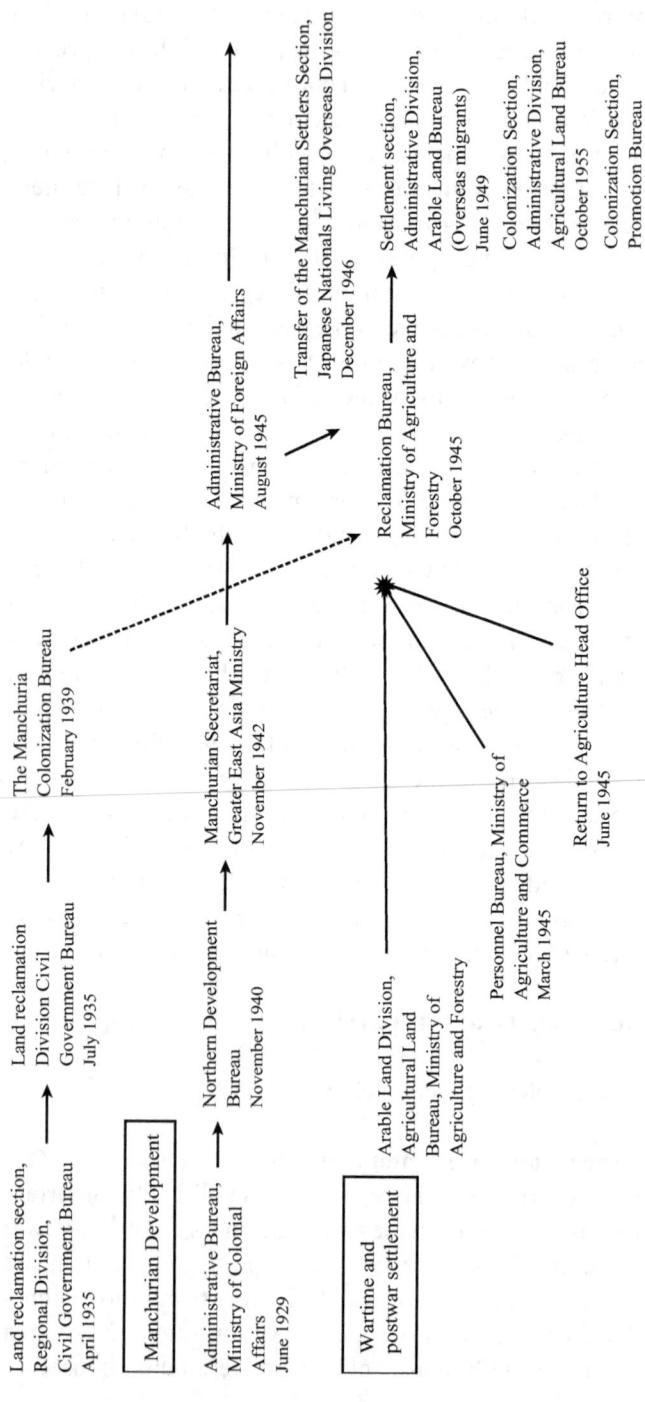

Figure 3.1: *Changes in government agencies related to settlement and emigration*

Source: Compiled by the author.

a temporary reception center in Tokyo suddenly occupied three elementary schools, demanding adequate housing.[35] This was reported both in Japanese and Japanese-American newspapers in the USA.[36] According to *Shinsō* (Truth), the action was organized by the Japan Communist Party activist, Iwata Eiichi, who led the repatriates in the reception center.[37] However, the important point in this case is that because 90% of the people in this group were Manchurian repatriates, Kohiyama Naoto, Chairman of the Manchuria and Mongolia Compatriots' Relief Association, declared his support and provided material assistance.[38] Kohiyama had been President of the South Manchuria Railway and then Transport Minister in the Suzuki and Tōjō cabinets. In other words, he was part of the ruling class. For such a figure to feel compelled to stand alongside the Japan Communist Party to support an illegal protest action reflects the complex circumstances that surrounded repatriates in this immediate postwar period.

One of the factors that contributed to this development was the increasingly outspoken criticism among repatriates of leaders such as Kohiyama who had left Manchuria before the defeat. *Junkan Tairiku Dōhō* (Thrice-monthly continental compatriots) (October 1946 issue) reported that within the Manchuria and Mongolia Compatriots' Relief Association, 'there is a deep rift in spirit between those Manchurian repatriates who risked their lives to come home after detention in a prison camp and the leadership, many of whom had returned from Manchuria before the end of the war ... [T]his is intensifying the reorganization mood within the association'. The question at issue was not only if one had a connection to Manchuria but whether or not one had experienced the 'war sacrifice' of repatriation after the war.

Those repatriates who had suffered as victims of the war and then found themselves in inadequately resourced reception centers comprised groups with the latent potential to be moved to direct action if they felt mistreated.[39] The government's inability to care for the needs of these people who had suffered so much as a direct result of national policies highlights the extent to which the issues of repatriates raised questions about the legitimacy of government. Two months after this incident, the directive 'Concerning Support for Overseas Repatriates' was addressed to all regional Directors in the name of the Under-Secretary for Home Affairs. This laid bare the impending sense of crisis:

Taking note of the fact that we are in the coldest period, there are some unsatisfactory aspects to treatment of repatriates, and this is not simply that even our best efforts cannot achieve our goals in this regard. Because there are concerns about the impact of problems of social stability on security, we are in close contact with the relevant authorities and devoting our efforts all the more to avoiding any unsatisfactory aspects in aid to repatriates.[40]

Repatriates' groups were still voicing the slogan 'Starvation or uprising?' in late 1947.[41] In March 1950, the number of repatriate households that had still not been provided with their own dwelling had climbed to 370,000, or 980,000 people.[42] There was still quite a distance to traverse between being repatriated and putting down new *roots*.

The claim that disputes concerning war victims formed the background to the actions of repatriates is not mere conjecture; it can be clearly seen in the sorts of issues that were expressed in repatriates' social movements. At the core of these was the demand for the 'equal sharing of war sacrifices'. The concrete expression of this demand came in the form of demands for the prompt repatriation of those still waiting, compensation for assets left behind, demands for the democratization of the regions, and demands for support (e.g., welfare; capital loans, and assistance finding employment). Before looking at the situation in the regions, I discuss arguments concerning war sacrifice, which can be seen as the foundation of movements by repatriates.

From the opinions expressed in their magazines and newspapers, it is clear that the demand for 'equal sharing of war sacrifice' was one of the key motivations for repatriates to come together and form groups. For example, a speaker at the rally of the National Federation of Overseas Repatriates on 15 July 1946 outlined their grievances as follows.

What we have seen, standing in the ruins of postwar Japan, is far too excessive inequalities of sacrifice with regard to this war. They suppress the questions of who it was that started the war and who that lost it, and they maintain that all of the people must share the burden of the sacrifices of war equally. But even if they pursue their deceitful policy in a positive way, the inequalities of the present situation are too excessive. Even if we divide it, the sacrifice that we repatriates are being made to pay is so excessively heavy. On this point, we demand the prompt enactment of a fair division of war sacrifice and the reinstatement to us of the life that normal Japanese nationals lead.[43]

At the same time that they were protesting about the uneven distribution of the burdens of war sacrifices, the repatriates were appealing for donations, as a 'ray of hope for the poor people' affected by the flood and wind damage caused by the Tone River bursting its banks in the Kantō region. They 'recollected just how grateful we were' at the time of repatriation for the 'merest kind words or deeds'. Their insistence that the suffering of the flood victims stirred their 'national affection' was another expression of their desire for social equity.[44]

Ideas of what it means to be a 'Japanese national' provided the logic that underpinned their arguments for a more even distribution of war sacrifice. As 'subjects', people were able to claim compensation under the Wartime Damages Protection Act for the sacrifices that they had made. Politically, however, they could either remain silent or insist that their burdens be shared by other people as well. In the end, it became a matter of honor.[45] At one of its meetings, the Kyoto Association of Taiwan Repatriates demanded a more equitable distribution of war sacrifices, making a 'demand to the government for the right to live as 'Japanese nationals'.[46] The issue of welfare payments became a touchstone for the claim that they were part of the 'Japanese nation' and ought to be treated equally. The Wartime Damages Protection Act, which contained some provisions for compensation for war victims, was repealed in September 1946 and the Public Assistance Act was enacted in its stead to address all types of poverty. This new law thus became the point of dispute for war victims.[47]

The Kyoto Prefecture Federation of Fellow Overseas Repatriates called its newspaper the 'publication for war victims' and entitled it *Minsei Shinbun* (People's Welfare Newspaper). This was a new title for *Kyōren Renrakuhō* (Newsletter of the Kyoto Federation), with the change reflecting the positive orientation of the Federation to the new system of welfare commissioners created under the Public Assistance Act. As an 'expression of this change of title', the newspaper published its intention to, fight boldly against political power and violence, report on the penniless existence of all war victims; and, attempt to contribute to the building of a peaceful and democratic Japan by befriending statesmen who have a heart, and playing a part in the implementation of measures that will assist the welfare of the people.[48]

We also need to recognize that the hardships facing repatriates were not only economic. In a survey of repatriates conducted in the mid-1950s, respondents were asked: 'What has been the most painful thing since your repatriation?' The largest group of respondents replied that it was being refused any cooperation and the attitude that, '*You lot have been living a thoroughly extravagant life in the overseas territories, so you are obviously going to have experiences that you find somewhat harsh*' (emphasis added).[49] This led many repatriates to feel that there was a hopeless gulf between them and those who had remained in the Japanese homeland. The repatriates saw their predicament as unfair, attributing their suffering to their war sacrifices and repatriation, but the general public's view (as the repatriate's saw it) was that their present suffering was in some sense a balancing of the inequity between those who had suffered through the depravations of the final stages of the war in the 'homeland' while the colonists lived in relative luxury overseas. Later accounts of repatriated settler-farmers also recall their time in the places where they settled, such as: 'It is hard to believe that, at this time, when people in Japan are in the midst of war, we are over here happily able to work without impediment. We really did do well to come over here'.[50] In other words, the general public's views were not unfounded. This is no doubt why repatriates stopped speaking about their experiences of colonization, which were inseparable from their war sacrifices, when collectively demanding equal treatment as citizens of Japan. These recollections and experiences were soon relegated to the group of things that should not be discussed in public.

In sum, the repatriates had been colonists. Their memories and experiences of prewar colonial rule were particular to them, and the difficulties of weaving them into the shared memories of the rest of the Japanese people had a major impact on the historical consciousness of postwar Japan.

Forms of putting down roots

As we have seen, poverty permeated all areas of life in the early postwar period, but it is exceedingly difficult to develop a detailed understanding of the situation in which repatriates found themselves in the regions. Only a small fraction of repatriates received any aid from the system, and how they managed to stay alive remains unclear (many collapsed and died in the streets). There was a significant influx of war victims and repatriates into Kyoto Prefecture immediately after the war. The administration expressed an awareness of their plight:

> This prefecture, as an area which has largely avoided war damage, is facing a foreseeable, impending and growing need to provide houses for the vast numbers of demobilized people and repatriates from overseas – war victims hoping to move into a new house – who disembark at the port of Maizuru.[51]

There was some assistance for repatriates landing in Kyoto from the Higashi Honganji Temple and the Student Alliance to Rescue Orphans and Fellow Compatriots Left Overseas (hereafter, the Student Alliance)), but subsequent measures to help them become established were inadequate.

We see from Table 3.1 that in 1946 more than 160,000 war victims, repatriates and demobilized military personnel poured into Kyoto. One index for looking at the lives of these repatriates is the qualifying conditions for receiving benefits from the new welfare system and the Livelihood Stability Fund.

To start with the conclusion, loans from the Livelihood Stability Fund to repatriates in Kyoto Prefecture were extremely limited and, furthermore, repatriates who were not affiliated with any formal support organization were effectively excluded from the welfare system. Table 3.2 lists the welfare and Livelihood Stability Fund payments made to repatriates, bereaved families and cooperatives in Kyoto Prefecture. As we can see, of the 80,000 repatriate households (120,000 people), only 379 households (1,179 people) received welfare payments; less than 1%.[52] A further 12.9% were receiving Livelihood Stability Fund payments, but that left the vast majority with no direct support. In contrast, in the Ōtsu and Senzaki Districts in Yamaguchi Prefecture, the proportions of repatriates receiving welfare payments were 21 and 47.2%,

Table 3.1: War victims, repatriates and demobilized soldiers in Kyoto Prefecture (1946)

	Total in Kyoto City	Total outside Kyoto City	Total
War victims			
Households	18,586	9,652	28,238
People	55,219	29,862	85,081
Repatriates			
Households	9,251	5,102	14,353
People	24,766	12,110	36,876
Demobilized soldiers from overseas territories	21,473	20,424	41,897

Document: Kyoto Prefecture Welfare Ministry documents.
Source: *Kyoto Nichinichi Shinbun* 14/10/1946.
Note: The author has revised obvious errors in the numbers.

respectively.[53] Considering that as of 1952, approximately 30 to 40% of households requiring welfare were repatriates, the figures for Kyoto are conspicuously low.[54] Thus we can see that there were striking disparities in the relief systems for repatriates in the different regions.

Table 3.2 details how many households were receiving welfare payments and Livelihood Stability Fund payments, broken down by 'bereaved families', 'repatriates' and 'cooperatives'. Since the purpose of the cooperative associations was mutual assistance for repatriates, it is possible that the members of these associations were more successful in their efforts to receive welfare payments. Nevertheless, the welfare system's budget was earmarked for the bereaved families, and 24.5% of widowed / fatherless families received payments. Although this is a small overall proportion, it is significantly higher than for repatriates in general.[55]

The hardships of repatriates continued for many years after the war. Hostels were established to receive them in every city, town and village in the prefecture, but they could only accommodate a very small portion of those in need. The administrative documents on the Takanogawa Dormitory, the largest reception facility for repatriates in Kyoto (opened 1/10/1946),[56] reveal that when the occupation ended (1952) there were still large numbers of people with no other option than to live in the reception facility. Close to

Table 3.2: Welfare and Livelihood Stability Fund recipients (Kyoto: 1950)

	Bereaved families	Repatriates	Cooperative associations
Target households	46,557	81,661	18,130
Target people	165,501	119,075	78,238
Households using Livelihood Stability Funds	450	10,564	–
Households receiving welfare	8,876	379	6,539
People receiving welfare	31,509	1,179	12,247
Widowed and fatherless families	22,036		
Households of widowed and fatherless families receiving welfare	5,406		
People in widowed and fatherless families receiving welfare	14,596		

Source: Compiled using Kyoto-fu Minsei Rōdōbu Engoka, 1950.

half of the residents were Manchurian repatriates. Only about half of the residents were officially permanent residents of Kyoto. The rest were from other regions.[57] Securing a place to live continued to be a central issue for repatriates. The Takanogawa Dormitory comprised hastily built single-story dwellings which, by 1952, were already in danger of collapse.[58] The activities of repatriates discussed below need to be understood against the background of the enduring hardships of their lives.

Organization of repatriate groups

'Repatriates' is simply the common term used in Japan to refer to people who were repatriated. In terms of both class and age, this was a loose group. Repatriations began with a trickle within weeks of the surrender, and were in full swing by the spring of 1946. Groups of repatriates began organizing themselves almost immediately with the goal of obtaining aid. The nature of these groups becomes clear from a simple listing of their names.

> Association of People in Kyoto from Central China (*Kyoto* 13/3/1946); Hebei Repatriates' Alliance (*Kyoto* 21/4); Tianjin Compatriots Association (*Kyoto* 5/10); Kinki Association of Taiwan Repatriates

Table 3.3: Place from which returned, household composition and permanent domicile of returnees living in the Takanogawa Dormitory

Returnees	'Manchuria'	China	Korea	Taiwan	Southern territories	Soviet Union	War damage	Other	Total
Households	90	24	27	19	3	3	0	12	178
People	393	109	123	93	10	13	0	44[a]	785
People in a household	1	2	3	4	5	6	7	8~	
Households	8	21	33	39	30	20	18	9	178

Permanent domicile	Kyoto	Osaka	Hyogo	Shiga	Nara	Mie	Wakayama	Fukui	Other
Households	76	16	8	9	1	1	3	3	61
People	362	62	30	52	4	2	11	15	247

Source: Kyoto-fu, 1955.
Note: [a] The author has revised this figure, from 144 in the original table, in the interests of consistency with the total.

(*Kyoto* 10/5, later renamed Kyoto Association of Taiwan Repatriates); Mutual Assistance Association of Repatriates from Korea (*Kyoto* 12/5); Association of People from Xuzhou (*Kyoto* 19/5); Kansai Branch of the Friends of the South Manchuria Railway Company; Let's Stay Alive Association;[59] Kyoto Alliance of Southern and South China Repatriates (*Kyōnichi*, 13/8); Kyoto Association of People from Saigon (*Kyōnichi*, 12/10); and the Branch of the Repatriates from Kwantung Territory Aid Society (*Kyōnichi*, 5/7).

Such a list clearly indicates that the overall trend was to organize by region of overseas residence and by occupation. Some evidence suggests that there was a group which some 6,000 households or 20,000 people had joined by February 1946, but the details are not entirely clear.[60]

With the repatriates organizing themselves so rapidly, the administration pushed for the creation of an alliance of these groups[61] to streamline resource distribution and management.[62] As if keeping pace with this demand, the Kyoto Prefecture Confederation of Fellow Overseas Repatriates (hereafter, Confederation of Repatriates)[63] also reorganized itself, on 12 December, as the Kyoto Prefecture Federation of Fellow Overseas Repatriates (hereafter, Repatriates' Federation). As a federation, it had been organized according to place of overseas residence and occupation, but as an alliance it was reorganized into branches based on 'school districts' and 'administrative districts in the City of Kyoto' for the convenience of distributing everyday goods throughout the alliance.[64] The Repatriates' Federation became the officially recognized group in Kyoto Prefecture.[65]

We should not conclude, however, that this led directly to the 'inclusion' of repatriates. Although the organization was restructured in order to obtain aid from the administration, decisions about the availability and allocation of aid still remained outside of this structure. The next section examines how these groups addressed that issue.

The politics of repatriates

Birth of the Repatriates' Political Alliance
The political demands of repatriates persisted in Japanese society even beyond this period, but almost all of the groups that emerged

at this time were short-lived. This does not mean, however, that they were without influence. Among other things, their politicization of the practical issues of everyday life had a lasting impact. The Kyoto case is unusual in that the repatriates' movement established a political group called the Kyoto Repatriates' Political Alliance. It also became deeply connected with the 'democratic front'.

Matsuo Takayoshi's research is indispensable for understanding the democratic front in Kyoto in the immediate postwar period. Matsuo demonstrates that postwar conditions reignited the personal connections that had been seeking democratization since the Taisho period, laying the groundwork for one of the leading democratic fronts in Japan.[66] Foreshadowing our conclusion, it is clear that the repatriates' social movement played a unique and important role in this democratic front. Let us look at the kind of actions that it took from this political position.[67]

The initial concerns of the democratic front in Kyoto were 'support for the labor movements, elections, food shortages and unity with women's groups'. It is also very significant that it included not only the Socialist and Communist Parties but the liberals of the Liberal Party of Japan. The connections between repatriation and politics lie in the fact that the support base for liberals of the Liberal Party of Japan included large numbers of repatriates from small and medium commercial and industrial concerns. Let us focus on the Repatriates' Political Alliance.

On 5 November 1946, representatives of the Confederation of Repatriates and other repatriate groups[68] met at the Kyoto Repatriates' Political Alliance Preparatory Committee. This was immediately after the proclamation of the new constitution and can be seen as anticipating the elections for heads of local government, which were to be held the following year.

The following points are contained in the draft mission statement produced at this meeting. The term 'semi-repatriates' here means the Japanese women who had married to colonized people such as Koreans or Taiwanese before the end of the war. They had transferred their family registers (koseki) to the colonial region of their husband. When these women repatriated to Japan after the war, the Japanese government officially dealt with them not as repatriates but as semi-repatriates.

- enhancing the political consciousness of overseas repatriates and semi-repatriates, concentrating political power...voluntarily participating in the Kyoto democratic front and actively cooperating in the democratization of our birthplaces,
- strengthening daily living support measures for overseas repatriates and semi-repatriates,
- the independent economic recovery of overseas repatriates and semi-repatriates,
- making public and unifying aid and relief projects for overseas repatriates and semi-repatriates,
- the preferential resolution of the housing problem for overseas repatriates and war victims in general,
- the cultural advancement of overseas repatriates and semi-repatriates and cooperation in achieving international friendship,
- making use of the overseas knowledge and experience of overseas repatriates and semi-repatriates for prospective peaceful trading,
- the implementation of impartial oversight concerning the aid policies and measures of the government and political parties.

Defining itself as an 'interim political party', the Alliance allowed dual party membership, because it limited its goal to relief for repatriates, some of whom had already belonged to various political parties. This is the peculiarity of this repatriate organization, distinctively different from other political parties at that time (*Kyōnichi* 5/11/1946).

On 9 November, the Preparatory Committee met again to discuss the 'equal sharing of war sacrifice' and to confirm a reversal of its previous 'attitude of entreaty' within the repatriate movement (*Yūkyō* 11/11/1946). The initial organization had excluded demobilized soldiers. There are reports that the Kyoto Military Government Civilian Intelligence Bureau issued a statement saying that not only was there no need to exclude them, but that it would rather like for them to be actively embraced by the organization. We are unable to confirm whether demobilized soldiers were ever included, though (*Yūkyō* 24/11/1946).

Following these preparations, a rally to form was held on the 25th of November. At this same venue, a 'Meeting to Hear Denunciations of Government Bureaucrats' was also held, and its militant political posture was clearly discernible (*Kyōnichi* 27/11/1946). Unable to narrow down the choices for Chairman, Takai Kenji, Konishi Hideo[69] and Makabe Futaba[70] were elected as acting Chairpersons (*Yūkyō* 27/11/1946, errors in the names were amended in an article in *Kyōnichi* 20/12). Kimata Shūsui, of the Kyoto Association of Taiwan Repatriates, was appointed as an advisor, and Sagawa Kazuo,[71] of the Association of People from Xuzhou, a member of the headquarters standing committee (*Kyōnichi* 20/12). Sagawa would later become the General Secretary of the Repatriates' Political Alliance (*Kyōnichi* 10/2/1947), but at the same time he held the post of General Secretary of the Kyoto Democratic Party, which was formed when the liberals of the Liberal Party (Chairman Takayama Gizō) broke away.[72] Sagawa was a key figure linking the democratic front and the repatriates' movement (*Kyōnichi* 19/6/1947). Little is known about Takai Kenji, but considering that Konishi Hideo was the Liberal Party candidate for Ehime in the Lower House elections of April 1947, we can assume that they had strong personal connections in the Liberal Party. With the aim of 'establishing protection for the livelihoods of repatriates and war victims in general via the concentrated use of their political power', the Repatriates' Political Alliance was unusual even in Japan at the time.[73] Of course, the participation of the liberals of the Liberal Party in the democratic front was also a rare occurrence in national terms.

Let us now look at the most important issue for regional democratic fronts – attitudes towards the first public gubernatorial and mayoral elections, which were to be decided in local polls on 5 April 1947. The participation of the Kyoto Branch of the National Salvation League for Democracy (founded on 13 October 1946) had been problematic from immediately after its inception but, ultimately, it was given permanent standing, and the participation of the Repatriates' Political Alliance in the democratic front was decided (*Kyōnichi* 14/1/1947). At this time, Takai Kenji was the Central Executive Committee Chairman and Sagawa was General Secretary (*Yūkyō* 14/1/1947). After many twists and turns, despite the fact that the National Salvation League for Democracy had already agreed upon Kawada Kenji – the Japan Communist Party endorsed candidate for governor – and Takeuchi Katsumi – the Japan Socialist Party endorsed candidate for mayor, the Repatriates' Political Alliance decided to support Ōta Tenrei for governor of Kyoto Prefecture and Kanbe Masao for mayor of the City of Kyoto (*Kyōnichi* 11/3/1947).

There were a mere 5,000 votes between Kanbe and Takeuchi in the mayoral election (121,883 to 116,345), pointing to the considerable influence of the repatriate organization.

The Kyoto Democratic Party – whose General Secretary, Sagawa, was concurrently General Secretary of the Repatriates' Political Alliance – endorsed the National Salvation League for Democracy candidate Kawada,[74] but, as mentioned, the Repatriates' Political Alliance endorsed Ōta and Kanbe. The ins and outs of these political affiliations are complex.

Repatriates established numerous cooperatives (*Kyōnichi* 17/4/1947), such as the Heian Cooperative and the Takasago Consumers' Union. The latter was set up by repatriates from Taiwan (*Yūkyō* 31/10/1946). In this context, in August 1947 the Federation of Kyoto Prefecture Repatriates' Cooperatives was established (*Kyōnichi* 20/8/1947). All of this would have bolstered support for Ōta Tenrei, who was also the representative of Kyoto's cooperative movement in the Repatriates' Political Alliance.[75]

After the April elections, Mayor Kanbe and Deputy Mayor Tabata Banmon (former Head of the Kyoto Branch Office of the *Asahi* newspaper) appointed Sagawa to be Head of the Secretarial Section of the City of Kyoto municipal offices. The following year he was appointed Head of the General Affairs Bureau.[76] Judging from these developments, although the Repatriates' Political Alliance was set up to participate in the democratic front, ultimately it seems to have followed a different path. From the perspective of the organized repatriates, it appears that their interests lay in making political demands and taking part in elections. They were somewhat successful in entrenching their leadership in the ranks of the administration. In June 1947, the Katayama Cabinet was formed, and the Kyoto Branch of the National Salvation League for Democracy was dissolved. After the elections, we see no further references to the Repatriates' Political Alliance, but we should not underestimate the important role played by repatriates' political groups in the immediate postwar period.

Kimata Shūsui, a repatriate from Taiwan, worked as an advisor to the Repatriates' Political Alliance while simultaneously contributing to lively discussions as a member of a newspaper editorial committee and a critic. He was an active city councilor, aligned with the All-Kyoto Democratic Front Unification Conference. The Kyoto Prefectural Settler-farmers' Union, which included large numbers of repatriated settler-farmers, also supported the Conference (see Chapter 2). These circumstances suggest that the links that sprouted here continued to be nurtured until the early 1950s.

The movement to re-elect district welfare commissioners

Repatriates' movements were not only concerned with elections. Repatriates found themselves outside the local community order. They made urgent demands about the state of their lives and repeatedly criticized the newly reorganized postwar community leadership, such as district welfare commissioners and members of agricultural land committees. Agricultural land committees made enormous changes, overturning the established local order, but people who came from outside the community were not well regarded (as noted in Chapter 2). The most pressing issue of this early period was discrimination against and exclusion of repatriates by district welfare commissioners, who played a key role in determining the payment of welfare benefits at that time.

In November 1946, the Public Assistance Act came into effect. The central role of regional district welfare commissioners in authorizing welfare payments in the early period of this legislation is a significant point of difference from subsequent laws. In November 1946, district welfare commissioners held a meeting at which they stated that they would 'concentrate efforts towards the smooth application of the Public Assistance Act, and aim to promptly rebuild the lives of all types of war victims'. The Repatriates' Political Alliance, however, criticized these officers for being nothing but *amakudari* (members of the old regime who have been given lucrative new appointments). The Alliance nevertheless confined themselves to holding a meeting to demand support to help people survive the winter.[77]

The re-election of municipal and prefectural district welfare commissioners was held between 28 March and 1 April 1948, but the Repatriates' Federation was critical of the process, saying that 'the bosses are still wielding influence behind the scenes', and that 70% of new committee members 'are seeing the rules of their revered occupations violated by a group of bosses who are purged officials, such as Heads of Neighborhood Association Federations, Heads of Neighborhood Associations, Deputy Chairmen and Chief Accountants of these associations'.[78]

Unlike the situation in late 1946, this time the repatriates' movement sympathized with the occupation administration's criticism of 'local bosses'. At a gathering of prefectural and municipal officials in leadership roles before this re-election, on 24 March, Emilie Putnam, Head of the Welfare Department of the occupying forces, said, 'I warn you about the air of indifference surrounding district welfare commissioners, and I hope that in the re-elections on 1 April large numbers of excellent officers will be selected via democratic methods'.[79] These concerns were not limited to district welfare commissioners; the situation was the same for the education administration. When Education Board members were elected, someone said that 'concerns that "bosses" donning PTA masks will seize the Education Board posts are increasing'.[80]

Possibly as a result of this criticism, as early as 5 April, at a session of the Screening Meeting for Prefectural District Welfare Commissioners (Chairman, Makino Toraji), a decision was taken that people who, between 8 December 1941 and 1 September 1945 had served as Heads of Neighborhood Associations, Hamlet Associations, and Heads or Deputy Chairmen of federations of these bodies would be 'asked to desist' as district welfare commissioners. This directive was sent to all relevant regional and municipal offices (*Kyōnichi* 7/4/1948). We can see the strong views of the occupation forces behind this swift response. Upon receipt of this directive, on 12 April, the Committee for the Recommendation of District Welfare Commissioners met and fiercely debated whether to change the selection of district welfare commissioners to a system of popular election or to continue with the established selection system (*Kyōnichi* 13/4). Putnam represented the occupation forces at this meeting. Miyamoto Yutaka, from the Repatriates' Federation assumed the post of Deputy Chairman of the committee (*Kyōnichi* 14/4).

This did not ultimately lead to a system of popular election, but 487 appointments were revoked of the approximately one thousand district welfare commissioners who had been appointed by the prefecture.[81] Ninety repatriates were then selected among the new district welfare commissioners who were subsequently appointed.[82] Putnam remarked that this had resulted in 80% of the commissioners being new (including non-expatriates), with 40% of these being women, an ideal outcome (*Kyōnichi* 19/5/1948).[83] At a Kyoto Prefecture Welfare Liaison Conference at the end of October that year, Putnam declared that 'while it is possible to find unsuitable people in the ranks of district welfare commissioners, they should be issued with one warning, and appropriate measures taken in the case of those with a bad record', which suggests that the democratization of district welfare commissioners was under surveillance. Thus, the repatriates' fierce resistance to the prevailing local order was somewhat rewarded, to the extent that their cause resonated with GHQ's democratization policies. Despite their successes in democratizing the appointment of district welfare commissioners, though, there were extremely limited funds available for welfare payments for repatriates in Kyoto Prefecture. The funds that were available appear to have been largely allocated to those who had managed to organize themselves, such as those in the cooperative movement. Then, with the enactment of the Public Assistance Act in 1950, the authorization of welfare payments was to be carried out by the administration, and thus ceased to be a basis for disputes.[84] In the process, the issue of war sacrifices ceased to be contested in local communities as well.[85]

The repatriates' movement was the most organized among the war victims' groups and had the greatest power to act. Judging by the reports of the time, we can see that its influence spread to other groups as the postwar democratic energies gained momentum. The Association of Bereaved Families was established and started to become active around 1947 (*Kyōnichi* 12/2/1947 and 2/3).[86] War victims' organizations were also formed around that time (*Kyōnichi* 2/3/1947) Some of these organizations appear to have built ventures such as the Yamashina Straw Factory (*Kyōnichi* 8/4/1947), but we have no details about this. There were also groups seeking compensation for forced wartime evacuees (*Kyōnichi* 23/12/1946).

The activities of the repatriates were not limited to demands for social security or welfare payments; they were primarily critiques of the society that discriminated against them. Many repatriates felt that, in the midst of extreme poverty, they were scorned, as can be seen in rally slogans such as 'Make the word "repatriate" a matter of pride not shame!' (*Minsei Shinbun*, 14, 15/4/1948).

Seeking awareness of ethnicity and solidarity
Repatriate groups fought against the established order and demanded equal treatment as 'Japanese nationals'. Judging from newspaper advertisements and the repatriates' relief actions, Japanese society appears to have presented a positive face towards repatriates. Popular songs of the period, such as *Ganpeki no Haha* (Mother at the Wharf),

reflect these images. These images differed considerably, though, from the personal experiences of repatriates in their daily lives.[87] Many of the repatriates' recollections share their mixed feelings, expressing hope upon sighting mountain ranges and ports from the ships that were bringing them 'home', but these feelings rapidly dissipated as they came to realize that they were no longer regarded as equals. Their feelings are clearly expressed in an entreaty by a repatriate group in Maizuru, which speaks of the profound emotions of 'returning to our native land', when it feels more like 'returning to our graveyard' (*Kyōnichi* (Yamashiro) 24/7/1946).

We need to take note of the ways in which the logic of the 'normal citizen' are formulated and mobilized. In many respects, the repatriates felt as though they were being treated as a different (and inferior) ethnic group – non-Japanese. The following passage by a repatriate leader is an explicit example of this.

> The looks that repatriates receive from people in general these days are not always warm by any means. At their most extreme, they not only give repatriates an icy stare, calling them thousand-yen beggars, they even say it with an air *as if* they were dealing with *someone belonging to a completely different ethnic group*. [emphasis added][88]

We must recognize that the repatriates' predicament did not compare to the suffering inflicted upon ethnic minorities such as *Zainichi* Koreans. Nevertheless, there were parallels in their discrimination, which they repeatedly pointed out in seeking equality for themselves as Japanese citizens.

An activist from the Student Alliance recalled 'the non-cooperation of railway employees; frowns from ordinary people; quarrels with shopkeepers; fights with non-Japanese – this was every day'.[89] This statement highlights that, even while repatriates were feeling discriminated against by mainstream society, they were also in conflict with members of other ethnic groups. Repatriation was in effect a violent collision between self and other. A strong awareness of the prevailing ethnic order can be observed among the repatriate leadership. In some respects, it appears that the antagonisms between groups of marginalized people – in this case, between repatriates and ethnic minorities – intensify the further down the social hierarchy they find themselves.

And yet, there were also many efforts to explore new relationships, using colonization as a point of connection. For example, Kimata Shūsui, editor-in-chief of the *Kyōtō Nichinichi Shinbun*, which was launched in 1946, used his experience as a repatriate from Taiwan to inform readers, frequently, of the plight of people connected with China. This is another important aspect of the various repatriate movements.

Another example of this is the editorial, 'Informing the Japanese people from the standpoint of the Chinese people' by the poet Wang Baiyuan (*Kyōnichi* 21/4/1946). This is seen as something sent to Japan, entrusted to the repatriates. According to Ho Yi-Lin, this text was originally published in the 3 March issue of *Jinmin Dōhō* (People's news guide) as 'Presented to all of the Japanese people'.[90] In this period, the repatriates published arguments in the media about decolonization that transgressed borders. In this vein, pieces such as Lin Tianmin's (Head of the Chinese Youth Corps[91] and frequent media contributor) 'Towards Joint Cooperation on China–Japan Friendship', Dōshisha University student Hu Qiujin's 'East Asian Peace will be Difficult without Japan's Cooperation' (both in *Kyōnichi* 8/7) and Wu Gongzhao's 'The Right Road to China–Japan Cooperation' (*Kyōnichi* 28/7) all discuss the future of Japan–China relations. In the discursive space of the immediate postwar period, these contributions by the people to discussions about international diplomacy are noteworthy.

Settler-farmers' experience of the emperor

Imperial tours for the people

I have outlined the conditions necessary for comprehending the process of resettling large numbers of repatriated settler-farmers. The two most important things to understand are: first, that, although there was policy guidance, there was otherwise only meager assistance from the state bureaucracy; and, second, repatriates were discriminated against and marginalized by mainstream society. In this section, I discuss the postwar imperial tours as mechanisms for linking repatriation with becoming established, and for conferring meaning on the lives of settlers.

The postwar imperial tours began in the cities of Kawasaki and Yokohama in Kanagawa Prefecture, in February 1946, and ended with the imperial tour of Hokkaido, in 1954. The imperial tours began with a coalescing of 'the motives of GHQ, which was attempting to use the imperial system to rule as an occupying force, and the intentions of the emperor himself.'[92] They differed from previous imperial visits by the Meiji and Taisho emperors in the appearance this time of a 'talking emperor'. The prevailing view expressed in the anti-establishment media, however, was that the emperor's 'talking' was limited to repeating the phrase 'Oh, is that so?' In this section, I want to shift the focus away from the emperor as a symbol of sovereign power, and toward the people who interacted with him.

The first point to note is that the emperor had conversations about various matters, depending on where he was speaking and the concerns of those to whom he was speaking. He did not simply say, 'Oh, is that so?' We need to consider the impact of these interactions on the people who met face-to-face with this man who in the very recent past had been revered as a living god. There are two typologies of the term 'talking emperor'. One is when appeals are made to the people in general, often through the mass-media, for 'acclamation and endorsement' as a confirmation of his charisma. The other is the case of face-to-face meetings and conversations. Proclamations in the mass media are prescribed, every time, by national politics. This is evident in the 1949 Kyushu Imperial Tour, when there were appeals for 'production increases'; and in the Shikoku Imperial Tour, which took place several months before the Comprehensive National Land Development Act was enacted in 1950, during which he announced that 'the prospects for comprehensive development were bright'.[93]

The second thing to note is the influence of these imperial tours on the formation of groups in the local community. Before the occasion of meeting the emperor, representatives of respective organizations were called together for a briefing, and all attended. In the process, new social unions were formed. Just as large-scale meetings such as the 'Rally to Welcome Home Liberated Activists Released from Prison' and the 'Rally to Welcome Home Nosaka Sanzō' provided opportunities for the left-wing to organize new social movements, we need to understand that the effects of these imperial tour briefing sessions were not confined to the place and time that they occurred. In this section, I will examine these two points, and then end by summarizing the function of imperial tours as catalysts in appeals 'from above' and responses 'from below'.

Media reports of the time clearly indicate that war victims and repatriates were among the principal audiences to be addressed by the postwar imperial tours. Repatriated settler-farmers are also frequently mentioned in the media as subjects of these meetings. These are just some of the large number of groups that those planning imperial tours had to cater for. Some of these meetings occurred in places where repatriates had already settled, while others occurred in repatriate dormitories. In the former cases, the meetings were intended to contribute to the continuation of reclamation activities in that area. In these places, a kind of dialogue was established where participants shared their experiences with the emperor and then listened to what he had to say. As we have seen, the suffering and discrimination that was common to experiences of repatriation was not recognized by Japanese society. For those who had suffered and then been marginalized for it, being able to talk about their experiences publicly and being publically acknowledged would have been considerably meaningful for their self-awareness vis-à-vis society.

The 1947 imperial tour

The emperor visited Kyoto as part of the Kansai Imperial Tour in 1947, the year when these tours were most frequent. The new constitution came into force on 3 March, but due to the chaotic political situation the dates of the imperial tour were only decided at the last minute.[94] On 24 May, the Katayama Cabinet was formed, the first cabinet under the new constitution. With the stability brought by the new cabinet, a decision was made for the Kansai Imperial Tour to begin on 4 June. Newspaper reports in the days leading up to the event said that its aim was 'to observe the condition of the people and to offer sympathy to war victims and overseas repatriates'.[95]

The response of the people was markedly different than on the emperor's visit to Kyoto in November 1945, when he had come to report the news of defeat at the Meiji Emperor's tomb in the imperial mausoleum (*Fushimi-Momoyama Goryō*). The throng of people crowded around, swamping the car in which the emperor rode after having alighted from the train.[96] Immediately after his arrival, the emperor made a gesture of solidarity with the masses, publically eating the 'substitute food' of 'bread with mixed grains in it'.[97] In light of the previous day's newspaper reports of Kyoto housewives barging into the prefectural offices shouting 'Give us Rice', the emperor's gesture was obviously a political attempt to acknowledge the social contradictions.[98]

The Association of Bereaved Families provides a good example of the new opportunities that the pre-tour briefing sessions provided for organizations. The formation of the Association of Bereaved Families was 'stimulated by the sight of the repatriates continually reorganizing their respective groups', but,

> when the emperor arrived at the Takanogawa Dormitory, more than thirty representatives of the Association of Bereaved Families, inspired by the warm words of His Majesty, confronted Matsuhisa, Chief of the prefectural Relief Division that same day. As a result of informal talks, it was arranged that there would be active appeals to bereaved families throughout the whole prefecture.[99]

Meetings with repatriated settler-farmers on the Kansai Imperial Tour, in contrast, were held in dormitories. Immediately after the war, dormitories were established as Compatriots' Relief Association facilities to house returnees and war victims.[100] The Kyoto meetings were held in the Takanogawa Dormitory, the largest dormitory in the prefecture, and were the most meticulously planned of all of the emperor's meetings to that point. Even the route that the emperor's entourage would travel inside the dormitory was decided in advance. Who would say what, and in what order, was rehearsed under the supervision of prefectural personnel.

Maehara Sekisaburō – founder of the Kyoto Settlers' Self-support Association, and former Company Commander of the Manchurian Youth Corps Brigade (hereafter, Youth Brigade) – represented the repatriated settler-farmers' at the meeting with the emperor in the Takanogawa Dormitory.[101]

Maehara and his family were late to be repatriated because they contracted typhus in Qiqihar. When he finally recovered, Maehara moved to Huludao, and was repatriated in October 1946. After repatriation, Maehara's family went to live in his parents' house in Fukuchiyama but, after two years, Maehara moved into the Takanogawa Dormitory, where he threw himself into relief activities for repatriated settler-farmers. In short, he was exactly the sort of war victim who was selected for meetings during imperial tours.

The following day, *Kyoto Shinbun* reported the imperial visit with the headline, 'His Majesty, Takanogawa Dormitory, Repatriates' Joy at the Honor and Inspiration', detailing the exchanges that took place.[102] The following letter was published in the Letters to the Editor column that day, 'With the words that He spoke to us when He said, "You were kind to come back, welcome home", we felt as if we had been compensated for everything; our aspiration to live once again returned to us' (a female repatriate).[103]

This was not a unique or individual response, but was a common experience among repatriated settler-farmers. A week after this meeting at the Takanogawa Dormitory, the National Settlers Self-support Association, in the name of its Chairman Sō Mitsuhiko, distributed a document titled 'His Majesty's Delivery of Encouraging Words' to every branch. In this, the following comments by the emperor are introduced as addressing all repatriated settler-farmers, reconfirming the determination to struggle once again to build a new Japan.

> All of you settlers, I understand that you suffered extreme hardship in Manchuria, and it was no doubt painful. Now that you have been repatriated, life is still full of hardship, but find a way to keep striving with bright spirits. I would like to see you recover as quickly as possible.[104]

In distributing this quotation, the Self-support Association, as a national organization, communicated their endorsement of the imperial tour; the emperor's promise of recovery became a shared experience and catalyst. It was as if the repatriates entered into a pact with the emperor, promising to keep striving with bright spirits, and to recover quickly.

Maehara, who had heard this appeal directly from the emperor, consulted with other Manchuria repatriates living in the dormitory and they devised a settlement plan. At the end of 1948, Maehara and the 19 households (80 people) who settled in the Haradani District in the City of Kyoto area formed the Rakuhoku Settlers' Agricultural Cooperative Union, stating that they were 'attempting to build a true paradise for settlers'.[105] Maehara served as Chairman of the Self-support Association until its dissolution, as well as being the inaugural Director of the National Self-support Association. He also served as Head of the Kyoto Prefectural Settler-farmers'

Cooperative, as Kishi Yamaji's successor (see Chapter 2). His activities with the Self-support Association continued, as can be seen for example, in his public acknowledgement at the 'Commemoration of the 10th Anniversary of the Postwar Farmers' Movement' in 1956,[106] and the inclusion of his name in *A History of Manchurian Settlement* as a special member of the Committee for Promoting the Publication of the History of Manchurian Settlement.[107] Immediately after repatriation, the 'sense of purpose' of this Company Commander of the Youth Brigade, who had 'felt irritated with the Japanese government's mistaken policies' during the war,[108] was strongly underpinned by his promise to the emperor.

The Kansai Imperial Tour included limited visits to repatriate dormitories in Wakayama and Hyogo, as the emperor met with repatriated settler-farmers there. Meetings were also held in repatriated relief facilities in Osaka. The type of responses and promises seen in Kyoto were reproduced in Hyogo. The emperor visited the Tamatsu Dormitory, a repatriated settler-farmer reception facility, on 13 June. Here, as elsewhere, the emperor appealed to former settlement leaders, 'Please do your best to rebuild Japan' and 'Please do your best to open up new land'. At these meetings again, as elsewhere, the repatriated settler-farmers, with tears of gratitude, vowed to build a new Japan.[109] This valorization of repatriated settler-farmers was repeated throughout the imperial tours. Their success in achieving their objectives can be seen in the following quote from Ōhinata Village, which had sent emigrants as *bunson imin* (to establish a branch village) and had preserved these groups upon their return and throughout the postwar resettlement:

> His Majesty coming to see us; that is enough for us to forget our hardships to date, and I think that even those who have passed away will be satisfied.[110]

After returning to Kyoto, following the tour of the Kansai region, the Grand Chamberlain commented on a different aspect of the events. He said:

> I often observed that on this imperial visit His Majesty, constantly saying something slightly hunched over and speaking in a metallic voice, clearly took the unornamented form of a human emperor;

particularly when he was encouraging people in repatriate reception facilities and children.[111]

The following day, 50,000 people gathered at the People of the Prefecture and City Welcome Rally, roaring '*Banzai* (Long live the emperor!)'.[112] As events aimed at validating the tale of building a new Japan, the imperial tours were a resounding success. The meetings with and promises made by the war victims group of repatriated settler-farmers were central to this.

Postwar settlement by repatriated settler farmers

Thus far, we have looked at the conditions and institutional structures affecting repatriated settler-farmers. I would now like to follow the process of their resettlement in Kyoto.

Let us start with the response of the Kyoto administration immediately after the war, and try to understand the conditions of repatriation for settler-farmers.[113] In October 1945, the Kinki Colonial Administration Conference met. People with responsibilities for this repatriation from two metropolitan regions and five prefectures, as well as the Head of the Kyoto Prefecture Military Affairs Social Welfare Division, held 'discussions regarding relief measures for the soon to be repatriated Manchurian settlers'.[114] These discussions appear to have focused on coming to terms with emerging trends. However, even this proved difficult, and dissatisfaction grew among the Japanese people who had been sent overseas.[115] The repatriation of Manchurian settlers was slow compared to that of other groups, with the first group of repatriates arriving in Japan in January 1946.[116] In April the 'Citizen's Rally Reporting on the Real Condition of Compatriots Living in Manchuria' was held.[117] Subsequently, information sessions were held, in particular, for families whose children had been sent to join the Youth Brigade.[118] Thus, the initial efforts of the repatriate leaders went towards providing explanations to the families of those whose whereabouts were unknown.[119]

After these activities subsided, some of the leadership were engaged in assisting the Relief Division in the Kyoto prefectural offices, while two months after the formation of a national organization, others were 'preparing for the quickening pace of settling repatriates' and organizing the Settlers' Self-support Association, of which Maehara Sekisaburō was Chairman, into 'an agency that 'worked closely with' the Settlers' Relief Association.[120] The first meeting of the Board of Directors, in early January 1946, secured the participation of the Kyoto Prefecture Relief Division, and made plans for settlements in Hokkaido, Komouno, Osadano and Uji. At the end of January, the freshly repatriated Youth Brigade was promptly sent to Hokkaido.[121]

Thus, in Kyoto, company commanders mediated re-settlement while dividing up duties between the Settlers' Self-support Association and the administration. After spring 1946, there was a steady arrival of settler-farmers being repatriated to Kyoto. Some went back to their places of birth, but those who could not went to live in repatriate reception facilities, where they waited for the intercession of the state. The majority of them were eventually settled in Hokkaido or in various places within Kyoto prefecture. According to reports in the *Minsei Shinbun*, a considerable proportion of Manchurian repatriates resettled as farmers in Kyoto Prefecture. It is believed that of 1,492 repatriated settler-farmer households, 825 households (55.3%) were re-settled, and there were plans to settle a further 150 households on newly obtained uncultivated land.[122] *Minsei Shinbun* subsequently reported that recruitment for re-settlement was continuing and that the application criteria was limited to repatriated settler-farmers.[123] The principal group re-settlement destinations in Kyoto for repatriated settler-farmers were: cleared land in Osadano, Fukuchiyama; cleared land in Ikari Kōgen; the Mutual Association for Agriculture and Industry (Kohata Village);[124] the Jōnan Plant in Terada Village; the Haradani cleared land in Kyoto City; and cleared land in Komouno. We will look more closely at the Jōnan Plant and the Haradani cleared land in the following sections.

Repatriates in farming areas: Terada Village and the Jōnan Plant

First, let us look at the case of Terada Village, which we mentioned in Chapter 1 as a place that had a sudden increase in Korean tenant-farmers during the final stages of the war.

From immediately after the war, statistics were collected in villages about Japanese demobilized people, repatriates and evacuees. With the successive repatriations of demobilized people, we see an increase in the numbers of ordinary compatriots from the spring of 1946.[125] Of the 243 people who had been repatriated or demobilized to the village by the end of 1947, as many as 167 were working in agriculture.[126] It can be assumed that, in the midst of growing demand on the land, people from the colonies who had been tenant-farmers during the war left the land in large numbers as this reflux of people was occurring.

There are reports of the appearance of an anti-repatriate settlement movement in Uji City, in response to the Jōnan Plant, which was a repatriate reception facility established by the prefectural government in Terada Village (*Kyōnichi* 21/12/1946). The discrimination faced by repatriates in the cities and the repulsion experienced by repatriates to their native villages[127] positioned repatriated settler-farmers in a bottleneck where discrimination and exclusion overlapped.

Let us now consider the conditions in the repatriate reception facilities, and the background to the opposition of local residents to repatriate settlement. During the war, the idea was promoted of the Shimazu Plant building a war plant in Terada Village.[128] Because this construction had happened after the acquisition of 100,000 *tsubo* (33 ha) of arable land,[129] there were continuous negotiations between the locals of Terada Village and the plant concerning the ownership of agricultural produce that had been grown on farms that were now within plant land. Relations were highly strained.[130] After the war, the land passed to the jurisdiction of the Ministry of Health and Welfare and was used as a facility for repatriates.

These circumstances contributed significantly to the less than favorable reception of repatriates by Terada Village. It would therefore be mistaken to attribute the villagers' hostility to the new arrivals to intrinsic nature. From the beginning of the wartime evacuations, they had accepted evacuees and provided facilities for them without receiving any official assistance. In September 1944, for example, although the village took in 27 households of evacuees and 29 schoolchildren evacuees, they did not have enough tables and chairs for the children.[131] While the state forcefully promoted evacuation, its efforts were limited to getting the people out of the cities; there was effectively no support for the villages that received them. Villagers were thus left to assume all of the 'costs' associated with the state's policy (including, for example, the administrative work of dealing with applications under the Wartime Damages Protection Act).

On 1 September, a request for space for repatriates arrived from the Military Welfare Division of the prefecture. The village responded that even though they might tentatively offer the town hall and the main temple building, 'these are unfit as residences as neither have gardens or any space around the buildings', which suggests that they rejected any further intake.[132]

Efforts in the village immediately turned to demanding the return of the maneuvering ground, which had been requisitioned from them in 1911. The earliest efforts to have the government sell back that land (which had been a private forest owned by the hamlet) were made in October. They also requested that the government sell the grounds to the villagers, and reconstruct the buildings because of the 'substantial destruction of the isolation ward building'.[133] When these grounds were surveyed their suitability as reclaimed land for agriculture, under the Emergency Reclamation Policy, the village contradicted its previous claims, arguing that the land was 'full of pebbles' and therefore unsuitable for reclamation. They wanted it to be returned to forest.[134] The maneuvering ground lands were eventually ear-marked to be reclaimed for agriculture, but in September 1946, it was requisitioned by the US military without ever going back to the village.[135] In sum, after the war the villagers had sought the restoration of former village land, which had been appropriated by the military-state. However, in this case, we see a demonstration of just how deeply entrenched the 'military' was in the land.[136]

It was against the background of these conflicts over land and the acceptance of war victims that, shortly after the war, the Terada Plant, with which the village had been negotiating over agricultural produce since before the war, became a plant under the direct management of Shimazu, and became the Jōnan Plant reception facility for repatriates.[137] This was the context for the village's opposition to accepting repatriates.

Nevertheless, large numbers of repatriates were received by Terada Village. The people from the Īrin Yamashiro Settlement Group and the Kyoto Byōrei Village Reclamation Group, who had been waiting in the facilities in Kyoto City for somewhere to go, were housed in Terada as repatriated settler-farmers.[138] In response to plans to receive 40 households (160 people), in 1947 and 30 households (150 people) the following year, Terada's village head made the following comments in a petition submitted to the prefectural government.

> Even from the point of view of the village's financial situation, in direct opposition to the scant ability of repatriates to pay taxes, this village has been placed in a situation of being forced by the prefectural government to inevitably incur considerable expenses in providing facilities for

repatriates, such as assistance for living and education. The village finds itself in circumstances that give cause for real concern for the urgent state of the village's financial affairs at this point in time.[139]

Thus, as villages were forced to provide assistance for needy war victims without any financial compensation, deep-rooted ruptures emerged between repatriates and local inhabitants, expressed in terms of differences in their war experiences.[140] In October 1947, the Ichinokubo neighborhood association, was established by repatriate households from the Jōnan Plant, and became Terada's eleventh hamlet.[141]

The Haradani district and its settler-farmers

The Haradani district is located at the base of the mountains in the northwestern part of the city and was incorporated into the City of Kyoto in 1918. It is hill country with undulations and gentle slopes. Its highest and lowest peaks are, respectively, 280 and 160 meters above sea level. At the time of this settlement, this region was concealed by pine forests. When settler-farming activities began, the soil was highly acidic with crumbly black topsoil and little organic matter. Postwar settlement began here in the late autumn of 1948, when twelve households from Manchuria became the first settlers. In this section, I will describe the history of this settlement largely on the basis of commemorative publications of the agricultural cooperative and interviews.

It appears that before the postwar settlements, several villages had formed and then disappeared in Haradani. Then, around 1940, part of the area was cultivated as a training farm of the Kyoto Prefectural School of Agriculture and Forestry, and the local farmers engaged in rice paddy farming. In 1944, the city council came up with a plan to relocate the Kyoto City Zoo to the area, but then realized that locating the zoo adjacent to the existing crematorium might create the wrong impressions. During the occupation, the site was mentioned as a possible site for a golf course, but this did not eventuate for the same reason.

In 1946, however, as a result of the Second Agrarian Land Reform, the privately owned uncultivated land of 27 landlords was compulsorily acquired, and Haradani was identified as postwar settlement land. The settlement cooperative would

Table 3.4: Background of settlers in the Haradani settlement

Background	Households
Manchuria Youth Corps Brigade Commander	1
Kyoto Fifth Youth Brigade members	1
Amada Township Pioneer Group	2
Songo Agriculture and Industry Settlement Group	1
Īrin Yamashiro Settlement Group	1
Ryūsō Settlement Group	1
Kokusekiton Settlement Group	5
Group name unknown	1
Demobilised navy personnel	1
Repatriated company employees	1[a]
Relatives of settlers	2
Unknown	2
Total	19

Document: From an interview with Mr. Hidehiko Maehara, 25/1/2006.
Note: [a] Worked in Shenyang

later have 'border issue' problems concerning the acquired zone, but in October 1948, Haradani received its first influx of new settlers.

Most of those who went to Haradani had experienced Manchurian settlement. However, they all had different places of origin (not exclusively inside Kyoto Prefecture), and different settlement experiences (see Table 3.4).

Those repatriated from Manchuria included: one household from each of the following: the family of the Company Commander of the Youth Brigade, members of the Fifth Kyoto Brigade, Ryūsō Settlement Group, Īrin Yamashiro Settlement Group, the Songo Agricultural and Industrial Settlement Group and a settlement group whose name is not known; two households from the Amatagō Settlement Group; and five households from the Kokusekiton Settlement Group. There were also two households from each of the following: naval returnees, families that had been employed by companies in Shenyang, and two families of settlers' siblings. There were two more households whose background details remain unclear.[142] Both the Amatagō and Īrin Yamashiro Settlement Groups were Kyoto Prefecture *bunson* (branch village) settlement groups, but aside from these, the Kokusekiton and others were mixed settlement groups, whose members came from a wide variety of places. Settlers from the Īrin Yamashiro Settlement Group were a family who had been in the Jōnan Plant, but relocated again to join this Haradani Settlement.

The leader of the settlers who moved into Haradani was Maehara Sekisaburō. Maehara became a central figure in the settlement, carrying out 'investigations to determine a suitable spot, acquisition of the land, recruitment of settlers, planning buildings and farms, and drafting requests to form a union'.[143] On 18 October 1948, those who had resolved to settle met in the offices of the Kyoto Prefecture Settlers' Self-support Association, loaded the tools that they would need for farming and timber to build temporary housing (provided by Kyoto Prefecture) onto two trailers towed by bicycles, and set off for Haradani.[144] Although various measures were introduced, such as a lottery to ensure the fair allocation of land, they opted for individual – not shared – housing. The smooth establishment of this settlement might be attributable to the fact that the leadership had been decided before settlement. However, the environment was so austere that two households left by the end of the first day of settlement. The houses in which the settlers were to live were still only half-built and only had cedar bark roofs. There was no electricity or well, and the toilets were inconvenient. Nevertheless, 40 years later, some women reflecting on this period said, 'Speaking for my family, we were happy';[145] 'Does my family get such a fine house?' I thought 'I was very deeply moved at the time';[146] and 'It may have had a cedar bark roof, but it was finished, and for us – who had been without a house – it was a happy time'.[147] There were no grand ideals here of the sort that the male leaders – politicians, bureaucrats and others – proclaimed in public; these women were focused on desires about their everyday lives.

Some settlers had married just before settlement, showing a strong commitment to the family unit. With the exception of minors from the Youth Brigade, these settlers were basically of the same generation, although there is at least one case of someone settling alongside their parents.

In the early days of the settlement, Haradani reverberated with the sound of trees being felled every day. With the arrival of a second wave of five households, the settlement satisfied the requirements to form a cooperative, and the Rakuhoku Settlers' Agricultural Cooperative

Union was established. A village of 80 people was born, counting all family members.

Union activities in the initial stages of settlement included: deciding the planting plan for each family; cooperative harvesting; adopting a joint freight system; and the adoption of a system whereby the union bundled all produce together and sold it in a central wholesale market. About half a year after the initial settlement, in April 1949, a general meeting decided to introduce livestock. The union planned to introduce three cows, 20 pigs, 10 goats, 150 chickens, 50 ducks and 100 rabbits. Union members initially pinned their hopes on pig farming, with the objective of securing a supply of manure and food self-sufficiency. They loaned one pig to each family. The settlers busied themselves building pigsties and acquiring fodder, but in the autumn the price for pork crashed, and almost everyone abandoned pig farming.

In other ways, too, farming did not proceed according to plan. From the beginning of 1950, they attended training courses run by the prefectural Agricultural Land Settlement Division, and tried cultivating chestnuts, roses and acacias as fodder, but did not achieve the expected results. They entered into a contract to cultivate garlic, but this was discontinued because of low yields and poor quality. Conscious of the fact that the decisive factor in the conditions that made farming difficult was the quality of the soil, they arranged to receive refuse from the City of Kyoto, with the intention of introducing organic matter into the soil. However, soon after deliveries began there were complaints: 'Is the union turning the settlement into a rubbish dump?'[148] and flies swarmed over the refuse. More troubling was that with the refuse, 'pathogens were introduced, resulting in deterioration of fruit trees and root vegetables' and a year later, they stopped this practice. The City Waste Bureau had not carefully selected organic matter that would decompose; some of the waste generated organic acids, which further damaged the soil. The waste also contained various usable items such as shoes, and the children started calling it the 'rubbish dump department store'. One settler recalls this period thus:

> One winter, the snow was piled knee high. My oldest son, who was in the first year of primary school, had to push my bicycle along from behind so that I could go over the mountain and into town to

collect tofu lees as fodder for the livestock. While scolding my son, who was dragging along behind me on the snow-covered mountain path looking like he was about to burst into tears, I just happened to notice that the soles of his rubber shoes, that we had picked out of the rubbish dump department store, had come off and that my son's feet were submerged in thawing snow. To this day, I still cannot shake off my wretched and pathetic feelings on that day.[149]

These vicissitudes continued until after 1953, when the union promoted the idea of concentrating on farming livestock. This decision was prescribed by the disadvantageous conditions of the land. Up to this point, the settlers had been rearing eight head of cattle, but now it was decided to add another twelve, and to build communal milking facilities. With the decision to introduce milk cows, each household began raising two cows. In hindsight, we can see that the settlement were early-adopters of dairy farming, beginning before the Act Concerning Dairy and Beef Cattle Production Promotion of 1954.

In 1958, the union's economic division, which had until then synthesized dairy farming, poultry raising and fruit and vegetable gardening, was restructured so that dairy and poultry operations would be managed under independent family accounting systems. The aim here was to foster the farmers' independence while the union shifted its focus to financial services and advice.

In 1960, the livestock producing households looked into expanding and commercializing their operations, under national and prefectural guidance. Ten households, including most of the poultry farmers, incorporated themselves as a separate corporation, Mitsuwa Poultry. Following their lead, three households of dairy farmers established the jointly managed Rakuhoku Farm. As new management bodies continued to be established, the system of joint management by the union dissolved. This joint management continued after this period, but after Haradani was zoned for urbanization, it rapidly became a residential area.

Urbanization proceeded from the late 1950s to the mid-1960s, with a corresponding reduction in the area dedicated to farming.[150] A prefecture-managed housing estate was constructed, and the settlers soon disappeared. Today, one can barely discern where the original settlement was located (see Photograph 3.2).

Farmers' lived experience of borders

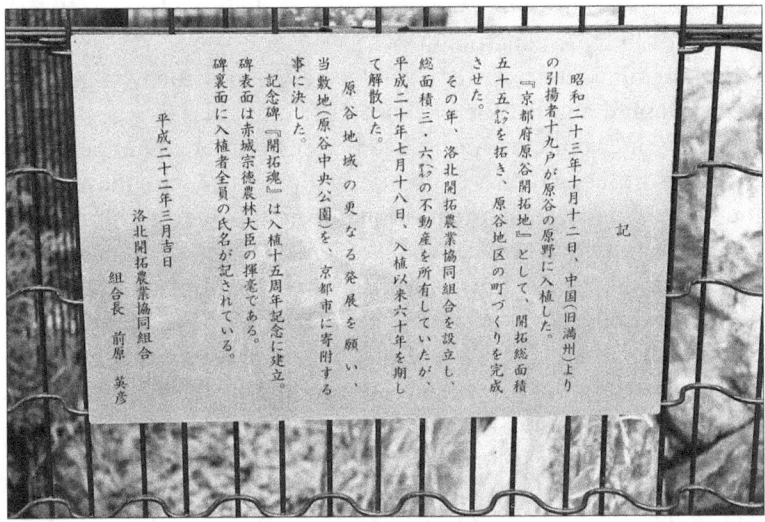

Photograph 3.2: Haradani Settlers' Monument (Haradani Central Park, Kyoto City) (author's image)

Repatriated settler-farmers and postwar Japan

The aim of this chapter has been to examine one aspect of the postwar repatriations. It has attempted to reveal the social forces behind the massive postwar resettlement of people who had suffered with the dissolution of the empire: repatriated settler-farmers. Many of them lived in a state of confusion.

Let me now synthesize the arguments thus far. Two key factors formed the background to the large-scale re-settlement of repatriated settler-farmers: the systems established by the bureaucrat class which had deployed colonizing-settlers to Manchuria before the war; and the responses of the repatriates to the poverty and discrimination that they faced upon their return. There are an increasing number of studies about postwar settlement policies, but it is imperative that we consider the matters raised above when considering individual cases in the context of postwar Japanese society. The formation of cooperative groups and the emergence of their leaders are direct responses to these conditions.

In the immediate postwar period, emergency settlement policies were adopted against the backdrop of social crisis. Repatriated settler-farmer policies were added later. Many bureaucrats who had been affiliated with Manchurian settlement policies moved into the new Reclamation Bureau of the Ministry of Agriculture and Forestry to implement emergency settlement, They cooperated with bureaucrats in the Administration Bureau of the Ministry of Foreign Affairs, which had inherited the functions of the Manchurian Secretariat, Greater East Asia Ministry to prepare for resettlement in the early period (we will see such cooperation again in Chapter 5, on postwar emigration policy). Bureaucrats who had been responsible for sending people to Manchuria before the war, adopted the slogan 'Building a New Japan' and reorganized prewar organizations to address the postwar conditions. Gradually, these various sections were moved into the Reclamation Bureau. Two points require particular attention. The first is that when we attempt to identify these changes on the part of the national government – whether the 'Outline of Emergency Measures Regarding the Employment of City Evacuees in Farming' or the 'Outline for the Implementation of Emergency Land Reclamation' – they are based on cabinet decisions. The second is that, while these measures were clearly taken as exercises of state power, they were not legislated, and thus were not legally binding. While a Settlement Act was considered, no such bill was ever presented to the Diet. Hence, postwar settlement had no foundational legal support (apart from the Settlers' Capital Finance Law), which undeniably cast a shadow over the insecure lives of settlers.

Large numbers of people re-settled on the basis of these policies, but – leaving out the democratization movements in the immediate postwar period and opposition to the social divisions that emerged in postwar Japanese society – the dominant images of repatriates were of excluded, subsumed and dependent beings. I have focused on the Kyoto repatriate movements, and attempted to depict the criticisms of the regional and national governments in order to reveal the repatriates' marginalization and their autonomous actions to demand equal treatment as Japanese people. In Kyoto, which escaped severe war damage, repatriates were largely excluded from the welfare system. However, they tried to organize themselves to protest their exclusion. Some of the repatriates who organized political groups became involved in the democratization movement, playing important roles, and assuming positions in local administration. Efforts to re-settle repatriated settler-farmers intersected with these movements. The poverty that pervaded their lives was far removed from the ideal of a nation of people who were equal and homogenous. Awareness of the gap between this ideal and reality can be seen in the slogan adopted by the repatriate movement: 'Making Repatriates Normal Nationals'.[151] Repatriates raised their voices in opposition to the government and the prevailing social order, asking to be treated the same as all other Japanese people. The path towards building a new Japan was forged by these demands to be seen as a nation.

However, assumptions about who should be regarded as equal within this nation retained a strong ethnic order, which excluded Koreans and Chinese. The repatriates' movement occurred in a period in which the citizenship of colonized peoples and non-Japanese ethnic groups had become uncertain. Against a background of widespread internal conflict, the strength of the repatriate movement was derived from the idea that the category 'Japanese people' equates to the 'Japanese ethnic group'. We have looked into this idealization, and we have seen that despite the leverage it gave to repatriates, there is also evidence of forms of solidarity that transcended ethnic groups and national borders, but we were not able to explore this in depth. I see this as a future research topic.

When we examined these issues in terms of the structures that differentiated the bureaucrat class from 'the people', we discovered the considerable impact of the conversations with the Showa Emperor during the imperial tours. During the 1947 regional imperial tours, large numbers of people enthusiastically greeted the emperor. These imperial tours were strategic events devised by the occupation authorities and the national government which sought to create a new national compact through direct dialogue between the emperor, war victims and repatriates. These meetings had a strong effect on how the individuals concerned approached rebuilding their lives in the austere conditions of the time, as well as providing strong shared experiences within the organizations to which they belonged. Individual actions were shaped by the people's determination to contribute to 'Building a New Japan', even as the shared experience of the tours became a driving force for the organizations' leadership class. In short, the imperial tours were effective in connecting the rebuilding of individual lives with the national objectives of rebuilding Japan. In the process repatriates, who had been marginalized, became active subjects who were building a new Japan by becoming settler-farmers.

However, while they lived as citizens, their memories and experiences have always been those of individual people and their self-selected groups. Although they were formally included within the class of citizens, their continuing economic poverty and, above all, their recollections of colonization and repatriation, severed their connections to the Japanese people as a whole.

Frequently, a nation is conceived as a homogenous group constructed through the exclusion of others who are different. There is, of course, some truth in this conception, but it also serves to mask the heterogeneity that is intrinsic to any group of people. The framework must therefore be re-examined. In the next chapter, we are looking at people who – even while being ethnically Japanese and Japanese citizens – had been cut loose from the land. The meaning of 'a nation' defined by exclusion also changes as conceptions of self and other are transformed through various encounters and experiences. To this extent, it is 'a floating signifier'. Although one distinction between self and other was drawn in the immediate postwar period, this did not resolve the matter indefinitely. Seen from one side, the lives of settlers have been the lives of 'others', whose stories have not been passed down. It has taken several decades for their voices to be heard.

4 Japanese expatriate 'others': Postwar land reform and migration

> For the quality of owning freezes you forever into 'I,'
> and cuts you off forever from the 'we.'
>
> Steinbeck, *The Grapes of Wrath*

Transnational history of postwar agrarian reform

Postwar agrarian reform in Japanese history has generally been represented as a wide-sweeping reform of the land system, rivaling Toyotomi Hideyoshi's nationwide land survey of 1582 and the land tax reform of 1873. It significantly changed the relationships between people and land. Such changes were essential in a nation facing a crisis of starvation, following the enormous social and personal sacrifices incurred during the war. According to Noda Kimio, the immediate aftermath of the Second World War was 'a period of agrarian land reform' on a scale unprecedented anywhere in the world.[1]

Previous studies of these reforms have focused primarily on issues of class; on changes in land ownership effecting landlords and tenants – in short, to conflicts between those who own property and those who do not (although some studies have focused on the role of villages as cooperative bodies that reconcile this conflict). This book has thus far focused on ethnic issues and the migration and settlement of people in rural villages, during and immediately after the war. In Chapter 1, I discussed the Koreans whose settlement was a contentious issue of agrarian reform. In Chapters 2 and 3, I discussed the experiences of the settler-farmers. In this chapter I will examine the agrarian reforms from yet another perspective that has been typically ignored: the transnational effects of this reform. As we will see, the farmers who migrated abroad before the war, especially to the United States – often with the government's encouragement, if not direct support (although sometimes that too)

– found themselves included among the 'absentee landlords' whose land in Japan was forcibly acquired under the reforms. My central concern is that, in the modern era, people have lives in multiple places. I hope to shed light on the complexities of this multiplicity through the issue of cross-border land ownership.

Research issue 1: Studies of the history of agrarian reform

In order to narrow the focus, I will re-examine two trends in the research history: studies of the history of agrarian reform, and studies of *Nikkeijin* in the US (Japanese immigrants and people of Japanese descent).

Up to this point, I have mainly discussed postwar settlers, but there has been a vast amount written about agrarian reform. Even now, 70 years after its implementation, cases from all over Japan continue to be researched.[2]

There were several layers to agricultural reform: the policies imposed by the occupying forces for establishing land-owning farmers to facilitate democratization and demilitarization; the farmers' movement following the 'Taishō Democracy'; and Japan's agricultural administration. The primary focus of historical research on agrarian reform has been to evaluate its effectiveness, as well as debates about continuity and discontinuity. After the 1990s, the scope broadened to comparisons with areas in Asia and Europe. Noda's observations that Japan's reforms must be situated within the context of worldwide agrarian reforms became well established. Despite this broader scope, however, the trans-national aspects remain unexamined. Akimoto Eiichi has studied how the particular history of the United States shaped the way agrarian reform policies were created,[3] but this still does not address what happened from the perspective of the people who were directly affected by these reforms.

Agrarian reform involves the state's compulsory purchase of land for re-sale to tenants, but there has been a continuous blind spot regarding the fact that overseas migrants from the prewar period were included in the category of absentee landlords whose lands would be compulsorily purchased. There are two exceptions to this trend: *Nōchi Kaikaku Tenmatsu Gaiyō* (Summary account of agrarian reform) compiled by Nōchi Kaikaku Kiroku Iinkai immediately after the reforms and *Nōchi Kaikaku Shiryō Shūsei* (Compilation of sources on agrarian reform) compiled by Nōchi

Kaikaku Shiryō Hensan Iinkai.[4] Research in this area remains scarce despite the official history written by the occupation authorities which pointed out the significance of the Japanese migrants' land issue.[5]

Perhaps researchers have tended to overlook the effected migrants because of their relatively small number. It is more likely, though, that their absence reflects the implicit world-view that the nexus between ethnic group and land ownership occurs within national borders (the idea of an ethnically homogenous nation).

There have been dramatic changes in migration since the dawn of the modern era. In prewar Japan, migration was sometimes curtailed and sometimes endorsed, but during the war it assumed a strong state policy character. Through these processes, new transnational connections were created between people and land, different from those in previous periods. The agrarian reforms threatened to rupture these connections.

Research issue 2: Studies of Japanese migration and *nikkeijin*

Agrarian reform impacted every prewar migrant who owned agricultural land in Japan. Precisely how many people were effected remains unclear However, to date there has been no research that examined the agrarian reform vis-à-vis Japanese migrants.

The focus of this chapter will be *nikkeijin* (hereafter, ethnic Japanese), and more particularly, those who lived in California. To date, most studies of ethnic Japanese during and after the war have examined: internment; subsequent repatriation, resettlement and the anti-deportation movement;[6] compensation for eviction; the movement to revise the California Alien Land Law;[7] and the acquisition of naturalization rights. Although this research addresses issues of generations, ethnicity, and identity, they are all focused on settlement in United States society.[8]

Little research in either English or Japanese has examined the effects of Japanese land reform on transnational Japanese. As Eiichiro Azuma pointed out, Japanese American experiences 'extended beyond the boundaries of a single polity'.[9] Yoneyama Yutaka has criticized the effective 'erasure' of Japanese migrants when historians reduce them to being simply people who 'crossed borders' or 'have gone to the United States'.[10] To date, research into the history of the relations between Japan and ethnic Japanese, during the war and postwar periods, has focused primarily on the role of the latter in reconstruction and relief operations such as LARA (Licensed Agencies for Relief in Asia), which provided relief supplies, and participation in GHQ.[11] Perhaps the term 'erasure' is too strong, but for people who left their land to improve their economic opportunities, having that land compulsorily acquired by the state must have been a severe blow to their transnational ties, and thus their self-identities, making them feel that their homeland had cast them adrift.[12]

Martin Dusinberre, focusing on prewar villages such as Kaminoseki Village in Yamaguchi Prefecture, has clearly documented the extent to which migrants sent remittances to their home villages, and that these were then used to provide public facilities. He also points out that over half of the migrants who still owned land in the village had it compulsorily acquired as absentee landlords, which disrupted transnational connections.[13]

This chapter will focus on social movements in the United States. The paths to land ownership there were many and diverse: people who were due to inherit as first-born sons; people who raised money for their voyage by mortgaging their land, and paid it back with their overseas earnings; and people who had no prospects of inheriting because they were younger sons, but bought land at 'home' through third parties with remittances that they sent back. I want to emphasize the depth and pervasiveness of a 'family-property consciousness' which was deeply rooted in modern Japanese society. Sakane Yoshihiro describes this as the 'triad' of family name, family property and family business.[14] How the agrarian reform affected these family values for Japanese emigrants has not been studied to date.[15]

A sense of the lived experience of border transgression emerges from examining the situation of migrants, who existed in the intersection between US and Japanese society throughout the postwar transformations. To what extent did these reforms transform relationships between self and others?

The first task for this section will be to examine the Japanese records and descriptions of the agrarian reforms to clarify how they addressed the issue of Japanese living overseas, and then to how these reforms were received by the ethnic Japanese immediately after the war. I will then consider the significance of the investigations before moving on to suggest areas of possible future research. One particularly significant aspect of this chapter is its consideration of local history in terms of Japan's relations with the United States.

The sources used in this research are *Tenmatsu Gaiyō* and *Shiryō Shūsei*; chronicles of the agrarian reform; and 'ethnic newspapers'.[16]

Outline of agrarian reform

Let us begin with an outline of agrarian reform. Less than two weeks after the 'Outline for the Implementation of Emergency Land Reclamation' had been decided, on 22 November 1945, the cabinet decided on the Agrarian Reform Guidelines. On 9 December, GHQ issued its 'Rural Land Reform' memorandum (SCAPIN-411), and agrarian reform was underway. In October 1946, following discussions within the Far Eastern Commission, the Special Measures Law Establishing the Owner-farmers Bill and the Amended Agricultural Land Adjustment Law were revised to produce an extremely powerful agrarian reform in which – in the space of a mere two years – the government would purchase two million hectares (initial objectives) of land and resell it to former tenant-farmers who would work the land themselves. The definition of one's domicile was crucial in this context; no absentee landlords were allowed to possess any tenant land, while those landlords were permitted to have land for tenancy as long as they had their address in the municipality concerned.

In the first agrarian reform, landlords were defined as those who owned tenant lands 'within the limits of the municipality of their address or place of temporary residence'. However, in the second agrarian reform this definition was refined and expanded to include all those who owned tenant lands 'within the limits of the municipality of their addresses'. This increased considerably the range of who would be considered 'absentee landlords'. By convention, some landlords had multiple addresses, but this agrarian reform directed that 'one's address is to be the base where one lives and (under Clause 17 of the Civil Code) this is *limited to just one*'. In subsequent directives, one's address was specifically indicated,

> under the Owner-farmers Law (Law Concerning Special Measures for the Establishment of Owner-farmers) and the (Agricultural Land Adjustment Law) as necessarily being the base where one lives and where one actually resides; people such as those leaving their families

in their hometown and returning themselves once or twice a week cannot be deemed to be residing there.[17]

The results of this reform were the sale of up to 80% of tenanted land and the disappearance of 'landlords' as a social class. In their place, there was a sudden increase in the number of small-scale owner-farmers. Tentative social stability was achieved through this reform, but economic stability for farmers, based on independent agricultural operations, remained a long way off. Nonetheless, this, combined with rapid economic growth, laid the foundations of Japanese agriculture today.

The issue of Japanese expatriates in agrarian reform

The beginning of the land issue for Japanese expatriates
The question of how Japanese expatriates were to be treated under agrarian reform was unclear from the outset, and passed through several stages before being decided. In this section, I will discuss the evolution of this process relying on the descriptions in *Tenmatsu Gaiyō* and *Shiryō Shūsei*. I am retracing the progress of this issue through these historical sources in order to highlight the disparities between the official Japanese record and the lived experience of Japanese expatriates, which we will look at later.

At the beginning of the occupation, this issue was entangled with that of the property of nationals of the Allied countries, which had been placed under Japanese government control pursuant to the 'Enemy Property Custody Law of 1941' during the war. Initially, the Minister of Finance's approval was required for any transactions concerning property in Japan owned by 'people residing in other countries', which effectively prohibited any such transactions.[18] Consequently, Japanese expatriates, regardless of their nationality, were prohibited from land transactions on their properties in Japan (proviso Clause 2, Ministry of Finance Ordinance Number 88, 1945).

At the beginning of the second agrarian reform, the Ministry of Agriculture and Forestry lobbied to establish agencies that would be authorized to purchase the lands of Japanese expatriates. In other words, it asked for the restrictions of the Ministry of Finance Ordinance referred to above to be lifted in the case of agricultural land.[19] This request was conveyed from the Ministry of Finance to the government, and then from the Central Liaison Office to

GHQ's Civil Property Custodian (hereafter, CPC). There were simultaneous requests made through GHQ's Natural Resource Section, with which the Ministry of Agriculture and Forestry had a particularly close relationship, but there was no reply from Washington. Subsequently, the Japanese government made no comment on this issue for some time.

It seems that, despite the government's reticence, local agricultural land committees, primarily in Tohoku, had begun acquiring land owned by expatriate Japanese, on the basis of the provisions for acquiring the land of absentee landlords. The Ministry of Agriculture and Forestry initially gave tacit approval to this process. However, many absentee landlords submitted petitions pursuant to the Ministry of Finance Order Number 88, and there was a pressing need to systematically elucidate the provisions of this ordinance.[20] In fact, from the time of the very first purchases in 1947, agricultural land committees throughout Japan submitted queries to the Ministry of Agriculture and Forestry about how to deal with the land of Japanese expatriates.[21]

In February 1948, when the fifth round of purchases had been completed, the Head of the Agricultural Administration Bureau finally released a directive 'Concerning the Treatment of Land Owned by Foreigners' (18/2/1948), which announced a suspension of purchases and of the resale of land already purchased (including un-repatriated people and Japanese expatriates).[22] There was a strong negative response to this decision from Japanese expatriates and, in particular, from those in Hawaii and California.

Eventual determination of compulsory purchase
More than a year after the reforms began, the policy concerning land owned by Japanese expatriates had not been decided. Ultimately, it was a GHQ memorandum, 'Application for General Permission to Dispose of Properties in Japan owned by Persons Outside of Japan According to Law Concerning Special Measures for Establishment of Owner-farmers' (SCAPIN–1911, 19/6/1948) that determined what the policy would be. The decisions concerning the property of foreigners in this were as follows.

> As of the present moment, 21 October 1946, the purchase of land registered as being owned by foreigners (people from Allied, neutral or Axis countries) is prohibited for the time being. *However, this does*

not apply in the case of people who hold Japanese citizenship (dual nationals). [emphasis added]

As we can see, only Japanese citizens were subject to compulsory acquisitions. In case there was any ambiguity, a condition was added which stipulated that Japanese expatriates who held only foreign citizenship would be exempted.[23] Then, a memorandum dated 19 June 1948, declared that the presence or absence of nationality would no longer be taken into account in determining the acquisition of lands.[24] This memorandum caused a sensation in January 1949, when it was reported in the pages of Japanese language newspapers overseas.[25]

Subsequently, in July 1948, the Head of the Agricultural Administration Bureau in the Ministry of Agriculture and Forestry issued a directive addressed to the Heads of all Agricultural Land Secretariats and to all governors 'Regarding the Processing of Agricultural Land Owned by Foreigners and Japanese Living Overseas' (5/7/1948). This directive proclaimed that 'land owned by Japanese living overseas was subject to purchase' – including people who had not yet been repatriated and second-generation Japanese (including those holding Japanese citizenship).[26] It is possible that the holdings of absentee landlords (including landlords from the former colonies) account for most of the land targeted under the seventh round of purchases immediately after SCAPIN–1911, but the details are not clear. The fact that in September that same year queries were still being received from Yamanashi Prefecture concerning being unable to complete purchases and difficulties with the paperwork suggests continuing confusion in local areas.[27]

Purchase decisions had to be communicated, not only to the various agricultural land committees that would determine their advisability, but also to land holders living overseas who, in principle, generally welcomed the agrarian reforms and yet were strenuously opposed to the compulsory acquisition of their own land. In August 1948, complaints arrived by telegram from the Hirano Law Firm in San Francisco and the 'Honolulu Chamber of Commerce' in Hawaii. The Japanese Refugees' Relief Committee complained that, 'making the land that Japanese people living overseas own in their home country the subject of purchase, despite the fact that these people are engaged in aiding their home country by sending money, is the act of people who do not understand gratitude'.[28] Following is part of a communication of purchase sent by the Ministry of Agriculture and Forestry.

> We must accomplish this work [agrarian reform] and continue striving in accordance with policy, as we have to date, in order to demonstrate our acceptance of the Potsdam Declaration, resuscitate a peaceful and democratic Japan, and take our place once again among the nations of the world. Therefore, while it is a profoundly painful matter not to be able to act in accordance with everyone's wishes, we hope that you will understand the need to put your land to use as agricultural land in your home country.

The Ministry did not take this attitude with absentee landlords living in Japan, which suggests that it was consciously drawing a distinction between ordinary absentee landlords and overseas landlords.

Purchase exclusions
At the end of 1948, 'Purchase and Resale of Agricultural Lands Owned by Persons of Dual Nationality' (SCAPIN-1911/1, 4/12/1948) was published, becoming the basis of a directive from the Under-Secretary of Agriculture and Forestry, 'Concerning the Purchase and Resale of Agricultural Lands Owned by Japanese Living Overseas and Dual Nationals' (20/12/1948). In accordance with this directive, all people recorded as Japanese in their family registers who were also dual nationals became subject to the compulsory purchase of land. In cases where family registers were unclear, it was decided to purchase the lands but defer resale for one year, in which time the presence or absence of records regarding the withdrawal of nationality would be verified. In February 1949, the restrictions in Ministry of Finance Ordinance Number 88 were rescinded and purchases became possible (Ministry of Finance notification no. 57). The problem in all of this was the issue of nationality; that is, the discrepancy between 'family register' and nationality.[29] In December 1949, approaching the end of the one year deferral period, cases were reviewed to determine which ones fell into the cancellation of purchase category.[30] In many cases extensions were granted until December 1949 and June 1950.

In July 1950, when the final purchases were about to be made, 'Purchase and Resale of Agricultural Lands Owned by Persons of Dual Nationality' (SCAPIN-1911/2, 25/7/1950) was released, followed by a directive from the Under-Secretary for Agriculture and Forestry, 'End of the Period of Deferment for the Resale of Agricultural Lands Owned by Japanese Living Overseas and Dual Nationals' (2/8/1950). In accordance with these directives, it was finally decided that the lands of people who had not applied for a revocation of purchase by 20 November would be sold after that date. (Another directive issued on 5 December stipulated that all resales would be completed within the 1950 financial year.)

As of the end of March 1950, there were 1,737 *chō* (1,721 ha) of land owned by landlords whose Japanese nationality status was being verified (there is no information for Hokkaido, Aichi, Mie and Wakayama). As of 21 November 1950, there had been 358 applications to revoke compulsory purchases, of which 51 cases (656 *chō* (651 ha)) had been successful (including pasture and uncultivated land). The total number of landlords is unknown, but *Tenmatsu Gaiyō* reports that 2,749 notifications of purchase were sent out.[31] As we will see in the next section, however, there are considerable doubts about this figure. While individual cases remain unclear, we have figures for the prefectures. In Kagoshima Prefecture, for example, by August 1950, more than 99% of purchased land had been sold, but 0.8% (around 277 *chō* (275 ha)) remained unsold. A total of 118 *chō* (117 ha), or 42.4%, of this belonged to Japanese expatriates, for which resale had been deferred. The vast majority of deferrals were because of the location of these migrants.[32]

The purchase of lands owned by Japanese nationals under the agrarian reforms was completed in the 1950 financial year. However, on 10 November 1951, the 'Memorandum on the Disposal of Lands under the Special Measures Law for the Establishment of Owner-farmers' was announced, making it possible to apply this law to people from Allied and neutral countries also, thus purchasing and reselling their land.[33] In the course of the agrarian reforms, then, we see that the laws were ultimately applied without regard to nationality. The 1952 Agricultural Land Act permanently grounded ownership of agricultural land on a cultivation principle which prioritized resident-cultivators. The impact of these reforms was not confined to the Japanese domestic sphere, but extended to 'Japanese' around the world. I will now shift our focus to Japanese migrants in the United States to develop an understanding of how these reforms were experienced by Japanese communities overseas.

Migrant responses: California

Conference of Absentee Landlords Living in the United States

So far in this chapter I have reviewed the development of the Japanese government's agrarian reform policies, especially as they pertain to Japanese citizens who lived overseas. In this section we will examine the responses of the migrants themselves, focusing primarily on those living in California. California had the largest number of Japanese living in the mainland United States. Their situation was unstable due to laws such as the California Alien Land Law and widespread discrimination, which became major issues in the debates in Japan about laws concerning lands owned by foreigners.[34]

For Japanese living on the west coast of the United States near the end of the war, the prospect of returning home from their wartime internment did not offer stability, either.[35] Attempts to apply the Alien Land Law in California more stringently after the war led to frequent property confiscations, making the lives of Japanese residents extremely unstable as they attempted to settle all over again. Against this backdrop, various groups formed, including, for example, the Civil Rights Defense Union in October 1945, as well as various groups of Japanese people who became more active (*Nichibei Jiji* (hereafter, *Nichibei*) 1/5/1946).

Despite the harsh conditions endured by Japanese in the United States, the democratization of their homeland was a matter of great interest and concern in their ethnic newspapers. The agrarian reform received considerable coverage. At this stage, there were no reports of the possibility that the agricultural lands of Japanese-Americans would be compulsorily purchased.[36]

As we have seen, the first round of compulsory land purchases began in late March 1947 – the end of the Japanese financial year. Responses from the migrant society began to appear in print around the time that notifications of purchase were sent to land owners.

The first case to appear in the newspapers is that of Chūgorō Nishimoto from Denver. When Minoru Yasui, a second-generation Japanese American lawyer acting on behalf of Nishimoto, sought further information from the US State Department, he received a reply that, 'All agricultural land within Japan would be disposed of pursuant to the provisions of the new Agricultural Land Act' (*Rafu*

Shimpō (hereafter, *Rafu*) 20/3/1947). This case was also featured in the Japanese American Citizens' League (hereafter, JACL), which reported that agrarian reform in Japan was dealing a blow to the property of first-generation Japanese-Americans (Yasui was a regional JACL leader).[37] There were also reports that during a visit to Japan in May, Roger Baldwin, Chairman of the Board of the American Civil Liberties Union, held discussions about the issue of land owned by Japanese expatriates with Colonel Schenk of GHQ's Natural Resource Section, and that the whole of GHQ was considering this matter (*Nichibei* 28/5/1947, *Rafu* 29/5/1947). Clearly, land reform was a matter of interest not only for the immigrants concerned, but also for US citizens' groups interested in human rights.[38]

That groups were formed identifying themselves as 'absentee landlords' to voice their opposition to land acquisition is quite interesting. Although numerous landlord groups formed in Japan to protest against the agrarian reforms during this period, none of them openly identified themselves as 'absentees'.[39]

San Francisco
The first group activity for which we have documentation occurred in San Francisco. On 30 March 1947, *Nichibei* ran the headline, 'Compatriot "Absentee Landlords" Living in the United States Victims of Japanese Agrarian Reform: Countless compatriots living in the United States who are landowners need to investigate countermeasures' (30/3/1947). The article reported that 'The implementation [of agrarian reform] has been confirmed through a recent exchange of correspondence with Japan, and absentee landlords living in the United States have been left dumbfounded with no means of acting'. However, it said, if 'the lands that they have bought in the hope of living off them when they return to Japan in their old age' are purchased from them, 'landlords living in the United States' will 'suffer a *double misfortune*' (emphasis added). (The first 'misfortune' had been the confiscation of their lands following their internment). One group stated that, 'Tenant-farmers would like to see a plan based on the principle of guaranteeing the possessions of all farmers, large and small, as they currently stand, applied also to absentee landlords living overseas'. They added, 'since there are no compatriot organizations to handle this for us, we are anxious for the mediation of the Civil Rights Defense Union'.

Nichibei reported that 'an emergency meeting' was planned, under the sponsorship of the San Francisco JACL which was taking up this issue from the perspective of 'protecting the interests' of ethnic Japanese (4/5/1947). It was decided that an 'Absentee Landlords Rally' would be held by land owners, sympathizers and sponsors, with the backing of the Civil Rights Defense Union on 18 May (*Nichibei* 13/5/1947). Articles in English described this as 'an issue confronting *Issei* [first-generation Japanese living in the United States] who own land in Japan'. It appears that once the implication of the reforms for landlords were understood, various parties began petitioning the Japanese authorities through GHQ (*Nichibei* 16/5/1947).

Sixty people assembled for the landlord rally and decided to found the 'Association of Japanese Absentee Landlords Living in the United States'. Masao Shinkai, Tatsuki Sakata, Shichijirō Hideshima, Fumio Okazaki and James Hirano were the inaugural committee members, and decided to send a telegram to the Ministry of Agriculture and Forestry and GHQ, which said:

> Having heard the news of compulsory purchases of agricultural lands owned by compatriots living in the United States, according to the Revised Agricultural Land Law Ordinance, the majority of compatriots aspire to return to Japan to cultivate their land, but are unable to travel abroad freely at present; we thus entreat you to postpone the compulsory purchases until the conclusion of a treaty between Japan and the United States. (*Nichibei* 21/5/1947)[40]

Los Angeles

Slightly later, organized activity also began in Los Angeles, the city with the largest number of Japanese residents in the state at that time. The 9 June meeting of the 'Monday Symposium', whose Executive Secretary was Chōei Kondō,[41] endorsed Katsuma Mukaeda's[42] call for a petition stating the united position of ethnic Japanese, and requesting that agrarian reforms be postponed (*Rafu* 10/6/1947). Mukaeda had only just returned to Los Angeles in February of the previous year following more than four years of internment, and was at the time working assiduously on Civil Rights Defense Union activities.[43] The first Absentee Landlords Rally was held to demonstrate support for this position at the Miyako Hotel on 20 June. Thirty-seven people attended, and decided to establish the Conference of Absentee Landlords (see Photo 4.1). The central

Japanese expatriate 'others'

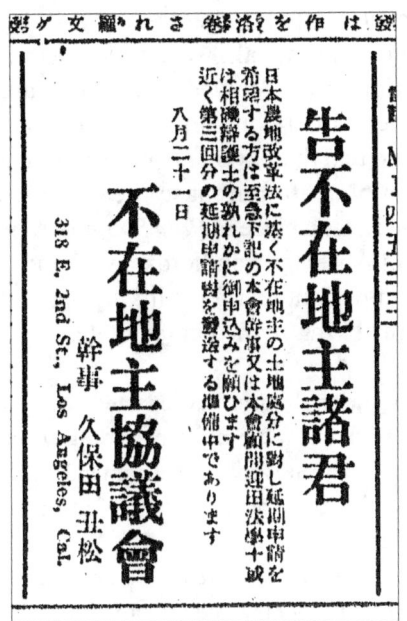

Photograph 4.1: Conference of Absentee Landlords advertisement (Rafu, 22/8/1947) (provided by Rafu Shinpōsha)

topic was petitioning GHQ to postpone the reforms. The members were: Chairman, Hirooka Shinichi;[44] Deputy Chairman, Motoe Satō; Executive Secretary, Ushimatsu Kubota; Treasurer, Ihei Sugimura; and Itsuyoshi Kagawa, Takaji Shimokubo, Kuichirō Nishi, Masayoshi Fujimoto and Manzō Tsutsui were permanent members (*Rafu* 21/6/1947).

The Chairman, Hirooka Shinichi, was from Hiroshima Prefecture and made his first trip to the United States in 1904. Having returned temporarily to Japan due to the vicissitudes of business, he went back to the United States in 1922 where he was relatively successful, opening the 'San Pedro Hotel' in 1924, and then a market on Hill Street in San Francisco City. Similarly, Kuichirō Nishi,[45] a permanent committee member, was from Wakayama Prefecture. He went to the United States in 1906, where he ran a business which earned him the nickname, 'the Rose King'. He had clearly been successful. There is insufficient information to say anything about the others, but we can assume that they all had considerable status in the immigrant community. There is also a strong likelihood that a significant majority, if not all, were first-generation migrants.

The information they received from Japan about the reforms may not have been either complete or entirely accurate, but they clearly understood that there were no provisions to exempt Japanese expatriates from plans to purchase their lands (*Rafu* 3/7/1947). Hirooka published a long piece in *Rafu Shinpō* setting out the aims of the Conference of Absentee Landlords. I will quote it in its entirety because it is an important text for thinking about the movement of absentee landlords living in the United States.

> The Japanese Agrarian Reform Law enacted last year does not take into account the particular circumstances of landlords living in the United States, and there are reports that our lands are to be purchased in the same way as large arable land holdings in Japan which are held in a feudal manner.
>
> We, Japanese living in the United States, not only have no right to be naturalized in this country and are prohibited from owning any land if we live on the Pacific coast, but we find ourselves in a situation in which even our freedom of residence is limited to a very small area because of prejudice against us as a race. I believe that tiny patches of farmland bought with meagre savings and minuscule patches of farmland handed over as a *token so that we do not abstain from festivals for ancestors* are far too small to become purchase objects and nor is this the intention of the legislation. These pieces of land belong to people who have lived in this environment and who *seek a place in their homeland where they can live in peace, making their farming implements their friends in their old age.*
>
> Those of us who have lived on the west coast were forcibly evicted at the outbreak of war between Japan and the United States, and we already feel that we are a long way off from our goal of getting back on our feet, having seen the toppling of the foundations of our livelihoods that we had built up over many long years.
>
> Therefore, *we absentee landlords living in the United States who had hoped to live out our old age in our homeland*, find ourselves in the predicament of it already being too late to recover in this country and of being about to lose the agricultural land that would be the foundation of our lives upon our return home. Moreover, because the present time, in which the new law has been enacted, is immediately after the end of the war, there has been no opportunity for stating

the standpoint of landlords living in the United States, and nor have we had the time to take any countermeasures. *I think that given that it has been enacted, there is no option but to obey the law; however, seeking a postponement of this law only in the case of landlords living in the United States and for a limited time is a matter of urgency, and possibly the sole course of action available.* It is because I thought that it would not be effective for everyone to mount their individual movement that I have humbly taken up the post of Chairman, putting to one side my own inadequacies. The fact that we have been fortunate enough to welcome John Aiso,[46] a lawyer and former army lieutenant colonel who has worked in MacArthur's headquarters, and Katsuma Mukaeda (Bachelor of Laws), who has extensive knowledge of this law in particular, as advisers to this organization and also to entrust all negotiations to them considerably strengthens its significance.

Consequently, I encourage all of you landlords living in the United States to give this organization your endorsement and to participate in creating one group and the realization of our aims.

> July 1947, Shinichi Hirooka, Chairman, Conference of Absentee Landlords Living in the United States (*Rafu* 14/7/1947, emphasis added)

The Los Angeles Conference of Absentee Landlords reported receiving a reply from GHQ and the Ministry of Agriculture and Forestry in late July acknowledging receipt of their petition (*Rafu* 26/7/1947). The San Francisco Association of Absentee Landlords also received a reply from GHQ and the Ministry of Agriculture. The Ministry's telegram simply read, 'Please wait as the matter is being investigated', which raised questions about earlier reports that there was no possibility of a postponement (*Nichibei* 29/7/1947). In November, there were reports that, as a result of these petitions, purchases would be postponed until the end of 1948.[47] As we have already seen, however, the Ministry of Agriculture made no such pronouncement in 1947. It is unclear whence came this information. John Aiso, adviser to the Conference of Absentee Landlords, and others sent a letter to the Minister of Agriculture dated 25 October 1947, reiterating the petition for an exemption from the agrarian reform, but the reply to this was that Japanese expats would be subject to the purchases, in the same manner as landlords in general. It also stated, however, that since it would not be possible to comply with the provisions of formal objections within the stipulated ten days from notification of a plan to purchase, consideration was being given to allowing three months before a purchase was completed.[48]

Other areas

Let us look now at cases in other areas. Initiatives were not limited to the parts of California where there were large Japanese expat populations. An Absentee Landlords Association was also formed a year later in the central part of California, which also petitioned the administration and relevant village headmen to postpone compulsory purchases (*Nichibei* 1/12/1948).

In Chicago, there were calls to form a discussion group, under the auspices of the 'Permanent Residents Association', to consider a petition for the 'postponement of the enforcement of agrarian reforms' (*Shikago Shinpō* 9/1/1948). However, I have not found any other reports of relevant movements in Chicago.

In Hawaii, the protest movement appears to have been even larger than in California. There are estimates of several thousand absentee landlords in Hawaii.[49] In April 1947, newspapers reported on the process for an application to postpone purchase (*Hawai Hōchi* 22/4/1947).[50] Within a few months, Sweden's Vice-Consul in Hawaii, Japan's Protecting Power in the US during the war, forwarded more than one thousand petitions that he had received to the Ministry of Foreign Affairs (*Rafu* 7/8/1947).

Several months after the events in California, reports appeared of communications from the Canadian Mission regarding agricultural lands owned in Japan. Explanations of the agrarian reforms were published several times in September and October (specific details of any collective action that ensued are obscure).[51]

In Brazil, I found only one newspaper which had reported on the reforms, but there may well be others. In April 1947, articles in *Burajiru Jihō* were still reporting that a bill to sell land owned by large-scale farmers and large landowners to tenants 'is scheduled to be voted on in the Diet', although the law had already been passed and the first round of purchases had been completed (*Burajiru Jihō* 1/4/1947).

Despite the discrepancies between countries, 'absentee landlord' initiatives erupted everywhere. Yet they do not appear to have been able to organize the majority of affected landlords. In fact, there are reports that most of the people affected in Los Angeles did not complete any formalities (*Rafu* 22/8/1947).

In addition to these group efforts, there were numerous individual land owners who attempted to apply pressure directly in the villages. In August 1947, there were reports of town and village Agricultural Land Committees postponing purchases in response to individual enquiries. These reports cited the importance of personal connections as the reason for the outcome in each case (*Nichibei* 9/8/1947). A typical example is the case of Yoshie Shiba from Ita Village, Mie Prefecture, who was informed that 'there will be no purchase right now under the rules' (*Nichibei* 4/12/1947). Accurate information was limited, making sources such as relatives and friends in Japan crucial for immigrant communities.[52] There was thus much confusion about the period of postponement, with some saying, for example, that it would continue until the peace treaty and others saying two years (*Rafu* 11/6/1947, 12/6/1947).

This suggests that an important characteristic of immigrant society in this period was the complexities of communication, as unreliable information was exchanged between families and within immigrant communities. Confusion grew more extreme as the Japanese government debated, and revised, the rules concerning nationality and compulsory acquisition.

Confusion about purchasing principles

Insecurity remained high until 1947, in both Japan and the United States. The situation began to change, however, in early 1948. On 19 January, litigation concerning the Alien Land Law – one of the most important issues for Japanese living in California, which had a significant impact on Japan–US relations – resulted in a victory in the Supreme Court, effectively rendering the law a dead letter, and opening the possibility for Japanese to own land in the United States. About the same time *Nikkei* people, using the wartime participation of the second-generation in US military service as a lever, began campaigning for full naturalization rights.[53]

It was also about this time that a GHQ memorandum (19 June 1948; SCAPIN-1911) declaring that there would be no exemptions for absentee landlords living overseas was finally reported in the United States in late July and early August. Judging by the manner in which this information was introduced, a notice sent by Captain Leahy to Mukaeda and published in *Rafu*, it seems that official channels were not functioning (*Rafu* 28/7/1948). *Nichibei* reported,

'150 hectares in *Amerika-mura* (America Village) Finally Released' using the same format as a newspaper from Wakayama Prefecture which had been sent by relatives to someone living in San Francisco. After this, the fact that the Japanese living in the US would not be exempt from the reforms was widely reported news from Japan.[54]

The news that Japanese living in Hawaii had set aside millions of dollars to purchase land in their birthplaces was reported via a similar process.[55] Many immigrants secured capital to purchase land in their birthplaces as the fruits of their hard work, an endeavor which made them reflect on the entire history of their migration.

When they learnt of this decision, Japanese expatriates were quite vocal in their criticism of the Ministry of Agriculture and Forestry. The activities of James Hirano (Hirano Law Firm) provide a typical example. In a telegram, on 3 August 1948, Hirano argued that compulsory purchases under conditions in which the effected parties were not free to travel to Japan were undemocratic, and violated the rights of the individual.[56] In October, the *Hokubei Mainichi* reported that as a result of Hirano's negotiations the purchase of agricultural land would be revoked for landlords living in San Francisco.[57] Hirano then repeatedly published advertisements in *Nichibei* (the first was 11/11/1948), and kept up his appeals on behalf of the Japanese community in the United States.

Also at this time, there were reports that there were 3,140 expatriate landlords from Hiroshima Prefecture, corresponding to almost 908 *chō* (900 ha) of cultivated fields (*Nichibei* 19/11/1948).[58] I mentioned above that the Ministry of Agriculture and Forestry estimates that there were only around 2,700 notifications of purchase, but these figures for Hiroshima Prefecture alone suggest that the real number is probably much greater, although the exact situation remains unclear. There were various exemptions from compulsory purchase, such as when the absentee head-of-household's family were his tenants, for example. When the Ministry of Agriculture and Forestry asked, 'What kind of agricultural land could easily escape purchase?' in a survey of all administrative areas, Hiroshima Prefecture alone replied that it was agricultural land owned by dual nationals.[59] In Hiroshima, from where large numbers had migrated, the inability to acquire the land of dual nationals had become a major problem.

In January 1949, Brigadier General Tansey, Head of the Civil Property Custodian Section (CPC) of GHQ, once again declared that agrarian reforms 'would be applied in the same manner to *Nikkei* living overseas including those in the second-generation', and sought to clarify the intent of the law, saying

> Whilst Japanese may live within Japan or overseas, the nature [of the law] is not such as to draw distinctions on the basis of these differing circumstances; it must be applied uniformly. This law shall, however, only be applied to agricultural lands, residential districts are excluded. Furthermore, lands owned by Americans and by other non-Japanese living in Japan are out of contention.[60]

The purchase exclusions provisions were announced through joint communiques from GHQ and the Ministry of Agriculture and Forestry, and reported in the Japanese press. The sources of information for *Nichibei* and *Hawai Hōchi* reports are not clear. Perhaps they received official communiques, but there is no evidence that they reported it. In California, as mentioned, local reporting was based on information conveyed informally through people connected with GHQ.

Notifications of the compulsory purchase of land were also frequently communicated through informal channels. In some cases, notifications were sent directly to the concerned parties, but where addresses were unknown, notifications were communicated via the *Nichibei Jiji* Newspaper Company, a private business. These notifications were sent by the Japanese Ministry of Foreign Affairs to *Nichibei Jiji* via the State Department in the United States.[61] *Nichibei* published the names of the people to whom the written notifications were addressed. The first list was published on 1 November 1949. There appear to have been three or four names published every day after this (*Nichibei* 4/11/1949)). A second list was published on 14 December, and a third on 26 January 1950 (26/1/1950, 15/2/1950).

In Los Angeles, such notifications were sent from the Governor of Fukui Prefecture to the *Rafu Shinpō* Newspaper Company via the US Department of the Interior (*Rafu* 29/4/1950). Even within Japan itself, the procedure of purchasing land from absentee landlords was described by the Ministry of Agriculture and Forestry as having 'presented unexpectedly extreme difficulties and considerable obstacles in terms of paperwork' in several administrative areas.[62]

Renunciation of citizenship

The renunciation of second-generations' Japanese citizenship symbolized this. Sakaguchi Mitsuhiro has highlighted how important the issue of dual nationality was to Japanese immigrants in the 1930s.[63] Activities to renounce Japanese nationality were initially made public in a report which said, 'as a result of complications arising in connection with rights issues back in Japan in the case of dual nationals, a trend to renounce their Japanese nationality has ultimately emerged among the second-generation' (*Nichibei* 19/1/1949).[64] This article does not articulate these 'rights issues' in Japan, but a follow-up report makes clear that the issue of absentee landlords under agrarian reform was central:

> It was unclear what form the formalities of renouncing Japanese citizenship amongst the second-generation living in the United States, *particularly in connection with issues such as postwar absentee landlords*, should take, but the Tokyo head office of the Committee for Oversea Compatriots has received the following confirmation from the Justice Agency and other relevant authorities who were approached (*Nichibei* 13/2/1949, emphasis added).[65]
>
> The Committee for Oversea Compatriots

There had already been reports in *Rafu*, on 21 October 1946, that nationality would become an issue (*Rafu* 28/7/1948). Because the decisions were to be made on the basis of nationality on that date, the renunciation of nationality at a later date became immaterial. However, there were reports in Hawaii that people who had applied to renounce their nationality received notices from the mayor of Hiroshima to the effect that they would be exempt from agricultural land purchases (*Hawai Hōchi* 7/10/1948). Another article in the *Hawai Hōchi* reported that there were substantial numbers of second-generation Japanese who had property assigned to them by their parents as a precaution against it being confiscated during the war as the property of people from enemy countries.[66] This was because the second-generation had American citizenship and relished privileges as Americans, whereas the first-generation could not obtain US citizenship.

There was some degree of ambivalence among second-generation immigrants on this matter. They felt they had to renounce the nationality of their parents' homeland to avoid the government acquisition of land that they had inherited in the family's hometown, in order to preserve their connections to a 'homeland' that many had never visited. From the perspective of the second-generation ethnic Japanese leaders, this was a positive outcome, conforming to the ideal of the child of the migrant who rejects the parents' aspirations of returning home, becomes a US citizen, and settles there permanently.[67] Beyond that, though, the wave of renunciations was largely meaningless: although there was a brief period in 1946 when the citizenship of absentee landlords was considered grounds for exemption from compulsory acquisition, as we have seen, those provisions were soon overturned, with the circular notice in November 1951 by the Japanese government affirming that the property acquisition laws should be applied to the citizens of Allied countries. Thus, nationality had no bearing on the acquisition of property owned by absentee landlords. Attempts by people to renounce their nationality were symbolic manifestations of the migrants' state of confusion in the absence of correct information from the government of their homeland.

Absentee landlords in the media and movements

In April 1950, reporting on absentee landlords begins again, possibly in response to the accelerating pace of land purchases. In San Francisco, there were reports to the effect that an 'Absentee Landlords' Discussion Group' would be organized by Kikumatsu Tōgasaki[68] and Hiroshi Morozumi (*Nichibei* 11/4/1950), and meet in the offices of the JACL as the 'Absentee Landlords' Rally' (*Nichibei* 12/4/1950). Rinji Kondō, a lawyer who had committed himself to this issue, reportedly argued that 'the constitutionality of the law to revise agriculture had still not been determined' (*Nichibei* 14/4/1950).[69] There were also calls from the San Francisco JACL offices for an Absentee Landlords Living in the United States Rally (*Nichibei* 18/4/1950). These events were followed by headlines such as, 'Purchase of Second Generation Agricultural Lands: Demands for Restoration Possible' (*Nichibei* 19/4/1950).

It appears, however, that the main focus of the Japanese in the United States was on litigation to declare the Alien Land

Law unconstitutional and to acquire citizenship rights. Although the issue of compulsory land acquisition in Japan was raised now and then, it hardly ever became a central concern for the community. Nevertheless, it is clear that these two issues became more interconnected once the Anti-Discrimination Committee of JACL began to act as an intermediary in negotiations with GHQ and the Ministry of Agriculture and Forestry in 1950.[70]

Meanwhile, if we look at the tenor of the media reporting of the absentee landlord issue, we see that while it expressed sympathy, it did not advocate for exemptions from the compulsory land purchases with the same vigor as it had pursued citizenship rights. Perhaps the newspapers did not see it as in their own interest to support causes that perpetuated people's hopes or desires to return to Japan – or at least, not as much in their interest as facilitating their readership's ability to settle down and make the United States their permanent home.

The following are several editorials that appeared in the media (the emphasis throughout is mine).

Tomie Yamada, Op-ed: *Rafu* **(7/7/1947)**

'Agricultural System Reform and Absentee Landlords'

> It will be painful for landlords living in the United States to easily let go of the agricultural lands that they have gone to pains to buy in Japan as a provision for their old age because they are absentee landlords. Since it is their intention to return to Japan in their old age and work for themselves, we would like to see the disposal of these lands postponed a little longer. This is the general opinion.
>
> There is not anyone who does not sympathize with the standpoint of these landlords living in the United States. I think that, if possible, we must help them by establishing some special measures.

At the same time, Yamada stresses that this is 'one of the important policies of the occupying forces'. He also notes that, *'Now that it has already been applied to absentee landlords in places like Manchuria and China, surely just granting an exceptional postponement to landlords living in the United States would stick in the throat.'* In other words, exemptions for landlords living in the United States are impossible when compared to the so-called 'repatriated landlords'.

Seigo Mutō,[71] ***Rafu* (31/8/1948–7/9/1948, five entries in total)**
'Advice to Compatriots Living in the United States re: the Agrarian Reform Law: Insights into Japan's Present Severe Conditions – An Entreaty to Consider'

Seigo Mutō had negotiated with GHQ and the Ministry of Agriculture and Forestry during his time in Japan as a representative of ethnic Japanese. He urged abandoning hopes of exemptions in several articles.

> Is it likely that suddenly going back to Japan after having lived overseas for twenty or thirty years and saying, 'I have not been able to return before now' would be sufficient reason for tenants to simply hand back land, or for agricultural land committees to readily approve this? And would not the economically privileged condition of compatriots living in the United States be particularly influential in their decisions? People must yield and reconcile themselves to numerous doubts. (*Rafu* 2/9/1948)

Furthermore, raising the issue of changes in the lifestyles of immigrants is important for Mutō's argument:

> Precisely because I have lived as one of my compatriots in the United States, I more than understand the feelings of people who own land in Japan in the hope of returning to their birthplaces and enjoying an easy life there in their old age… I think that *the anticipation of 'old age' should not be returning to Japan and living there permanently, but become instead visiting one's hometown and sightseeing in Japan.* (*Rafu* 7/9/1948)

As we can see here, agricultural land ownership is an issue of the immigrants' way of life.

'Magnifying Glass' (*Nichibei* 16/1/1949)
The final example is an anonymous article. After quoting the statement by Tansey of the CPC, mentioned earlier, that there would ultimately be no exemptions, the author appeals for 'noble sacrifices' in the interests of reforming the homeland.

> The requests for exemptions by our compatriots back in Japan, on the grounds of special circumstances, have also proved ineffective. If the

purpose of this is also to improve the lives of the farming masses via this new age's social reform of liberating Japan's tenants, then it is *an inevitable noble sacrifice*... The law has made temporary allowances but finally, with the issuing of the recent statement, while these are extremely painful circumstances for our compatriot landlords, we must also resign ourselves to the fact that we are caught up in world trends and that we are in a situation which cannot permit exemptions.

This statement might be viewed as the mainstream attitude of ethnic Japanese. Mike Masaoka, one of the community's leaders, articulated the changing attitudes of the Japanese immigrant community in the early postwar years as follows:

The first-generation – from the standpoint of guardians, having passed on everything to the second-generation – have also clearly abandoned their aspirations of returning to their native land after defeat, and discovered an attitude of wanting to return to their immigrant nature and settle down on their land in the United States. (*Nichibei* 18/10/1946)

This appears to be a fairly accurate description of the prevailing attitude of ethnic Japanese, and the attitude that the community leaders hoped to foster. Throughout this period, while the immigrant community maintained its connections in Japan, major effort was put into movements to acquire civil rights, and citizenship rights. These went hand-in-hand with an intention to settle permanently (*Nichibei* 7/12/1947). Hence, the efforts of 'absentee landlords', which expressed aspirations to return to their birthplace one day, was inevitably limited to peripheral demands for a community whose primary struggle was the quest for permanent residence.

'Overseas representatives of empire' or 'parasitic landlords'

Agrarian reform treated the land owned by people who lived beyond the borders of towns and villages as being owned by 'absentees'. This position was at odds with customary village practices of family property management, which had included 'trans-boundary' forms of cultivation since early modern times, as cultivators moved around, following seasonal demands for labor. It was even more at odds with the modern system, which had commodified and normalized the distinction between ownership rights and tenancy or 'presence'. It was thus natural that migrants, who by definition had traversed borders, would become 'absentee landlords'.

Recognizing that land owners' rights had been normalized, though, does not mean that they were universally accepted. In fact, one of the premises underpinning the agrarian reforms was a critique of absentee landlords that had pervaded Japanese agriculture since the war. In Onogō Village in Kyoto Prefecture (now within the Kyoto City limits), 70% of fields, forest and mountain land was owned by absentee landlords in 1944, a situation that the media described as a 'colonial village' and which inspired the Association for the Restoration of Lost Land.[72] And this was despite repressive policies towards absentee landlords that had already been adopted in the prewar period.[73]

At the same time, though, prewar Japan strongly encouraged emigration. Japanese migrants living in the United States had frequently been ignored by the Japanese government, and particularly at times such as the attack on Pearl Harbor, but we should also recognize that later, when internment in an 'enemy country' was reported, the Committee for Compatriots Living in Enemy Countries was established by the Japanese government to encourage Japanese nationalism among expatriates.[74] With Japanese expatriates in mind, the committee resolved to make the following 'pledges of overseas compatriots':

- We are 'subjects' of the Japanese empire. With piety and reverence, we report our debt of gratitude to the Emperor.
- We are on a mission from the empire of Japan. We will display the ideals of founding a state with selfless devotion.
- We are overseas representatives of the empire of Japan. We will enhance national prestige in solidarity as one group.
- We are pioneers of the development of the Japanese empire. We will accomplish our mission by acting according to our principles.
- We are people who will build a new world order (*Kyoto* 25/4/1942).

These pledges present emigrants as people on a state mission; as representatives of both the nation and its people. The nation, with its contradictions between, on the one hand, oppressing absentee landlords – even under a modern land ownership system in which it could not get its hands on their land – and, on the other, endorsing overseas development by its subjects, was far removed from most people, whose aims were protecting their family property and maintaining and developing this property through their labor.[75] Hence, the tendency to either ignore or make light of the importance of migrations during the empire, results in a failure to recognize the importance of land issues in Japanese history.

Emigrants who owned land were simultaneously disadvantaged within Japanese society and honored as representatives of the Japanese people. The prewar 'distortions' of imperial Japan were reformed after the war ended in defeat. Only a tiny portion of the voices of the people who lived through this experience have been recorded, and there has been no in-depth analyses that have connected their experiences to the nature of postwar society. Agrarian reform rendered it practically impossible for farmers in Japan to follow the well-worn path of working overseas to acquire capital to invest in Japanese property. Within the postwar Japanese territory, the provisos of agrarian reform were applied in enormously disparate ways, depending on where one lived – and its implementation had enormous impacts on how people lived.

Let us summarize the behavior of Japanese expatriates. The mainstream of their communities welcomed agrarian reform as democratizing their homeland, but the absentee landlords who were directly affected sought exemptions from or postponements of its application. For this reason, before July 1947 absentee landlord groups were formed with primarily first-generation expat members. Papers such as the *Nichibei Jiji* – the 'ethnic media' – initially supported efforts to protect people's interests. But its support waned rather quickly, and it began calling for 'noble sacrifices', appealing to its readers to see the homeland not as a place to retire to, but as a place to visit for sightseeing. In a society in which xenophobic pressures against Japanese were strong, the community and its media sought civil rights, focusing on the rights of permanent settlement and naturalization. The demands of absentee landlords, who aspired to return to Japan in the future, were of very little concern to most of the community. Agrarian reform eliminated the prospects of people from farming villages returning to live out their old age in their birthplaces, which in turn affected the way in which they were Japanese. For the first-generation especially, losing property in their birthplaces held particular meaning during this period when they could not become naturalized as US citizens, and the Alien Land Law had not been repealed. The second generation had seen no improvement in their social standing despite their military service. Moreover, the reforms did not only impact those who were absentee landlords at the time; it also changed the future prospects of others who hoped to purchase land 'at home' once they had succeeded as migrants. Thus, its effects were felt across the immigrant community. In the small number of demands and actions of these migrants we can see a rupture between prewar and postwar Japan. Hence, to understand changes in the postwar identities of Japanese immigrants in the United States, in addition to local conditions, it is necessary to come to terms with the part played by postwar agrarian reform in Japan, which decisively changed the migrant's sense of family property. It is in this sense that this book takes the position that overseas Japanese were 'othered' via the postwar agrarian reforms.[76]

It is also worth bearing in mind that the Japanese were not the only migrants buying land in their birthplaces. The following passage is Park Chaeil's (1957) description of the situation of land purchases in people's birthplaces.

> The resolution of the *Zainichi* Korean issue will not occur unless it is premised on the resolution of the Korean issue. And there is one essential condition in order to resolve the *Zainichi* Korean issue by means of resolving the Korean issue. This is agrarian reform in South Korea. *Consistently throughout the prewar and postwar periods what many Zainichi Koreans have bought with their savings is not their residences or shops in Japan but farmland in South Korea...* Only agrarian reform of the rice fields owned by *Zainichi* Koreans in South Korea will bring a fundamental resolution of the *Zainichi* Korean issue.[77] (emphasis added)

While, as discussed in Chapter 1, there were people who acquired land and settled in the society to which they had migrated, many others sought to buy land in their birthplaces. Analyzing the locations of the property that migrants own would help to develop a more multifaceted understanding of modern history.

Let us finally turn to the second of the topics that I mentioned at the beginning of this chapter – points for future research. We find very little evidence of any campaigns or actions by absentee landlords in the Latin American countries. We need to review why there were such different responses. Even if we conclude that there was no concerted action in Brazil concerning Japan's agrarian reforms, we could not say that there was no impact. Kiyotani Masuji, an intellectual in a migrant society says:

> When I visited my birthplace ten years ago [around 1970], while experiencing tortured feelings about the fact that the lands of my parental home had been handed over to the people whom I left on the land as tenants when I departed for Brazil as a result of the 'unreasonable' measures known as the postwar 'compulsory purchasing of the lands of absentee landlords', I loitered on the road in front of the home in which I was born many times, but I was finally unable to go in. Running my hand along the boards of the old-looking main pillar, the window shutter boxes and the stiles of YK's house, I pieced together various memories of the house of my birth.[78]

For Kiyotani the main objective of agrarian reform vanished; all that he was able to write about was the compulsory purchase. Postwar reforms may well have forged relationships between people and land, but alongside these new relations we also have the image of migrants who walk around the villages of their birth yearning for the homes where they were born. The absentee landlord issue significantly changed the meaning of 'in group' and 'out group' in relation to privately owned agricultural land; the extent to which it did this calls for further research (as mentioned in ethnic newspapers, comparisons with Japanese people in the former colonies are also important). There is also a need to collect a variety of case studies that might reflect the significant regional differences in the responses and attitudes of Japanese villages – the sites where agricultural lands were being purchased.[79]

Furthermore, the foundational principles of this law had an important effect on later waves of migration. In Chapter 5, I point out that many of the people involved in developing Manchurian settlement policies were later engaged in formulating postwar emigration policies. Disposing of their property before they set off had been regarded as a given by this group of emigrants. I am jumping ahead a little, but I think that one of the background factors to the establishment of this policy was the necessity of locating this postwar agricultural land into the prewar legal system, which did not recognize the ownership of agricultural land by people who were 'absent'. We can also see a connection with this issue in the emphasis some technical officers who took part in postwar migration and colonization placed on ruptures with the prewar period; they commented that overseas emigrants had to renounce their nationality at the same time as they left Japan because the postwar Japanese overseas emigration policy was totally different from the Manchurian migrants who migrated under the Japanese flag.[80]

Finally, while agricultural lands are an important part of family property, we must be careful to note that they are not the only family property.[81] The most important things in relation to the *ie* (family) are typically the family residence and tombs. The particular importance of the word 'gravesites' is apparent from the frequency with which it is uttered by immigrants. In this sense, the question of how Japanese and *Nikkei* coped with thoughts about their ancestors, their own burials, and 'tombs' needs to be examined alongside the issue of agricultural lands.[82]

Put quite simply, both migration and settlement are issues of 'population', 'borders' and 'productivity' for states. But, for the individual, they are nothing more nor less than issues of how they live and die as they carry a multitude of burdens. We need to take a fresh look at the issue of 'ownership', which mediated all of this.

From the research notes

The Honolulu Petition

On 20 January 1949, the following petition was addressed to the Hiroshima Prefecture Agricultural Land Committee by Japanese residents of Honolulu who were associated with the Chamber of Commerce and Industry (individuals have been de-identified).

> When I learnt from a letter that I recently received from my nephew that the agricultural and residential property that I own as my private property in Village X in Y district would be purchased it was truly a bolt from the blue, and although I immediately sent an enquiry to the agricultural committee in Village X they did not take up the matter; thus, having no opportunity to make a formal complaint I address my petition to your distinguished committee.

I have received no notification whatsoever concerning plans to purchase the aforementioned agricultural and residential lands from the agricultural committee, nor have I been served with any purchase decree. The fact that I am the owner of these lands and also their whereabouts are, I think, sufficiently well known to the members of the agricultural committee given that I have recently forwarded funds for items such as leisure facilities, school supplies, exercise equipment and school funds, as well as having made donations via the Hiroshima War Damage Relief Society. And yet, there has been no notification whatsoever regarding the purchase – particularly the purchase of the residential land: I find this most unsatisfactory.

I humbly entreat you to exclude the aforementioned agricultural and residential lands owned by me in Village X, in particular the residential land in Section C of the village, from your purchase plans.

(Agricultural Land Development Section, *Sogan Ikken Daijūichiji, Jūniji Baishū* (One petition: purchases 11 and 12) Hiroshimaken Gyōsei Bunsho [S1–90–156], held by Hiroshima Kenritsu Monjokan)

Chapter 4 has essentially been about the importance of agricultural land, but we can read this petition as placing more importance on residential land. There will naturally be variations in the feelings tied up with land depending on the form of land use and on the personal life histories of individuals, but this source expresses the feelings, of those whose lands were compulsorily acquired, that agrarian reforms were unfair in every sense.

On 2 March, the Hiroshima Prefecture Agricultural Land Committee – on the basis of a letter concerning this petition from the agricultural committee in Village X – dismissed the petition for the following reasons.

1. The petitioner's arguments that he did not receive either notification of the plan to purchase or a purchase directive cannot be recognized as grounds for exemption from purchase.
2. The petitioner states that his address is on territory in the United States, but as this makes him a dual national, as a foreigner, he cannot be granted exemption from purchase.
3. The provision of articles of comfort and donations cannot in any way be acknowledged as grounds for a petition.

(Agricultural Land Development Section, *Sogan Ikken* [S1–2009–278], held by Hiroshima Prefectural Archive (Kenritsu Monjōkan))

However, because the applicant declared his intention to withdraw his application regarding the residential land, this was ultimately excluded from purchase. Even so, there can be little doubt that one relationship had been severed.

There were only a small number of petitions of this type sent to prefectural agricultural committees. A slightly larger number were sent to city, town and village agricultural committees.

5 Putting down roots: Postwar administration of overseas agricultural emigration and farmers

You may well complain about life in the country,
But how many people actually end up there, in that situation?
Oh, everyone!

Niigata Nippōsha (ed.) '*Wakai Nōmin* (Young farmers)'

Postwar emigration, agriculture, and villages

An overview of postwar emigration

This chapter deals with two themes. One is an explanation of the nature of the postwar administration of overseas agricultural emigration, with particular attention to the activities of the Ministry of Agriculture and Forestry. The other is a consideration of how the inhabitants of farming villages reacted to emigration policies.

The government's postwar policies for assisting overseas migrants resumed in 1952. The numbers of people emigrating were initially quite small, but then steadily increased, reaching a peak around the mid-1950s, before falling sharply. The turning point for emigration policy was in 1961, when social questions were once again raised about the carelessness of emigration administration in the case of 'groups of emigrants who had gone to the Dominican Republic returning home'. Throughout the 1960s, the number of people choosing overseas emigration remained small, and by the 1970s there were hardly any references to emigration as a social issue. (By 1970, however, more than 100,000 people emigrated each year with no government assistance, constituting the majority of overseas emigrants).[1]

Table 5.1: Number of Japanese postwar government-assisted overseas emigrants (1952–1991)[a]

Year	Total number	Agricultural sector[b]	Year	Total number	Agricultural sector
1952	54	54	1972	1,012	428
1953	1,498	1,482	1973	631	174
1954	3,741	3,730	1974	534	126
1955	3,512	3,471	1975	506	187
1956	6,168	6,121	1976	502	191
1957	7,439	7,372	1977	467	174
1958	7,606	7,527	1978	483	188
1959	7,610	7,494	1979	549	151
1960	8,386	8,229	1980	597	122
1961	6,263	6,113	1981	600	123
1962	2,201	2,104	1982	357	51
1963	1,526	1,415	1983	217	91
1964	1,105	761	1984	137	69
1965	818	450	1985	109	28
1966	1,531	585	1986	146	46
1967	1,543	442	1987	171	47
1968	1,129	338	1988	157	26
1969	1,146	365	1989	88	19
1970	1,236	343	1990	41	8
1971	1,098	434	1991	52	16
Total				72,966	61,095

Source: Compiled by author using Kokusai Kyōryoku Jigyōdan, 1992.
Note: [a] These emigrants include those who were issued with 'notifications of eligibility' by the administration (later, from the Japan International Cooperation Agency, via the Overseas Emigrants Association) and also who presented a 'migration card' upon migrating to Canada and Australia. See p. 1 of the source document. [b] The figures for the agricultural sector have been based on the total 'independent cultivators', 'public appeals' and 'designated' for 1952–1965; the total for 'cc' for 1966–1979; and the numbers for 'agriculture' for 1980–1991.

From 1952 until 1991, over 80% of migration was connected to agriculture. In fact, in the period 1952–1965 – which will be given particular attention below – 56,323 out of 57,297 overseas emigrants, or 97.2%, were connected to agriculture. This is why it is essential that the period of rapid growth of overseas emigration policy be dealt with through the lens of agricultural emigration.[2]

We do not have a clear picture of the personal backgrounds of emigrants, but it is likely that a considerable number were from farming villages. This assumption is based on the contemporary awareness of the seriousness of the problem of surplus population in rural areas. In the period before rapid economic growth and before there were structures in place for the cities to absorb a large labor force, this surplus agricultural population, symbolized by the problem of second and third (or, non-inheriting) sons, became a major social problem.[3] Farming villages were poorer than the cities, and the government intervened using various means to encourage emigration for those whom the village could not provide a livelihood. Some of these people achieved their aims of becoming established and succeeding in local society overseas. More than a few people died, however, as a result of the careless manner in which these initiatives had been researched and promoted. For most of the others, agricultural emigration was a path of terrible hardship.

Studies of the administration of postwar overseas emigration have to date been based on the actions of the Ministry of Foreign Affairs as the ministry responsible for the program. This research includes a substantial body of work by Wakatsuki Yasuo, who was directly involved in overseas emigration ventures.[4] There have also been frequent references to fierce jurisdictional battles – both within the emigration administration and between the Ministry of Foreign Affairs and the Ministry of Agriculture and Forestry. For a long time, however, many aspects of the role of the Ministry of Agriculture and Forestry remained unexamined. In recent years, this point has started to attract the attention of a few researchers.

Itō Atsushi conducted an examination of youth policy throughout the prewar and postwar periods which highlighted the importance of the Ministry of Agriculture and Forestry's role within migration administration. He also outlined the development and continuity up to the present day of private groups – such as the Association for International Collaboration of Farmers – in promoting migration. Through this work, Itō has broadened the discussion to include *Nikkei* Brazilian workers of the 1990s. He is also raising the issue of cross-referencing research on Manchurian settler emigration, postwar emigration and foreign workers. The present book is in some respects simply a response to questions raised by Itō.[5]

Fujihara Tatsushi discusses the significance of focusing on the behind-the scenes role played by the agricultural economist, Sugino Tadao, who worked on Manchurian settlement and postwar overseas emigration policies. Sugino is representative of the logic that transformed 'agricultural colonization studies' from abstract learning to practical knowledge applied in the field.[6] Fujihara highlights important aspects of the study of postwar Japanese agriculture, but does not address how the implementation of policies affected the local people.

Itō's and Fujihara's achievements and the questions that they have raised might be summarized as follows. The state's promotion of emigration was not confined to the implementation of administrative policies; rather, the execution of state policies conferred a scientific basis to knowledge and policies generated by private groups, and was also inter-related with spontaneous and proactive student movements (for example, the Japanese Students' Overseas Emigration League). The connections between the core players who dispatched postwar emigrants should be made clear by future research. My focus here is on how postwar farmers – the intended audience for state appeals – responded. I am also interested in whether postwar farmers refused to become deracinated 'others'. Future research needs to overlap with analyses of the countryside. As a milestone along the way to fuller analysis, I would like to begin by tracking the actions of the bureaucracy, which was the axis for state actors in emigration administration.

The people confronting the policies

A further objective of this chapter is to attempt to elucidate how people came to decisions about whether to migrate across national borders, or attempt to stay in their villages, where farmers come into direct contact with the administrative mechanisms of power. Overseas emigration trends have increased and declined. What I would like to explore in this chapter is why people did not emigrate. Both policies and a variety of other means were deployed to promote emigration; and yet, most people did not respond. Why was this? It is easy to see that, in most cases, a decision is made before one migrates. But staying put is no less a decision, whether due to resignation, inertia, a strong sense of attachment, for any other reason.

It is important to recognize the relationships between these issues and the mass-migration from farming villages to cities during the period of rapid economic growth. Of particular importance is the relationship with the structures of city formation, which has at one of its extremes the *yoseba*: sites where laborers gather hoping to get hired for the day. There had been, of course, connections between farming villages and urban underclass workers before this period. What is distinctive is that now, unlike earlier periods – after the prewar Depression, and immediately before and after defeat – people did not return to the villages when conditions changed in the cities; the move was now 'final'.[7]

It is generally well-known that the migration from farming villages provided the basic source of an urban underclass of labor. So too is the fact that this migration was triggered by changes in farming villages which resulted from the pursuit of modernization during the period of rapid growth. The peak of overseas emigration in the late 1950s occurred when the population problem in farming villages was on the cusp of changing from one of oversupply to one of depopulation. The massive flow of males out of these villages, migrating for long periods for work, and forced closures of entire villages forged the pathways for migration to the cities. The contemporary expression, 'It is no longer postwar' reflected anxiety in the face of new conditions. Similarly, the Japanese nation and the social consciousness of its people were not as stable at this time as is suggested by the phrase 'the 1955 system' – the classification subsequently applied to it. Various attempts were made to come up with a solution for these migrations before some structure was imposed, which happened after the 1960s.

The more vigorous pace of postwar overseas emigration was in part a response to this period of searching for solutions. Postwar migrants differed from wartime migrants. The latter had been part of national policy and assistance, albeit limited, was given to them. Fierce selection procedures for postwar emigrants, in contrast, suggest that this group should be regarded as having been able to fund themselves which, therefore, also distinguishes them from the lowest stratum of people who were flowing from farming villages into the urban underclass. These differences in the social strata to which villagers belonged notwithstanding, overseas emigrants were yet another group of people who had been separated from the particular dynamic of the space that was the traditional village. That the numbers of overseas emigrants remained small is no reason for ignoring their experience. Rather, it is precisely by conjecturing about the diverse life-experiences of the people who were attempting to make something of the new conditions while continuing to suffer that we can gain a multifaceted understanding of this period. The late 1950s, the golden age of overseas emigration, also coincides with the beginning of efforts to 'repatriate' *Zainichi* Koreans.[8] These multiple ways in which national borders were being traversed, at a time in which the Japanese public did not really feel the fruit of economic growth, is intimately bound up with a social consciousness characterized by intense discrimination.

This research helps to clarify the processes by which urban social groups and their individual distinctiveness are formed. Through increased understanding of the interdependence of the widespread changes in farming villages and cities, we can begin to develop a more holistic picture of the structures of postwar governance and the lives of the people who they affected. The following section summarizes changes in the population of farming villages from the immediate postwar period until the period of rapid economic growth. The next two sections endeavor to clarify who attempted to do what and why within emigration administration. The final section uses contemporary surveys of farming villages to consider the manner in which farmers reacted to this administration.

The unfolding 'population problem' in postwar villages

As we have seen in previous chapters, farming villages experienced an overall labor shortage under the wartime system. From the final stages of the war, however, both the population and the number of households in farming villages increased sharply as a result of evacuations, demobilization and repatriation. The number of households reached a peak of 6,170,000 in 1950, and then declined slowly until the late 1960s, when there was a sudden drop as 80–90,000 households began leaving farming villages annually (Table 5.2).

The farming villages had to cope with waves of people unleashed by a series of general mobilizations during the war, followed by the abrupt end of the mobilizations as the empire collapsed. GHQ analysts argued that the absorption of people by farming villages had allowed the unemployment rate to appear statistically low in

Table 5.2: *Number of postwar farm households (1944–1968) (unit: 1,000 households)*

Fiscal year	Households
1944	5,502
1945	—
1946	5,697
1947	5,909
1948	—
1949	—
1950	6,176
1951	6,099
1952	6,148
1953	6,142
1954	6,105
1955	6,042
1956	6,040
1957	6,013
1958	5,991
1959	5,973
1960	5,935
1961	5,906
1962	5,829
1963	5,750
1964	5,667
1965	5,576
1966	5,500
1967	5,419
1968	5,351

Source: 1944 *Nōrinshō Tōkeihyō* (Ministry of Agriculture and Fisheries statistical tables); 1951–1954 *Nōgyō Dōtai Chōsa Zenkoku Kekka Gaiyō* (Outline of national results of the agricultural surveys); 1956–1959 (*Nihon Nōgyō Nenkan 1962 Nenban*). Figures for 1955, 1960 and 1965 come from agricultural censuses, and for 1961–1964 and 1966–1968, Ministry of Agriculture and Forestry, *Nōgyō Chōsa Kekka Hōkokusho* (Report on agricultural survey results).

the midst of extremely serious postwar unemployment, but further analysis suggests that this is not entirely accurate.[9] In fact, farmers responded to rapid increases in the numbers of people engaged in farming in their villages by reducing their working hours.[10]

Furthermore, the number of farming households that made up this increase were extremely small. As of August 1947, out of around 5.9 million farming households 1.4 million owned less than 3 *tan* (0.3 ha) of agricultural land, and of these around 320,000 owned less than 1 *tan* (0.1 ha) of land.[11] During the food crisis immediately after the war, farming villages experienced a very brief economic boom. But the agricultural land reform's owner-farmer system turned this population, once again, from a driving force for democratization into an impediment for farming villages.

The Dodge Line was introduced to Japan in 1949 by the occupying forces to reduce inflation. Its budget austerity created an economic crisis for farming villages in general and small-scale farmers in particular. These farmers once again found themselves in a distressing predicament, following the agricultural land reforms. In May 1949, a 'Resolution Regarding the Population Problem' received all-party support during a plenary session of the lower house of the Diet. The three matters agreed under this resolution were: increasing the food supply via national land development; curbing the population through birth control; and, initiating investigations into sending migrants overseas.

A Diet resolution was not, of course, going to resolve the crisis. Applications flooded in from unemployed youth from farming villages to join the newly-formed police reserve corps, and newspapers frequently reported stories of the uncovering of human trafficking as families took desperate measures in their efforts to survive.[12]

The crisis in farming villages in the early 1950s clearly reveals a wages gap between agriculture and industry. Japan's low wages compared to other advanced nations was no doubt crucial to its ability to achieve rapid economic growth (Table 5.3), but it was the even lower wages of agricultural labor that underpinned this Japanese structure of cheap labor in manufacturing. Immediately after the war, the gap between agricultural and industrial laborers' wages began to close, but by 1948 the wages gap began to widen and thereafter the disparity continually increased. By 1953, the wages gap rivaled the prewar period of agricultural crisis (Table 5.4).

Against this backdrop, there were massive changes in the employment structures for new middle school graduates (Table 5.5). Agricultural economist Namiki Masayoshi, analyzed the number of these graduates employed in agriculture by academic year and

Table 5.3: International comparison of hourly average wages (manufacturing) (Japan = 100)

Year	Japan	United States	United Kingdom	Germany[a]	France
1959	100	986	385	258	178
1965	100	577	271	228	134
1969	100	400	168	181	95
1973	100	203	104	148	75
1985	100	178	97	136	114
1990	100	110	105	157	120

Source: Until 1973, Teruoka, 2008, p. 185.
Notes: For figures after 1985 I have used Rōdō Seisaku Kenkyū-Kenshū Kikō, 2007 and 2010. I have used the conversion values for the exchange rates in each given period. [a] Data for Germany until 1990 is from the Federal Republic of Germany (West Germany).

Table 5.4: Wage disparities between Japanese agriculture and industry

Fiscal year	Agricultural wages (yen)	Industrial wages (yen)	Percentage
1934–1936	0.84	2.44	34.8
1947	74	70	107
1948	185	193	96.1
1949	236	329	71.7
1950	201	398	50.5
1951	209	481	43.5
1952	230	559	41.1
1953	257	672	38.2
1954	286	675	42.4

Source: *Nihon Nōgyō Nenkan*, 1956 *nenban*, p. 31.
Notes: Prewar agricultural wages are wages for young males hired on a daily basis, based on Ministry of Agriculture and Forestry surveys. Prewar industrial wages are daily wages for young males based on Ministry of Labor surveys. Postwar agricultural wages are daily wages for male agricultural laborers based on cost of living wage surveys in farming villages. Postwar industrial wages are daily wage amounts for males in manufacturing industry, based on Ministry of Labor surveys.

Table 5.5: Number of school graduates employed in agriculture (1950–1960)

	Newly employed graduates (1,000s)	New graduages employed in agriculture	(%)	Middle school graduates (1,000s)	High school graduates (1,000s)	High school graduates (%)
1950	831	439	52.9	414	25	5.7
1951	998	432	43.2	391	40	9.3
1952	1,079	420	38.9	363	57	13.6
1953	1,016	286	28.1	244	42	14.6
1954	943	233	24.8	186	48	20.4
1955	1,039	263	25.3	205	58	22.1
1956	1,188	252	21.2	193	58	23.2
1957	1,292	220	17.0	170	50	22.5
1958	1,222	185	15.2	139	46	24.7
1959	1,282	166	12.9	119	46	28.0
1960	1,256	127	10.1	84	42	33.4

Source: Yearly editions of Sōri-fu Tōkeikyoku, *Sangyō Kōzō Kihon Chōsa* (Basic Survey of Industrial Structure).
Note: The definition 'new graduages employed in agriculture' changed after 1953 to 'people principally employed in agriculture throughout the year'.

background. At the beginning of the 1950s, the proportion employed in agriculture fell, as if in line with the growth in the wages gap. Also, the increase in the proportion of high school graduates in these employment numbers indicates that middle school graduates were actively, and as a matter of preference, entering areas other than agriculture. Namiki has produced many studies of the population problem. In 1959 he observed that, 'This fact is sufficient to show that some sort of extremely drastic change is underway'. In the 1960s such changes were patently obvious.[13]

Together with the 1961 establishment of the Agricultural Basic Act, the clear objective for agricultural administration was 'structural improvement policies' (expanding the scale of operations, increasing productivity via mechanization, and selective expansion). This has been called 'fickle agricultural policy' because of the confusion in the villages generated by its haphazard changes, but its central goal remained focused on increased productivity. The expression 'landslide' began to be used in this period to describe the rapidly accelerating departures from both agriculture and villages. This was soon followed by problems with the continued survival of agricultural land as depopulated regions began to appear. At the time, the central problem of farming villages had become one of 'depopulation', while the overcrowding in cities was problematized in terms of factors such as pollution. The framework shaping the discussion of the population problem in this context is one about disparities between cities and farming villages.[14]

The number of farming family households returned to its prewar level of 5.5 million between 1965 and 1966, but there was a significant change in the composition of such families during this period. Farm families now experienced feminization of the workforce, an ageing population, and increasing reliance on sideline occupations. One of the clearest responses to this population problem is the concurrent sharp decline in the number of overseas emigrants. The following section discusses this trend and the facts surrounding it.

Postwar emigration administration to 1954

This section deals with the development of the agricultural administration for overseas emigration. A two-volume archive edited by the Agricultural Settlers Association, called *Jurisdiction and Organization of Postwar Overseas Agricultural Emigration* (1965; hereafter *Jurisdiction and Organization*) is one of the basic sources for tracing developments in the Ministry of Agriculture and Forestry regarding overseas emigration. *Jurisdiction and Organization* is composed of documents from the Colonization Division of the Ministry of Agriculture and Forestry, and other sources (such as Ministry of Foreign Affairs documents and newspaper articles) accumulated by the editor Ishihara Haruyoshi.[15] The directives and internal documents contained in these volumes provide an extremely valuable collection of sources, including official documents not yet available to the public. These volumes cover the transitions that occurred inside the administration of overseas emigration policy. The following discussion will rely heavily on this work.

The Settlement Division in the Administrative Department of the Agricultural Land Bureau had administered settler affairs, but a new provision, 'Concerning the selection and sending off of overseas settlers', was added under the 'Ordinance to amend the organization of the Ministry of Agriculture and Forestry' (Ordinance Number 389). Before its reorganization as the Agricultural Land Bureau, the Reclamation Bureau had such a large number of bureaucrats who had taken part in the colonization of Manchuria that some asked, 'Isn't this the return of the Manchuria Colonization Bureau?'[16] Following the reorganization, the Agricultural Land Bureau was still staffed with personnel who were deeply imbued with a clear prewar pedigree of economic revitalization and Manchurian emigration.

Hirakawa Mamoru was a Ministry of Agriculture and Forestry bureaucrat who had served as Head of the Agricultural Land Bureau from 1951–54 at the time of the inception of the administration of emigration (then as Deputy Minister of Agriculture and Forestry). He continued to display his enthusiasm for emigration administration even after retirement from office. After graduating from the Law Department of Tokyo Imperial University in 1931, Hirakawa worked in the Agricultural Affairs Bureau of the Ministry of Agriculture and Forestry, transferring temporarily to the Manchurian Industry Department in 1935. He began participating in the administration of settling Manchuria as the very first Division Chief of the Development Office. Then, in 1939, as Director of the Development Secretariat he became one of the principal leaders in the colonization of Manchuria.[17] After the war, having served as Head of the Agricultural Land Bureau from 1951 until December 1954, Hirakawa became Under-Secretary of Agriculture and Forestry under Kōno Ichirō, the Minister of Agriculture. He retired in June 1956 and began assisting in efforts to establish the *Zenkoku Takushoku Nōgyō Kyōdō Kumiai Rengōkai*, or *Zentakuren* (Federation of Agricultural Cooperatives for Colonization) while also engaged in editing activities as the head of the Committee for Promoting the Publication of the History of Manchurian Settlement. Hirakawa was known as a strong proponent of emigration. The Minister, Kōno Ichirō, is said to have remarked, 'Hirakawa is a type that surprised me – he may be Under-Secretary, but all he ever talks about is emigration'.[18] In short, Hirakawa was a key Ministry of Agriculture and Forestry figure in the administration of overseas emigration who appears to have overseen preparations for resuming it.

Jurisdiction and Organization regards the 'Research Society of Volunteers Affiliated with the former Ministry of Colonial Affairs' as driving these efforts. This 'research society' was very small, comprised of only three senior bureaucrats, who met to form a research group looking into restarting overseas emigration, basing their efforts on information brought along by a foreign affairs administrative official. Waguri Hiroshi (Head of the Settlement Division, Agricultural Land Bureau in the Ministry of Agriculture and Forestry from September 1951 until it was abolished in 1955)[19] and two other men – Yoshizaki Chiaki, a leader of the Settlers' Self-support Association and Kawada Isao, Assistant Secretary for Colonial Affairs in the prewar period – met regularly in Kawada's office. From 1950, the group was preparing to reestablish overseas emigration programs.[20]

Waguri Hiroshi was in charge of the practical business of the Ministry of Agriculture and Forestry (previously discussed in Chapter 3). In 1933, he passed the examination for high-grade civil officials, and started his career as a colonial bureaucrat in the Police Affairs Office of the Governor-General of Korea. After that, via the Ministry of Colonial Affairs, he participated in emigration to Manchuria as Head of the Settlement Division, Manchurian Secretariat in the Greater East Asia Ministry. After the war, he took part in supporting repatriation from his position in the Administration Bureau of the Ministry of Foreign Affairs, and then transferred to the Reclamation Bureau in the Ministry of Agriculture and Forestry in order to implement the domestic resettlement of repatriated Manchurian settler-farmers. Such was Waguri's singular career. The experience of Hirakawa and Waguri in the settlement of Manchuria can be seen as having strongly prescribed both the developments in and the quality of the Agricultural Land Bureau, and thus also of the Ministry of Agriculture and Forestry.

In the preparatory stages, at least, the Ministry of Agriculture and Forestry and the Ministry of Foreign Affairs cooperated in promoting the reestablishment of emigration and were joint supporters of the policy. The bureaucrats who had worked together in the prewar Ministry of Agriculture and Forestry and the Ministry of Colonial Affairs continued to cooperate, capitalizing on their personal links and shared experiences in the economic revitalization movement and dispatching settlers to Manchuria. Thus, emigration administration was re-established in 1952 with the Ministry of Foreign Affairs and the Ministry of Agriculture and Forestry sharing the duties inherent in dispatching emigrants – a process that stretched from recruitment, selection and induction all the way to the port of departure. The initial lack of conflict between these two ministries can be seen in the fact that the selection of recruits for emigration was left to the Ministry of Foreign Affairs.[21]

This changed in 1953, immediately after the resumption of emigration, when the Ministry of Foreign Affairs began to act according to its view that there ought to be centralized control over all emigration administration. *Jurisdiction and Organization* begins its account of these changes from the period when Taneya Seizō assumed responsibility for emigration. Taneya had been a foreign affairs administrative official in charge of repatriation until then.[22] His appointment marks the start of the jurisdictional conflict referred to as the 'Hundred Years War', over emigration administration between the Ministry of Agriculture and Forestry and the Ministry of Foreign Affairs.

The first change to appear in the Ministry of Foreign Affairs was the establishment of the Federation of Japan Overseas Associations as the umbrella organization for overseas associations, of which ten had already been set up in various places. The next change to emerge was the Ministry's attempt to construct a system that encouraged the establishment of overseas associations in every region via the mediation of this new federation.[23] Furthermore, The Ministry of Foreign Affairs also attempted to start up a Council for Overseas Emigration under its own leadership. The Ministry of Agriculture and Forestry's response to these developments can be seen in an internal document from the Settlement Division of the Agricultural Land Bureau, 'Concerning Overseas Emigration', which mentions the activities of the Overseas Emigration Colloquium, which was the forerunner to the Council for Overseas Emigration (established 1955, Government Ordinance 111). This document points out that 'the Ministry of Foreign Affairs has appointed Mr. Murata Shōzō as the head of this new body and that it has organized it around central figures who share the pedigree of having been in emigration companies in the old Ministry of Colonial Affairs.[24] It also notes that only a single individual with Ministry of Agriculture and Forestry pedigree, Kodaira Gonichi, was included in this new body. The conclusion is that the 'pedigree' of the Overseas Emigration Colloquium was that of the 'emigration companies' in the old Ministry of Colonial Affairs.[25] Beyond this critique, the Ministry of Agriculture and Forestry responded more concretely to this new system by urging the governors of every administrative area of Japan to establish regional branches of the Association for International Collaboration of Farmers.[26]

Nasu Shiroshi and Kodaira Gonichi made repeated attempts to mediate the discord between the sections of the two ministries. They submitted private plans such as 'Understanding between both the Ministry of Foreign Affairs and the Ministry of Agriculture and Forestry Regarding Emigration Matters'; however, both ministries appear to have rejected their efforts.[27]

The Ministry of Foreign Affairs tried to take care of all aspects of emigration administration on its own, including recruitment and selection. In reality, however, since practically all of the people involved were agricultural migrants, when it came to selecting migrants with agricultural experience there was no other option than to rely on the Ministry of Agriculture and Forestry's administrative system, which extended all the way down to the regional level. According to a survey conducted by the Settlement Division, in 1954 the agricultural administration actually conducted all recruitment and selection of emigrants at the regional level. Specifically, in 31 prefectures, the management sections of regional operations overseeing overseas emigration administration were located in agricultural administrative units; eleven were based in general and civil affairs branches; and four under both types of supervision.[28] The Ministry of Foreign Affairs argued that the Ministry of Agriculture and Forestry had had no connection with emigrants going to Brazil in the prewar period, and nor had it conducted any practical training. Furthermore, it rejected any participation by the Ministry of Agriculture and Forestry on the grounds that the principle of free migration made any recruitment and selection unnecessary. The Ministry of Foreign Affairs' position did not prevail, however.[29] In the end, these various divisions of duties created an administration of emigration that was a strange amalgam which varied depending on the administrative area.

These conflicts even made their way into the Diet, where they were discussed at a meeting of the Lower House Agriculture and Forestry Committee on 7 April 1954. At the time of the compilation of the budget, the Settlement Division stressed to the Ministry of Finance the role that had been played by the Ministry of Agriculture and Forestry in Manchurian settlement, and advocated that budget funds be allocated to the latter ministry.[30] The result of these disputes was that on 20 July 1954 a 'Cabinet Decision Concerning the Regulation of Operations in Overseas Emigration' was taken, which established a system giving the Ministry of Foreign Affairs overall oversight. The Ministry of Agriculture and Forestry was put in charge of the recruitment, selection and training of agricultural emigrants. The final selection of emigrants was now subject to directions from both Ministries.[31]

The provisions of this cabinet decision did not end the jurisdictional disputes between the Ministry of Agriculture and Forestry and the Ministry of Foreign Affairs. There were, for example, renewed attempts at centralization through expanding the Immigration Office; budgetary disputes concerning the route for issuing assistance payments; and disputes within the Council for Overseas Emigration. In terms of the larger framework, however, this cabinet decision remained in place until the 1963 inauguration of the Japan Emigration Service. Thus, we can see the continuation of prewar personalities and sectionalism in the bureaucratic organization of postwar emigration administration. The central point of contention was, however, the question of the kind of continuity that would be created. In the following section, we will look at the logic that underpinned these conflicts.

The logic and policies behind encouraging emigration

The definition of emigrants in the draft Overseas Emigration Bill

According to Wakatsuki's schema, the basic policies that fueled complex internal conflicts in the administration of postwar emigration were characterized by: a policy of mass migration; a focus on the receiving country; and an emphasis on permanent residency.[32] In this section, I will delineate the Ministry of Agriculture and Forestry's policy as well as the logic that it employed in thinking about how to promote overseas emigration. The conflicts within the bureaucracy were not only manifest in disputes between personalities, and not only about departmental interests, but also about the underlying logic behind it. Although sectionalism is intrinsic to bureaucracy, the logic that justifies it differs according to time and place.

The two ministries had different definitions of emigrants from the outset. These were plainly evident in the arguments that arose in the process of drafting a bill concerning overseas emigration. Up until this point, the only law regarding migration had been the 1896 Emigrants Protection Act, which was in reality a dead letter.

The initial act of the newly created Emigration Bureau in the Ministry of Foreign Affairs was to draw up a 'Draft Outline Overseas Emigration Bill'. The first draft, in January 1956, explicitly stated that permanent residence was not a requirement: 'not exclusively people seeking permanent residence, but people who go overseas with the intention of engaging in work – even if their aim is not permanent residence – and also others who accompany them'.[33] The Ministry of Agriculture and Forestry's Colonization Division informed the Emigration Bureau of its contrary view that 'emigrants ought to be defined as people whose goal is "permanent residence"'.[34] The following year, in 1957, the Colonization Division defined emigrants as 'people who travel abroad in order to earn a livelihood overseas, and their accompanying family members, with specific exclusions'[35] and reiterated its opinion that the term emigrant ought to be applied to 'people who travel abroad with the goal of permanent residence and those who accompany them'.[36] Although there appears to have been some reconciliation between the members of the two bureaus later in 1957, the bill was not submitted. *Jurisdiction and Organization* is unclear on why. We can, however, discern why the Ministry of Agriculture and Forestry vigorously opposed centralization of emigration administration within the Ministry of Finance, and insisted that the definition of emigrant must stipulate 'permanent residents'. The first of these points is addressed in the following passage.

> The bulk of emigrants are farmers, and the participation of the Ministry of Agriculture and Forestry – with its agricultural expertise – in their recruitment and selection will result in the selection of excellent farmers and the successful building of new villages. Our long years of experience in recruitment and selection will ensure that all goes smoothly.[37]

The next passage indicates that the emphasis on permanent residency was based on an understanding that the migration program was intended, above all, for the benefit of the whole of 'Japanese agriculture'.

> Overseas agricultural migration, on the one hand, guarantees, through emigration overseas, a stable livelihood to those who were born and reared in a farming family and who wish to considerably advance their opportunities in agriculture. On the other hand, emigration can give those who remain in the home village the opportunity to expand the size of the plots that they work. Consequently, it is essential that we strongly promote overseas agricultural emigration as one link in the structural policies for improving the quality of Japanese agriculture.[38]

This pamphlet clearly states that emigration policy was merely part of a broader framework for advancing the economic development of those who remained behind. The reference to 'building new villages' is twofold, referring to both structural improvement in the migrants' destination societies as well as the 'domestic' villages. Yet, although the benefits at both ends are recognized, the emphasis was squarely on the latter. It was from this perspective that the Ministry of Agriculture and Forestry insisted on permanent migration: if the door was left open for migrants to return at some unspecified time in the future, the redistribution of their arable land and other property to the remaining villagers would merely store up trouble for the future.

Although we cannot know for certain, it seems unlikely that many of those who emigrated did so with the intention of becoming permanent residents in their destination countries. Although researchers outside of Japan have attributed a 'sojourner mentality' to the first-generation emigrants,[39] this was strongly rooted in the cultural value of the family in Japan. There is little doubt that a significant proportion of emigrants held onto the dream that one day they would retire to their own plot of land in their place of birth; this dream was behind the family property consciousness that we saw in Chapter 4 among the absentee land-owners living in the United States. The Ministry of Agriculture and Forestry's arguments fundamentally contradicted these aspirations.

There is considerable overlap between these arguments and those that had informed policies to promote emigration to Manchuria. First, the surplus population was identified as the cause of the dire poverty of prewar farming villages, made inevitable by the tiny holdings of farming families. Then, the revitalization of the farming village economy was pursued in a military-like campaign. In the postwar period, though, the plight of the villages was made worse by the bureaucrats' failure to provide assistance to bring about the wellbeing of individuals and families. Instead, the ministry attempted to persuade those affected that they ought to live in a way that contributes to the structural improvement of the farming village, which was of greater value than the individuals.

Another feature of the Ministry of Agriculture and Forestry's arguments for emigration was that it should be perceived as a continuation of internal development. In fact, the domestic settlement system used by the Ministry of Agriculture and Forestry was appropriated in the recruitment, selection and training of overseas agricultural emigrants. We could, on the one hand, see this as a case of defending its sphere of influence in the face of the sudden decline in the numbers of new settlers domestically. It might also be seen as a reallocation of resources that had temporarily been put into domestic development, towards overseas agricultural migration policies. For example, when the preliminary training of overseas emigrants began in the 1930s, training methods were devised by village mainstays in farming villages. Then, in the postwar period, training was carried out using 'management training farm facilities' which had been established in each prefecture for emergency settlement training. The teachers employed in these facilities included technical officers who guided people in farming, many of whom had performed the same role in the Manchurian settlement. Nakamura Kōjirō, one of the leaders of Manchurian settlement, remained deeply involved in postwar development, under the official title of 'former Director of Manchurian Development Corporation'.[40]

However, the poverty of the settler-farmers created by the postwar emergency was a well-entrenched social problem by the end of the 1950s, and the mainstream of agricultural administration had shifted its focus from building villages to creating individual farms run as large-scale operations. This resulted in a threefold approach to existing settler-farms. Where there were no prospects of running a going concern, people were urged to leave farming for another profession. 'Subsidy Measures for Settler-farmers to Abandon Farming'[41] were put in place to contribute to the stability of the remaining settler-farms. Even larger assistance payments for overseas emigration opened up an additional administrative line away from postwar development towards overseas emigration. This alternative would certainly have appealed to those settler-farmers who, ten years after having settled on the land, still had to engage in long periods of work away from home in order to survive. There was a significant number of these farmers in need of a cash income, who were burdened by debt, and could see no prospect of running a stable business.

The Ministry of Agriculture and Forestry's view that emigration was one link in 'building villages' survived into the postwar period. This thinking was evident in projects from the economic revitalization movement to the ministry's wartime ideas about 'embarking overseas'. These Ministry of Agriculture and Forestry positions, however, ran completely counter to the Ministry of Foreign Affairs' arguments about free emigration, which in some respects could be seen as contemptuous of 'grass roots' emigration.

The National Federation of Colonial Agricultural Cooperatives

Next, let us look at the kind of projects that emerged as a result of this way of thinking about emigration. I said previously that the Ministry of Agriculture and Forestry arguments about emigration regarded emigration as one link in the 'building of villages'. The policy devised to realize this was a postwar *bunson imin* (emigrating in groups to establish a branch village) emigration policy. This 'emigration of a set portion of villagers' is a reformulation of prewar policies to develop Manchuria – for example, cases such as Ōhinata Village in Nagano Prefecture. This practice was revived and to some extent realized in the postwar period.[42] The postwar overseas group emigration of a set portion of a village population began in the countryside, such as that in 1955 from Taishō Town in Kōchi Prefecture. This phenomenon is dealt with in detail in the 'Agricultural Almanac' of that time.

This postwar *bunson* emigration began with individual villages, but was soon adopted systematically by the Federation of Agricultural Cooperatives for Colonization (*Zentakuren*). *Zentakuren* was established in 1955, on the occasion of the participation of the Central Union of Agricultural Cooperatives (*Zenchū*) in the Cotia Youth Migration, to promote the overseas emigration of farmers. *Zenchū*'s written statement of aims says:

> There needs to be a reasonable solution to the surplus population in farming villages, in order to improve the economic and social position of farmers. We think that the promotion of overseas emigration by farmers

in agricultural cooperatives from our group – as one form of policy for second and third sons in farming families and also for farming families with tiny holdings – should be one link in the building of new villages.[43]

As this activity deviated from the main object of agricultural cooperatives, its establishment was achieved by pushing hard against fierce criticisms from the Cabinet Legislation Bureau, not to mention the Emigration Bureau. Because this shows that the movement encouraging emigration, including the establishment of *Zentakuren*, was promoted in quite a highhanded manner within Japan's agricultural administration, I will quote the opinion of the Cabinet Legislation Bureau at length.

1. Under the Agricultural Cooperatives Law, the business of improving the culture of everyday life, under Article 10, should be understood, fundamentally, as aiming to increase improvements given the current state of farmers' cooperative lives; and not in terms of forecasting ventures such as the promotion of overseas emigration with a view to bringing about change on this basis.
2. Similarly, Article 10 must in practice be directly, and substantially, linked with things that union members can use such as facilities like crèches. Surely, it is unreasonable to expand it in a limitless manner stretching even as far as ventures aimed at benefitting the union, such as the promotion of overseas emigration.
3. However, conceiving of agricultural cooperatives as village communities – on the basis of the fact that ventures under Article 10 are restricted to improvements in the lives and culture of farming villages – does not mean that overseas emigration ventures, such as those that prevent the fragmentation of arable land and the increasingly tiny size of farming operations, cannot reasonably be understood to be ventures intended under this article. Even in these cases, however, the purchase of land overseas by *Takushokuren* (*Zentakuren*) for the purpose of sending off the second and third sons of farming families is substantially no different from agricultural cooperatives operating steel works in cities, and surely this would be difficult to accept.[44]

The opinion of the Cabinet Legislation Bureau, the official opinion of the Ministry of Foreign Affairs, was delivered to the Chief Cabinet Secretary of the Ministry of Agriculture and Forestry from the

Chief Cabinet Secretary of the Ministry of Foreign Affairs. In these circumstances, this problem of *Zentakuren*'s establishment became a much larger dispute than the various battles over jurisdiction, moving beyond the departments with direct responsibility.

> The foundational principle of colonial agricultural cooperatives should be stated as being the revival of the 'movement to build villages' that had been carried out during the era of Manchurian settlement by people from all prefectures. As such, it is something that will deal a death blow to emigration policy with our Latin American partners, who have seen an extreme increase in nationalism as a result of World War Two.[45]

These criticisms notwithstanding, common ground was ultimately reached according to which agricultural cooperatives would not take a leading role in overseas land purchases.[46] In August 1956 the Head of the Promotion Bureau effectively approved the establishment of Central Union of Agricultural Cooperatives (*Zenchū*).[47] Its foundation meeting was held in November 1956, with the Ministry of Agriculture and Forestry giving its permission that same month. At a general meeting the following year, in 1957, however, *Zentakuren* changed its articles of incorporation in order to be able to purchase land overseas, distribute it and conduct direct agricultural guidance.[48] In the 1958 and 1959 fiscal years, *Zentakuren* specified about 50 towns and villages as 'villages designated for collective emigration'.

In 1961, the *bunson* policy – following the same designation system as previously used by agricultural cooperatives – identified 100 'cities, towns and villages encouraged to engage in collective emigration'.[49] The Agricultural Settlers Association drew up the reports concerning individual *bunson* settlements, but we need further research into this process.[50]

Although the number of emigrants decreased sharply, as if in response to this systematic preparation, this was not simply a quantitative change. The Agricultural Almanac states that:

> A declining tendency for second and third sons from farming families to emigrate emerged alongside the increase in employment opportunities domestically. Applications for family emigration are on the rise in areas with relatively few employment opportunities,

such as fishing villages, outlying islands and domestic reclaimed land. There are also considerable numbers of retired coal miners applying for emigration as a transition period phenomenon.[51]

Consequently, at the same time as conjecturing about the overall state of affairs on the basis of declining migration numbers, it is also necessary to examine the qualitative changes within these numbers, such as the increasing tendency for migrants to be dispatched from more remote places and marginal regions.

This emigration policy, however, became largely ineffective, for two main reasons. First, structures emerged for migration to domestic cities; and, second, the return to Japan of entire groups whose emigration had been unsuccessful. For example, recruitment of emigrants for a new settlement in the Dominican Republic was promoted with catch phrases such as 'Paradise in the Caribbean Sea', but the destination did not live up to these promises. Surveys of proposed emigrant destinations were, however, not conducted until months after the sites had been determined. It was thus not uncommon for emigrants, such as those to the Dominican Republic, to find that their new residences were considerably different than the sites that had been described in the government's survey reports.[52]

The remarks of people who took part in postwar emigration reveal that they were uniformly different from prewar emigrants. A clear and important difference is that the latter was carried out as an integral part of colonial rule and occupation. However, at a 1936 symposium, 'Talking about Manchurian Settlement', Katō Kanji said of local conditions, 'during the time that it would take to insist on surveys because we do not know what [the proposed location] is like, emigrants' enthusiasm would be lost. Therefore, I would like the Japanese nation to have faith in going ahead and sending over a steady stream of people'.[53] Katō's words echo the views of the postwar emigration administration: both invoke a hierarchy in which the village is paramount and individuals are subordinate.

Farmers' reactions to immigration administration

Even at the emigration administration's high point, the numbers being dispatched remained below projected estimates. Various groups involved with migration policy – such as the Agricultural Settlers Association, *Zentakuren* and university researchers –

continually searched for the main causes of policy stagnation even while conducting repeated surveys of farming villages in order to stress the importance of migration.[54] In this section, I will describe the farming village that emerges from these various sources.

The preceding examination of the actions of Ministry of Agriculture and Forestry bureaucrats showed that their postwar emigration policy was in effect a continuation of the wartime policies, albeit this time pursued peacefully, not militarily. It continued, however, to be based in the logic of improving the structure of agriculture in pursuit of the ideal of 'building villages'.

Meanwhile, the people living in farming villages also had accumulated experiences of confronting and coping with these state interventions. These experiences can be discerned in people's actions, without the need for theorization or formulization. The experience of war undoubtedly had powerful effects on the lives of people in farming villages.

A very interesting phenomenon that emerges frequently from surveys of emigration is the extreme divergence between people's evaluation of policies and the actual situation. In a 1951 questionnaire in the *Asahi Shinbun* on 'Policies for Resolving the Population Problem', overseas emigration emerged as the top policy (28%; followed by birth control 24%; and then emigration and birth control 14%). In response to a question about whether readers thought that they might like to emigrate in future should the opportunity arise, 25% said that they would and 65% that they would not.[55] The promoters of emigration within the Ministry of Agriculture and Forestry would have greeted these figures with delight. The people appeared to understand that Japan's 'population problem' was one of surplus population, and there was a commonly shared view that overseas emigration was a viable solution. The results of door-to-door surveys, however, differ markedly from those produced by unsigned questionnaires.

For example, Achi village was designated as a special guidance district by the Ministry of Greater East Asia and saw large numbers of its people sent to Manchuria. Emigrants from this village were dispatched to several Manchurian settlement groups, such as the Achigo settlement group. The proportion of Achi village's population who emigrated was about 14 times the national average.[56]

A *Zentakuren* investigation reports conditions in the village at the time as follows.

Fewer than half of the people who emigrated to Manchuria have returned, and there are aspects of the psychological impact of the failure of this emigration that still cannot be completely swept away. The prevailing situation is that the village, on every level, is still unable to actually contemplate the question of emigration.

Many Manchuria settler-farmers lost their lives and many more were victims of the processes of repatriation. It might be thought that those same villages that had sent off large numbers of prewar emigrants would welcome new emigration opportunities, but the wartime experiences of the villagers led them to oppose postwar emigration policy. Having returned to the villages whence they came, they found that they were unable to settle there. The *Zentakuren* report continues.

> The expansion of the size of farm operations is regarded as being of fundamental importance to rebuilding the village and, as will be discussed below, the systematic implementation of the group emigration of small-scale farm households is progressing, but these plans are for emigration to places within Japan.[57]

At the end of the 1950s, there were very few new domestic settlements. However, what might, on the one hand, make those who remained un-settled in one way or another into potential recruits for the postwar *bunson* plan, on the other hand, had lead many repatriates to resolve 'not to cross the seas again', thus rendering them quite unreceptive to further overseas migration. So the Ministry of Agriculture and Forestry turned its efforts towards creating new domestic settlements.[58] For example, Goka, part of Achi village, was designated under the Plan for Building New Farming Villages, in 1955, and – under a *bunson* plan – twenty households settled on reclaimed land that had been cleared in the Yatsushiro Sea area of Kumamoto Prefecture.[59]

The former village of Yamato, in Yamagata Prefecture, had also sent off prewar *bunson* emigrants.

> As mentioned previously, 35 households have migrated to domestic settlement sites in the postwar period, but there are as yet no overseas emigrants. It is said that this is not the influence of the Manchurian emigration of the past. In the immediate postwar period, returnees

from Manchuria – dissatisfied because they were frowned on – tended to hesitate also when it came to migration to domestic reclaimed areas such as Hokkaido. These days, however, returnees and ordinary villagers see the failure of Manchurian emigration as an inevitable consequence of defeat. These days, this should no longer exert any negative influence on future emigration.[60]

Despite the researchers' conclusions, this village did not accept overseas emigration policies again. Farmers reported that their Manchurian emigration experiences were, in fact, a 'negative influence'.

All of the farming villages in these examples experienced either the prewar dispatching of Manchurian settlers or an influx of postwar settlers, and both groups reacted to postwar changes. Although these various surveys are all labeled opinion polls, they were, in fact, tools for promoting emigration; the people conducting the surveys were invariably agents for emigration. The Terayama hamlet in Wajima City in Ishikawa Prefecture responded harshly to contact with these surveys.

> The vast majority of the people in the Terayama district, as mentioned at the outset, were totally unaware of, and indifferent to, overseas emigration. Moreover, should some mention of overseas emigration slip out, they would, on the contrary, close their minds and cover their ears. Alternatively, they were also quite likely to object and repulse this sort of talk.[61]

The report declares that the farmers are 'unaware and indifferent', but then goes on to describe behaviors which clearly contradict this conclusion. His report suggests rather clear signs of revolt, but these signs are too vague for him to clearly describe. The report cites a particular repatriated farmer from *Karafuto* (Sakhalin) as saying, 'We emigrated to Karafuto and tirelessly built up assets, which we had to leave behind. When it comes to talk of overseas emigration, we are prepared to listen to it only after the government has compensated us for the assets that we have left overseas'.[62] This seems to be fairly representative of the attitude of former colonists, sentiments tinged with a sense of misfortune. They clearly reveal that postwar experience of repatriation and their ensuing social marginalization had left them anything but 'indifferent'.

Nevertheless, people's 'indifference' is a common theme in these surveys. Let us look at an extreme case – the survey carried out in Namie Town in Fukushima Prefecture. This survey targeted villages that had sent a specified number of emigrants overseas in the past. It began with an introductory pitch, 'Some people in the places to which emigrants have gone are saying that they would like to coax the farmers who stayed behind to take the decision to emigrate'. The survey then introduces a questionnaire to be conducted with people who were in contact with emigrants from the same village. In response to a question asking whether respondents, hearing that all was going well in the emigration destinations, felt that they would like to emigrate, 39 out of 41 answered 'no'. In response to, 'When told about "local good news" by other people who had emigrated, how did you feel about emigration?' 41 out of 41 uniformly replied 'indifferent'. This survey concluded that 2 out of 41, or 5%, of people surveyed hoped to emigrate.[63] The survey team that went to Namie did not report that it had the third largest number of postwar settlers of the Hamadōri (easternmost) district of Fukushima.[64]

Between population and people

The 'population problem' remained a major issue throughout the postwar period, but its emphasis shifted. In the 1950s, there was an increase in overseas emigration activity. Then, around the mid-1960s, as the era of rapid economic growth continued to pick up pace, the emphasis shifted to the 'disparity' between the depopulated rural areas and the overpopulated cities. The problem of an ageing population also began to appear at this time. Of course, much of this change was driven by the need for a stable urban labor supply. The Civil Rights Act in the United States in 1965 and the revolutionary change in immigration restrictions that followed were of considerable significance for emigration in Asia and for Asian immigration into the United States. The sudden increase in migrants from South Korea and the Philippines to the United States brought new influences to the complex ethnic minority society in the United States.[65] A period of rapid economic growth and social change in Japan changed the course of migration between Asia and the United States, as Japan turned inwards. The administration of emigration continued in Japan, but its focus gradually shifted away from seeking to recruit emigrants as a response to the population problem, towards repatriating migrants who had previously been sent away, and attracting skilled migrants.

In the initial stages, postwar emigration administration progressed as planned by people who had been involved in the prewar economic revitalization movement and Manchurian settlement policies. The failure of this administration began as a result of the attitude of the Ministry of Foreign Affairs. Fierce conflict arose between the Ministry of Foreign Affairs, the agency responsible for this policy, and the Ministry of Agriculture and Forestry, which challenged its authority. It can be argued that these disputes were about conflict over the nature of the emigration administration. In this chapter, I have been able to reaffirm Wakatsuki's observation that if we ignore trends in the Ministry of Agriculture and Forestry we will not be able to understand the characteristics of postwar emigration administration – particularly, its focus on permanent residency.

The logic of the Ministry of Agriculture and Forestry emigration administration was consistently and firmly rooted in the 'building villages' perspective; the idea of dispatching emigrants to achieve structural improvements of Japanese agriculture, especially by achieving a suitable scale of farming. Consequently, a *bunson* emigration policy was also partially implemented in the postwar period. In an interview published in 1973 in *Nōrinshō Kōhō* (Ministry of Agriculture and Forestry Public Relations), Hirakawa touches on the significance of dispatching emigrants in a way that is a major departure from the administration of Japanese emigration, as he had himself promoted it up to that time.

> The main purpose of agricultural emigration these days is to send off settlers who have the ability to bring about development that contributes to the advancement of the countries to which they go. Emigration these days is not invasion. There are countries that cannot grow by their own efforts. Would neglecting them not be regrettable in terms of human development?[66]

Migration figures as a whole were persistently low. Reports about dispatching emigrants, mainly from the mid-1950s to the late-1960s, suggested various schemes that might be used to encourage emigration. But the farmers' wartime experiences left them indisposed towards proposals that they should move permanently to other countries. The people conducting these surveys came face-to-face with these sentiments. (Wartime experiences were, of course, interpreted in extremely broad ways, and we see cases of the re-emigration of leaders of postwar settlement.)

People understood Japan's population problem, but while they did not say anything to the contrary when publicly asked for their opinion, they resoundingly rejected emigration as a solution to the problem. This is in striking contrast to birth control which was put into practice, albeit gradually, through support for women to learn about it voluntarily and in groups. Like emigration, it had been advanced as a method for solving the population problem. The fact that women's actions, even in the postwar period, were consistent with state policy has led to a tendency to see unity with the state. We need to keep in mind, however, the deliberately selective nature of people's actions. Naturally, 'individuals' within the 'population' were mediated by the nature of various interim groups, such as being members of a village or a family. This manifested itself as an assortment of variations, one of which was domestic settlement.

The migration of people away from their homes, be it as part of the periodic recruiting of new middle school graduates or long-term working away from home arrangements, emerged during the period of high economic growth. Some of this internal migration to the cities may have resembled individual challenges of the 'trying one's luck' variety. However, because the vast majority of those who left for the cities were responding to the heterogeneity and instability inherent in the national economy, the factor that made this migration ultimately possible was the sundering of family unity. The resultant pain in the relations between countless parents and children and between married couples became the backdrop that colored family stories. Only by abstracting out this aspect are we able to call the postwar period of rapid economic growth a 'miracle'. The implications for those engaged in the typical form of migration in this period of rapid economic growth call for further investigation. These types of migration contrast with both settlement and overseas emigration, in which migration occurred on the basis of the family unit.

The first part of this chapter examined the nature of state intervention on the policy front, with a primary focus on trends within sections of the Ministry of Foreign Affairs and the Ministry of Agriculture and Forestry responsible for emigration. They are presented as representatives of their respective ministries in order to explain the logical structure of inter-ministry conflict. We should bear in mind that on the whole neither ministry was enthusiastic about emigration. The focus on individual bureaucrats is, in effect, a function of the state's lack of enthusiasm for emigration. This general lack of enthusiasm serves to highlight the actions of the segment that was enthusiastic.

In this chapter, I have focused narrowly on wartime experiences and have described the manner in which people attempted to put down roots in the soil. There are, however, also frequent reports about the feelings of first sons who remained in the villages in this period. As second and third sons headed off to the cities in the period of rapid economic growth, one response of the first sons who managed the families left behind in the villages was to accept their lot with resignation. Alternatively, they felt a sense of dissatisfaction, a feeling akin to having been left behind. In a society that is undergoing modernization, even staying behind in a certain place steadily assumes a self-contradictory nature.

Conclusion

We are, in the end, another kind of soil.

Tokutomi Kenjirō '*Mimizu no Tawagoto* (Ramblings of an Earthworm)'

Migration, nation and village

This book is an attempt to present a new history of the interconnections between migration and Japan's rural villages from the perspective of the 'others' who migrated during the Asia-Pacific War and in the following decades. Here, I would like to expand on the topic that I raised at the outset: transformations in the connections between the people and the land. The people discussed in this book were all positioned at the periphery of society. However, by focusing on their relationships with the 'center' rather than on their isolation as peripheral figures, we end up with a history that goes well beyond the periphery. By tracing and retracing the borders between 'self' and 'other' it is possible to conclude that while this relation is mutually constitutive and ambiguous, the hierarchy between the two was maintained during this era.

Let us briefly review the topic of each chapter. Chapter 1 examined questions surrounding nation. The commencement of colonial rule was an epochal moment that greatly transformed the nature of labor in Japanese society, which until then had severely restricted the participation of 'foreigners' in the labor market. As wages in the domestic labor market increased during the 1920s, the increasingly disadvantageous place of agriculture, which had been a topic of concern throughout the modern period, became even more conspicuous. As a whole, the so-called landlord system and family management developed further, but in large agricultural operations and orchards in the urban peripheries that were dependent upon hired labor, people from the colonies flowed in as low-waged workers. In particular, in western Japan there was large-scale substitution of male farmhands by new workers from the colonies. The pace of this transformation accelerated after 1937 and even more during the final stages of the war as Koreans were progressively accepted as tenant-farmers. While the Japanese empire publicly advocated a policy of assimilation through imperial subjectification, officials grew increasingly concerned about the dangers associated with the settlement of colonial populations in the farming villages, which had been officially identified as *the source of the nation*. The defeat of imperial Japan in the Second World War imposed a complex burden on Koreans who had lived under colonial rule. It brought both liberation and fear. In the end, the fear that had been simultaneously created and masked by colonial rule came to the surface, and most Koreans left the farming villages. No doubt these events had an impact on urban areas, too, but that is beyond the scope of this book. However, the people who put down roots in various parts of mainland Japan after surrender endured a vast array of battles along the way.

Chapter 2 explored the relationship between city and countryside. The evacuations in the final stages of the war were on a massive scale. Even for a successful writer such as Kishi Yamaji, life in a wartime city was incredibly difficult. Food shortages, unemployment due to wartime regulations, and war damage made evacuation the only choice for many. As a result, the population of Japan's major cities was reduced almost by half by the end of the war. This chapter presented the Agricultural Land Development Corporation's reclaimed land as one example of a place of settlement for someone like Kishi, who had no connections to people in the countryside. Conditions there were not immediately hospitable. The military government sought to divert all 'resources' to wartime pursuits in the name of total war mobilization. Vast numbers of people were cut off from their homes and livelihood in a time when the value of life itself was diminished, and moved voluntarily or under coercive conditions in search of new connections to the land. Very rarely were their efforts successful.

It is virtually impossible to come to terms with sacrifice and death as it comes in the midst of danger. It only became possible to face the enormity of the sacrifices of war once it was over. However, problems like the food crisis and unemployment continued long after the war. Japan's defeat provided the occasion for evacuee settler-farmers to organize themselves into groups that made demands about matters that were crucial to their continued survival.

In Kyoto, these demands linked the settler-farmers together with broader democratization movements that had arisen. However, the majority of evacuees returned to cities within a few years of the end of the war. Further research is necessary to reach a comprehensive understanding of the experiences of the wartime evacuees, but their return to the cities is an extremely important component of this picture.

The post-surrender experiences of Manchurian settler-farmers were considerably different from those in the Japanese 'homeland'. One issue is how to understand the connections between those who ventured to Manchuria and settled there and Korean farmers and evacuees who settled in Japanese farming villages discussed above. At the very least, the visions of Manchurian settlers were inextricably tied to the broader vision of Manchuria as a land of reclamation (though there were undoubtedly people who 'opted out' of the vision). The extent to which the land they sought was tied to Japanese military rule, and how this contradiction was managed became evident for all to see once the apparatus of that rule collapsed. Land ownership by Japanese in Manchuria was inseparable from Japanese colonial rule. There is some documentary evidence which suggests that settlers did in fact try to forge connections with the land in Manchuria,[1] but a careful treatment of these materials is beyond the scope of this book.

The repatriation of the Manchurian settlers to Japan was already underway when, on 31 August 1945, the Japanese government announced that people waiting to be repatriated should remain where they were, as repatriation would only occur in 'unavoidable' cases. This did not change until GHQ decided to assist with repatriation.[2] Settler-farmers were once again abandoned in a foreign land. Even with assistance of the victorious Allied powers, particularly the United States, repatriation did not mean resettlement in their hometowns. Repatriates streamed into cities, formed groups based on shared personal experiences and demanded full inclusion into the category of people who sacrificed during the war. The repatriate groups' demands for compensation were closely tied to their claims for inclusion in the welfare system. Although at times their status as nationals was questioned, the fact that their shared experience of colonial control was overlooked by Japanese society in general has important implications for postwar historical consciousness. Further, one of their main demands during these struggles was over the provision of land for settlement. These demands were strongly supported by the bureaucratic leadership and its postwar settlement policies. Consequently, considerable numbers of repatriated settler-farmers became settlers once again in areas throughout the new 'Japan'. The now symbolic emperor played a mediating role in this process as interlocutor and guarantor.

The 'equalization of sacrifices' which the architects of the total war system insisted upon in the final stages of the war was far from lived-reality. The gap between ideal and reality during the wartime period surfaced as diverse energies as people gained newfound political freedoms and knowledge, and provided the prerequisite for the creation of a new image of the nation and the motive force for social change. Consequently, critiques of the concept of 'the nation' are meaningless if they ignore the ways that understandings of the nation were shaped by the various and compelling *accidental* demands made by the people within concrete historical processes.

The movement of people took place periodically at the community level from the final stages of the war and into the immediate postwar period. What can be read from the movement of various 'others' over a set period, whose perspectives and experiences overlapped partially, but were in fact, each imbued with difference? More detailed studies of these perspectives and experiences are required before we can draw conclusions about the whole on the basis of individual case studies. Yet, one conclusion that we can safely draw is that, when faced with a society on the brink of collapse, people turned to the land. Living in a time of total war meant continuously responding to mobilization demands while trying to feed oneself. The problems with the food supply, which grew severe from the middle of 1944, greatly affected people's lives. According to Nakai Hisao, the main concern at this time was not 'a matter of not eating for three days', but 'not knowing how long one could make the tiny amount of food last.'[3] These concerns turned people towards the land. Working the land, and even the land itself, has its own temporality. Even without any agricultural skills, having a connection to the land and cultivating it (leaving aside actual yields) allows one to imagine a harvest that is to come. Both the people who silently left the collapsing cities during the war and the people who began to speak out after it lived with the will to remain connected with the land. Repatriated emigrants who had dreamed of living out their 'remaining years' on agricultural land in their birth places also poured their labor into newly settled lands, despite having few connections to it.

From a grass-roots perspective, far more than any official policies, it was the energy of these settler-farmers that shaped the 'land reform period' following the Second World War. We cannot ignore the fact that the will of the people to survive expressed itself in a variety of ways, at times through the farmer's unions, at others through a nationalism that extended well beyond the narrow confines of agriculture, in a manner that, following earlier research, also reveals continuity between: prewar colonization, wartime mobilization, war damage, the collapse of the empire, and finally, the postwar reconstruction.

The postwar agrarian reforms were partly designed as top-down responses to social crisis, but the formation of postwar society is unthinkable without the bottom-up determination of the people to survive. Chapter 4 examined this from the perspective of Japanese expatriates. The cases presented there highlight the extent to which postwar reforms exceeded people's expectations and transformed relationships to the land. Further, the chapter revealed that the history of Japanese migration to Asia and across the Pacific underscores the need to recognize the particularities of the period in question. The discursive space of the postwar era occluded the history of colonial rule and emphasized the idea of an ethnically homogenous nation. This nationalist discourse ignored the presence of and roles played by domestic minorities, including those from the former colonies and indigenous people. In addition, we must recognize the fact that the very nature of what it meant to be 'Japanese' changed after the war as a result of severing Japanese expatriates from land ownership relations.

The final chapter's examination of postwar emigration policies required tracing the policies of the Ministry of Agriculture and Forestry bureaucrats who had been involved with emigration administration since before the war, and highlighted the unchallenged hierarchy between villages and individuals. The emigration policies were consistently aimed at ensuring that the 'whole' would endure. There was, however, no correlation between national-level policy objectives and individual concerns about personal well-being. Hence, few people responded to the administration's postwar emigration policy. Wartime experiences were deeply etched in people's minds. Although conditions in Japan remained harsh, most chose to stay.

This is yet another instance of the state treating the people as a monolithic 'population', while individuals continued their efforts to enhance their living conditions under the circumstances in which they found themselves. Both parties were deeply alienated from one another. This does not mean, though, that the people were opposed to the state; rather, they were selective about accepting and putting into practice state policies which they saw as necessary or personally beneficial such as family planning.

Heterogenous mixture or imperial order?

Next, let us consider the new understandings of the past that emerge from a synthesis of these realities. The most significant is the importance of the ethnic issue in agriculture for Japanese imperial rule. That being said, during the war, one can discern early signs of changes which would completely undermine the foundations of Japanese agriculture. To date, the connections between agriculture and ethnicity in modern Japan have only been addressed by research on the history of ideology known as *nōhonshugi*, the idea that agriculture should form the basis of Japan's economic and social life. Further empirical research is necessary, but there seems to be a need to re-examine this issue from a trans-regional perspective. Earlier studies treated the relationship between agriculture and nationalism as axiomatic. However, we must also take account of the significant changes that occurred in agriculture in different regions, for they reveal a latent conflict between the state and the village concerning production.

We also need to reconsider the vectors of social transformation during the war. Earlier studies have highlighted transformations brought about by the feminization of the labor force and the increasing presence of 'factory-worker farmers' but an investigation of changes that the presence of ethnic others brought to agriculture has been lacking. Social changes during the wartime period have to be rethought from these overlapping realities. The war plans drafted by the central planners of the total war system in order to strengthen their control produced unexpected outcomes.

The connection between ethno-nationalism and land remained central to the ideology of state rule from its first formulations following the Meiji Restoration. In pursuit of this ideology, the government did not permit other ethnic groups to become established in 'the realm'. Contradictions were brought into the system as the state expanded its territory though colonial rule, incorporating other nationalities into the empire. By the final stages of the war, a labor force was procured from the colonies and other controlled areas through violent means. Some consideration was given to policies that would serve to maintain this labor force by allowing settlement in the 'homeland'. Agriculture, however, was imbued with special meaning and the settlement of other ethnic groups in farming villages remained taboo. Governing authorities remained consistent on this point until the end of the war.

The responses of the farming villages to these developments were twofold. On the one hand, they were at one with the state in taking advantage of the asymmetric power relationships of colonial rule. That is, they enthusiastically employed people from the colonies as cheap labor in order to profit from the emerging market economy. On the other hand, despite the taboo on other ethnic groups settling in farming villages and administrative efforts to prevent it, villagers were flexible about taking in others when necessary. In matters such as growing produce, farming villages in the homeland submitted to the state's leadership until the surrender. Yet when it came to the ethnic issue, Japanese farming villages *ignored* the state's wishes, instead doing what they deemed necessary to maintain their agricultural lands.

Farming villages existed in a space where they were regarded by the state as *the source of the nation* and, for many critics of the modern state, as being its indigenous element – its *ethnically pure* community. However, the villages were rapidly changing in ways that challenged these perceptions. Ethnically mixed villages, in which the colonizer and colonized worked side-by-side emerged in western Japan – the vanguard region for developments in Japanese agriculture. Collective relationships developed as people engaged in activities of production and reproduction. There seems to be a correlation between these changes and postcolonial views that stress the 'necessary deformation and displacement of all sites of discrimination and domination'.[4]

This mixing of different ethnic groups appears to stem from a seemingly upward movement in social class and from the rate of social change, which accelerated sharply under the total war system. It would be mistaken, however, to read these trends as any sort of levelling. It was, in fact, a widespread expansion

Conclusion

Figure C.1: People movements and connections to land in the prewar and imperial periods

Japanese	Japanese homeland settler farmers *or* Settler farmers in Manchuria[a] (Japanese = land owners)
	Homeland settlement = becoming land owners / Manchurian settlement = becoming land owners
Koreans	Japanese homeland agricultural laborers / Laborers for foundation work for reclamation
	Japanese homeland tenant farmers (Koreans = cultivators and laborers)

Note: [a] Japanese settlement in Manchuria often caused a chain reaction of the migration of Chinese and Koreans who had been its indigenous occupants.

of the imperial landlord system in which Japanese owned the land and people from the colonies farmed it. The relationships between people and land during the war can be summarized as per Figure C.1.

The impact of business curtailments and military mobilization in order to conduct a total war was felt everywhere, as was the cumulative disruption to everyday life by war damage and the looming prospects of a ground battle. Under these conditions, the implicit hierarchy of empire was carried over into the structures of migration, settlement, and land ownership. This hierarchy manifested in multiple forms: Japan and its Korean colony; Japanese who were becoming landlords and owner-farmers through Manchurian settlement;[5] and Koreans becoming tenant-farmers. From the countless ranks of those who had lost their livelihoods through colonization and war, those who were able to find work or become tenants in Japanese farming villages may have been extraordinarily diligent and adaptable. However, even in these exceptional cases, it was generally, as might perhaps be expected, differences in ethnicity that separated people into the haves and have-nots. Throughout the empire and its sphere of influence, new farming villages made up of rulers and ruled were being constructed in accordance with structures of dominance.[6] *Imperial villages* had a consistent ownership hierarchy, which was continually prescribed by the social order. The main point of this study has been to examine the multilayered and multi-ethnic site of the new agriculture.

Figure C.2: Composition of postwar people movements

Japanese	Homeland cultivation farmers → Postwar cultivation farmers (Rapid increase in those who left agriculture)
	Cultivation farmers in Manchuria → (Some 30%, about 90 thousand, deceased because the areas became battlefields) → Repatriation to homeland → Postwar cultivation (40%)
Koreans	Korean farmers → Returning to Korea *or* Either migration to cities or settlement after agricultural reform

Another point of discussion in this study is the nature of the postwar developments in agriculture. Figure C.2 attempts to depict this.

Admittedly, there are many points about the postwar era that I have not been able to clarify. However, as the regionally based sources analyzed here reveal, what is certain is that the connection between land and people was significantly disrupted by the war and transformed by the postwar liberation of the colonies. The people who devoted their lives to the future of the puppet state of Manchukuo, for example, made enormous sacrifices for the empire. These were people who had been recipients of generous state support and accorded high social status as the 'leading ethnic group'. The sudden loss of land, prestige and livelihood they had worked for must have come as a terrible shock.

During a war with no end in sight, people used their ingenuity to stay alive under ever-changing conditions. Defeat resulted in even further and more profound changes to these conditions. Marginalized others experienced this most directly. Defeat completely severed the possibility that any of the changes that may have begun to sprout during the development of capitalism in these new imperial villages would take hold.

The military defeat of the empire signaled the end of everything that had accrued to that point. The people responded by turning once again to the land in their quest for a stable and reliable livelihood. As previous studies have correctly observed, postwar agrarian reform was premised on various prewar actions; my research does not challenge this. My point is that neither the postwar reforms nor the subsequent research about these reforms took ethnicity into account. Moreover, the reforms applied to all absentee landlords without exception. The fact that the reforms would be so far-reaching could not have been predicted on the basis of the various prewar changes. Another characteristic of the postwar period is that it began with severing expatriates' ties with their hometowns, transforming them into 'others'. As such, it is necessary to re-examine the issue of modern land ownership; not in simple economic terms, but from a pluralistic political perspective.

I have not been able to discuss the indigenous Ainu people in this project. This is a major shortcoming of this book. I hope to pursue further research that will address this issue in combination with an analysis of Hokkaido, which was a designated settlement destination during both the wartime and postwar periods, and has continued to be an important place for Japanese to settle.[7]

Examining the experiences of repatriated settler-farmers in various regions in terms of postwar settlement policies highlights the significant role they played in postwar nation-building, which was certainly not limited to food and social policies. The resolve of large numbers of people who, with the loss of colonies and controlled territories, were determined to build a new postwar Japan by reconnecting with the land has generally been overlooked in research about postwar reconstruction. However, with scant financial backing, postwar setter-farmers were forced into the gap between national consciousness and isolation. Thus, their experiences were closer to a sense of being besieged, which is accompanied by a loss of identity, than to inclusion.[8]

The idea of a nation is intrinsically exclusive of those who do not belong, but despite ideological notions of purity, there is invariably heterogeneity within every nation. Nevertheless, the concept of nation has survived in the postwar period by acquiring successive new meanings which serve to mask its internal heterogenous characteristics. One of the questions that historical research must address is the social costs of efforts to define a homogenous nation, with particular focus on differences in treatment of excluded others.

Whether or not one was present in the Japanese homeland at the moment that the empire collapsed and the colonies were lost determined the kinds of connections with the land one might be permitted to develop in the early postwar period. This orientation became the basis of the new postwar Japanese consciousness, a consciousness that refused to recognize the mere presence, much less the contributions of ethnic minorities in the farming villages. I have tried here to reconcile the achievements and criticisms of previous studies of imperial history. I cannot claim to have escaped the discourse that places Japan at the center, a discourse which had been widely criticized, but I have focused on the ways in which the expanding empire fundamentally transformed Japan – a transformation which in many ways it continues to deny. It is not yet possible to predict where such revelations might lead, but it is a topic that I will continue exploring.

Liberation from a 'fragmented history': future topics

This study, while touching on events following the postwar migration policies, is primarily focused on the 1940s. As well as continuing efforts to compensate for the inadequate research in this area to date, we also now need research that examines developments after the 1940s.[9]

Almost all of the areas settled during the initial stages of the postwar period experienced poverty due to lack of resources, capital and technology. The lives of settler-farmers were rife with complications. Aside from poverty, the most high-profile issue in settlement areas was the requisitioning of sites for the purpose of rearmament; detailed studies of this issue are sorely needed. Since the early 1950s, many settlement areas have organized opposition to attempted requisitions of new military land throughout Japan, even as large areas have in fact been requisitioned. In my discussion of settlements in Kyoto Prefecture (Chapter 2), I mentioned the liberation of military land, but much of this land was quickly returned to the military. From around the time that Kishi Yamaji left the settler-farmers' movement, Japan began rebuilding its military, both for the purpose of providing support for the Korean War and towards its independence. Throughout this process, opposition to bases and requisitioning intensified across the country. The settler-farmers' movement would become an important part of these protest movements.[10]

Furthermore, in this period, the 'Shimagurumi Tōsō (All Okinawa Struggle)' protested against land confiscation and military bases that were located in Okinawa under the direct military rule of the US. The postwar separation of Okinawa from the 'homeland' is another issue that must remain in our sights. We should also attempt to come to grips with postwar Japan by retracing the struggles for land in the Japanese 'homeland' during this period.

Furthermore, while criticizing wartime analyses which left out war sacrifices, the same criticism applies to this work. The otherness which was produced through the catalyst of divide and rule during the occupation period continues to severely challenge our historical consciousness to this day.

We also must address the issue of rapid growth. Efforts to survive were intertwined with postwar agrarian reform, but they were far from stable. Families were separated once again in the period of rapid economic growth as a result of overseas agricultural migration policies; the movement of groups of children to urban areas to be employed; and leaving home to find work elsewhere in Japan. Although the traditional form of the family had changed substantially on the legal front, there were still strong concerns about the inheritance of family property and a belief that the eldest son should remain in his home town. In the midst of all of this, women were increasingly taking over the management of agriculture, which was called 'housewife agriculture', and gender hierarchies underwent considerable change. Developments such as birth control, the implementation of family planning and the legalization of abortion were all part of efforts to stabilize the birth rate. Possession of land did not automatically lead to stability or security; there were numerous other issues that had to be overcome. The movement of young people to the cities as well as the hardships endured by women in childbirth resulted in the destabilization of the family, which in turn became a major social welfare issue due to the ageing population in regional farming villages from the 1960s. Experiences of living and dying were considerably transformed around this time.

Looking at all of these factors as a whole, the period of rapid growth can be seen as a transition period for the population problem. Farmers have had many experiences: they have seen poverty and discrimination; searched for ways to cope in the midst of these experiences; tasted growth in their agricultural enterprises; and better health and fewer injuries due to new technology. In the course of all of this, they do not forget their suffering or their achievements; they continue to create new connections and to press on with their work. This is another topic for future research.

It is important that we use historical sources in order to improve our understanding of the state, which has treated people as a population, and intervened in their lives on this basis, as well as the various ways in which people have contested state intervention.

In other words, historical research should be used to identify the ways in which the state utilizes policies to mobilize and intervene in the lives of ordinary people, the individual activities of the people confronting these government interventions, and finally, the ways in which these competing tendencies coexist.

Throughout human history, the future that people and groups aim for rarely coincides with what comes to pass. Postwar Japan is no exception. To understand the present, however, it is worth asking of the historical record: who were the main actors; what were they seeking; and how did their actions combine and produce the society that we live in today? Present day Japan suffers from a lack of historical perspective on these various 'prospects' and the assumptions that underpinned them, papering over key questions that need to be posed. It is not surprising, then, that a certain kind of nostalgia imbues recollections of a 'united' society during the war, a time in which there was no tolerance for 'individuality' and the people in Japanese society were particularly brutal towards 'others.'

Why was Japan's rapid economic growth not predicted, and why did it leave so many people confused and surprised? Why was socialism so attractive to large numbers of people? Why did a portion of the people in economically advanced countries feel a 'revolutionary' sense of urgency in the late 1960s? And, what results did this produce? What kind of future did people aspire to as Japan reached the height of its economic prowess in the late 1980s? Also, why is it that today – when all of this has transpired – we are so incapable of understanding that our pasts will influence our futures?

I think that one of the reasons for this is a weak conceptualization of the 'common people'. The use of the term 'common people' has been criticized for its ambiguity (of course, it has also been a useful term precisely because it is ambiguous). However, if we consider the mobility of people in modern times, as discussed in this book, it is to be expected that the connections made by people should be at least somewhat ambiguous. The use of any single social category – whether national borders, class, ethnicity, or gender – to encapsulate the countless things that come with mobility, would simply end in fragmentation.

Liberation from a fragmented state will not be achieved by abandoning the idea of the 'common people'. It is a concept that provides a basis for complex and integrated analyses which entail otherness. It also connotes the space to which the people freely belong. However, as we attempt to identify new, united and historical 'subjects' there is always the risk that these subjects will once again be seen as homogenous people 'from below', or 'grassroots' people. This sort of representation relies on simplified conceptions of small-scale traditional societies (for example, collective communities). This book has, however, even if only partially, revealed the great complexity and plurality that has been effaced by the idea of agriculture that has been mobilized in the name of Japan, in which certain collectivities of people were naturalized as representing 'common people'.

Everyone is an 'other' in certain relationships. Those who are different must interact and craft particular relationships in asymmetric conditions. Constantly restricted by historical paths and circumstances, this is yet *another tradition* that has survived for a long time. It is never the single 'us', but the collective 'we' that exists at the meeting point between self and others. From this perspective, this book has painted another fractured 'self-portrait'.

Notes

Introduction

1 Amrith, 2011, pp. 5–6.
2 Foucault's arguments hint at the view that the ruling powers intervene in the 'population'. See, Foucault, 2007, especially the 25/1/1978 lecture.
3 Both in the past and at present there is no clear separation into 'human trafficking' and the sort of migration that my research assumes to be an independent action. Since the mid-1990s, increased attention has been paid to the international problem of human trafficking (particularly forced prostitution and child labor), and in 2000 the so-called 'Palermo Protocols' were established (see the entry on human trafficking in Scholte and Robertson (eds.), 2007, pp. 600–603. It is very significant that as part of this increased attention the U.S. State Department pointed out in its 'Trafficking in Persons Report' that 'some migrant workers are reportedly subjected to conditions of forced labor through a "foreign trainee" program'. We must always be cautious about demarcations when it comes to migration.
4 I am thinking here of Minamikawa Fuminori's arguments about the 'composition of racial ethnicity', which re-positioned the concepts of ethnicity and race in relation to nationalism (Minamikawa, 2007).
5 Gaimushō Kanrikyoku Keizaika, 1949, p. 48.
6 Regional history has seen an increase in studies dealing with the migration of people in recent years. But in, for example, Asao, et al. (eds.), 1994, there are practically no studies of the migration of people, with the exception of studies of the evacuation of school children.
7 Hall (ed.), 1974, pp. 124–125. I use the English title of *Kokutai no Hongi* from De Bary et al. (eds.), 2006.
8 Yoon, 1989.
9 This does not mean that I have a negative view of the general results of descriptions with a strong theoretical load. An awareness of the theory-laden nature of all observations is now a postulate in modern science, but this does not lead directly to a confrontational orientation. It results instead in a movement towards dialogue, in which there is a battle between various approaches while researchers remain cognizant of the limitations of the respective theories upon which they are relying. It might be thought that after the stage when the meaning of 'scientific' in the social sciences practically came to equal Marxism-Leninism, the favorable reception of these sorts of scientific theories would have become inevitable. It is rather the frequent concern with problems of paradigm theory such

as, for example, 'from Marxist studies of history to X' that is creating difficulties in Japanese historical studies. The groundbreaking nature of paradigm theory was that it raised the problem of incommensurability between different paradigms. Reflecting back on this, it seems that the result of applying paradigm theory to today's methodological disputes would simply encourage unproductive fragmentation.
10 Tanaka, 1978.
11 Kurihara, 1943.
12 Saitō, 1989 and 1999.
13 For more on this organization, see Noda, 2008. For the results of this viewpoint see also, particularly, Sakane, 2011.
14 Kumagai, 2004, 'suggests ways to overcome the frames of 'family and village' and 'theory of the stratification of the peasant class', and proposes a consolidation along the lines of a shift in various points of view such as – from settlement to migration; from group to individual; from productivity to sustainability; and from regions to a broader overview. A tangible result of this can be found in the appearance of research on new people coming to work in agricultural villages and on foreign brides.
15 Sakaguchi Mitsuhiro, 'Shutsuimin no Kioku (Emigrants' recollections)' in Nihon Imin Gakkai (ed.), 2011, pp. 100–101. Also, Sakaguchi, 2012, pp. 6–7.
16 Yamada Moritarō established the 'colonial Korean pattern' in his typological analysis of the 'Japanese' landlord system. This understanding also carried over to the critics who came after him, in the form of a division of scholarship into Japanese history and Korean history. Asada Kyōji's work (1989) mainly focused on the colonies, but also attempted to deal with the 'Japanese' landlord system on the level of the empire as a whole. Ōishi (ed.), 1985, analyzed the activities of landlords who expanded the sphere of land management in Korea. However, discussions of the landlord system in subsequent Japanese agricultural histories show no signs of tackling the problem of colonial rule.
17 Ōtsuki, 1939, p. 23.
18 Tobe, 2008.
19 Komagome, 2005.
20 Mori, 2005.
21 Amemiya, 2008.
22 Satō, 2005.
23 Fujita, 1958.
24 The meaning of historical events is not necessarily perceived at the very instant when they take place. We retroactively construct our perceptions concerning the meaning of the experience by repeatedly looking back at the event and in the midst of various communications.
25 Ōkado, 2008, see 'Jidai o kubunsuru koto (On periodization)'.
26 Kitagawa, 2000.
27 Akazawa, 2005.
28 As Kuroda Toshio pointed out in the 1970s, it is difficult to set up the premise that the division of time periods adopted in specific regions and those used in the 'centre' (the whole) are consistent, and also the idea that

we ought to take into account the independent changes in tempo in each region (Kuroda, 1977). This argument about the division of time periods has the additional limitation that it sees this kind of consistency as also being possible, particularly, in a period of total war. Another important point about Kuroda's arguments as they relate to the present book is the identification of differences between people's history (*minshūshi*) and regional histories. Although Kuroda concurs with the argument that people's history is an important part of regional histories, he does not see them as being of equal value. This is because the concept of 'common people' (*minshū*) goes 'beyond the regional'. Kuroda argues that the concept of people is essentially one lacking in regional opportunities, but contains elements that still ought to be examined today. The various matters that 'regional histories' have not referred to in recent years are the reason for putting together this history of research.
29 Benhabib, 2004, p. 18.
30 Laclau, 2007, p. 95.
31 This is a reference to Chantal Mouffe's view that politics cannot be unified by 'classes'; she foresees the construction of a new hegemony via the implementation of a new democracy arising from circumstances in which all 'conflicts' of an individual nature within diverse social relationships produce 'chains of equivalence' (Mouffe, 2005, p. 53).

Chapter 1

1 '*hantōjin*' is a highly derogatory term for Koreans.
2 Tōa Nōgyō Kenkyūjo, 1942a, No page number provided. This conference was on 7 and 8 October, attended by people concerned with agrarian policy, including Ishiguro and Ishii as well as Tomabechi Gizō, Nasu Shiroshi, Aruga Kizaemon, Kawashima Takeyoshi, Ōtsuki Masao, Kondō Yasuo, Hirakawa Mamoru, Mizuno Takeo and Ōuchi Tsutomu. This document was kindly provided to me by Itō Atsushi, for which I am especially grateful.
3 Higuchi, 1998, and Yoshizawa, 2003.
4 Tsukasaki, 2004.
5 Ōkubo, 1996.
6 Takano, 2009.
7 By 1940, Korean farmers were producing a large variety of crops and were making important contributions to the broader agricultural sectors, for example, in seedling and landscaping businesses.
8 Suzuki, 2006.
9 Mori Hatsuya, *Naichi Zaijū Hantōjin Mondai: Nōkō Tenkan Keikō to no Kanren ni tsuite* (The problem of Koreans living on the homeland: Links with changing agricultural trends), (1945 graduation thesis, Agriculture and Forestry Economics Division, Faculty of Agriculture, Kyoto Imperial University). During the final stage of the wartime period, the Agriculture and Forestry Economics Division, Kyoto Imperial University's Faculty of Agriculture conducted collective studies related to national policies

and a multitude of achievements were produced. The fact that police-related documents were made use of in this graduation thesis points to the possibility that it was written as part of this research activity.

10 At around this time, a substantial number of migrants travelled from northern Italy and southern China, which had been the major suppliers in the global sericulture market. These movements around production and distribution of silk, a global product, are essential for understanding migration in Japan. A comparison of the economic history of sericulture between Italy, China and Japan can be found in Federico, 2009.

11 The Japanese scholar Adachi pointed out the ethnic dimension of Weber's argument, which had traditionally been understood only from the perspective of social stratification associated with capitalism (see, particularly Adachi, 1997, pp. 12–15). For this paragraph, I also referred to Hizen, 2003.

12 Uesugi, 1998, p. 61.

13 In 1920, out of 6,448,343 farm operators (that is, the total of owners, managers and tenants excluding laborers), 6,892 were Japanese (of which 6,052 were tenants), accounting for 0.1% of the total. The area cultivated by Japanese was around 500,000 acres, which is 0.05% of the total of approximately 950 million acres. The figure varies greatly between regions – for example, in California, Japanese nationals constituted almost 80% of the 'colored' agriculture-related population; Japanese made up 4.4% of farm operators and were associated with 1.2% of the farm land (USDA, 1920, Census of Agriculture, http://www.agcensus.usda.gov/Publications/Historical_Publications/index.asp (accessed 7 July 2011).

14 Ngai, 2004.

15 In 1871, Minamiyamashiro Tea Products Company invited Wu Dewan from China to teach Japanese workers how to produce Chinese green tea for export to the United States. Tea production was targeted for industrial promotion by Kyoto Prefecture. Several other Chinese nationals were involved in tea production in southern Kyoto (Chen, 2004, pp. 202–203).

16 'Jūgyō o kyokasubekarazaru rōdō narabini rinshi no ue kyohi wo kessubeki rōdō no shurui shitei (Specification of types of work that must not be permitted and those for which the decision to reject must be made upon consultation with the superior)', compiled in Murakami and Hashimoto (eds.), 1997, p. 146. Details on this issue can be found in Yamawaki, 1994.

17 *Shinajin Rōdō ni Kansuru Ken Shireian (Okayama)* (Draft instructions on matters regarding Chinese labor (Okayama)), 1916, Japan Center for Asian Historical Records, reference code [A05032487100]. 'Shinajin rōdō hukyoka ni kansuru ken (Matters regarding non-permission of Chinese labor)', Murakami and Hashimoto (eds.), 1997, p. 244.

18 Compare this stance with the following statement about the sudden increase of Chinese workers in Korea under Japanese colonial rule (while rice monoculture was being imposed in the Korean colony, the Chinese played an important role producing vegetables): 'This is essentially a natural trend in which demand is driven by differences in labor wages and efficiency; thus the rampancy of Chinese workers is

truly unavoidable' (Chōsen Sōtokufu (ed.), 1924, p. 44). It appears that what was 'natural' in the colonies was not natural in mainland Japan.
19 Meanwhile, Chinese people were valuable producers of vegetable crops in colonial Korea. See, Lee, 2012.
20 Teruoka (ed.), 2008, pp. 104–105.
21 Senda, 1971, p. 56. These comments about farming practices are based on the discussion in Takahashi, 1926.
22 Nakamura, 1991, p. 243.
23 Yokoyama, [1899] 1985, p. 317.
24 Ōtsuki, 1941, p. 87 and Embree, 1972, p. 80.
25 The data is from a table titled 'Nōsaku Chinsen (Farming wages)' in Kyoto Furitsu Sōgō Shiryōkan, 1970, p. 194.
26 Hisama Kenichi views this as transplanting Japanese-style agriculture (Hisama, 1943). We might need to complement our study of 'people' in this chapter with similar research about farming methods.
27 Hong, 1987.
28 The most popular destinations were the Malay Peninsula, Sumatra and Manchuria. Amrith, 2011, p. 193.
29 According to Amrith, these three destinations stimulated the following mass-migrations: the migration of Vietnamese farmers from the Red River Delta and its riverside regions to the Mekong River Delta; the migration of Burmese farmers to the Irrawaddy River Delta; and the settlement of Thai cultivators in the Chao Phraya River's riverside regions (ibid, 2011, p. 31).
30 Some Koreans may have considered employment in Japanese agriculture as unconventional, despite the large proportion who did so, possibly because they were widely dispersed. Jeong Cheongjeong (1924–) commented on this after visiting an older male cousin who was working as a farmer in Hiroshima: 'It is no wonder that we, who originally come from farming villages, engage in farming; but at that time, it seemed strange to me that Koreans who had migrated to Japan, in whatever form, worked in agriculture in Japan' (Jeong, 1984, pp. 106–107).
31 Article 3 of the Gando Convention, for example, permits the settlement of 'ethnic Koreans' in Manchuria. Article 5 stipulates that land and properties owned by 'ethnic Koreans' should be protected by the Qing Government in the same way as those owned by Chinese and Manchurian people (Gaimushō (ed.)), 1966, pp. 792–794. See also, Park, 2005. Park described the link between land and people in Manchuria in terms of nationality and sovereignty.
32 Hong, 1987, pp. 15–25.
33 For the Wanpaoshan Incident, see, Park, 1981.
34 Young, 1998, pp.362–373.
35 For example, the local newspaper *Nanshin* (4/12/1915), published around the Shimoina District of Nagano Prefecture, reported that a Korean laborer who had been employed in a fruit orchard in the district since 1912 committed suicide, distressed over a love affair with a woman from Niigata Prefecture who was working at the orchard as a servant.
36 *Shiga-ken Nōkaihō* (Report of the Shiga Prefecture Agricultural Association), 1923, 125, pp. 13–14. There were 163 male and 10 female

Korean day workers recorded. Their wages were classified merely as 'upper', 'middle' and 'low', providing no clear indication of either the position of Korean people in the labor market or their employment status.

37 *Yamaguchi-ken Nōkaihō* (Report of the Yamaguchi Prefecture Agricultural Association), 1924, 249, p. 32. The contents of the discussion are unknown.

38 Osaka-shi Shakaibu Chōsaka, 1924, 'Chōsenjin Rōdōsha Mondai (The problem of Korean workers)', in Park (ed.), 1975, pp. 350–351.

39 *(Taishō 9 nen) Kokusei Chōsa Hōkoku: Zenkoku no Bu Dai 2 kan Shokugyō* (The 1920 national census report: Nationwide part 2, occupation), 1925, p. 240.

40 See, *(Shōwa Go-nen) Kokusei Chōsa Hōkoku: Dai 2 kan Shokugyō Oyobi Sangyō* (The 1930 national census report: Part 2, occupation and industry), 1935, pp. 224–225. While male farmhands topped the list, other major forms of employment included 4,027 'other agricultural laborers', 2,001 charcoal burners and 1,248 herdsmen and livestock farm laborers. There are another 827 people in this category, most likely tenant-farmers or farm owners. There were also two who 'depend on rents from tenant-farmers', one male and one female.

41 For example, Lee Choonja's (1941–) father worked as a farmhand while running a junk shop in Higashi Osaka City. Osaka-shi Jinken Hakubutsukan and Osaka Kokusai Rikai Kyōiku Kenkyū Sentā, 1999, pp. 46–47.

42 Seo Byeongil (1914–) initially worked in mines in Yamaguchi Prefecture after migrating to Japan around 1940. Meanwhile, he was also engaged in agriculture. Later, he purchased some farm land within the prefecture, in Mine City, where he ran a farm while taking up a variety of work including railway jobs and charcoal burning. In the national census of 1940, the number of Koreans who worked as charcoal burners rose sharply to 9,206 from 2001 in 1930. One interesting point in Seo's recollection is that he quit farming because it became too difficult to meet compulsory delivery quotas and it became 'ridiculous' in the end. The point is that Korean rice farmers abandoned agriculture, just like their Japanese counterparts, once farming was no longer aimed at self-sufficiency and self-consumption. The interview is found in Osaka-shi Jinken Hakubutsukan and Osaka Kokusai Rikai Kyōiku Kenkyū Sentā, 1999, pp. 18–22. For Korean laborers who worked as mowers, see Chapter 11 of Iida-shi Kyōiku Iinkai (ed.), 1976. This document also describes the multiple hats worn by those long-term stayers, including: sericulturalist, farmer and charcoal burner.

One interesting fact is that the wooden back carrier used by Korean laborers for mowing became widely established as '*Chōsen seita*' (Korean back board), replacing the Japanese '*shoiko*' that had been traditionally used in the area (see Photo 1.2). It would be helpful to ascertain the processes through which changes in basic practices and methods, such as everyday tools, equipment and knotting methods, spread across the regions.

43 Tōa Nōgyō Kenkyūjo, 1943, pp. 99–101.

44 Another reason that it is difficult to establish accurate figures is that Japanese regional administrators often excluded areas where Koreans were concentrated in groups. A report of a preliminary survey conducted

in preparation for a structural improvement project noted that it excluded from the survey 'the Ibaraki area and the 219 farming households consisting of Koreans within the jurisdiction of the practice association, for which it [the preliminary survey] was deemed unnecessary in light of the current local condition' (Ibaraki Shiyakusho Keizaika, 1965).

45 A graduation thesis in the Agriculture and Forestry Economics Division, Faculty of Agriculture, Kyoto Imperial University, 1929.

46 More than 600 Koreans came to work in construction in the immediate aftermath of the earthquake. A branch of the *Soaikai* (Mutual Friendship Society) was established in Mineyama Town of Naka District to help them transition to agricultural work. For the Mutual Friendship Society, see Manfred, 1981. The Naka District branch reportedly hosted a 'Korean laborers movement rally' around that time with 700 people attending (*Osaka Asahi Shinbun*, 22 April 1928).

47 Kawamura, 1929, pp.54–56.

48 For the details of this case study, I referred to 'Hitotsuya Kyōdō Kōsaku Kumiai nōjō Taishō 15 nendo seiseki gaiyō (Hitotsuya Cooperative Farming Association: Fiscal 1926 summary of performance of agricultural land)', in Osaka-fu Naimubu, 1927.

49 According to data by the Ministry of Home Affairs, the daily wages for Korean agricultural laborers in Kyoto Prefecture at the time averaged about 1 yen, ranging from 80 *sen* to 1 yen 30 *sen*, and it was normal to work 30 days per month. See, Naimushō Shakaikyoku Daiichibu, 1924, 'Chōsenjin rōdōsha ni kansuru jōkyō (Situation regarding Korean workers)' in Park (ed.), 1975, p. 500.

50 Studies on the structure of the urban underclass workforce can be found in Shimada, 2001.

51 Tokunaga, 1997, pp. 119–120. Yamamoto Kisaburō was village headman of Otogi Village (present-day Tenri City).

52 For example, in Saga Prefecture, it is said that workers hired by the year remained indispensable for the operation until power-operated water lifting devices were introduced in place of the 'three-step' treadle water pumps. See Namiki, 1959, p. 114.

53 Fukuoka Chihō Shokugyō Shōkai Jimusho, 1928, p. 1.

54 Ibid, p. 1.

55 See 'Kamoto-gun Nōkai nōgyō rōekisha koyō jōken naiyō gaiyō (Kamoto District Agricultural Association's overview of conditions of employment of agricultural laborers)' in ibid., pp. 2–3 and 8.

56 Ibid. pp. 8–9.

57 On this point, see Higuchi, 2010, pp. 37–38. This document describes the 'vocational course' as being part of the compulsory elementary school curriculum for Korean children in colonial Korea in 1929, which focused on agricultural education in order to nurture 'farmers' – or 'colonial farmers (agricultural humans)' in Higuchi's words. Whether there is any direct connection to the case study is unknown; but the underlying principles of the 'trainee program' and this 'vocational course' are strikingly similar.

58 One report praised young Korean contractors extremely highly, and reported that the farmers who engaged them treated them with kindness

and compassion. A kind of paternalistic relationship may have existed in some cases. Kim Chanmo, born in 1918, went to Saga Prefecture to work for a farming family through his cousin's referral around 1933. He noted his experience of being treated kindly by the family who took him in until his departure (Kim, 1991, pp. 35–43). The situation may have been rather different if it had been during the war. We can see this in the recollections of Jeong Seunbak, who migrated to Japan at the age of nine in 1933. After working for some time in a construction camp in Wakayama Prefecture, he was sold to a farming family as a servant. He noted that he suddenly started to be treated much more harshly as soon as the Sino–Japanese War broke out. He says that the family he was serving was pressured by reservists to not treat Koreans in the same way as they treat Japanese (Jeong, 2001). Note, however, that we cannot make any straightforward comparison between this and institutionalized cases.

59 Fukuoka Chihō Shokugyō Shōkai Jimusho, 1928, p. 11. The employment of Koreans in agriculture continued into the 1930s in Kamoto District. An autobiographical novel by Jeong Heejung depicts her journey to Kamoto District with her mother and describes her brother and sister working in a variety of jobs including baby-sitting and silk farming (Jeong, 1984).

60 *Tokkō Geppō* (Special Higher Police monthly bulletin: July 1934), pp. 131–132. They were arrested on charges of failing to obtain permission, violating the regulation to control mediation businesses set forth by the Oita Prefectural Ordinance. They allegedly recruited and smuggled to Japan a total of 116 people to work on farms, mainly from North Gyeongsang Province, between February 1927 and May 1934. Although they were arrested for acting as intermediaries for others, they also employed Koreans on their own farms. One of them employed as many as 15 Koreans. The bulletin reported that: 'This type of activity is considered as a risk that may cause and facilitate illegal travel of Korean workers to mainland Japan, and thus requires a substantial consideration from the regulatory perspective in the future'.

61 The list of people indicted for alleged violation of the Peace Preservation Law in a Police Affairs Bureau monthly bulletin includes a young man from South Jeolla Province who worked as an agricultural laborer as well as a greengrocer and was a member of the Osaka Branch of the National Farmers' Union (*Tokkō Geppō* (Special Higher Police monthly bulletin: January 1932), p. 3). He was prosecuted for belonging to the Japan Communist Youth Union. Although allegations by the Special Higher Police cannot be regarded as factual evidence, it seems safe to assume that some Koreans were involved in the movement in one form or another. Around the same time, Haneda Ichirō, a member of the Japan Proletarian Artists Union who had been involved in various activities in Osaka since 1930, was running a series of cultural events with members of the Writers' League and the Theater League, hosting small traveling exhibitions and other gatherings in industrial districts and farming villages where he endeavored to distribute and expand readership of the organization bulletin *Senki* (Battle Flag) (Fukumoto (ed.), 1979, p. 50). In fact, the posters advertising *Senki*, drawn by artists such as Haneda, directly appealed to Koreans by slogans written in Korean.

62 Zennō Seinenbu Osakafuren, 1931, p. 24.
63 'Oretachi no Nyūsu (Our news)', 1930 [date and issue unknown]. This is contained in Zennō, Osaka 1930 (National Farmers' Union, Osaka 1930), held by the Hosei University Ohara Institute for Social Research.
64 'Nōgyō kōryō (Kōryō Iinkai sōan) (Agricultural mission statement (drafted by the Mission Statement Committee))'; and Ōshima, 1975. This draft mission statement of the JCP was written in 1931 according to Ōshima. Part of its 'theses' states that the 'five million agricultural proletarians' are 'the most trustworthy comrades for proletarians on the whole', and that 'the party must pay special attention to this particular group of agricultural proletarians, the ones who migrated from the colonies, as they are expected to play the most active role in rural villages in times of the proletarian revolution due to their anti-imperialist revolutionary activism'. This draft, however, was not adopted in the well-known theses of 1932.
65 The Haui Island Dispute is an example of a tenant dispute that crossed the boundary between Korea and 'mainland Japan' (Iwamura, 1972, pp. 152–154).
66 Kikakuin Sangyōbu, 1938, p. 21.
67 Ibid., pp. 2–3.
68 Ibid., p. 23.
69 Ibid., p. 25.
70 Ibid., p. 27. It should also be pointed out here that lower wages were not the sole motivator for employing Koreans; they also had exceptional skill sets. They were 'outstanding learners of farming techniques' and their work is 'very often far superior to that of Japanese' (ibid., p. 28). As the employment of Korean labor had become accepted as an 'absolute necessity', Onga District began dispatching Korean 'trainee farmers' from Shōwa House in Shimonoseki City of Yamaguchi Prefecture to rural villages in 1932 through the 'agricultural work student' program, in order to secure a more skilled workforce. The program reportedly came to a temporary halt between 1936 and 1937, then resumed in 1938. Shōwa House was officially called 'Yamaguchi Prefecture Social Service Association Shōwa House' (Yamaguchi-ken Shakai Jigyō Kyōkai Shōwakan). For a study of Shōwa House, see Kimura, 2006.
71 Kikakuin Sangyōbu, 1938, p. 27.
72 Ibid., p. 28. Of those hired laborers, only 20 were Japanese men; the rest were Japanese girls. Of the 45 Koreans, 12 were from the 'agricultural work student' program.
73 Ibid., p. 29.
74 Ibid., pp. 82–83.
75 See the case study on Yano Village of Hyogo Prefecture (present-day Aioi City), in Kurata, 1938, p. 156. According to Kurata, the landlords in the area preferred and sought 'new migrants' over those who were already in Japan. Similarly, in Hokkaido, the police did not permit importing agricultural laborers directly from Korea. However, it seems that the controls implemented varied depending on the region and time period. A landlord in Asada Village of Oita Prefecture, arranged for a Korean worker to travel to Japan in 1926 as an 'agricultural employee'. Three years later, the Korean worker brought over his wife and three children

from Korea. One of the children, Park Gyeongsik, became a prominent *Zainichi* Korean historian. This demonstrates the possibility of bringing over one's family while living as an employee of a farming family (Park, 1981, pp. 5–11).

76 On the wartime mobilization of Koreans for forced labor and its development process, see Yamada, Koshō and Higuchi, 2005.

77 This refers to the Cabinet decision of 30 October 1934, 'The Matter of Measures for the Immigration of Koreans', in which policies to suppress migration to the Japanese mainland and direct them instead towards the northern areas of Korea and Manchuria as well as to assimilate Koreans living in the mainland were formulated. Moreover, it was determined that instructions would be given to employers in Japan not to seek workers from Korea but rather employ mainland Japanese or Koreans who had already migrated to the mainland. It is clear that the authorities' policies were contrary to the landlords' preferences, as discussed previously.

78 The goal of policies of the Movement to Establish Imperial Farming Villages was to nurture farms of appropriate size with long-lasting business operations in mind. Its specific vision was set out in seven points by Mizoguchi Saburō of the Ministry of Agriculture and Forestry as follows:
  1. It should be an owner-managed farm with no sideline business.
  2. Management should be fundamentally run by family labor.
  3. The farm land should be of size that is suitable for the geographical and social conditions of the location.
  4. Staple food should be the main produce, accompanied by animal husbandry.
  5. It should enjoy advanced farming techniques and high production efficiency.
  6. The living standard should be of a level that allows a modest life with a moderate level of economic self-sufficiency while fostering a unique culture that is relevant to agriculture.
  7. Long-lasting commitment to agriculture should be made with the management principle of ensuring timely response to the state's requests.

See Mizoguchi, 1943, p. 20.

79 Nōchi Seido Shiryō Shūsei Hensan Iinaki (ed.), 1972, pp. 719–726.
80 Tonomura, 2012.
81 Tōa Nōgyō Kenkyūjo, 1942a. No page number is provided.
82 Ibid.
83 The quote is from Tōa Nōgyō Kenkyūjo, 1942b, pp. 16–17. Ishiguro continued: 'Specifically, one idea I can think of is to allocate Koreans to the south'. Ishiguro's view was that, given that the objective of maintaining the population could not be compromised for the agricultural sector, they should bring in Koreans to address labor shortages, but only in the industrial sector. This was met with a great deal of opposition by those who regarded 'mixed marriage' as problematic, to which he responded that that was a 'leap of logic' (ibid.). An example of discourses in opposition to mixed marriage at the time can be found in Mizushima and Miyake, 1942. Ishiguro's response provides some clue about where he drew a boundary. It

would appear that he did not view mixed marriage in general as a problem; but in the context of the 'blood' of farmers it becomes a problem. The point is that Japan's racism is not uniform, and this *agrarian racism* needs to be examined in more detail.

84 It was even more so because, in the colonial agricultural administration more directly, 'the life one should lead as an Imperial farmer' was preached under the slogan of 'the establishment of the Imperial farmers' way'. For the Imperial farmers' way, see, for example, Tominaga, 1944. If we consider this together with the fact that *Chōsen Nōkaihō* then contained a document titled 'Nōdō Shinsei (Pledge to the farmers' way)' to promote *Kōminka* (imperialization) that read: 'We shall earnestly and faithfully look up to the Emperor and serve his Imperial land', the political nature of the agricultural bureaucrats and politicians of Imperial Japan becomes even clearer. On the transformation of Korean rural society during the war, see, Shin, 1996.

85 Tōa Nōgyō Kenkyūjo, 1942b, pp. 64–65.

86 Ishiguro said: 'It is doubtful whether we can consider the population we sent [to Manchuria] as the root of the Japanese ethnic group' (ibid., pp. 15–16).

87 At that time, as part of the survey effort, a research group was established, headed by Sakimura Shigeki of Tokyo Imperial University. One of the group's reports is Kawano, 1940b. Although the Agricultural Administration Bureau's survey conducted in 1942 has not been uncovered, the research is assumed to have begun that year, based on the fact that much of the 1943 report is a comparison with the previous year.

88 According to Senda Shōsaku's research into agricultural employment and labor: 'It is likely that it was very rare for agricultural laborers such as those hired by the year to be able to become tenant-farmers or to even take the first step up the so-called 'agricultural ladder'' (Senda, 1971, p. 60). Taking this into account, should we consider the ethnic 'substitution' discussed earlier in this chapter as being not a result of a simple replacement? Regarding the decline of agricultural laborers, I referred to Nōseikyoku Nōson Sōmushitsu,1944a and 1944b. In Fukuoka Prefecture, female workers from the Amakusa region of Kumamoto Prefecture are reported to have been brought in to substitute for Korean laborers who were no longer available.

89 Naimushō Keihokyoku Hoanka, 1944, *Kokumin Dōin Keikaku ni Tomonau Inyū Chōsenjin Rōmusha Narabi Zaijū Chōsenjin no Yōchūi Dōkō* (Trend requiring attention regarding migrant Korean workers and resident Koreans resulting from the National Mobilization Plan), Japan Center for Asian Historical Records, reference code [A05020292800].

90 Yamada, Koshō and Higuchi (eds.), 2005, p. 101. Previous research has revealed that after September, when Koreans began to be conscripted, the use of violence in the process was prevalent. However, some Japanese revisionists insist that Koreans and Japanese were conscripted *without discrimination* as Japanese nationals. I disagree with such claims and am more inclined to the view that the mobilization system was ethnically discriminatory. For example, around the same time, the Kujō Jūjō Plant of Kotobuki Heavy Industry Company (*Kotobuki Jūkōgyō*) in Kyoto, a munitions factory with 3,250 employees, was troubled by a spate of long-term absences without notice; absenteeism soared from 152 cases in January 1994 to 207 in February (see Tokubetsu Kōtō Keisatsuka, 'Rōmusha no shisō

dōkō (Thought and trend of workers)', *Shōwa Jūkunen Shigatsu Yukizawa Zen Chiji Arai Chiji Jimu Hikitsugi Enzetsusho* (The April 1944 written instructions on administrative handover from Former Governor Yukizawa to Governor Arai), Administrative Documents of Kyoto Prefecture [Shōwa 19–18–1–1], p. 432). While both Japanese and Korean workers were involved in the conscription process, it is undeniable that the mobilization system entailed ethnic discrimination.

91 Gunjushō Sōdōinkyoku, 'Gunjushō shukan kakugi kettei jikkō jisshi jōkyōshirabe (Report on the implementation status of the cabinet decision supervised by the Munitions Ministry)', 31 May 1944, in Gunjushō Sakitani Gunjikan, *Sankō Shiryō Zattetsu: Shōwa Jūkyunen Nigatsu–Shōwa Jūkunen Jūichigatsu* (Miscellaneous collection of references: February–November 1944), The National Institute for Defense Studies Library. According to this document, a notice titled 'Matters regarding the use of Korean laborers' was issued on 3 March, based on the Cabinet decision under the joint signatures of Labor Affairs Bureau (*Kinrōkyoku*) and National Health Bureau (*Kenminkyoku*) of the Ministry of Welfare. This seems to have been issued in conjunction with 'Outline of Instructions on Extension of Contract Period with Migrant Koreans', which followed immediately.

92 Kawano, 1940a.

93 Teruoka (ed.), 2008, pp.140–142.

94 There have been many studies of urban areas around Kyoto City, including Gotō, 1991. One of the main topics of discussion was the large number of *Zainichi* Koreans living in urban enclaves and the discrimination that they experienced. More recent work includes Sugimoto Hiroyuki's research, which considered both the history of *Zainichi* Koreans and the history of the *burakumin* in which they lived in Kyoto City. See, Sugimoto, 2015.

95 *Shōwa Nijūnen Arai Zen Chiji Miyoshi Chiji Jimu Hikitsugi Enzetsusho* (The 1945 written instructions on administrative handover from Former Governor Arai to Governor Miyoshi), Administrative Documents of Kyoto Prefecture [Shōwa 20–15–1], p. 551.

96 Koreans swarmed into the mining industry. According to Mori, Koreans 'are everywhere, overthrowing the general dogma that the proportion of Korean employees must not exceed 30%. They are now increasing to 40 and 50% before we know it, occupying as much as 80% in extreme cases' (Mori, 1945, pp. 25–26). As for wartime reclamation, Ōkubo Yuri's aforementioned thesis indicates that there were many Koreans working for the reclamation projects operated by the Agricultural Land Development Corporation, and among those working at the site were many Koreans who had escaped while being forcibly relocated to Japan.

97 See, *Shōwa Jūkyūnen Shigatsu Tōkei ni Kansuru Tsuzuri* (Documents related to the statistics of April 1944), Terada Village document [2289]. For Terada Village, I used documents archived in the Jōyō-shi Rekishi Minzoku Shiryōkan (Folk Heritage Museum).

98 See, 'Sonsei no gaikyō (Village overview)', *Sankō Shiryō* (Reference materials), Terada Village document [2377]. It should be noted that I calculated the percentage of tenant land based on 'Ta no bu (Category: Rice field)', *Shōwa Nijūichinendo Tōkei Hōkoku Zairyō Tsuzuri* (The file of resources for fiscal 1946 statistical report), Terada Village document

[2319]. There is a slight discrepancy here, though, as the total area of rice field is recorded as 2,479.7 *tan* in this document.
99 Kyoto-fu Nōchi Kaikakushi Hensan Iinkai (ed.), 1980, p. 28.
100 'The farmers' union's class movement should be deemed to have come to an end with the establishment of the All-Japan Farmers' Union Kyoto Prefecture Federation coupled with the dissolution of the prefectural branch of the National Farmers' Union that followed immediately after that' (Kyoto-fu Nōchi Kaikakushi Hensan Iinkai (ed.), 1980, p. 175).
101 *Tokkō Geppō* claimed that the majority of members had been involved in the National Farmers' Union (Naimushō Keihokyoku, 1939, *Tokkō Geppō* (Special Higher Police monthly bulletin), April, p. 117. The Japan Farmers' Federation (*Nihon nōmin renmei*) was formed under the umbrella of Nakano Seigō's Tōhōkai under the lead of Koyama Makoto from the Nagano Federation of Rural Revitalization (*Nagano nōson kōsei renmei*), joined by Kimura Takeo from Yamagata and others. It is understood that the All-Japan Farmers' Union lost its power as more prominent organizations including Niigata, Hyogo and Aomori joined this move (Watanabe, 1959, pp. 1517–1518). The Kyoto union joined the Patriotic Farmers' Union Alliance after having seen Osaka and Hyogo withdraw from the All-Japan Farmers' Union and switch to the Patriotic Farmers' Union Alliance (*Shōwa Jūrokunen Kawanishi Zen Chiji Andō Chiji Jimu Hikitsugi Enzetsusho* (The 1941 written instructions on administrative handover from Former Governor Kawanishi to Governor Andō), Administrative Documents of Kyoto Prefecture [Shōwa 16–21–1], p. 14.
102 Tanaka Yoshio became a director in charge of liaison with the farmers' union at the inaugural rally of the Kyoto chapter of the Social Democratic Party of Japan on 12 November 1945 and was appointed as an advisor in the election in March 1946 (Matsuo, 2002, pp. 157–158 and p. 324).
103 *Shōwa Jūrokunen Kawanishi Zen Chiji Andō Chiji Jimu Hikitsugi Enzetsusho* (The 1941 written instructions on administrative handover from Former Governor Kawanishi to Governor Andō), Administrative Documents of Kyoto Prefecture [Shōwa 16–21–1], p. 15.
104 Mori, 1945, p. 36.
105 Ibid., p. 40.
106 For the activities of *Kyōwakai*, see Kinoshita 1939 and 1940.
107 *Kyōwakai*'s Uji branch seems to have been proactive in efforts aimed at 'harmony' such as hosting a soccer tournament in Terada Baseball Stadium (*Kyoto*, 4/1/1943). There are reports of an enterprise magazine featuring these activities, but it has not been uncovered (*Kyoto*, 30/1/1943).
108 Mori, 1945, p. 37.
109 Ibid., p. 46.
110 Ibid., p. 39.
111 Kurata, 1938, p. 514.
112 Mori, 1945, p. 39.
113 A former industrial cooperative chairman commented: 'I heard from Terada Village Industrial Cooperative's former chairman Mr. Nishimura that the majority of them [Korean farmers] not only work in farming but also have other jobs. They provide labor in the slow season for farming

and they are building up a good amount of savings from extra cash they receive. Considering that the wage for construction workers used to be 17 to 18 yen per day before the regulation, and 8 yen 20 *sen* to 10 yen after the regulation, their income is expected to be quite substantial' (Mori, 1945, p. 51).

114 Jang Boksun (1932–), who evacuated to a rural village in Hiroshima from Osaka towards the end of the war, wrote in his autobiography how his father, who decided to start farming 'as a tenant-farmer's tenant-farmer or something of the sort', was brooding over the paddy field he was allocated, grumbling, 'They think Koreans are stupid. That's why they gave me land like this... How on earth am I supposed to make rice here?' Importantly, Jang also mentioned that as he worked on the farm, his father 'began to show a smile that he never showed while he was working at construction sites', which he speculated was due to the fact that farm work was in his blood, something he felt nostalgic about (Jang, 1999, pp. 47–50).

115 Mori, 1945, pp. 46-47. There was a news report of the 'heroic act' of a man called Lee Wangnae in Kitakatsura District of Nara Prefecture, who ended up running farmland of 9 *chō* 7 *tan* on his own as a result of agreeing to take over the land of enlisted farmers, and returning it to them upon their demobilization (*Kyoto Nichinichi Shinbun*, 4/8/1946). The article introduces Lee as an advisor to (former chairman of) the Nara Headquarters of the League of Koreans Residing in Japan (*Zai-Nihon Chōsenjin Renmei*). Likewise, the father of one of the most famous entrepreneurs in Japan, Son Masayoshi, was a tenant-farmer who returned to his land around the time of the agrarian reform. His comment 'Can't you tell the difference between what's yours and what's not' speaks to the mistaken sense of ownership many tenant-farmers developed from working the land belonging to someone else (Sano, 2012, pp. 120 and 127).

116 Some Koreans might have been included in Japanese households through marriage, especially in the form of a man being adopted into a bride's family, but the numbers are unknown. For our purposes, let us assume that such cases were rare, given that the authorities attempted to dissuade Korean men from marrying Japanese women after all of the Japanese men had left for military or industrial service, as pointed out in Tonomura, 2006.

117 Mori, 1945, p. 52.

118 The name '*Kyōwakai*' continued to be used locally despite the fact that it had been reorganized into *Kōseikai* by that time. For the structure of governing Koreans through *Kōseikai*, see, Higuchi, 2009.

119 Mori, 1945, p. 50.

120 Ibid., p. 52.

121 See, 'Shōwa nijūnen jinkō chōsa daisanji tōkeihyō sōfu no ken (Matters regarding the forwarding of third edition of the statistical tables of the 1945 population survey)', *Shōwa Jūkyūnen Jinkō Chōsa Ikken* (Matters related to the 1944 population survey), Terada Village document [2278]. There were 4,052 Koreans in the Kuze District as a whole, second only to the Funai District (5,242) in Kyoto Prefecture (*Shōwa 22-nen Saishū Hōkoku Kankei Tsuzuri* (Files on the 1947 final report), National Archives of Japan).

122 The data is from 'Ta no bu (Category: Rice field)', Terada Village document [2319]. A similar trend is discernible in northern Osaka. A survey by Miyamoto Tsuneichi showed that, in Abuno Village's Tsukahara hamlet (Osaka Prefecture), Korean farmers increased from two to 14 households from March to July 1945. Note that this village is unusual; it received 300 evacuees when the local population was only approximately 100 (Miyamoto, 2006).
123 Nōseikyoku Nōson Sōmushitsu, 1944a.
124 Notice from the Head of Terada Village to the Head of the Uji District Office titled 'Chōsenjin Chūkaminkokujin Hontōjin honseki o Okinawa-ken ni yūsurumono no tōrokurei ni yoru tōroku shūkeihyō sōfu no ken (Matters regarding the forwarding of the summary of registration made under the registration order for Koreans, Chinese, Islanders and people who are legally domiciled in Okinawa Prefecture)', 20/3/1946, *Chūkaminkokujin Hontōjin Honseki o Okinawa-ken ni Yūsurumono no Tōrokurei ni yoru Ikken Tsuzuri* (Filed documents relating to the registration order for Chinese, Islanders and people who are legally domiciled in Okinawa Prefecture), Terada Village document [2337].
125 O Gisun-san Tsuitō Bunshū Kankō Iinkai (ed.), 1980, p. 34. Oh Gisun also wrote that they had settled in the village to avoid conscription. This is a digression, but some young Koreans from Shūzan joined the Manchurian Youth Corps Brigade and lost their lives there. This was a particularly harsh blow for their poverty-stricken parents who struggled to survive in wartime Japan. Minakami Tsutomu was working as a recruiter in Shūzan in 1937 for Kyoto Prefecture's Employment Division where he was in charge of reclamation-related businesses. The state of affairs is documented in his essay, Minakami, 1977. I imagine there were constant tensions between them and the local farmers, although of varying intensities, amid the constant changes in agricultural villages. Park Heonheang (1918–) recalled that when he evacuated his family from Amagasaki in Hyōgo Prefecture to an agricultural village in Shimane Prefecture, he was treated with extreme hostility by the local farmers (Park, 1990, pp. 194–195).
126 The citation is from Osaka Prefecture administrative document titled '*Shōwa nijūichinen hachi, kyū, jūgatsu fusangikai gian gengi tsuzuri* (Compilation of agenda proposals for August, September, October 1946 prefectural council)', Osaka Prefectural Archives.
127 Ju Seok (1926–2002) reported that he moved to Hiroshima City, where he could live in a group, due to the rumors of attacks on non-Japanese in the rural areas (Chu, 2002, p. 51).
128 One repatriate whose background has been identified was an officer in the Office of the Governor-General of Korea who worked as a welfare commissioner after the war (*Shōwa Nijūichinendo Minsei Shorui* (Documents on welfare fiscal 1946), Terada Village document [2388].
129 '*Hi-Nihonjin sōkan ni kansuru ken* (Matters regarding the repatriation of non-Japanese)', 15/5/1946, Terada Village document [2337].
130 According to an occupation activities report of the 109th Military Government Company which was stationed in Osaka 'Osaka-fu military occupational history' (20/5/1946), the military government authority demanded that the prefectural Social Welfare Section discontinue the

practice of assigning a quota of returnees to each zone and, instead, tell the *Chōren* representative of the zone to meet the required number (Ōya (ed.), 2007, p. 296). Also, see Chapter 3, Section 2 of Kim, 1997, pp. 247–254.

131 It has been argued that, by issuing this document, GHQ declared that *Chōren* should have nothing to do with the repatriation program (ibid., p. 62). The following statement confirms this: 'in light of the issuance of the order from General MacArthur's HQ to the effect that "any Korean union or organization shall not be made liable for, in whole or in part, the repatriation of Koreans"', made on 14 June 1946, 'the captain of the local occupation force Major Wright ordered the dissolution [probably of *Chōren*'s office inside concentration camps for Koreans] on 12 July and the duties of repatriation now belonged to the Repatriation Relief Bureau, both in name and reality' (Senzaki Hikiage Engokyoku (ed.), 1946, *Senzaki Hikiage Engokyoku Shi* (History of the Senzaki Repatriation Relief Bureau)' in Kato, 2001).

132 Notice from the Head of the Uji District Office to the heads of respective municipalities titled 'Chōsenjin sōkan ni kansuru ken (Matters regarding the repatriation of Koreans)' (25/6/1946), contained in Terada Village document [2337]. The notice 'Hi-Nihonjin no sōkan ni kansuru ken (Matters regarding the repatriation of non-Japanese)' (25/4/1946), which was sent from the Repatriate Relief Authority to the heads of the prefectural Education and Citizens' Affairs Departments (Kyōiku Minseibu) in April prescribed that, from then onwards, the repatriation of Koreans shall take a new form, in which the prefectures take leadership with cooperation from *Chōren*, as opposed to the arrangement in which *Chōren* played the central role with support from the prefectures. Hence, it is possible that the process seen in Terada Village was the mainstream, and that Osaka and Senzaki were exceptions (Tottori-ken Kōseika, *Shōwa 22-nen Hi-Nihonjin Sōkan Yusō Kankei Tsūchō Tuzuri* (The collection of 1947 circulars related to repatriation and transportation of non-Japanese), Tottori Prefectural Archives. I wish to thank Mr. Miyamoto Masaaki for pointing me towards this document.

133 Uji Chihō Jimushochō, '*Chōsenjin no sōkan ni kansuru ken* (Matters regarding the repatriation of Koreans)' (2/9/1946), Terada Village document [2337].

134 '*Chōsen mikikansha meibo* (List of non-repatriated Koreans)', Terada Village document [2337].

135 Nōchi Kaikaku Kiroku Iinkai, 1951, p. 276.

136 Ibid., p. 277.

137 Zainihon Chōsenjin Renmei, 'Dai jukkai Chūō Iinkai gijiroku (The 10th Central Committee Meeting proceedings)', in Park (ed.), 1, 2000, p. 166.

138 Zainihon Chōsenjin Renmei Chūō Sōhonbu, 'Dai jūsankai Chūō Iinkai gijiroku (The 13th Central Committee Meeting proceedings)', in ibid., 1, p. 289.

139 'Chōren dai 13-kai Chūō Iinkai zokuhō seikatsu kiki toppa ae banzen tōsōteki soshiki eui kyōka (The 13th Chōren Central Committee Meeting updates: Organization to undergo reinforcement to prepare for a fight to break the livelihood crisis deadlock)', *Haebang Shinmun*, 10 February 1948.

140 'Yon nīyon kinen tōsō ae sōkekki (All-out rally for the commemoration of the 4.24)', *Daejung Shinmun* (*Taishū Shinbun*), 17 April 1949.
141 Zainihon Chōsenjin Renmei Chūō Sōhonbu, 'Zentai Soshiki Tōkeihyō (Statistics table of the entire organization)', Park (ed.), 2, 2000, p. 16.
142 'Kosakuken kakutoku Kyoto Kuze shibu Minsei katsuyaku (Minsei plays an active role in helping Kyoto Kuze branch acquire tenant farming rights), *Haebang Shinmun*, 1 April 1948. The article was printed in Korean and is somewhat difficult to read in some parts, but the gist is as follows: 'Chōren Kyoto Headquarter's Kuze branch carried out a struggle to demand that the Agricultural Committee abolishes racial discrimination and grants tenant farming rights to Koreans under the lead of Minsei [League of Korean Democratic Youth in Japan (Zainihon Chōsen Minshu Seinen Dōmei)]. On the 16th, they formally acquired the tenant rights for 14 *tan* 8 *se*, which was distributed to fellow Korean farmers. As a result, five households began working in agriculture in this region'. Another struggle broke out when Minsei's office was searched under the pretext of a crackdown on black market cigarettes, sparking protests against unjust oppression (*Rakunan Taimusu* (Rakunan times), 1 June 1948). It appears that this movement was in collaboration with Japanese labor unions and the Communist Party (See, 'Kyoto Kuze futō danatsu hantai (Objection raised against unjust oppression in Kyoto's Kuze)', *Haebang Shinmun*, 25 June 1948.)
143 On 21 January 1950, the Head of the Uji District Office instructed respective heads of municipalities to report any collective demonstration by Koreans (Jōyō-shishi Hensan Kenkyūkai (ed.), 1977, p. 155).
144 'Tochi Baishū o bōgai (Land acquisition interfered)', *Haebang Shinmun*, 9 April 1949.
145 A farmer in Yasu District of Shiga Prefecture, Kawase Yoshio, recalls an extremely troublesome experience he encountered around 1947, when he was the head of the Nodanuma Reclamation Agricultural Union. He negotiated with the prefectural office after receiving a request from Koreans working at reclamation construction sites to purchase subdivided land, but the prefecture insisted that 'subdivided land cannot be sold to foreigners' (Kuwahara (ed.), 1976, pp. 80–81).
146 This information is from an interview with Yokota Jintarō, a Japan Communist Party member in the House of Representatives, in *Daejung Shinmun*, 5 February 1949. Yokota participated in the movement as a farmer activist before the war. In particular, he was involved in the formation of the Japan Communist Group (*Nihon Kyōsan Shugishadan*). The interview was conducted on the occasion of his election as a member of the House of Representatives in 1949. In the interview, he argued that 'the acquisition of places to work or arable land as the issue of securing Korean people's livelihood rights' is directly linked to the issue of the acquisition of political rights'.
147 Teradamura Nōchi Iinkai, 1949, *Nōchi Iinkai Ikken Tsuzuri* (Filed documents relating to the Agricultural Committee), Terada Village document [no document number].
148 Gaishi Iinkai Jimukyoku, 1952, pp. 41 and 42.
149 O, 2009, especially, Part 2, Chapter 4.

150 The people most seriously affected by this ordinance were the Chinese in Japan. There was intense tension between Japan and China over land ownership at this particular time, as the Chinese revolution was looming.
151 *Nōchi Kaikaku Shitsumu Sankō* (Administrative references for agrarian reform work) contains examples. I will refer to this source in Chapter 4.
152 Morita, 1955, pp. 77–78. We are yet to confirm if any Koreans were candidates for membership on this committee. There is, however, a report indicating that there was a Korean candidate for *Nōgyō Chōsei Iinkai* (Agricultural Adjustment Committee) in Ōta Town, Ibaraki Prefecture (present-day Hitachiōta City) (See, Nihon Kyōsantō Kantō Chihō Iinkai, 25 November 1948, *Joseon eui Byul* (Stars of Korea), 4).
153 Notice from the Agricultural Land Bureau of the Ministry of Agriculture and Forestry to the Legal Opinion First Bureau (*Hōsei Iken Daiichikyoku*) of the Attorney-General's Office titled 'Gaikokujin no senkyoken oyobi hisenkyoken ni tsuite (Regarding the right to vote and right to stand election of foreigners)' (20/6/1949) (in Hōmufu, 1950, pp. 187–188).
154 A 'Korean agricultural cooperative union' referred to as 'the only "agricultural cooperative" in the Korean community', was reportedly formed in Ibaraki City, Osaka Prefecture with 160 participating households. See, Zainihon Daikanminkoku Kyoryū Mindan Osaka-fu Chihō Honbu, 1980.
155 It is difficult to trace exact numbers, because the Japanese local administrations excluded areas with a concentrated Korean population from their data. For instance, the Economic Division of Ibaraki City Office's publication in 1965 (see Ibaraki Shiyakusho Keizaika, 1965), which was a preliminary report for the implementation of projects for structural improvements, states: 'The study excluded 219 agricultural households in the Ibaraki area as well as the communities in which Koreans lived, because of their particular circumstances'.
156 One post-war change that is worthy of attention is the male to female ratio in agricultural employment. According to *Zairyū Gaikokujin Tōkei* (Statistics of foreign residents), the total number of Koreans employed in the agriculture and forestry industry as of 1959 was 10,659, accounting for 7.2% of all employed persons. There were 8,109 men and 2,550 women. This means that the agriculture and forestry industry was the largest sector for employment of women, employing 17.7% of 14,427 women who were employed at the time. Considering 94.7% of Korean women in Japan did not have a job, there is great potential for future studies to investigate the way they were connected to agriculture.
157 The prefectures with the highest number of approvals for migration were Saga, Yamaguchi, Okayama, Hiroshima and Oita, according to [Tōyō Takushoku Gaisha] Chōsen Shibu Nōgyōka, 1935, *Tōtaku no Shokumin Jigyō* (Oriental development company's colonial enterprise), which was later included in Mizuta (ed.), 1976, pp. 326–327.
158 Immediately after the surrender, on 30 August, before any specific reform plan was suggested, the following report was submitted to the central government as the demand from the people: '1. A variety of measures should be implemented with resolution based on nation-building by agriculture, 2. The method of guidance for agricultural management should be revised to one that breaks the traditional one-size-fits-all

malpractice and utilizes to the maximum the knowledge and experience of farmers while providing instructions so as to drive agricultural management with concentrated diligence, 3. The elimination of absentee landlords and the establishment of owner-farmers should be implemented promptly, 4. Since cultivation is of immediate necessity in order to establish the system of domestic self-sufficiency, the state must ensure that it carries through with cultivation until there remains not even an inch of land left uncultivated (Kobayashi, Chiaki 'Shinjitai ni taisuru kokumin no yōbōjikō ni kansuru ken (dai-ippō) (Matters regarding the demand of the nation's people in response to the new situation (first report))', 30/8/1945, in Awaya and Kawashima (eds.), 1994, p. 196.
159 Noda, 1989.

Chapter 2

1 'December 1944 Shimominochi local office circular on the implementation of the Joint Campaign for Receiving Urban Evacuees', Nagano-ken (ed.), 1988, p. 293.
2 Maeda, 1991, p. 18. Some scholars of farming village populations estimate that the figure was nine million people at the end of the war (Nojiri, 1947, p. 13). These figures are, of course, limited to the Japanese 'homeland', they do not address all of the evacuations throughout the empire, such as in Taiwan or Korea.
3 Shimaki, 1947, p. 8. (From the entry for 15/9/44).
4 Nōrinshō Sōmukyoku Tōkeika, 1946, p. 20.
5 The statistics on the number of evacuees in Tatsuoka Village in Nagano Prefecture, a village with a population of around 4,500 which received more than 1,700 evacuees, shows that approximately 75% of all evacuees arrived in the period after April 1945. The figure is calculated based on the following documents held in the Iida City Institute of Historical Research: Tatsuokamura, 1940, *Sonsei Ichiran* (Village outline); and Tatsuokamura Bunsho, *Ji Shōwa 20-nen Toshi Sokai ni yoru Tenyūsha no Jūtaku Jukyū Jōkyō Hōkoku: Sokaisha Ukeire Jōkyō Hōkoku* (Report on the supply–demand status of housing for the people who moved in as urban evacuees from 1945: Status report on evacuee acceptance).
6 Although lumped together under one term, evacuation comprises a variety of forms of migration; some occur in order to adapt to the situation at hand, involving some degree of voluntariness such as the case discussed in this chapter. Others are forced such as by building evacuations, which should, under normal circumstances, be addressed separately as 'forced migration' or 'displacement'. These various items ought to be categorized and synthesized in future research.
7 *Kishi Nikki* (Diary of Kishi) is in the possession of Itō Jun, Kishi's eldest son. The parts written from 1919 to 1971 survive today. The density varies day to day; there are days he writes three days' worth of entries at a time and other days he describes interactions with people he met and his thoughts in minute detail. The sections with historical

significance for proletarian literature were first reprinted in Uranishi Kazuhiko's 'Kishi Yamaji "nikki" (The "diary" of Kishi Yamaji)', (Uranishi, 2001–2003).
8 Kurokawa, 2006. The evacuation referred to by Kurokawa in this work is restricted to the evacuations of people, such as group evacuations of school children. Further research is needed on building evacuation policies which created problems that persisted into the postwar period in Kyoto. For a case study on Kyoto, see Kawaguchi, 2014. *Kyoto* (3/12/1945) reported the formation of the Kyoto-wide alliance of evacuees under the headline 'We deserve better: Angry 75,000 forced evacuees in Kyoto demand privileges'.
9 Kitagawa, 1997.
10 Nōchi Kaikaku Kiroku Iinkai, 1951, p. 157.
11 Uranishi Kazuhiko (2009) pointed out that *Bungaku Annai* was active in developing communication links with writers in Korea, Taiwan and China.
12 A detailed discussion of *Jitsuroku Bungaku* can be found in Kōno, 2007. Miyanishi Naoki praised Kishi's activities from the dissolution of the Writers' League until 1937, identifying them with the 'popular front' movement of the time (Miyanishi 1982).
13 For a more detailed profile of Kishi, see Itō, 2007.
14 According to Iwagami Junichi, the topic of 'dispatching writers to the countryside' was raised under agenda item 5 (Iwagami, 1946, p. 64).
15 Nakano, 1998, pp. 561–564.
16 Koshōji, 2010, is another work undertaken with the same initiative. Tsuruta Tomoya was involved, with Kishi, in the launch of the magazine *Nōmin Bungaku* (Peasant Literature) in 1955.
17 The exhibition titled 'Saitama e Sokai Shita Bunkajintachi' (Cultured people who evacuated to Saitama) was held in the Saitama Peace Museum in 2001, where a collection of resources about ten highly-educated evacuees were displayed. The event catalogue contains a list of the professionals in the arts and literature who evacuated to Saitama Prefecture (Saitama-ken Heiwa Shiryōkan, 2001, p. 43).
18 Kishi, 1934a, no. 3, 12 May.
19 Kishi, 1934a, no. 4, 13 May.
20 In an entry dated 19 January 1950, having seen the muddled response of the JCP to the Cominform criticism, Kishi wrote, somewhat self-mockingly: 'If Kurahara [Korehito] and Miyamoto [Kenji] turn out to have failed as men, I will have nothing to be afraid of in this world any longer. Rather, the world will become a comfortable place'. It appears that Kishi was tormented by regrets over his 'conversion' during the war and that this had turned into a sense of inferiority compared to those who remained steadfast.
21 Kishi had written an article entitled 'The principles in the new phase and directional change to the dispersed form' just before his arrest in 1934 (Kishi [1934] 2009).
22 Kishi, 1934b.
23 *Tokkō Gaiji Geppō* (April 1937), pp. 7–8. This movement is described as an extension of the so-called '*Tasūha* (majority) movement' in Kansai by those involved (Zadankai, 1978). I also referred to 'Hikokunin Wada Shisashi ni taisuru Chian Ijihō ihan jiken yoshin shūketsu kettei (Osaka

Chihō Saibansho hōkoku) (Conclusion of the preliminary examination concerning the Peace Preservation Law violation incident for Defendant Wada Shisashi (Osaka District Court report))', *Shisō Geppō*, 55, pp. 87–91.
24 These charges were dropped on 20 May 1938 (20/5/1938). I am reluctant to consider this a 'conversion'. Is an ideological change under conditions of indefinite detention and violence an independent enough act to be called a 'conversion'? Perhaps it should be interpreted as 'brainwashing' through torture. Regular interviews were conducted after his release.
  Frantz Fanon described colonial rule's psychological campaigns and their results, mentioning 'emotional and intellectual change and mental disorder following torture' as one of the types of mental disorders produced by colonial wars. Of course, recognizing brainwashing and responsibility for subsequent collaborations may be separate matters. Nonetheless, what is of interest here is the order of occurrence. I cannot help thinking that the distance between a local movement, which seems to have successfully negated feelings of guilt by directly facing up to military oppression, and the sort of movement in which Kishi participated calls for further historical analysis. See, Fanon, 1967, particularly Chapter 5 'Colonial war and mental disorders'.
25 Maruyama Yoshiji (1903–79) was from Hyōgo Prefecture. He became acquainted with Ōya Sōichi and Kishi Yamaji while he was working as a journalist for the newspaper *Yorozu Chōhō* and was involved in editing the Writers' League's paper *Bungaku Shinbun*. Maruyama worked with Kishi and Eguchi in producing *Bungaku Annai*, and became a permanent council member of Nihon Nōmin Bungakukai (the Japan Peasant Literature Society) in 1955.
26 In the column entitled 'Sakka seikatsu shōmetsu (Annihilation of writers' livelihoods)', Inoue Tomoichirō wrote: 'This thing called writers' livelihoods has completely disappeared from Japan' (*Tokyo Shinbun*, 3 May 1944).
27 Sasayama Shigetarō (1902–1974) was appointed head of the Personnel Office when Ishiguro Tadaatsu was appointed as Minister of Agriculture and Commerce in the Suzuki Kantarō cabinet, as the end of the war was approaching. He recalls that Ishiguro's aim for the Personnel Office was to promote the return of capable farmers from the front lines to mainland Japan. Along with Hirakawa Mamoru, they worked hard to secure an agricultural workforce by negotiating with the military's *Fukuinka* (Demobilization Division) (Sasayama, 1978, pp. 9–10).
28 Teruoka (ed.), 2008, pp. 150–153. When we use the expression 'increasing food production', however, we should not overlook the fact that there was a major shift from agricultural export promotion to measures to address basic food shortages resulting from the drought of 1939. In 1938, the Cabinet Planning Board's policy makers had envisaged reducing domestic consumption and increasing exports of high-value-added and relatively more competitive products such as butter from Hokkaido. See the comment by Yagizawa Zenji in Kyōchōkai, 1939, p. 4.
29 Hashimoto, 1939. Hashimoto presents the development of cold highlands as part of the efforts aimed at self-sufficient fodder production, positioned parallel to the Asia Development Youth Patriotic Labor Service Corps

(*Kōa Seinen Kinrō Hōkokutai*) and the millet-sowing movement (*hiemaki undō*). Related studies can be found in Tonooka Kazuo, '*Teito jinkō kyūyō no anzen ni shisuru kokudokeikaku no hitsuyō to sono ichian* (The need for national land planning that contributes to the safety of food supply to the population of the imperial capital and one proposal)', in Jinkō Mondai Kenkyūkai (ed.), 1941,and Yamaguchi, 1942.

30 For details on how the corporation was established during the war and its operations, see Sakane, 2002.

31 Nōrinshō Kōchika, 1941.

32 In the 'Matters Concerning Increased Production and Securing Food' under the 'Matters Concerning the Determination of Prior Deliberation of Important Policies Regarding the Fiscal 1944 Budget' submitted to the Cabinet meeting of 26 November 1943, land improvement was raised as the first priority item among measures to increase food production. During the meeting, someone remarked that this was 'already being implemented' (*Asahi* (Tokyo) 27/11/1943).

33 Kyoto-fu Tōkeika, 1945, *Shōwa Nijū-nen Sōgō Sakuzuke Jisseki Chōsahyō* (Survey into the comprehensive planting record of 1945), Administrative Documents of Kyoto Prefecture [Shōwa 20–62].

34 Useful references regarding the evolution of policies on cessation of and changing occupation discussed in this section are found in Ōkado and Yanagisawa, 1996, and a subsequent work by Yamazaki, 2004.

35 This comes from a pamphlet issued by *Manshū Ijū Kyōkai* (Manchurian Immigration Council) in 1941 entitled *Tairiku Kinō Kaitakumin* (Return to Agriculture Continental Emigration).

36 'Chūshō shōkōgyōsha ni taisuru taisaku ni kansuru ken (Matters regarding measures for small and medium-sized merchants and craftsmen)' *Kōbun Betsuroku* (Separate official records), Japan Center for Asian Historical Records, reference code [A03023594600].

37 For example, see, Shibano, 2010. People who had ceased working or changed occupation already constituted as much as 20–30% of the population of settlers in 1941, proving to be a very important part of the Manchurian settlement policy (Yamanaka, 1941, p. 23).

38 Nakai, 1943. See the first section of Chapter 3.

39 The citation is from 1943 'Dai hachijūikkai Teikoku Gikai Shūgiin Yosan Iinkai gijiroku (sokki) dai jūnikai (Minutes of the Lower House Budget Committee of the 81st Imperial Diet (stenographic record) no. 12)', Database System for the Minutes of the Imperial Diet, p. 261. At the time, the destruction of superior agricultural land by the influx of factories was a major problem for the government. There was a contradiction between the prevention of urban concentration and the preservation of agricultural land over factory locations.

40 The diary entry for 8 August 1944 in Itō, 1983, p. 71 reads:
When the rumor went around last year that school children would be assembled and forced to evacuate as a group, we thought it was all made up; newspaper reports also publicly denied it. Look at us now, it has become reality in the blink of an eye. I must say the authorities executed it very well; but more than anything, I am astonished by how quickly time flies.

41 *Asahi* (Tokyo) 27/11/1943.
42 Tokyo Daikūshū, Sensaishi Henshū Iinkai (ed.), 1973, pp. 516–518.
43 For example, Kamiizumi Hidenobu, 'Waga sokaiki: Sokai to kinō (My memoirs of evacuation: Evacuation and return to agriculture)', *Yomiuri Hōchi*, 2/2/1944; 4/2/1944; and Shimomura Chiaki, 'Waga sokaiki: Musashino no naka ni (My memoirs of evacuation: Into Musashino), *Yomiuri Hōchi*, 9/2/1944.
44 I, however, doubt that the evacuation of elderly, children and expectant mothers was motivated by the recognition that these people needed protection, which was the propaganda used at the time. I suspect it was rather because they were seen as a 'burden', as can be seen in a notice sent from the air defense headquarters: 'The promotion of the evacuation of especially elderly, children and expectant mothers, who would be an encumbrance to air defense activities, is in progress' (Bōkū Sōhonbu Jichō, 'Sokai kuiki eno tennyūsha toriatsukai ni kansuru ken tsūchō (Note on the handling of people who are moving into evacuation zones)', 22/12/1944, in Gunjushō Daijin Kanbōkyoku, *Hatsu Rai Kan Tsuzuri Shōwa Nijū-nen Ichigatsu Yokka–Ichigatsu Sanjūichinichi* (Corresponding file for the period from 4 to 31 January 1945), The National Institute for Defense Studies Library).
45 Naikaku Seido Hyakunenshi Hensan Iinkai (ed.), 1985, p. 265. Referring again to Shimaki's diary, immediately after this: 'the neighborhood association's office was plagued by several dozen telephone calls about evacuation every day' (Shimaki, 1947, p. 101).
46 See, 'Toshi sokaisha no shūnō ni kansuru kinkyū sochi yōkō (Outline of emergency measures regarding the employment of city evacuees in farming)', *Kōbun Ruiju* (Classified public documents), National Archives of Japan Digital Archive, Microfilm number 071700, frame 1372–).
47 Yamashita, 1948, p. 781. *Asahi* (Tokyo) (28/6/1945) reported that the Head Office of Return to Farming was established by the Cabinet meeting of 26 June under the headline 'Sensaisha yonjūmanko no kinō sokushin (Forty-thousand war-affected households are encouraged to return to farming)'. According to the article, the immediate target of promoting a return to farming was set at 100,000 households in mainland Japan and 250,000 households in Hokkaido. Nishimura Shōichi, who was at the time Director General of the Administration Bureau, was appointed to lead the Head Office of Return to Farming. Nishimura later became the first Head of the Reclamation Bureau which was established after the war.
48 Sugihara, 2002.
49 This is the wording used in the section introducing the Tokyo Metropolitan Government's policy to encourage people to change occupation and return to farming in 'Sundo mo tagayase shokuryō jikyūda: Teito no ten-haigyōsha Ibaraki-ken ka kaitakuchi ni kinō (Cultivate every inch of land for food self-sufficiency: Those who changed occupation or ceased working in the Imperial capital shall return to farming in the settlement in Ibaraki Prefecture)', 1943, *Shashin Shūhō* (Weekly photographical journal), 277, p. 6.

50 Despite inspecting rental properties on 13 and 14 November, and even after promising to rent a property on the 16th, he ended up cancelling on the 24th. One of the likely reasons for this was that when he visited the principal of the region's elementary school to discuss his first son's school transfer on the 21st, he sensed that the local people 'do not like having children from Tokyo joining them after all'.
51 From Kishi, 1945. It is accompanied by the notation 'Spring of 1945'.
52 Nōrinshō Kyoto Nōchi Jimukyoku, 1949, pp. 3–5.
53 Suenaga, 1954, p. 185.
54 Kyoto-fu Nōchi Kaikakushi Hensan Iinkai (ed.), 1980, p. 34.
55 *Shōwa Nijūni-nendo Rinji Nōgyō Sensasu* (Fiscal 1947 special census of agriculture); and Nōrinshō Kyoto Nōchi Jimukyoku, 1949, pp. 1–2.
56 For this passage, I referred to Hiyoshi Chōshi Hensan Iinkai, 1987, pp. 883–885; and Anonymous, 1948, p. 656.
57 *Kyoto Hinode Shinbun*, 21/2/1942. This article refers to the *Nōgyō Zōsan Hōkoku Suishintai* (Patriotic Implementation Teams for Agricultural Production Increase). For the events leading up to the formation of these teams and their development in the postwar period, see, Itō, 2013.
58 *Kyoto Hinode Shinbun*, 7/3/1942. When did this mobilization of students end? *Kyoto* (22/12/1945) reported that a group of students from Kyoto Imperial University's Division of Agricultural Machinery in the Faculty of Agriculture, went to Osadano in Fukuchiyama city to engage in reclamation. According to the report, these activities were carried out in cooperation with 1,000 members of the prefectural farmers' armies (*nōheitai*), namely, Tanba Corps (Tanba-tai) and Tango Corps (Tango-tai). Another report from *Kyoto* (5/7/1946) has it that the Ritsumeikan Agricultural Corps (*Ritsumeikan Nōkōtai*) was mobilized to Yawata.
59 Kishi, 1955. According to *Kyoto* (1/8/1942), the initial objective was to create paddy fields. To this end, a dam was being built for securing water supplies. Therefore, it could have been that they were mobilized to construct the dam.
60 *Shōwa Jūhachi-nen Nashimotonomiyahi Denka Goshisatsu Ikken* (The 1943 inspection by Her Highness Princess Nashimoto), Administrative Documents of Kyoto Prefecture [Shōwa 18–24].
61 Nōrinshō Kyoto Nōchi Jimukyoku, 1949, pp. 4–5. This data uses a different notation for the year of the settlement than other historical records but it provides reliable data about the number of the settled households.
62 Anonymous, 1948.
63 See, *Shōwa Jūroku-nen Kawanishi Zen Chiji Andō Chiji Jimu Hikitsugi Enzetusho* (The 1941 written instructions on administrative handover from Former Governor Kawanishi to Governor Andō), Administrative Documents of Kyoto Prefecture [Shōwa 16–2–12], pp. 17–18. The textile weaving and dyeing industry including Nishijin fabrics suffered a serious setback following the '7 July Prohibition' (*Shichi Shichi Kinrei*), with 364 factories closed and 705 changing their business category, leaving 14,553 people unemployed. 'Shichi Shichi Kinrei no eikyō ni yoru jigyō no kyūhaishi, shitsugyō jōkyōshirabe (Report on the status of the suspension or discontinuation of business and unemployment due to the impact of the Prohibition on 7 July)' contained in Kawanishi's handover document

provides a breakdown of the industries entered by those who changed occupations.

64 'Senryoku Zōkyō Kigyō Seibi ni tomonau jūgyōsha tenkan jōkyō (Shōwa jūku-nen san-gastu genzai) (Status of workforce conversion pertaining to the Curtailment of Industries for Increasing War Potential (as of March 1944))', *Shōwa Jūku-nen Shi-gatsu Yukizawa Zen Chiji Arai Chiji Jimu Hikitsugi Enzetusho* (The April 1944 written instructions on administrative handover from Former Governor Yukizawa to Governor Arai), Administrative Documents of Kyoto Prefecture [Shōwa 19–18–1–2], p. 677.

65 *Shōwa Nijū-nen Roku-gatsu Arai Zen Chiji Miyoshi Chiji Jimu Hikitsugi Enzetusho* (The June 1945 written instructions on administrative handover from Former Governor Arai to Governor Miyoshi), Administrative Documents of Kyoto Prefecture [Shōwa 20–15–1]. This document lists the First Amata Settler Group, the Yamashiro Village Settler Group and the Kyoto Byōrei Village Reclamation Group as already dispatched to Manchuria; it also reports the Second Amata Settler Group, the Daisen Kyoto Settler Group and the Heian Village Settlement Group as in preparation for deployment. Of these, Byōrei and Heian were the two settler teams that returned to farming on the continent consisting of people who had changed occupation. See, p. 206.

66 Kyoto-fu Nōgyō Kyōdō Kumiai Chūōkai (ed.), 1968, p. 229.

67 While reclaimed land was in surplus in Gomagō, Hirabayashi Taiko, who evacuated to her birthplace, the village of Nakasu, Nagano Prefecture at the end of March 1945, around the same time that Kishi evacuated, recalls in her diary that she had to make a journey from her own village – where there was no available land – to neighboring villages to steal crops to meet the compulsory delivery of grass allotted to the village (Hirabayashi, 1979, p. 131).

68 Uemura Yoshio, 'Kaikon kinō ni kanshi Nōchi Kaihatsu Eidan Fuku Rijichō to kaidan yōshi (Summary of conversation with the Deputy Director of the Agricultural Land Development Corporation regarding reclamation and return to farming)', 2 September 1945, National Diet Library Modern Japanese Political History Materials Room (Kensei-shiryōshitsu) Mōri Hideoto Papers [181–11]. In their subsequent meeting, the Corporation's representatives reported that they have 'promptly initiated reclamation work after immediately accepting 20,000 convicts in 200,000 *chō* of training ground across the country, and further several dozen thousand people in munitions factories'. The Nippon Steel Corporation responded that they would make a decision based on the degree of the shrinkage of the business (Uemura Yoshio, 'Nōchi Kaihatsu Eidan kanbu to saikaidan yōshi (Summary of conversation of the follow-up meeting with the Agricultural Land Development Corporation leader)', Mōri Papers [181–10]). With regard to penal labor, there were reports in the newspapers of the time that they were mobilized for land reclamation but the facts remain unknown. Meanwhile, there was also a report that homeless people from Osaka were sent to coal mines (*Asahi* (Osaka) 23/5/1948).

69 Sasayama,1978, pp. 73–74. The importance of this statement is that it indicates what was going on among the bureaucrats administering

agriculture and forestry before they had good prospects for agrarian reform.

70 'Shūnō taisaku jisshi no ken (Matters regarding the implementation of measures for employment in agriculture), *Kyoto-fu Kōhō* (Gazette of Kyoto Prefecture), 18 December 1945. In March of the following year, the Reclamation Department was established (*Kyoto* 20/3/1946). On 15 November 1946, 'Outline for the Implementation of Emergency Land Reclamation of Kyoto Prefecture' was announced. Its policy was prescribed as to 'make strong attempts to promote the emergency land reclamation work by cultivating the uncultivated and improving the cultivated land within Kyoto Prefecture in line with the national plan designed to promptly establish food self-sufficiency by leveraging the national land that remains after accommodating to the new postwar state of affairs to the maximum advantage, and at the same time help resolve the unemployment rate' (*Kyoto-fu Kōhō*, 15 November 1946).

71 The calculation is based on the table titled 'Nyūshoku jisshi kosū (Number of settled households)'; and the table titled 'Ikko atari nōka jinkō, nōgyō jūjishasu no suii (Fluctuations of the farm population and number of agricultural workers per household)' in Sengo Kaitakushi Hensan Iinkai (ed.), 1967, pp. 702–703, and pp. 774–775 respectively. The data in the latter is from the 1950 financial year. It should be noted that these figures represent the numbers of new settlers. For example, the number of settled households for 1955 was 140,000, which suggests that at least 50,000 households had left agriculture (p. 776).

72 The entries for 14 and 17 September and 1 November 1945 in *Kishi Nikki* recount how he purchased the household goods of Korean families who were returning to Korea.

73 A villager who used to go to school with a Korean child told me that upon leaving the village this schoolchild had said, 'I would be killed just like when the [Great Kanto] earthquake happened!' There were many Koreans living in Gomagō towards the end of the war, so much so that it was nicknamed 'Korean Village'. I heard from a person who I happened to meet in an eatery in Gomagō while I was visiting for research in April 2007 that there were five to six Korean children per class of 50 children. I record this here as a field note since it is not adequate to use as a historical source. According to an article titled 'Hanshin giseisha kyūen katsudō mōretsu (Tremendous relief activities for the Hanshin [educational struggle] victims underway)' in *Haeban Shinmun* (1/7/1949), which is representative of the newspapers run by Koreans in Japan in the postwar period, we can confirm that the villages of Wachi and Tonoda (near Gomagō) had local chapters of the Funai branch; however, it is not yet known if there was a chapter formed in Gomagō Village or if there were any other Korean organizations.

74 While this kind of connection was evident in Gomagō Village and Terada Village, there were also Koreans who became settlers after the war, as discussed in Chapter 1. One source states that leaders of the Settlers' League included members of Korean origin but this has not been substantiated by other documents (Momose, 1987, p. 213).

75 For *Jiron*, see Ureshino, 1980.

76 For Kyoto Workers' Institute, see Ueno, 1978, p. 74.
77 About two years after the organization of the union, the people from Nishijin who had had to change occupation were allowed to return to their former production activities ('Nishijin niman ten haigyōsha gyōkai fukki tsuini jitsugen mazu go seisan kumiai katsudō (Former Nishijin workers are finally returning to the industry, starting with five union activities)', *Kyōnichi*, 12/7/1947).
78 Kyoto-fu Nōchi Kaikakushi Hensan Iinkai, 1980, p. 271.
79 Nōrinshō Kyoto Nōchi Jimukyoku, 1949, p. 6.
80 Shimizu, 1967, pp. 44–45.
81 *Kishi Nikki*, 13/6/1946. Kyoto-fu (1973) mentions that the Gomagō Settler Farmers' Union was established in May 1946 but this is incorrect.
82 Katsuragi Hachiro, 1947, Jagaimo to Makiyama no Kyōdōjigyō ni Seiko (Cooperation in potatoes and mountain management succeeded), *Kaitaku Nōmin Shinbun* (Settler-farmer News), 1, 20/4/1947.
83 Kaga 1947. See Taniguchi (reprinted), 1972. Taniguchi criticized Kishi in his field report on Gomagō. Having read this, Kishi wrote in his diary that he and Taniguchi 'have not talked since this spring, (14/12/1947). Five years later, Kishi criticized Taniguchi (Kishi, 1952).
84 According to *Kyoto* (*Yamashiro*), 18/12/1946, when the Kyoto Prefectural Land Reclamation Society was established, Yamagami Shūkichi from the Agricultural Association and Kishi were appointed as Chairman and Deputy Chairman, respectively. There were 17 participating organizations, including the Farming Union (Shūnō Kumiai), Agricultural Association (Nōgyōkai), Compatriots' Relief Association (Dōhō Engokai) and the Agricultural Land Development Corporation.
85 *Asahi* (Osaka), 30/1/1946. Shimizu Seizō, a leader of the settler-farmers in Osaka, was appointed Deputy Chairman of the All-Japan Settlers' League.
86 *Asahi* (Osaka), 16/5/1946. This article explains that settlers 'have returned to agriculture but are unable to make ends meet' and that the 'General Meeting to Overcome Settlers' Problems and Bottlenecks' was planned for this reason. No date for the meeting was provided.
87 Kishi 'Kaitaku zange (Confessions of settlement)', p. 1. When this was written is unclear, but it is recorded in the notebook titled 'Kaitaku Jidai: Sōsaku Nōto 1951.9 (Settlement times: Creative notes 9/1951)' (Kishi, 1951).
88 *Kaitaku Nōmin Shinbun* (Settler-farmer news), 1, 20/4/1947.
89 The editing was performed in cooperation with Maruyama Yoshiji, according to the diary.
90 Kishi 'Kaitaku zange (Confessions of settlement)', in Kishi, 1951, p. 4.
91 See the meeting minutes of 26 May 1947 in Kyoto-fu Nōchibu Nōchika, 'Kyoto-fu Nōchi Iinkai gijiroku (Kyoto Prefectural Agricultural Committee meeting minutes)', Administrative Documents of Kyoto Prefecture [Shōwa 26–133–1]. Kishi was also appointed as Secretary to the Director of the Federation of Funai District Agricultural Committees (Funai-gun Nōgyō Iikai Rengōkai). *Kyoto* (*Ryōtan*), 6/7/1947.
92 'Sensaisha ga hiraku "Osakamura": Kyū Maizuru gunkōnai no mujintō ni ("Osaka Village" developed by war victims: On the deserted island in the former Maizuru naval port)', *Asahi* (Osaka), 16/6/1946.

93 Shimizu Kaoru, who was in charge of the reclamation, recalls that the problem was that they made people settle in Maizuru without any assessment of whether the city was suitable for reclamation or not. The reclamation turned out to be unsuccessful and was opposed by the local residents (Shimizu, 1967, pp. 45–48).
94 Osaka-fu Nōchibu Nōchika, 1952, p. 459.
95 *Kyōnichi*, 22/3/1947.
96 Kishi, 1947, pp. 33–34.
97 Kishi, 1949.
98 The figures from this and next paragraph are from Kyoto-fu Nōchibu Nōchi Kaitakuka, 1953.
99 Nozoe Kenji, 1976, is an excellent document on this topic. Research to date also includes case studies on cooperative management which became a common practice among settler farmers in the postwar period; for example, Nishida and Kase (eds.), 2000 and Nagae, 2001. There is no doubt that the application of cooperative management on postwar reclaimed land provides an interesting case study within the context of postwar agricultural history. However, it is more fitting to say that the absence of foundations for management to function was the most fundamental characteristic of Japanese settlers' communities during this period.
100 It seems that he began developing the idea towards the end of 1947 with fellow editor Tezuka Hidetaka. After he returned to Tokyo, they held a monthly editorial meeting at Kurahara Korehito's house. They found a complete notebook containing *Orugu* (The organizer) at the residence of Kawanami Hideo of Kansei Gakuin University on 6 October 1948. This work was published over nine volumes, as Shin Nihon Bungakukai, 1948–1949, *Kobayashi Takiji Zenshū* (Collected works of Takiji Kobayashi), Nihon Hyōronsha.
101 In 1948, one and a half pairs of work footwear equaled one sack of rice in black market value (Tanaka, 1976, p. 81).
102 For a summary of the incident, see Shimizu Seizō, 'Kinkyū hōkoku: Renmei honbu Jikatabi Jiken no shinsō gaiyō (Emergency report: The summary of truth about the Settlers' League Headquarters' Work Footwear Incident)', 23 June 1948, Tokushima Kenritsu Bungaku Shodōkan.
103 Yamada (ed.), 1948, p. 200.
104 Nōrin Daijin Kanbō Sōmuka, 1972, p. 500.
105 Zadankai, 1949, pp. 2–3.
106 Ibid., p. 8.
107 Kishi also frequently visited Osaka and Kobe. He wrote, in the diary entry for 26 April 1948, 'Today, in Osaka, I saw a demonstration by Koreans against the closure of elementary schools', and on the following day, 'I am going to Kobe. Martial law has been imposed in connection with the demonstration by Koreans'. These are the only descriptions related to the Hanshin Educational Struggle.
108 The articles of incorporation of the Kyoto Prefectural Settler Farmers' Cooperative were drafted by Kishi. See, *Kishi Nikki* 9/1/1948. The Agricultural Co-operatives Act was passed on 19 November 1947.

109 *Kyoto-fu Kaitaku Nyūsu* (Kyoto Prefecture reclamation news), 1, 1949.
110 Note that this did not mean that he completely severed his ties. Maehara Sekisaburō, who I mention in Chapter 3, often came to Tokyo from Kyoto to collect payments for the money that Kishi had borrowed from the cooperative.
111 Published on the website *Kishi Yamaji Netto Shiryōkan* (Kishi Yamaji online archive) as Kishi Yamaji and Itō Jun (ed.), 'Watashi no Bungakushi (My literary history)': http://www.kisiyamaji.com/
112 Kishi, 'Zetsubō Keikaku nōto (Notes on Project Despair)' is written in a section of a notebook where union receipts were pasted for accounting. Date unknown. Currently held by Itō Jun.
113 Suenaga, 1954, pp. 191–193. This was written in 1954, before the so-called 'Morinaga Arsenic Milk Poisoning Incident' came to light in August 1955. Arsenic was detected in powdered milk produced at the Tokushima Plant of the Morinaga Milk Company, resulting in a large number of victims and immense disruption for dairy farmers in the western part of Japan, where farming was experiencing good growth at the time.
114 Itō (ed.), 2006, pp. 194–195.

Chapter 3

1 The period of interest in this chapter is from immediately after the war up to and including 1948, when discourses on repatriate issues changed. This change occurred when the problem of Siberian detainees, known as 'red repatriates', became an issue for the anti-communist policies formulated as the Cold War escalated. As well as an extensive study of the 'red repatriates', a general history of Japanese repatriates can be found in Watt, 2009.
2 Nōrinshō Daijin Kanbō Kōhōka (ed.), 1950, p. 111.
3 For an analysis of the political discourses concerning repatriates, see 'Oritatamareta teikoku (Folded empire)' in Asano, 2008.
4 For the policies behind repatriation, see, Katō Yōko, 2005; Sekiguchi, 2003; and Katō Kiyofumi, 2012.
5 Michiba, 2002, and 2008.
6 Araragi, 1994.
7 Miyoshi, 2008; and Kitazaki, 2009. Itō (2006) is critical of the first publication of Kitazaki's paper.
8 Aoki, 2011.
9 Kimura, 2005.
10 Shimizu, 1953; Bix, 2005; and Hara 2008. Another work focused on the imperial tour in November 1945 is Sebata, 2010. The depiction of occupation policy regarding hoisting the national flag at imperial visits is found in Osa, 2013.
11 Maruyama, 1969, p. 151. Narita Ryūichi attempted to retrace what is gained through analysis of the notes left by repatriates from a social-history perspective (Narita, 2003).
12 The first large-scale protests by 'red repatriates' was in front of Kyoto Station in July 1949. Other books about Manchurian Emigrants in Kyoto Prefecture include Futamatsu, 2005.

13 'Nōrin Suisanshō Hyakunenshi' Hensan Iinkai (ed.), 1981, pp. 22 and 34–35. The Reclamation Bureau was later reorganized into *Nōchikyoku* (Agricultural Land Bureau) in 1949, and then into *Kōzō Kaizenkyoku* (Structural Improvement Bureau) in 1972. It had jurisdiction over the training abroad program in the United States as well as postwar agricultural emigration from 1952 (see Chapter 5).
14 'Gunyōchi no nōkōchi tenyō ni kansuru ken (Matters regarding conversion of land for military use to arable land)', Nochi kaikaku shiryō hensan iinkai, 16, 1982, p. 460.
15 Tōda, 1967, p. 612.
16 Waguri passed the examination for high civil servants in 1933. He began his career as a bureaucrat in the Police Administration Bureau of the Governor-General of Korea, then after working in the Ministry of Colonial Affairs, became involved in Manchurian emigration as the head of the Settlement Division of the Greater East Asia Ministry's Manchuria Secretariat. After the war, he held a post in the Administration Bureau of the Ministry of Foreign Affairs, and then in the Reclamation Bureau of the Ministry of Agriculture and Forestry before he was appointed as head of the Hokkaido Settlement Department in 1948. See the relevant documents in Kokuritsu Kōbunshokan, *Ninmen* (Appointments and dismissals); and Hata, 1981.
17 Tanigaki worked in the Settlement Division of Manshūkoku Kōnōbu (Manchuria Agricultural Promotion Department) alongside Hirakawa Mamoru, who would play an important role in the postwar overseas agricultural emigration policy. After working in the Reclamation Bureau, he was assigned to the Agricultural Land Bureau (Hirakawa, 1989, pp. 142–143). Also, Terayama, 1974.
18 Sasayama, 1978, p. 78.
19 This perception was already present in the early days (*Tairiku Jōhō Tsūshin* (Continental information communication), 8, 16 February 1946, p. 12. The Administration Bureau was responsible for the border control administration until the Immigration Bureau was established (Hōmushō Nyūkoku Kanrikyoku (ed.), 1981).
20 This was formed from the Reclamation Bureau; the Repatriation Relief Board of the Ministry of Welfare; the General Affairs Division of the Ministry of Home Affairs' Local Affairs Bureau; the Overseas Legal Entity Department's (*Zaigai Hōjinbu*) Settlers Division (*Kaitakuminka*) of the Ministry of Foreign Affairs' Administration Bureau; the Settlement Department of the Agricultural Association; the Agricultural Land Development Corporation; and the Compatriots' Relief Association (Dōhō Engokai).
21 A copy held by Osaka Jikōkai of Gaimushō Kanrikyokuchō, 'Hikiage Manshū Kaitakumin no Engo ni Kansuru Ken (Matters regarding relief for returning Manchurian settlers)', 27/5/1946, *Raishin Tsuzuri (Ji Shōwa Nijūichi-nen Jūnigatsu Shi Shōwa Nijūni-nen Jūnigatsu* (The filed circulars (from December 1946 to December 1947)).
22 A copy of Gaimushō Kanrikyokuchō, Kōseishō Shakaikyokuchō and Hikiage Engoin Hikiagekyokuchō, 'Hikiage Manshū Kaitakumin no Engo ni Kansuru Ken (Matters regarding relief for returning Manchurian settlers)', 17/7/1946, ibid.

23 This draft plan is compiled in *Noda Bunko* (Noda Papers), the documents of Noda Testugorō, who worked in the Reclamation Bureau, held by the Zenkoku Kaitaku Shinkō Kyōkai.
24 *Kaitaku Min Hikiage Kankei: Kaitakumin Kankei Zengo Shori Jimu no Nōrinshō Ikan* (In relation to settler repatriation: Transfer of jurisdiction over administration of settler-related remedial measures to the Ministry of Agriculture and Forestry), [K–0014], held in the Diplomatic Archives of the Ministry of Foreign Affairs of Japan.
25 Kaitakuka, *Jinji ikken* (A personal case), Administrative Documents of Kyoto Prefecture [Shōwa 21–92].
26 There are reports that a large number of employees from the Manchurian Development Corporation, an immigration assistance agency in Manchukuo, also found positions in sections responsible for settlement in the prefectures (Momose, 1987, p. 242).
27 *Tairiku Jōhō Tsūshin* (Continental information communication), 4, 12/1/1946 and 19/1/1946, p. 5.
28 Manshū Kaitakushi Kankōkai, 1966, p. 756. This association was dissolved in 1948. All its assets were transferred to the Settlers' Self-support Association.
29 Manshū Kaitakushi Kankōkai, 1966, p. 756.
30 'Shōwa Nijūni-nen Nigastu daiikkai Kaitakumin Jikōkai Sōdaikai ketsugi jikō (Resolution at the first Meeting of Representatives of the Settlers' Self-support Association in February 1947)', *Raishin Tsuzuri* held by Osaka Jikōkai. It was also decided in this meeting that they would collectively join the Settlers' League as the Self-support Association.
31 *Tairiku Jōhō Tsūshin* (Continental information communication), 87, 29/9/1947.
32 Nakamura, 1973, p. 180. This document was kindly pointed out by Mr. Sakashita Akihiko.
33 *Tairiku Jōhō Tsūshin* (Continental information communication), 87, 29/9/1947.
34 *Kaitaku Nōmin Shinbun* (Settler-farmer news), 9, 15/3/1948.
35 *Asahi*, 21/8/1946.
36 *Nichi Bei Jiji* (Nichi Bei Times), 29/8/1946.
37 Henshūbu, 1946, 'Hikiagesha Gakkō Senryō Jiken no Shinsō (The truth about the repatriates' school occupation incident)', *Shinsō* (Truth), 6, November. Iwata Eiichi is said to have led various direct actions including the Kyūjō (imperial palace) Incident, 'the Mayday for Food Supplies', the Itabashi Incident (where concealed goods were exposed) from immediately after the defeat, presumably in a 'revolutionary atmosphere'.
38 *Asahi*, 22/8/1946.
39 Needless to say, not everyone was able to stand up for themselves or voice their demands. A survey of repatriates in Tokyo, revealed that 933 out of 4,720 households (19.8%) responded that they were not aware of the repatriate relief organizations such as livelihood consultation centers, the Assistance Association for Compatriots, and welfare commissioners (reported in the third issue of *Dōmei Jihō* (Alliance reviews) (26/2/1947),

the bulletin of the Student Alliance to Rescue Orphans and Fellow Compatriots Left Overseas).
40 Kaigai hikiagesha no engo ni tsuite (Concerning support for overseas repatriates)' (14/12/1946), *Kairan Zattetsu* (Miscellany of circulated notices), Administrative Documents of Kyoto Prefecture, [Yūki (document to be preserved for a limited period) Shōwa 22–2]. The specific actions mentioned include preferential employment in public works and preferential approval for eatery businesses, taking appropriate measures in regard to collection of local taxes and giving consideration to providing winter survival goods.
41 The phrase is from a newspaper advertisement of the Niigataken Kōsei Renmei (Niigata Prefecture Welfare League) placed in *Niigata Nippō*, 17/10/1947. There are also reports of other cases of 'illegal occupation'. For example, an ex-army institute for technology in Kokubunji city, *Tairiku Jōhō Tsūshin* (Continental information communication), 85, 15/9/1947.
42 Sangiin Kōsei Iinkai Senmoninshitsu, 'Zaigai dōhō hikiage mondai ni kansuru shiryō (Materials regarding overseas compatriot issues)', in Katō (ed.), 2005, pp. 589–590.
43 *Fukushima Repatriates' Newspaper*, 5/8/1946. There are reports that a bitter feud between the local repatriate organizations and the central leadership developed into a scuffle during this rally, leading to the dissolution of *Hikiagesha Chūō Renmei* (Central League of Repatriates), which had hosted the event (Koizumi, 1946).
44 *Kyōren Renrakuhō* (Newsletter of the Kyoto Federation), 7, 25/9/1947.
45 One example of the burdens imposed upon imperial subjects is Hirabayashi Taiko's experience during her evacuation. Hirabayashi evacuated to Nagano Prefecture towards the end of the war. She noted, with some surprise, that her 70-year old mother was summoned for the 'mobilization' at three o'clock in the morning, as if this was to be expected (1 July 1945 in Hirabayashi, 1979, p. 128.)
46 'Songai o wakachiae (War Damage should be shared)', *Kyōnichi*, 13/8/1946.
47 The Wartime Damage Protection Act, which was intended to provide compensation for war victims, was abolished, together with the Military Assistance Act, upon promulgation of the Public Assistance Act in 9 September 1946. The government defended abolishing the Wartime Disaster Protection Act as 'the provisions regarding the provision of aid and gratuity are no longer necessary in this day, where a considerable time has elapsed since the war's end'. This did not accurately reflect the situation of repatriations. Akazawa (1993) pointed out the inappropriateness of integrating the Wartime Damage Protection Act, which combined social security and compensation (for war victims) into the Public Assistance Act. This sense of inappropriateness is reflected in the repatriates' struggle.
48 *Minsei Shinbun*, 11, 1/3/1948.
49 Miyoshi, 1959, p. 16.
50 Mizumoto Misa, *Shōwa jūkyū-nen kara: Manshū no omoide: Byōrei Taiheiton* (From 1944: Memories from Manchuria: Byōrei Taiheiton), p. 26.
51 'Fukuinsha, sensaisha narabini hikiagemin ni taisuru jūtaku taisaku no ken (Matters regarding housing measure for demobilised people, war

victims and repatriates)', Administrative Documents of Kyoto Prefecture, [Shōwa 20–16–1], p. 126.
52 Kyoto-fu Minsei Rōdōbu Engoka, 1950.
53 Kimura, 2005, p. 126.
54 Miyoshi, 1959, p. 9.
55 Of course, there is no doubt that government support was absolutely indispensable for bereaved households who had lost their breadwinner. My point here is to highlight that government subsidies were insufficient, reflecting its financial crisis. Kikuchi and Ōmura (eds.) (1964) is a chronicle of a widow who confronted the old Public Assistance Act system.
56 The Takanogawa Dormitory used to be the Takanogawa branch of the Kyoto Army Hospital (*Kyoto*, 20/9/1946). It is reported that residents of the Takanogawa Dormitory campaigned for extension of the period of stay and democratization of the operation as the dormitory only offered several months short-time accommodation and the person in charge was high-handed (*Kyōnichi*, 26/11/1946 and 27/11/1946).
57 Lee Huipal (1923–), for example, is a Korean who had been working in Sakhalin since before the war, who was able to repatriate to Japan because he married a Japanese woman in 1958. In an interview he discussed moving into a repatriates' dormitory after returning to Japan (Oguma and Kang (eds.), 2008, p. 163).
58 Shakaika, *Shōwa Nijūnana-nendo Takanogawa Jūtaku Kokuko Hojo Ikken* (Documents relating to the government subsidy to Takanogawa Dormitory in 1952), Administrative Documents of Kyoto Prefecture, [Yūki (Limited period) Shōwa 27–6].
59 This organization engaged in volunteer activities at the rest area for repatriates in front of Kyoto Station. Nawata Hidetaka was its representative (*Yūkyō*, 12/8/1946).
60 *Tairiku Jōhō Tsūshin* (Continental information communication), 20/4/1946, p. 15.
61 In March 1946, the existing regional repatriation relief bureaus were abolished and the Repatriate Relief Authority was established. This was immediately followed by a consultation headed by Director-General Saitō Sōichi aimed at forming a unified organization, which led to the establishment of the Central Federation of Repatriate Groups (*Hikiagesha Dantai Chūō Rengō Kai*) in October of the same year (which would later be reorganized into the National Federation of Repatriate Groups (*Hikiagesha Dantai Zenkoku Rengō Kai*)). See, Rusu Kazoku Dantai Zenkoku Kyōgikai (ed.), 1959, pp. 75–76.
62 Tadekura, 1967, p. 154. Ikeda, who returned to Kyoto in 1946 after working for the Legal Affairs Bureau of the Taiwan Governor-General's Office as a chaplain, was participating in the repatriate movement with the assistance of a painter, Dōmoto Inshō, when he was asked by the head of Kyoto Prefectural Citizens' Affairs Department to 'create repatriates' organizations by [administrative] regions' (the timing is unknown). Ikeda later served as the director general of the Kyoto Prefecture Federation of Fellow Overseas Repatriates, and then as the vice-chairman of the Kyoto Prefecutural Council of Social Welfare.

63 *Yūkyō*, 22/5/1946. *Kyoto* dated 19 May, reported that 19 organizations, including the Association of People in Kyoto from Central China, had established a preparatory committee towards unification.
64 *Kyōnichi*, 14/12/1946.
65 *Kyoto*, 29/12/1946. It should be noted that an internal dispute erupted between the new and former executives about operations of the organization in the course of this transition (*Kyōnichi*, 23/12/1946 and 28/12/1946).
66 Matsuo, 2002, in particular, Chapter 4, 'Haisen chokugo no Kyoto Minshu Sensen (Kyoto Democratic Front immediately after the defeat)'.
67 Fuke Takahiro includes an analysis of the Kyoto Democratic Front in and after the 1940s, utilizing the resources held in the National Archives and Records Administration of the United States and the Hoover Institution (Fuke, 2013).
68 The Association of People in Kyoto from Central China (Ōtorī Takehiko), As Long as We are Alive Association (Nawata Hidetaka), Commerce Comrades Society (Nakanishi Issei), the Association of People from Xuzhou (Sagawa Kazuo) and the Kyoto Association of Taiwan Repatriates (Kimata Shūsui).
69 Konishi was born on 26 November 1911 in Kōzato Village, Ehime Prefecture. He went to a private school known as Jikyōsha while working in a Sumitomo Machinery plant as well as an assistant farmer. He participated in the inaugural conference of the National Farmers' Union as the representative for Ehime at the age of nineteen. Recognized for his skills by Washio Kageji, he found employment in Sumitomo Pipe & Tube in Amagasaki City as a technical researcher. In 1932, he was sent to Anshan (in Manchuria) as a technical expert, and later became a manufacturing director at Seikō Manufacturing Plant in Fengtian. He established Konishi Ironworks at the age of 24. He then established Kōtoku Metal Manufacturing Company, which developed an integrated process of steelmaking and rolling and became involved in manufacturing locomotives for logging railroads. In 1944, he returned to Japan and became chief of the Headquarters of the Manufacturing Corps in the Munitions Ministry's General Directorate for Aircraft and Weapons Bureau. After the war, he became president of Hirano Steel in Osaka, and then moved on to become the president of Japan Fossil Fertilizer Company (Aomori) and Shinwa Development Company, (Tokyo). Immediately after the war, in December 1945, he formed the Overseas Compatriot Assistance Association in Kyoto and became its chairman. In April 1947, he ran for a seat in the House of Representatives from the Liberal Party in Ehime, but was not successful. In May 1948, he was invited to become the board secretary from outside the House by President Yoshida and participated in the party headquarters' political affairs research committee as an industry planning commissioner. In 1949, he was elected to the House of Representatives from Ehime. After that, following a series of unsuccessful election bids, in 1956, he stood for the House of Councillors by-election from Kyoto and won. This personal history is based on *Ehime Shinbun*, 6 January 1949; and *Kyoto*, 17/1/1956 and 10/12/1945.
70 Makabe Futaba was a repatriate from North China, but her background is unknown. Newspapers reported that she was the representative of the

'Kyoto repatriate women's league' (*Kyoto*, 8/10/1946) which was probably the 'Kyoto Overseas Repatriates Women's League'. The inaugural rally was held on 3 November 1946 at Kikoku-tei with over 200 attendees, where Makabe was appointed chairperson; and Nakajima Seki (later the chair of the Federation of Friendship Societies of Piecework in Kyoto) and Manabe Akiko were appointed as the vice-chairs. After setting up a vocational center at Senbon Kaikan, they opened the Yoshidayama Home for Mothers and Children on 15 January 1947, which would come under the direct management of the prefectural government under the name of Yoshida Home for Mothers and Children (Yoshida Boshiryō) upon the reorganization of April 1948 (Kyoto Fujin no Ayumi Kenkyūkai (ed.), 1976, pp.31–33).

71 Sagawa Kazuo was born on 25 March 1910 in Miyazu Town in Kyoto Prefecture. He joined the left-wing student movement after entering the Law Faculty of Kyoto Imperial University in 1930; then in August 1931, he was arrested as a sympathizer during the crackdown of the local Communist groups in Kansai (the so-called 'August 26 Incident') but released without charge on 29 September. He graduated from the university in 1933. After graduation, he worked in Daimaru until 1938; from then to Japan's defeat, he engaged in research on the Chinese economy at the Japan Institute of Chinese Studies (Sina Mondai Kenkyūjo) in Tianjin, which would later be renamed the Japan Research Institute of Chinese Economy (Chūgoku Keizai Kenkyūjo) headed by Kokushō Iwao. After repatriation, while being involved in a local politics study group (*Yūkyō* 16/10/1946), he formed the Association of People from Xuzhou where he was engaged in the repatriate movement discussed above. Subsequently, he was an official at Kyoto City Hall, but resigned when Takayama Gizō assumed the office of Mayor of Kyoto City. He joined the Japan Socialist Party in 1951 and was elected to the prefectural assembly in 1959. At the Kyoto gubernatorial election of 1974, he supported the chairman of the Kyoto prefecture federation of the Socialist Party Ōhashi Kazutaka against the incumbent Governor Ninagawa. As a result, he was expelled from the Socialist Party along with Ōhashi and others. He served sixteen years in four terms as a prefectural assemblyman during which time he held the post of the 51st Chairman (see, Kyoto Fugikaishi Hensan Iinkai, 1983, pp. 77–82; Kyoto Teikoku Daigaku Gakusei Undōshi Kankōkai, 1984, p. 230, 242 and 310; and Sagawa (ed.), 1974, p. 68). He reportedly handled liaisons and negotiation with the occupation forces during his time as a Kyoto City government official (from interview with Sagawa Kimiya [Kazuo's eldest son] and Arakawa Sueo).

72 The Kyoto Democratic Party formed after the left-wing faction of the Liberal Party of Japan broke away when the first Yoshida Cabinet was installed. It was founded on 10 October 1946 with Takayama Gizō (Mayor of Kyoto City from 1950) as Chairman. For a detailed account, see Matsuo, 2002, pp. 237–238.

73 Hirotani, 1947; and *Kyoto*, 8/11/1946.

74 Matsuo, 2002, p. 246.

75 In December 1945, the Kyoto Consumers' Union was founded by Ōta Tenrei. It was reorganized into the Federation of Kyoto Cooperatives in August 1946.

76 From Kyoto Fugikaishi Hensan Iinkai, 1983, p. 78.
77 *Kyōnichi*, 18/12/1946. The meeting was called 'rally to call for self-support promotion for repatriates'.
78 *Minsei Shinbun*, 13, 1/4/1948.
79 'Kyoto Jimukyoku Hangeppō (Kyoto administration office bi-weekly report)', 24 March 1948, in Ara (ed.), 1994, p. 65.
80 'Shitsumu Hangeppō (Official bi-weekly report)', 14, in Ara (ed.), 1994, p. 108.
81 *Minsei Shinbun*, 14, 15/4/1948.
82 *Minsei Shinbun*, 17, 1/6/1948.
83 Note, however, that a circular from the regional offices asked the municipalities to not appoint non-Japanese nationals as welfare commissioners. It is unclear specifically who was referred to as non-Japanese nationals here, since colonized subjects were Japanese citizens at the time. Nevertheless, it is worth noting that, while compromising in response to the repatriates' criticisms, this is the first time that measures were put in place to narrow the scope of welfare to 'Japanese nationals'. The notice sent from the regional offices of Kyoto Prefecture to the municipalities titled 'Matters regarding appointment of welfare commissioners' (15/4/1946) reads, 'appointing non-Japanese nationals as a welfare commissioner is inappropriate given the intent that welfare commissioners are servants of the whole community who handle certain regions or special circumstances and not of any group thereof, and that they cannot represent particular interests. Hence, we ask to ensure that the appropriate action is taken upon consideration of the aforementioned' (*Minsei Iin Kaisen ni Kansuru Shoshorui* (Various documents regarding reselection of welfare commissioners), Terada Village document [2405]).
84 'Kyoto Jimukyoku Shitsumu Hangeppō (Kyoto Administrative Office official bi-weekly report)', 17, in Ara (ed.), 1994, p. 127.
85 Before the new Public Assistance Act was enacted, a circular 'Concerning the Field of Activity Covered by the Duties of District Welfare Commissioners and their Selection' (15/3/1949) was sent to the governors of all administrative areas from the Head of the Social Bureau in the Ministry of Welfare, directing district welfare commissioners to stop making welfare determinations. The circular asked that consideration be given to appointing people such as repatriates when district welfare commissioners were to be replaced. 'Concerning the Sphere of Activities of District Welfare Commissioners (Children's Officers) in the Administration of Official Care' (31/10/1949) was issued under the signatures of the Heads of the Social Bureau and the Children's Bureau. It announced a policy of 'gradually changing' District Welfare Commissioners, who 'have had responsibility for being in charge of and managing the majority' of official welfare work to date, to a system of collaboration with 'salaried officials' operating on a legal basis. The regional disputes with repatriates in Kyoto contributed to bringing about these changes. Their effect was to take decisions about war damages and social welfare away from local officers engaged in face-to-face discussions with their communities, and give them to government officials removed from the community by the layers of bureaucracy. This change in direction also impacted on later

understandings of war responsibility in Japanese society. The circulars mentioned above are contained in: Zenkoku Shakai Fukushi Kyōgiai (ed.), 1964, pp. 485–489.
86 The Association of Bereaved Families was quiet at that time. Its activities would reach their peak after the Peace Treaty, when they fought for the reinstatement of annuity for their military services, which had been prohibited during the occupation.
87 These differences were voiced countless times in the newspapers. Most of the voices were those of repatriates themselves, but others also expressed their concerns about the way that refugees were treated. For example, one writer said: 'there are those that look and laugh at repatriates; worse still, I see some people even point at them and say abusive things' ('Hikiagesha ni atatakai te o (Give a warm helping hand to returnees)', *Kyōnichi*, 18/7/1918).
88 *Nakagyō Nyūsu* (Nakagyō News), September, 13/9/1947.
89 Kyoto Chiku Gakusei Dōmei no Kiroku Henshū Iinkai (ed.), 1996, p. 52.
90 Ho, 1999, p. 363.
91 The Chinese Youth Corps was later renamed the China Youth Association (Chūka Minkoku Seinenkai) (*Kyōnichi* 5/9/1946), which operated and managed the China Democratic Academy (Chūgoku Minshu Gakuin), the China Youth Academy (Chūgoku Shonen Gakuin) and the China-Japan-Philippine Academy (Chū, Nichi, Firipin Gakuin) (*Kyōnichi* 17/9/1946).
92 Hara, 2005, p. 347. John Dower argues that the 'mass-communications emperor system' came into being because of changes brought about by these imperial tours (Dower, 2000, p. 330).
93 *Tokushima Shinbun*, 25/3/1950.
94 'Heika no gojuraku wa itsu? Seikyoku antei seba yokka (When is His Majesty the Emperor arriving in Kyoto? On the 4th if the political situation is stable), *Kyoto*, 1/6/1947.
95 *Kyoto*, 27/5/1947.
96 *Kyoto*, 5/6/1947.
97 *Kyoto*, 4/6/1947.
98 'Shufuren imaya sōdachi: Fu e "Kome yokose" (Housewives are now standing up *en masse* to the prefecture: "Give us rice")', *Kyoto*, 3/6/1947.
99 *Kyoto*, 13/6/1947.
100 At least, twelve temporary reception centers for housing repatriates and war victims were established ('Onshi Zaidan Dōhō Engokai Kaishi (Ge) (History of the Imperial Gift Foundation the Assistance Association for Compatriots (Second volume))', in Katō (ed.), 2001, pp. 481–482.
101 Maehara Sekisaburō was born in Fukuchiyama, Kyoto Prefecture in 1907. After completing his compulsory military service, he was appointed leader of a Youth Brigade. In March 1942, the Second Kyoto Company of Manchurian Youth Corps Brigade, which Maehara would later serve as Company Commander, was formed by drafting members from regions under the jurisdiction of the Kyoto prefectural government. They travelled from the Japanese port of Tsuruga to the port of Rajin in North Korea, and entered the Dagang Training Camp. Conditions there were so harsh that they lost their first man during their first winter from typhus caused by 'extremely cold weather and malnutrition'. After one and a half years

of field training, the advance team settled in the Kankō Volunteer Army Settlement Group. It was not until March 1945 that the main force followed. At the same time, the age-based drafting of trainees began. Maehara was called into the Qiqihar Defense Command, also in March. The Soviet Union entered the war on 9 August, and most of the remaining trainees were enlisted by the 11th. The remaining settlers began retreating on 12 August. However, the repatriation was exceedingly difficult due to the conscription of young trainees and the detention of leading figures. They continued repatriation in groups but more than 50 people died in the process. The repatriation picked up speed from May 1946; trainees returned to Japan separately. Among 186 trainees who were send to Manchuria, 50 were confirmed dead, 18 went missing and 118 returned home (as of 1970). Kyoto-fu Manshū Kaitaku Seinen Giyūtai Renraku Kyōgikai, 'Giyūtai Damashī' Henshū Iinkai (ed.), 1970, pp. 42–44. See also Iguchi, 1988.
102 *Kyoto*, 6/6/1947.
103 *Kyoto (Yamashiro)*, 8/6/1947.
104 Manshū Kaitaku Osaka no Rekishi Hensan Iinkai, 1995, p. 52.
105 Rakuhoku Kaitaku Nōgyō Kyōdō Kumiai, 1990, p. 83.
106 *Hyōshōsha Meibo* (List of honors), Sengo Nōmin Undō Jusshūnen Kinensai, 24 March 1956, in Shimosaka Masahide Papers of the Ohara Institute for Social Research.
107 'Kanmatsu Kaiin Meibo (Appendix list of members)', Manshū Kaitakushi Kankōkai (ed.), 1966, appendix.
108 Rakuhoku Kaitaku Nōgyō Kyōdō Kumiai, 1990, p. 45.
109 Hyōgo-ken Minseibu Engoka and Hyōgo-ken Rusu Kazoku Renmei (ed.), 1964, p. 213. In Wakayama Prefecture, the tour visited the repatriate relief facilities (*Kyoto* 9/6/1947).
110 'Senroku [East Nagano], Heika no hannichi: Kasanaru kaitaku no shinrō ni sasuga ome mo kasumu (His Majesty's half day in Senroku region: Naturally tears well up in His Majesty's eyes)', *Shinano Mainichi Shinbun*, 8/10/1947.
111 *Kyoto*, 14/6/1947.
112 *Kyoto*, 15/6/1947.
113 In the public notices section of *Kyoto* (13/10/1945), Kyoto Prefecture called for the Manchurian settlers and the Youth Brigade members to 'present themselves or provide a notification' to the Military Affairs Social Welfare Division.
114 *Kyoto*, 20/10/1945.
115 This development is reported in *Tairiku Jōhō Tsūshin* (Continental information communication), 3, 5/1/1946 and 8, 16/2/1946.
116 *Tairiku Jōhō Tsūshin* (Continental information communication), 6, 2/2/1946, p. 10.
117 *Kyoto*, 6/4/1946. The event was co-hosted by the Committee of Relief Measure for Compatriots in Manchuria and the Student Alliance.
118 *Kyoto*, 18/6/1946.
119 *Kyoto (Yamashiro)*, 18/8/1946; *Kyoto (Ryōtan)*, 20/8/1946.
120 *Kyoto*, 23/12/1946 and Kyoto-fu Manshū Kaitaku Seinen Giyūtai Renraku Kyōgikai 'Giyūtai Damashī' Henshū Iinkai (ed.), 1970, pp. 42–44. There

was a mention of the Manchuria and Mongolia Compatriots' Relief Association's Kyoto branch in a report made in April 1946 (*Tairiku Jōhō Tsūshin* (Continental information communication), 16, 20/4/1946, p. 13).
121 'Kokomo onaji kōya: Manshu hikiage seishōnen o Hokkaidō e (Same old wasteland: Sending young Manchurian repatriates to Hokkaido)', *Kyoto (Ryōtan)*, 14/1/1947 and *Kyoto*, 30/1.
122 'Hikiage nōmin no sainyūshoku: Fu jikōkai no igyō (Resettlement of repatriated farmers: The achievements of the prefectural Self-support Associations)', *Minsei Shinbun*, 13, 1/4/1948. In Chapter 2, I mentioned that there were 568 households of postwar settlers in Kyoto Prefecture. There is a considerable gap in the numbers here, in part, perhaps because those who settled outside the prefecture are not accounted for. Other cases were not included in government statistics. For example, the Jōnan Plant in Terada Village had farm land which may have been considered a 'settlement' by the people who moved in but was not classified as such by the administration.
123 *Minsei Shinbun*, 22 and 23, 1/9/1948. As well as those settled by administrative initiative, there were also instances of repatriates voluntarily moving into settlements. Some reported cases include the alliance of North China repatriates settling in the Atsumi Peninsula (*Yūkyō*, 23/8/1946) and the Shima Peninsula (*Yūkyō*, 9/9/1946).
124 The reclamation of the Uji region was disrupted in the course of rearmament and the Peace Treaty, which brought about the restoration of the Uji Ammunitions Arsenal, expansion of the maneuvering ground, and occupation by the US military.
125 'Fukuin gunjin (gunzoku) sū sensaishasū narabini gaichi (fukumu Karafuto)' kankei hikiageminsū teiki hōkoku no ken (Matters regarding the proposition and report on the number of demobilized servicemen (and civilian employees), war victims and returnees related to external territories (including Sakhalin))', *Shōwa Nijū-nen Kugatsu Ikō Heiji Ikken Tsuzuri* (Filed documents related to military affairs from September 1945), Terada Village document [2299]. This document reports the number of people moving into and out of the village for the period from November 1945 through April 1946 on a biweekly basis.
126 Even after taking into consideration that Terada Village was home to the Jōnan Plant, a reception facility for repatriated settler-farmers, the proportion of civilian repatriates and demobilized servicemen who found employment in agriculture was substantial ('Shūgyō jōtai betsu, sangyō betsu, danjo betsu (hikiagesha o fukumu) rōdōryoku jinkō (Workforce population (including repatriates) by employment status, industry and gender)', *Shōwa Nijūni-nen Jūgatsu Tsuitachi Rinji Kokusei Chōsa* (Provisional national census on 1 October 1947), Terada Village document [2335].
127 There was, for example, a case in Taga Village where the entire village opposed the arrival of unemployed manganese ore mine workers, leaving the settlement plan at a standstill (*Kyoto* 10/7/1947).
128 Near the war's end, from July 1945, students from the course of literature of the Third Higher School (*Daisan Kōtō Gakkō*) were mobilized to work in factories and to engage in agricultural work. The main task in

the agricultural work was reportedly to clear the bamboo grove around the hostel and cultivate the land into potato fields. Based on this, we can presume that this type of mobilization of students was part of the premise for the settlement of postwar returnees. For details on the everyday lives of mobilized students, see, Sonoda, 2008.

129 Nishimura Yoshikazu, 'Chihō bunyozei tsuika bunyo shiryō sankō gushinsho (Full report on document reference of additional distribution of the local distribution tax)', 14/9/1947, *Shomu Ikken Tsuzuri* (Filed documents relating to general affairs), Terada Village document [2275].

130 'Shimazu kōjō kensetsuyōchinai nōsakubutsu shutoku kyōgikai (Council concerning obtainment of agricultural produce within the land for construction of Shimazu plant)', *Shokōchō Jikō* (Public hearing items), Terada Village document [2274–2].

131 'Sokai jōkyō chōsa (Survey on state of evacuation)', *Chōsonchōkai Teishutsu Mondai Jūkyū, Jū, Nijūhachi* (Questions submitted to the heads of municipality meeting 28 October 1944), (*Shōwa Jūkyū-nen Hachigatsu Chōsonchōkai Ikken* (Documents relating to the heads of municipality meeting of August 1944), Terada Village document [2280]). Across all areas under the management of Uji regional office, there were only enough desks and chairs for 44% of evacuated schoolchildren.

132 'Kinōshatō ni taisuru ukeire tatemono chōsa no ken kaihō (Circular on matters regarding investigation of buildings to accommodate people returning to agriculture)', *Shomu Ikken Tsuzuri* (Filed documents relating to general affairs), Terada Village document [2275].

133 'Rikukaigun shoyū tochi narabini tatemono haraisage shinsei no ken (Matters regarding the disposal of land and buildings owned by the Army and Navy)', 16/10/1945, *Shomu Ikken Tsuzuri* (Filed documents relating to general affairs), Terada Village document [2275].

134 'Kokuyūrin kaitaku yoteichi shirabe no ken kaihō (Circular on matters regarding the investigation of the national forests planned for reclamation)', 6/2/1946, *Shomu Ikken Tsuzuri* (Filed documents relating to general affairs), Terada Village document [2275].

135 'Nagaike Enshūjō narabini sono fukin sesshū ni tsuite (The Nagaike Maneuvering Ground and the requisition of neighboring land)', 9/9/1946, *Shomu Ikken Tsuzuri* (Filed documents relating to general affairs), Terada Village document [2275].

136 A survey by the Ministry of Home Affairs revealed that immediately after the war, before the 'oppressive legislation' such as the Peace Preservation Law ceased to exist, the anti-military sentiment was salient among the general public. Demobilizing military personnel became targets of dissatisfaction and taunted with insults, such as 'Remnant of defeated troops are passing by' or 'You useless soldiers who can't put up a fight are so irritating'. They were even victims of robbery in extreme cases. 'Kikan gunjin no gendō ni kansuru ken (dai ni-hō) (Matters concerning the speech and conduct of returning military personnel (the second report))', 10/9/1945, *Tokushu Jōhō Tsuzuri: Hoan Kachō* (The file of special information: Public Safety Division director); Awaya and Kawashima (eds.), 1994, 1, pp. 101–102; and Wakayama-ken Chiji Kobayashi Chiaki 'Kikan gunjin no tokui gendō ni kansuru ken (Matters concerning peculiar

speech and conduct of returning military personnel)', in Awaya and Kawashima, (eds.), 1994, 1, pp. 244–245.
137 'Mikensetsu kōjōtō shikichi chōsa no ken kaihō (Circular on matters regarding the investigation of sites for unbuilt plants)', 20/11/1945, *Shomu Ikken Tsuzuri* (Filed documents relating to general affairs), Terada Village document [2275].
138 From an interview with Hirano Tsuyako, a former member of Īrin Yamashiro Settler Group (5/10/2005).
139 'Chihō bunyozei tsuika bunyo shiryō sankō gushinsho (Full report on document reference of additional distribution of the local distribution tax)', 14/9/1947, *Shomu Ikken Tsuzuri* (Filed documents relating to general affairs), Terada Village document [2275].
140 There are clear overlaps with the experiences of bereaved families in rural villages during the war. Payments for the acceptance of these families during the war were made to the village fund, rather than the individuals concerned. These funds were supposed to provide farmers an opportunity to 'recognize the unfolding situation' and 'contribute to the promotion of national spirit' but were, instead, appropriated to support local families whose husbands and sons went to the war. It is likely that this also generated discrimination at the time (Sasayama, 1939, p. 48).
141 Jōyō-shishi Hensan Kenkyūkai (ed.), 1977, p. 148. According to the document titled 'Jōnan Nōkōjō no kanri unei ni tsuite (On management and operation of the Jonan Plant)' by Tabata Tomoo (plant manager of the Jonan Plant), as of March 1952, 43 households resided in the plant among which two-thirds worked in agriculture. It reports that, in addition to fruit, vegetable and tea, the plant operated 4.5 *chō* of rice fields in total, consisting of 3 *chō* within the plant and the rest elsewhere (*[Ryō] Kankei Tsūchōtō Tsuzuri: 25, 26, 27-nendo* (Filed documents of [residence]-related circulars: Fiscal 1950, 1951 and 1952), Administrative Documents of Kyoto Prefecture, [Yūki shōwa 27–9].
142 From an interview with Maehara Hidehiko, Sekisaburō's eldest son (26/1/2006).
143 Rakuhoku Kaitaku Jigyō Kumiai et al. (ed.), 1968, p. 6.
144 Ibid., p. 18.
145 Ibid., p. 71.
146 Ibid., p. 69.
147 Ibid., p. 71.
148 Ibid., p. 29.
149 Ibid., p. 49.
150 'Hikiagesharyō seiri jōkyō ichiran (List of the arrangement status of repatriates' dormitories)', *[Hikiagesharyō Oyobi Hikigesha Jūtaku Kankei]* ([Matters related to returnees' hotels and returnees' housing]), Administrative Documents of Kyoto Prefecture, [Yūki shōwa 38–6]; and *Jōnan Danchi Hikiagesha Jūtaku (35-ko) Nyūkyo Ikken* (Documents relating to the occupation of the Jōnan Housing Complex for repatriates (35 households)), Administrative Documents of Kyoto Prefecture, [Yūki shōwa 43–2].
151 *Minsei Shinbun*, 14, 15/4/1948.

Chapter 4

1 Noda, 2006, pp. 6–28.
2 I will not delve into the research here but one recent representative work is Shōji, 1999. Of particular relevance to my discussion is Chapter 6 '"Fujiyūna tochi shoyū" no keisei to senjiki nōchi seisaku (Formation of "restricted land ownership" and wartime agricultural land policies)'. For a general history, see Watanabe and Gomi (eds.), 2002. In relation to my discussion, see Part 4, in particular, Chapter 2 by Sakane Yoshihiro and Chapter 3 by Iwamoto Noriaki. Another work that discusses matters of contemporary significance is Noda, 2012.
3 See section two of Chapter 5 of Akimoto, 1989.
4 In the prefectural-records of agrarian reforms, there was no direct mention of the issue of Japanese landlords living overseas. Some of these records, including Tokushima Prefecture, did mention the large number of petitions seeking exemptions for repatriated landlords from Japan's colonies and sphere of influence from land acquisition, which was also controversial at the time.
5 The issues of particular concern regarding exemption from purchase of land were: (1) allocation of agricultural land used for official or public purposes, (2) use for residential and urban purposes, (3) handling of agricultural land used for mining purposes and (4) handling of agricultural land owned by people living outside the country (Takemae and Nakamura (supervising eds.), 1997, pp. 65–69).
6 Murakawa, 2007.
7 Numerous lawsuits were filed and the movement to revise the law grew. In the case of Fred Ōyama, which started with his alleged violation of the Alien Land Law in 1944, the US Supreme Court upheld Ōyama's rights of land ownership in its ruling of 19 January 1948. While they did not render the Alien Land Law unconstitutional, it nonetheless practically became a dead law. A verdict of unconstitutionality was reached in the 1952 trial of Fujii Sei and the law was abolished following the state public opinion poll of 1956.
8 Minamikawa, 2011.
9 Azuma, 2005, p. 5.
10 Yoneyama, 2000, pp. 142–143.
11 Tatara, 1999; Iino, 2006; and Ozawa, 2009.
12 Miyata, 1986 is a pioneering study that discusses consciousness of one's native place from a range of perspectives, including annual events, and views on life and death.
13 Dusinberre, 2012, p. 114.
14 As pointed out by Sakane, in Japan, 'to own land' was the very foundation of the family name and family business, which thus was used as a basis for the family's honors and status (*kakaku*) within communities largely driven by the village mentality (*mura shakai*) (Watanabe and Gomi (eds.), 2002, p. 413).
15 This issue was not mentioned by either *Nichibei Jiji*, 1949 or Ochi, 1957.

16 Sakaguchi Mitsuhiro used this term to collectively refer to various newspapers issued within the communities of Japanese living in the US, positioning them as 'the newspapers that provided the backbone of the social bond among immigrants' (Sakaguchi, 2001, p. 14).
17 For the description in this paragraph, I referred to Kobayashi, 1975, pp. 203–204.
18 Ministry of Finance Ordinance Number 88 of October 1945 '*Kin, gin, yūkashōkentō no yushutsunyū in kansuru kinyū torihiki no torishimari ni kansuru ken* (Matters regarding the supervision of financial transactions involving import or export of gold, silver and securities)'. Article 2 specified that transactions of 'any property in Japan owned or managed, directly or indirectly, in part or in whole, by people residing in other countries on and after 7 December 1941' were prohibited (necessitating approval the Minister of Finance).
19 In June 1947, '*Shōwa nijūnen Ōkurashōrei dai hachijūhachigō dainijō tadashigaki no kitei niyoru seigen no kaijo ni kansuru ken* (Matters regarding the removal of the restrictions pursuant to the proviso of Article 2 of Ministry of Finance Ordinance Number 88 of 1945)' was submitted to the Ministry of Finance by the Head of the Agricultural Administration Bureau.
20 Nōchi Kaikaku Kiroku Iinkai, 1951, p. 276.
21 For example, the Head of the Aichi Prefectural Agricultural Land Bureau sent a query titled 'Amerika shiminken o yūsuru mono no shoyū suru nōchi no toriatsukaitō ni tsuite (Regarding the handling of agricultural land owned by US citizenship holders)' addressed to the Head of the Agricultural Administration Bureau in the Ministry of Agriculture and Forestry (19/6/1947, Nōchi Kaikaku Shiryō Hensan Iinkai, 1981, p. 39) and the ministry indicated that they saw no issue with the application. Similarly, the Head of the Agricultural Land Bureau of the Kyoto Agricultural Land Secretariat issued a query 'Gaikoku kyojūsha no shoyū nōchitō no baishū ni kansuru ken (Matters regarding the purchase of agricultural land etc. owned by people residing in other countries)' to the Head of the Agricultural Land Bureau of the Ministry of Agriculture and Forestry concerning the agricultural land that had already been purchased (9/10/1947, Nōchi Kaikaku Shiryō Hensan Iinkai, 1981, pp. 70–71). Their question was whether it was sufficient to cancel purchases only when a lawsuit was filed. Within the jurisdiction of the Kyoto Agricultural Land Secretariat, Wakayama Prefecture was singled out as having a large number of such cases.
22 Nōchi Kaikaku Shiryō Hensan Iinkai, 1981, p. 836. The Japanese expatriates referred to herein did include people who had not been repatriated from the former colonies, but conscripts were not classified as overseas residents, and were thus exempted from the purchase restrictions. This had a significant influence on the Siberian detainees, who were excluded from the category of 'overseas residents', and whose land was therefore compulsorily purchased. The primary focus of this chapter, however, is on voluntary migrants to the Americas who, for simplicity, I will refer to as Japanese expatriates.

23 Later, in June 1950, a directive was issued to reconfirm the applicability of the Agricultural Land Adjustment Law to those who hold foreign nationality. Yamazoe Risaku [Under-Secretary for Agriculture and Forestry], 15/6/1950, 'Gaikoku kokuseki shoyūsha ni taisuru Nōchi Chōseihō no tekiyō ni kansuru ken (Matters regarding the application of the Agricultural Land Adjustment Law to people with foreign nationality)', Nōchi Kaikaku Shiryō Hensan Iinkai, 1976, pp. 713–714).
24 This decision also prescribed the treatment of people from Japan's former colonies. Specifically, it was determined that '*hi-Nihonjin* [*non-Japanese persons*, which refers to Koreans, people of the Taiwan Province, and people of Japanese descent living abroad] who resided in areas under the control of Japan in the past and do not reside in the homeland of Japan as of the date of this memorandum' (19 June 1948) shall be treated in the same manner as foreigners, rendering it possible for the Agricultural Committee to purchase land owned by Koreans who returned to their homeland immediately after the defeat. There is a detailed account of this in Chapter 1.
25 Nōchi Kaikaku Shiryō Hensan Iinkai, 1978, p. 519.
26 Nōchi Kaikaku Shiryō Hensan Iinkai, 1976, p. 663. The attachment to the directive specified that 'Koreans who reside in the homeland will be treated as Japanese' (Nōchi Kaikaku Shiryō Hensan Iinkai,1976, p. 667). The preceding paragraph declared that 'Taiwanese persons who have been issued a nationality certificate by the R.O.C. mission will be treated, regardless of the certificate, as Japanese persons with regard to any private rights and legal matters, except for criminal jurisdiction, as long as they are in Japan. GHQ's Legal Affairs Division affirmed that certificates have effect only when regarding criminal jurisdiction. However, it is imperative that guidance be given on the handling of Korean and Taiwanese persons so as to avoid futile conflicts. In case of a complicated matter, a logical and reasonable explanation should be provided by citing official documents of relevant ministries of the Japanese government.'
27 A query from the Head of the Yamanashi Prefectural Agricultural Land Bureau to the Head of the Agricultural Land Bureau of the Ministry of Agriculture and Forestry titled 'Zaigai Hōjin (nijū kokuseki o yūsuru mono o fukumu) no shoyū suru nōchi baishū uriwatashi ni tsuite (Regarding the purchase and resale of agricultural land owned by Japanese living overseas (including people with dual nationality))', 9/9/1948, Nōchi Kaikaku Shiryō Hensan Iinkai, 1981, p. 142.
28 Nōchi Kaikaku Kiroku Iinkai, 1951, p. 280.
29 For the main instances where a mismatch between family register and nationality could occur, see Gaimushō Kanrikyoku Zaigai Hōjinka, 9/1948, 'Zaigai Hōjin kankei no koseki to kokuseki no jittai ga souisuru omonaru jirei ni tsuite (Regarding the main instances where the states of family register and nationality are in disagreement with respect to Japanese living overseas)', Nōchi Kaikaku Shiryō Hensan Iinkai, 1976, pp. 855–858.
30 The directive issued by the Agricultural Administration Bureau titled 'Zaigai Hōjintō no shoyū nōchi baishū ni kansuru ken (Matters regarding

the purchase of land owned by Japanese living overseas)' described in specific terms when the purchase of agricultural land must be revoked and when it should not.
31 Nōchi Kaikaku Kiroku Iinkai, 1951, p. 280.
32 Kagoshima-ken, 1954, p. 805. We have data on the total area but the number of people involved is unknown. There are statistics on deferred area by cities and districts within Kagoshima Prefecture in the table presented op cit. p. 808 from which we can deduce that almost half of the land was concentrated in Kanawabe District with approximately 55 *chō* (54.5 ha). It is likely that it also varied significantly from municipality to municipality within the district.
33 Kanazawa, 1953, p. 68.
34 The law which allowed foreigners to own land in Japan was passed in the Diet in 1910 but was not really enforced until 1925, when very similar legislation was enacted again. In this process, however, a lack of reciprocity between Japan and the USA was debated. It was pointed out that it would be wrong for Japan to permit US nationals to own Japanese land, while state laws in the US do not allow foreigners' land ownership. The California Alien Land Law affected the debate in the Japanese legislation process.
35 Chan, 1991, pp. 122–139. There is a vast literature on the internment of Japanese American.
36 One of the articles featured a story about Seiei Wakukawa's paper on the Japanese tenant-farming system being sent to GHQ from Hawaii ('Newsman's article utilized in land reform program', 15/2/1947, *Pacific Citizen*, 24 (6).
37 'Japan land reform hits property owned by *issei*', 15/3/1947, *Pacific Citizen*, 24 (10).
38 Reports that Baldwin mentioned the issue of agricultural land during an informal talk with people from the Central Liaison Office and GHQ is substantiated by the Ministry of Foreign Affairs document *Nikkei Gaijin Kankei Zakken* (Miscellaneous documents relating to aliens of Japanese descent), [K'1–1–0–5].
39 'Jinushi no soshiki suru dantai (Organizations formed by landowners)', 1948, *Nōchi Kaikaku Shitsumu Sankō* (Administrative references for agrarian reform work), 8, p. 113.
40 It was reported that, in response to the enquiry from the Association of Absentee Landlords, GHQ's Colonel R. M. Levy replied that the matter was currently under examination (*Nichibei* 24/7/1947).
41 Kondō was born in Komatsu City of Ehime Prefecture in 1878 and migrated to the US in 1920. He was a graduate of Aoyama Gakuin University. He became the chief secretary of the Southern California Central Japanese Association in 1919 and later moved to Long Beach where he worked as an employee of New York Life Insurance (*Nichibei* 1922[1995], p. 316). He was also a contributor to the *California Daily Newspaper*, offering commentaries on current news (Katō (ed.), 1961, p. 577).
42 Mukaeda was born in Mitake Village, Kamoto District in Kumamoto Prefecture in 1890. He migrated to the US in 1908 upon graduation from the Kumamoto Agricultural School (Kumamoto Nōgyō Gakkō). He

began his career in legal services after a period of schooling and then returning to Japan. He played a leadership role in the Japanese-American community. After the end of his internment, he continued to serve in leadership positions for the Civil Rights Defense Union, the Council of Japanese Descendants (Nikkeijin Kyōgikai) and the Southern California Branch of the Anti-Discrimination Committee (ibid., p. 591).

43 See the interview with Katsuma Mukaeda by Paul F. Clark on 22 May 1975 for the California State University, Fullerton, Oral History Program Japanese American Project.

44 Hiraoka was domiciled in Kuba Village in Hiroshima Prefecture. His children are Ristuko, Sakae, Yuriko and Juichirō (Takeda, 1929; Sakata (ed.), 1994, p. 290)

45 Nishi was from Ryūmon Village in Wakayama Prefecture where he worked in agriculture and started a rose nursery in 1920. He continued to expand his business and later entered into joint management with his younger brother Nishi Akira (*Nichibei Shinbunsha*, 1922[1995], p. 451), and Matsumoto, 1929, p. 112.

46 John Fujio Aiso (1909–1987) was born in Burbank, California. He began his law career after studying at Harvard Law School. He went to study abroad in Tokyo and worked in Manchuria helping companies manage their legal affairs from 1937 to 1939. He returned to the USA in 1940 and entered the military the following year. After the war, he was involved in the purge of public officials as a member of staff of GHQ's Civilian Intelligence Agency, from which he resigned in 1947 ('Hall of Famers', Japanese-American Veterans Association, available at: http://www.javadc.org/Hall of Famers.htm (accessed 26 April 2012). See also Takemae, 1977.

47 The article read: 'this petition for the postponement is valid until the end of 1948; and if no peace conference is held and the person concerned is unable to travel to Japan to deal with the matter themselves by then, it will be a matter of course that another petition for the postponement will be submitted' (*Nichibei* 18/11/1947).

48 John Aiso '(Letter)' and the Head of the Agricultural Administration Bureau in the Ministry of Agriculture and Forestry 'Zaigai Hōjin no shoyū suru nōchi no toriatsukai ni tsuite kaitō (Response regarding the handling of agricultural land owned by Japanese living overseas)' (addressed to John Aiso, Maeno and Aiso Law Firm in Los Angeles, California, the US), Nōchi Kaikaku Shiryō Hensan Iinkai, 1981, pp. 82–84. Aiso's letter stated that the petition represented 143 Japanese living in the US who, I assume, made up the members of the Los Angeles Conference of Absentee Landlords.

49 The estimate of the number of absentee landlords is based on 'Nōchi mondai ni tsuite: Nippon Hawai Kyōkai Renrakubu hatsu (On agricultural issues: from the Liaison Office of the Nippon Hawaii Kyōkai)' in the 14 December 1947 issue of *Hawai Hōchi*.

50 This move also attracted wide press coverage in North America two months later. See *Nichibei* 27/6/1947.

51 See *New Canadian* 20/9/1947, 27/9/1947, 4/10/1947 and 18/10/1947.

52 *Nichibei* (25/5/1947) also reported that Yamaguchi Prefecture had decided to postpone; that the response varied across prefectures; and that the

seizure of tenant lands was problematic. An official response stating that the purchase was being temporarily postponed was finally delivered to the Hirano Law Firm in March the following year (*Nichibei* 18/3/1948).
53 'Fight to continue against state alien land law', *Nichi Bei Times* 22/6/1948.
54 One article read: 'on the issue of the purchase of land belonging to our fellow Japanese living abroad who own but are absent from their land, the Committee of Overseas Compatriots reported that they had decided not to accept any special circumstances based on the spirit of constitutional equality as Japanese nationals' (*Nichibei* 25/8/1948).
55 One report said: 'the Ministry of Agriculture and Forestry released an official announcement regarding the enquiry from the Hawaii negotiation to the effect that our compatriots living in Hawaii, the US will not be granted exemption from the purchase of the agricultural land of absentee landlords' (*Nichibei*, 24/9/1948). This article was also featured in the JACL bulletin 'U.S. Japanese informed of land reform', 2/10/1948, *Pacific Citizen*, 27 (14).
56 Nōchi Kaikaku Kiroku Iinkai, 1951, p. 280.
57 *Hokubei Mainichi* 20/10/1948.
58 This works out to be 3 *tan* 5 *se* (0.35 ha) per household, which, though only an average, is consistent with the fact that many absentee landlords were small land owners.
59 *Nōchi Kaikaku Shitsumu Sankō* (Administrative references for agrarian reform work), 1948, 11, pp. 10–11. One of the prefectures cited a case where the tenant land of an absentee landlord was treated as the tenant land of a resident landlord because their family was living in the village. It is possible that such cases were quite common for migrants (*Nōchi Kaikaku Shitsumu Sankō* (Administrative references for agrarian reform work), 1948, 10, p. 10).
60 '"Nōkaihō ni jogairei mitomezu zaigai Hōjin nimo tekiyō" Sōshireibu tōkyoku, gokai o issō no seimei ("Agricultural revision law applies without exception, including to Japanese living overseas": GHQ releases a statement to clear up misunderstanding)' (*Nichibei* 14/1/1949).
61 'The US State Department could not deliver these themselves as they were unsure of the addresses of the recipients. They then found the name of the *Nichibei Jiji* Newspaper Company on the letter of request from the Japanese Ministry of Foreign Affairs. With no other way of locating the recipients, they sent all relevant documents to our head office the day before yesterday requesting that we forward them'. The request was said to have been made by John Allison, the Director of the Office of Northeast Asian Affairs (*Nichibei* 1/11/1949).
62 Cited from Nōrinshō Nōchibuchō, 16/2/1949, 'Tafuken (to, dō) zaijū jinushi uketorinin ni taisuru nōchi taikatō shirahai jimu shori ni kansuru ken (Matters regarding the administrative process for payments such as compensation for agricultural land to landlords living outside the prefecture)' (*Nōchi Kaikaku Shiryō* (Resources on agrarian reform), 1949, 72 and 73, p. 7).
63 See Chapter 7 'Zainichi Nihonjin no "nijū kokuseki mondai" kaiketsu undō (Movement to resolve the "dual nationality issue" of Japanese living in the US)' in Sakaguchi, 2001.

64 The likely motivation for this was the speculation that the law would not apply to people who were nationals of Allied or neutral countries (*Rafu*, 17/1/1949).
65 The headline read 'Nihonseki ridatsu no tetsuzuki Zaigai Dōhō Taisaku Iinkai chōsa (Study by the Committee of Overseas Compatriots on how to renounce Japanese nationality)'. Although I cannot give a full account in this book, the movement of the Committee of Overseas Compatriots acted as a contact point and is of considerable importance. This was followed be a further article titled 'Nihon ridatsu no tetsuzuki (Process for renouncing Japanese nationality)' (*Nichibei* 15/2/1949).
66 The *Hawai Hōchi* of 19 August 1947 pointed out that many of the Japanese living in Hawaii made arrangements to transfer all their properties to their sons who were US citizens in fear that their assets could be seized for belonging to persons from enemy countries. It should be noted, however, that the actual story featured in this article was the perceived problem of the properties given to the sons in this fashion being transferred to their wives upon the sons' deaths in the war. It did not make any reference to the issue of agricultural land. Nonetheless, if the wives had inherited all property, this would have included properties in Japan.
67 Mike Masaoka, *Nichibei* 18/10/1946 (discuss below).
68 Tōgasaki was born in Kawane Village in Ibaraki Prefecture in 1867, the second son of Tōgasaki Hyōgorō (Katō (ed.), 1961, p. 470).
69 In May, a newspaper reported that Yoshikazu Yamamoto, who was living in Monterey, filed a lawsuit in Japan to challenge the constitutionality of the law through the Morozumi Law Firm (*Nichibei* 8/5/1949). Morozumi, who was assigned to the trial, cited a letter from Hozumi Shigetōon, asserting that the Supreme Court had not affirmed the constitutionality of the agrarian reform and that the suit had only failed in lower courts (*Nichibei* 4/8/1949). On the other hand, a bureaucrat from Japan's Ministry of Agriculture and Forestry (Ōwada Keiki) said in an interview upon his visit to the US that no one can evade the application of the agrarian reform (*Nichibei* 5/10/1949).
70 See, *Pacific Citizen*, 7/1/1950, 30 (1) and 22/4/1950, 30 (16).
71 Domiciled in Iwade Village in Yamanashi Prefecture, Seigo Mutō migrated to the United States in 1903. He then worked as a journalist for the *Rafu Shinpō* Newspaper Company (Hirose, 1934).
72 'Tachiagaru Onogōmura (jō) (Onogō Village standing up (1))' (*Kyoto* 13/12/1944).
73 The wartime Japanese authorities took some measures to impose restrictions on landowners by the Rent Control Order of 1939, and the Land Control Order. See Dore, 1959, Chapter 4.
74 Kumei, 2008.
75 In Manchuria, to motivate settlers to settle permanently, the Reclaimed Farm Law was enforced, making reclaimed land hereditary property. This is another issue that needs to be explored from the perspective of the divergence between the state and people over immigration and settlement. For the Reclaimed Farm Law, see Manshū Kaitakushi Kankōkai, 1966, pp. 385–389.
76 This is by no means intended to suggest that Japanese and their descendants living in the US and those in the homeland completely severed all ties after

this. What was severed was an important connection, but it was one of many. We can see from looking at regional newspapers in the 1960s that large donations were made by Japanese descendants living in South America in times of crisis such as natural disasters ('Hisaichi koji ni mimaikin Brajiru zaijū kyōdo shusshinsha no aijō (Natives from this area, now living in Brazil, show their love through donation to children orphaned in the disaster)', *Nanshin* 6/10/1962).
77 Park, 1957, p. 167.
78 Kiyotani, 1985, p. 192.
79 The single term 'absentee landlords' may contain different concepts within it; for example, a response from a survey indicated that there was a rough distinction between 'gone forever' and 'temporarily away'. The perception of the farmers who were living in the villages is yet another topic awaiting exploration in the future. I referred to the comment made by Mr. Yoshimoto from Mikanohara Village in Kyoto Prefecture in Noda, 1989, p. 122.
80 Kawai, 1952.
81 The purchase of residential land belonging to Japanese living overseas became possible under SCAPIN–1911, as an 'incidental purchase' to agricultural land. The timing, however, seems to vary. Nōrinshō Kanribuchō, 'Zaigai Hōjin oyobi nijū kokusekisha shoyū nōchi no baishū, uriwatashi ni tsuite (Regarding purchase and resale of agricultural land owned by Japanese living overseas and people with dual nationality)', 5/10/1950, Nōchi Kaikaku Shiryō Hensan Iinkai, 1981, pp. 254–255.
82 Apropos the gravesites, one major issue of the time was discrimination over interment in the US. Some considered that, in California, it was almost impossible to bury the descendants of Japanese nationals in privately-owned cemeteries ('Segregation to the grave', 4/1948, *Pacific Citizen*, 27 (22)).

Chapter 5

1 Except for the people who received government assistance, the main postwar migration destination for people travelling on a Japanese passport was the United States (Shiode, 2015). Since US restrictions on new immigration continued until 1965, this category was probably almost all women married to occupation personnel (troops stationed in Japan after it regained its independence). In December 1945, US Public Law 271 was passed, allowing the immigration of partners who had been married in occupied territories, but excluding Asian women (oriental war brides). This changed in June 1947, and in the period up until 31 December 1952, 10,517 Japanese women married men from the United States who had been engaged in the occupation (Strauss, 1954, p. 99). We suspect that, even after this period, the majority of people immigrating to the United States from Japan were 'war brides'.
2 The focus here is on postwar Japan, but does not include Okinawa, which was under a different form of rule at the time. Araragi Shinzō (2013)

contrasts postwar emigration from Okinawa with that from the rest of Japan.
3 Kase, 1997, contains a detailed discussion of this. See also Morita, 2005.
4 Wakatsuki and Suzuki, 1975.
5 Itō, 2013, especially Chapters 5 and 6.
6 Fujihara, 2007.
7 Ōkōchi Kazuo characterized the deteriorating living conditions immediately after the war and the mismatch between employment and labor at that time as generating 'increased vagrancy'. He sees the origins of this in the highly fluid labor force that existed between the cities and agricultural villages. He argued that 'cutting off this flow was of fundamental importance' (Ōkōchi, 1946, pp. 60–61).
8 Morris-Suzuki, 2007.
9 Takemae and Nakamura (supervising eds.) 1996, pp. 79–80.
10 Nōgyō Fukkō Kaigi (ed.), 1951, *Nihon Nōgyō Nenkan 1951 Nenban* (Japanese Agricultural Almanac, 1951 edition)), Ie no Hikari Kyōkai, p. 41. (Hereafter: *Nihon Nōgyō Nenkan 19xx*.)
11 Nōrinshō Tōkei Chōsabu, 1949, p.1. If we look, in particular, at the proportion vis-à-vis the total number of agricultural households, this census indicates that there were few in the Tōhoku, Kantō and Hokuriku regions but many in regions to the west of the Tōkai area; we can also assume that many areas experienced the kinds of situations that are the main discussion of this book. There are also reports that at this time there was a sudden increase in overseas emigration consultations at the service for returnees in the Ministry of Foreign Affairs (*Tairiku Jōhō Tsūshin 90* (Continental telecommunications), 20/10/1947).
12 For example, 'Smuggling nowadays, Even girls in Tōhoku being sold off, A Rush for relentless supervision', in *Asahi* (Osaka 14/3/1949). A detailed discussion of postwar human trafficking can be found in Fujino, 2012.
13 Namiki, 1959, p. 168.
14 Regional development after the 1970s can also be understood in terms of this framework, which changed once again from the 1990s, as the low birth rate and ageing population became central policy concerns.
15 Ishihara Haruyoshi, after graduating from a practical course in the Agriculture Department of Tokyo Imperial University, was connected with a movement for people to rehabilitate their lives in the Hyōgo Prefecture Agricultural Association. After this, he participated in the movements to revitalize the economy while he was in the Economic Revitalization Section of the All Japan Federation of Youth Groups, and was closely involved in youth policy. In the postwar period, he was attached to the Settlement Bureau, Agricultural Land Bureau and the Promotion Bureau, as well as being connected with departments that supervised settlement and migration. One of his publications was Ishihara, 1949.
16 Tōda, 1967, p. 612.
17 Manmō Shiryō Kyōkai, 1989, p. 752.
18 Terayama, 1973, p. 68.
19 Nōrin Suisanshō Hyakunenshi Kankōkai (ed.), 1981, p. 286.
20 *Jurisdiction and Organization I*, p. 5. The draft mission statement drawn up by the Settlers' Self-support Association at the start of 1949 declares that,

'we must engage in sufficient mental preparation and technical training to enable us to voyage as leaders in peaceful colonization come the day that we are again permitted to do so'. While strongly advocating new domestic settlement, emigration policy was being formulated (*Murazukuri* (Village building) 1, 1/1/1949).

21 'Amazon imin no boshū oyobi senkō jimu ni kanshi irai no ken (The matter of requests regarding the business of the recruitment and selection of emigrants for the Amazon)' addressed to the Under-Secretary of Agriculture and Forestry from the Under-Secretary of Foreign Affairs (27/6/1952), *Jurisdiction and Organization I*, p. 10.

22 *Jurisdiction and Organization I*, p. 14.

23 'Kaigai kyōkai nado setsuritsu kyoka ni kansuru ken (Regarding permission for establishing bodies such as overseas associations)' directive to the governors of all administrative districts from the Under-Secretary of Foreign Affairs (29/9/1953), *Jurisdiction and Organization I*, pp. 27–28. This contains a request that 'the flood of applications for private group migration be prevented' as the plan is for overseas associations to carry out the duties associated with sending people overseas.

24 Settlement Section, Agricultural Land Bureau, Minister of Agriculture and Forestry, 'Kaigai imin ni tsuite (Concerning overseas emigrants)', in *Jurisdiction and Organization I*, p. 24. Murata Shōzō (1878–1957) went from working for *Osaka Shōsen Gaisha* to taking part in colonial development during the war. Under the second Konoe cabinet, he was appointed Minister of Communications and Railroads. In 1942, he became special adviser to the Philippines Expeditionary Force. After the war, having survived the purge of public officials, Murata assumed the role of special adviser to the Ministry of Foreign Affairs and was an ambassador plenipotentiary for reparations to the Philippines (Itō (ed.), 1959).

25 Kawada Isao, who offered his office for the initial meetings of postwar emigration administration, had also been President of the Taiwan Development Company towards the end of the war.

26 'Nōgyō imin sonota kaigai nōgyō kankei jigyō suishin taisei no kakuritsu ni tsuite (Concerning the system for promoting agricultural emigration and other works related to overseas agriculture)', directive to the governors of all administrative districts from the Under-Secretary of Agriculture and Forestry (9/1/1954), *Jurisdiction and Organization I*, pp. 60–61.

27 'Imin jimu ni kansuru gaimu nōrin ryōshō no ryōkai jikō (Nasu-Kodaira Plan)', September 1953, in *Jurisdiction and Organization*, pp. 21–23. Also, Ishiguro Tadaatsu, Tsubogami Teiji, Kodaira Gonichi and Yoshizaki Chiaki, 'Kaigai nōgyō imin jimu no toriatsukai ni kansuru gaimu, nōrin ryōshō no ryōkai jikō (draft)' (Memorandum of understanding between the Ministry of Foreign Affairs and the Ministry of Agriculture and Forestry regarding administrative work concerning overseas emigrants), 26/1/1954, in *Jurisdiction and Organization I*, pp. 63–64.

28 *Jurisdiction and Organization I*, p. 66.

29 Agricultural Land Bureau, 'Imin jigyō jisshi ni kansuru gaimu nōrin ryōshō no iken no sōiten genkyō' (Present points of disagreement between the Ministry of Foreign Affairs and the Ministry of Agriculture

and Forestry about the implementation of emigration projects), 8/3/1954, *Jurisdiction and Organization I*, pp. 68–73.
30 *Jurisdiction and Organization I*, p. 75.
31 Ministry of Agriculture and Forestry and Foreign Ministry, 'Kaigai ijū ni kansuru jimu chōsei ni tsuite no kakugi kettei' (Cabinet decisions on administrative coordination about overseas emigration), 20/7/1954, *Jurisdiction and Organization I*, pp. 84–85. In 1964, Emigration Agency Regional Offices were established in every prefectural capital (*Jurisdiction and Organization II*, p. 32).
32 Wakatsuki and Suzuki, 1975, particularly section 4 of Chapter 2, pp. 104–121.
33 *Jurisdiction and Organization I*, p. 267.
34 *Jurisdiction and Organization I*, p. 268. The Ministry of Labor also commented that 'in principle, employment security institutions should take charge of the introduction of job opportunities and recruitment of emigrating workers (employment emigrants)' (Employment Security Bureau, Ministry of Labor, 'Ijū kankeihō no rippō ni taisuru rōdōshō no iken' (The views of the Ministry of Labor about legislation for emigration), 12/3/1957, in *Jurisdiction and Organization I*, p. 274. It appears that the later emigration path for coal miners was established via this Ministry of Labor process.
35 'Kaigai ijūhō no kihon yōkō (Basic outline of the Overseas Emigration Act)', in *Jurisdiction and Organization I*, p. 271.
36 'Ijū kankeihō no rippō ni taisuru nōrinshō no iken (Ministry of Agriculture and Forestry opinion regarding the enactment of laws concerning emigration)', in *Jurisdiction and Organization I*, p. 273.
37 Mainichi Shinbun Jinkō Mondai Chōsakai (ed.), 1968, p. 348.
38 Zenkoku Takushoku Nōgyō Kyōdō Kumiai Rengōkai (ed), 1961, p. 12.
39 Masterson and Funada, 2003, pp. 114–115.
40 See, Nihon Kaigai kyōkai Rengōkai (ed.), 1957, p. 64. Nakamura had surveyed Hokkaido as the next possible destination for settling Manchurian farmers immediately after their return to Japan (see Chapter 3). For more on management and training farms, see *Nihon Nōgyō Nenkan 1955*, p. 312.
41 Directive from the Under-Secretary for Agriculture and Forestry, Sengo Kaitkaushi Hensan Iinkai (ed.), 1968, pp. 197–199.
42 There were efforts towards implementing a *bunson* policy at the prefectural level in the settlement immediately after the war. For more on cases in Nagano Prefecture, see Yasuoka, 2014.
43 Zenchū Shidōbu, 'Takushoku Nōkyōren no setsuritsu ni tsuite (On the establishment of the Federation of Colonial Agricultural Cooperatives)', 12/3/1956, in *Jurisdiction and Organization I*, p. 286.
44 Nōgyō Kyōdō Kumiaika, 'Takushokuren no setsuritsu ni kansuru hōsei kyoku no iken (Opinion of the Cabinet Legislation Bureau regarding the establishment of the Federation of Agricultural Cooperatives for Colonization)', 7/8/1956, in *Jurisdiction and Organization I*, pp. 298–299.
45 Ministry of Foreign Affairs, 'Nihon Takushoku Nōgyō Kyōdō Kumiai Rengōkai' (Federation of Colonial Agricultural Cooperatives), 24/7/1956, in *Jurisdiction and Organization I*, p. 314.

46 'Takushoku Nōgyō Kyōdō Kumiai Rengōkai no setsuritsu ni tsuite (toi) (The establishment of the Federation of Colonial Agricultural Cooperatives (questions))', 26/8/1956, in *Jurisdiction and Organization I*, pp. 319–320.
47 Head of the Promotion Bureau, Ministry of Agriculture and Forestry, 'Takushoku Nōgyō Kyōdō Kumiai Rengōkai no setsuritsu keikaku ni tsuite (On the plans to establish the Federation of Colonial Agricultural Cooperatives)', in *Jurisdiction and Organization I*, p. 323.
48 *Jurisdiction and Organization I*, p. 336. This was how *Zentakuren's* efforts in the Guatapará settlement began. For more on Guatapará as a place of emigration, see Shiraishi, 1997 and 2001. Shiraishi participated as a technical officer at the Guatapará emigration site.
49 *Nihon Nōgyō Nenkan* 1961, p. 79.
50 Zentakuren 1958, for example, is a source from the early period. See also, Gotō, 1966; Nōgyō Takushoku Kyōkai, 1965 and 1966.
51 *Nihon Nōgyō Nenkan* 1962, p. 91.
52 Wakatsuki, 2001, Chapter 14.
53 Katō, Kanji et al., 'Manshū Imin o Kataru (Talking about Manchurian emigrants)', in Yamada (ed.), 1978, p. 421.
54 I have not been able to deal with it in this chapter, but there were also repeated surveys of eligible emigrants. An implicit premise in these surveys was that it was possible through proper screening to identify people who were likely to cause problems at the emigration destination; the relentless attempts to survey and supervise people who were going to travel across borders is quite likely in keeping with the structure of the immigration control policy in postwar Japan.
55 'Jinkō mondai no kaiketsu saku: Honsha yoron chōsa (Policies for resolving the population problem: opinion poll by this company)' (*Asahi* (Osaka) 4/11/1951).
56 In 1940, 5.6% of the population of Goka went off as emigrants; nationally, the figure was 0.4%. Calculations from Achi Sonshi Henshū Iinkai (ed.), 1984, pp. 351, 571 and 573.
57 Zentakuren, 1958, p. 149.
58 When Yoshizaki Chiaki, leader of the Chifuri Pioneering Group, asked members of his pioneering group about the conditions they would look for if they were to engage in colonization again in the postwar period, they replied: 'a place from which I would not cross the seas again' and 'a place with no snow'. See Yoshizaki Chiaki, 'Manshū kaitaku ni tsuzuku naichi kaitaku (Domestic pioneering carrying on from Manchurian pioneering)', in Chifuri Kaitaku 60 Shūnen Kinen Jigyō Iinkai (ed.), 2006, p. 191. This work, edited by people who took part in pioneering activities, commemorates postwar settlement.
59 Achi Sonshi Henshū Iinkai (ed.), 1984, p. 586.
60 Zentakuren, 1958, p.107.
61 Nōgyō Takushoku Kyōkai, 1964, p. 51.
62 Nōgyō Takushoku Kyōkai, 1964, p. 13.
63 Nōgyō Takushoku Kyōkai, 1968.
64 According to Shōji Kichinosuke, in 1968 there were 478 settlers out of 2,422 households – that is, 19.6% ('Kusetsu 20 nen no kaitaku nōka

(20 years of unswerving determination of a settler-farming family)', in Fukushima-ken Nōchi Kaitakuka (ed.), 1973, p.306.
65 Chan, 1991. See Chapter 8.
66 Terayama, 1973, p. 67.

Conclusion

1 The 25th issue of *Tairiku Jōhō Tsūshin* (22/6/1946) provides an account of the organisation of the Tohoku Japanese Farmers' Union (*Tōhoku Nihonjin Nōmin Kumiai*). It reports that in Fengtian, for example, there were 1,800 union members led by Tanaka Magohei, who would later become the chairman of the All-Japan Settlers' League. The union's members collectively held 800 *chō* (793 ha) of rented land from Chinese people.
2 *Shūsen shori kaigi* (Council for Managing the Termination of the War) titled 'Sensō shūketsu ni tomonau zaigai Hōjin ni kansuru zengo sochi ni kansuru ken (Matters regarding remedial measures relating to overseas Japanese associated with the end of the war)', 31 August 1945.
3 Nakai, 2011, p. 88.
4 Bhaba, 1994, p. 159.
5 Given the intended policy goal for the Manchurian settler-farmers was to make them self-employed, the trend was that they, almost inevitably, became landlords. On this topic, see Imai, 2007.
6 Those who look closely at this space come upon documents that indicate that, where there was discrimination and violence, there often was 'love' at the same time. However, not enough studies have been conducted on this subject, due to the difficulty of objectifying love.
7 Discussions of the Ainu and their experience of agrarian reform can be found in Higashimura, 2006. For a discussion of the land policy which preceded that, see, Yamada, 2011.
8 For the term 'besieged', see 'Yakusha atogaki (Translator's afterword)' in Habermas, 2004, p. 396.
9 If the fundamental purpose of research is to contribute to discussions based on shared resources, the limited availability of the resources that I have relied upon must be seen as one of the shortcomings of this work. Although it is an immense challenge, I hope I will, by some means, be able to find a solution to this problem.
10 Koseki (1977) presents documents about the anti-base movement. Sugiura (1954) is a report on these movements from the time. Details of these can be found in 'Kichi: Kashika sareru sensō to bōryoku (The base: Visualising war and violence)' in Toba, 2010. Yasuoka (2013) focused on the politics of resistance against the installation of the Self-Defence Forces base in Kashima village of Ibaraki Prefecture in the 1950s.

Glossary

Administration Bureau	Kanrikyoku	外務省管理局
Administrative Department	Kanribu	農林省農地局管理部
Agricultural Administration Bureau	Nōseikyoku	農林省農政局
Agricultural Affairs Bureau	Nōmukyoku	農林省農務局
Agricultural Basic Act	Nōgyō Kihonhō	農業基本法
Agricultural Land Bureau	Nōchi Kyoku	農林省農地局
Agricultural Land Committees	Nōchi Iinkai	農地委員会
Agricultural Land Development Corporation	Nōchi Kaihatsu Eidan	農地開発営団
Agricultural Land Development Law	Nōchi Kaihatsuhō	農地開発法
Agricultural Settlers Association	Nōgyō Takushoku Kyōkai	農業拓殖協会
All-Japan Settlers' League	Zen Nippon Kaitakusha Renmei	全日本開拓者連盟
All-Kyoto Democratic Front Unification Conference (or Mintō)	Zen Kyoto Minshu Sensen Tōitsu Kaigi	全京都民主戦線統一会議
Arable Land Division	Kouchika	農林省農政局耕地課
Asia Development Youth Patriotic Labor Service Corps	Kōa Seinen Kinrō Hōkokutai	興亜青年勤労報国隊
Association for International Collaboration of Farmers	Kokusai Nōyūkai	国際農友会
Central Federation of Repatriate Groups	Hikiagesha Dantai Chūō Rengō Kai	引揚者団体中央連合会
Central Union of Agricultural Cooperatives	Zenkoku Nōgyō Kyōdōkumiai Rengōkai (Zenchū)	全国農業協同組合中央会（全中）
Civil Rights Defense Union	Minken Yōgo Kyōkai	民権擁護協会
Colonization Division	Takushokuka	農林省拓殖課
Committee for Compatriots Living in Enemy Countries	Tekikoku Zairyū Dōhō Taisaku Iinkai	敵国在留同胞対策委員会
Compatriots' Relief Association	Dōhō Engokai	同胞援護会

Glossary

Concordia Society	Kyōwakai	協和会
construction camps	hanba	飯場
Council for Overseas Emigration	Kaigai Ijū Shingikai	海外移住審議会
Curtailment of Business Operations Ordinance	Kigyō Seibirei	企業整備令
emigrants to establish a branch village	bunson imin	分村移民
Emergency Measures Controlling Movement into Urban Area	Tokaichi Tennyū Yokusei Kinkyūsochirei	都会地転入抑制緊急措置令
Emigration Bureau	Ijū kyoku	外務省移住局
Farm Household Economic Survey	Nōka keizai chōsa	農家経済調査
Federation of Agricultural Cooperatives for Colonization	Zenkoku Takushoku Nōgyō Kyōdō Kumiai (Zentakuren)	全国拓殖農業協同組合連合会(全拓連)
Federation of Japan Overseas Association	Nihon Kaigai Kyōkai Rengōkai	日本海外協会連合会
Foreign Investment Committee	Gaishi Iinkai	外資委員会
General Plan for Managing the National State of Affairs under the Current Situation	Gen Jōsei ka ni okeru kokusei unyou yōkō	現情勢下ニ於ケル国政運用要綱
Head Office of Return to Farming	Kinō Taisaku Honbu	農商務省帰農対策本部
Immigration Office	Iminkyoku	外務省移民局
Imperial Farming Village	Kōkoku Nōson	皇国農村
Japan Emigration Service	Kaigai Ijū Jigyōdan	海外移住事業団
Japan Farmers' Union	Nihon Nōmin Kumiai (Nichinō)	日本農民組合(日農)
Japan Reclamation Association	Nihon Kaitaku Kyōkai	日本開拓協会
Japanese Literature Patriotic Association	Nihon Bungaku Hōkoku Kai	日本文学報国会
Jurisdiction and Organization of Postwar Overseas Agricultural Emigration	Sengo Kaigai Nōgyō Ijū no Shokan to Kikō	『戦後海外農業移住の所管と機構』
Kyoto Branch of the National Salvation League for Democracy	Kyūkoku Minshu Renmei Kyoto Shibu	救国民主連盟京都支部
Kyoto Prefectural Settler-farmers' Union	Kyoto-fu Kaitaku Nōmin Kumiai	京都府開拓農民組合

Kyoto Prefecture Confederation of Fellow Overseas Repatriates (Confederation of Repatriates)	Kyoto-fu Kaigai Hikiage Dōhō Rengōkai	京都府海外引揚同胞連合会
Kyoto Prefecture Federation of Fellow Overseas Repatriates (Repatriates' Federation)	Kyoto-fu Kaigai Hikiage Dōhō Renmei	京都府海外引揚同胞連盟
Law Concerning Special Measures for the Establishment of Owner-farmers	Jisakunō Sōsetsu Tokubetsusochihō	自作農創設特別措置法
male farmhand	Sakuotoko	作男
Manchukuo Repatriates' Relief Association	Manshūkoku Kankei Kikokusha Engokai	満州国関係帰国者援護会
Manchuria and Mongolia Compatriots' Relief Association	Manmō Dōhō Engokai	満蒙同胞援護会
Manchuria Colonization Bureau	Kaitaku Sōkyoku	満洲国開拓総局
Manchurian Immigration Council	Manshū Ijū Kyōkai	満州移住協会
Manchurian Settlers' Remedial Treatment Plan	Manshū Kaitakumin Zengo Shori Yōkō	満洲開拓民善後処理要綱
Modern Literature	Kindai Bungaku	『近代文学』
Mutual Friendship Society	Sōaikai	相愛会
National Federation of Overseas Repatriate	Hikiagesha Dantai Zenkoku Rengōkai s	引揚者団体全国連合会
National Farmers' Union	Zenkoku Nōmin Kuminai (Zennō)	全国農民組合（全農）
National General Mobilization Law[ii]	Kokka Sōdōinhō	国家総動員法
National Settlers Self-support Association	Zenkoku Kaitakumin Jikōkai	全国開拓民自興会
New Japan Literary Society	Shin Nihon Bungakukai	新日本文学会
Office for Increasing Reclamation	Kaitaku Zōsan Honbu	農林省開拓局開拓増産本部
Outline for the Implementation of Emergency Land Reclamation	Kinkyū Kaitaku Jisshi Yōryō	緊急開拓事業実施要領
Outline for the Implementation of Settlement Operations	Kaitaku Jigyō Jisshi Yōryō	開拓事業実施要領

Glossary

Outline of Emergency Measures for the Decisive Battle	Kessen Hijōsochi Yōkō	決戦非常措置要綱
Outline of Emergency Measures Regarding the Employment of City Evacuees in Farming	Toshi Sokaisha no Shūnō ni kansuru Kinkyūsochi Yōkō	都市疎開者の就農に関する緊急措置要綱
Overseas Emigration Colloquium	Kaigai Ijū Kondankai	海外移住懇談会
Patriotic Agricultural Association	Nogyō Hōkoku Renmei	農業報国連盟
Personnel Office	Yōinkyoku	農林省要員局
Plan for Establishing Population Measures	Jinkō Seisaku Kakuritsu Yōkō	人口政策確立要綱
Promotion Bureau	Shinkōkyoku	農林省振興局
Reclamation Bureau	Kaitakukyoku	農林省開拓局
Repatriate Relief Authority	Hikiage Engoin	引揚援護院
Repatriates' Political Alliance	Hikiagesha Seiji Dōmei	引揚者政治同盟
Settlement Division	Kaitakuka	大東亜省満洲事務局開拓課
Settlement Division	Nyūshokuka	農林省農地局管理部入植課
Settler-farmer News	Kaitaku nōmin shinbun	開拓農民新聞
Settlers Division	Kaitakuminka	外務省管理局在外法人部開拓民課
Settlers' Relief Association	Kaitakumin Engokai	開拓民援護会
Settlers' Self-support Association	Jikōkai	全国開拓民自興会
Student Alliance to Rescue Orphans and Fellow Compatriots Left Overseas (Student Alliance)	Zaigai Fukei Kyūshutsu Gakusei Dōmei	在外父兄救出学生同盟
Wartime Damages Protection Act	Senji Saigai Hogohō	戦時災害保護法
welfare commissioners	minsei iin	民生委員
Work Footwear Incident	Jikatabi jiken	地下足袋事件

Bibliography

Books and articles

Achi Sonshi Henshū Iinkai (ed.), 1984, *Achi Sonshi* (History of Achi Village), 2, Achi Sonshi Kankō Iinkai.
Adachi, Yoshihiro, 1997, *Kindai Doitsu no Nōson Shakai to Nōgyō Rōdōsha* (Rural communities and farm workers in modern Germany), Kyoto Daigaku Gakujutsu Shuppankai.
Akazawa, Shirō, 1993, 'Senji Saigai Hogohō Shōron (Monograph on the Wartime Damage Protection Act)', *Ritsumeikan Hōgaku* (Ritsumeikan law review), 225 and 226.
———, 2005, *Yasukuni Jinja: Semegiau 'Senbotsusha Tsuitō' no Yukue* (Yasukuni Shrine: Tracing the struggle over 'mourning the war dead'), Iwanami Shoten.
Akimoto, Eiichi, 1989, *Nyū Dīru to Amerika Shihon Shugi* (The New Deal and American capitalism), Tōkyō Daigaku Shuppankai.
Anonymous, 1948, 'Kaikon no nirei (Two examples of reclamation)', *Nōgyō Oyobi Engei* (Agriculture and horticulture), 23(11).
Amemiya, Shōichi, 2008, *Senryō to Kaikaku* (Occupation and reform), Iwanami Shoten.
Amrith, Sunil S., 2011, *Migration and Diaspora in Modern Asia*, Cambridge: Cambridge University Press.
Aoki, Takeshi, 2011, 'Gaichi Hikiagesha Shūyō to Sengo Kaitakunoumin no Sōshutsu: Nagano-ken shimoina-gun igara-mura no jirei (Returnees and agrarian emigrants in postwar rural communities in Japan, 1945–1956: a case study of Igara village, Shimoina district, Nagano prefecture)', *Shakai Keizai Shigaku* (Socio-economic history), 77(2).
Ara, Takashi (ed.), 1994, *Nihon Senryō, Gaikō Kankei Shiryōshū Dainiki* (Compilation of sources on the occupation of Japan and diplomatic relations part 2), 7, Kashiwa Shobō.
Araragi, Shinzō, 1994, *'Manshū Imin' no Rekishi Shakaigaku* (Historical Sociology of 'Manchurian Emigration'), Kōrosha.
———, 2013, 'Sengo Nihon o meguru hito no idō no tokushitu: Okinawa to hondo no hikaku kara (Characteristics of the migration of people in postwar Japan: Comparison between Okinawa and the mainland)', in Tsuneo Yasuda (ed.), *Shakai no Kyōkai o Ikiru Hitobito (Shirīzu Sengo Nihon Shakai no Rekishi 4)* (People who live on the social boundaries (History of postwar Japan series 4)), Iwanami Shoten.
Asada, Kyōji, 1989, *Zōhoban Nihon Teikoku Shugi to Kyū Shokuminchi Jinushi*

Sei (Japanese imperialism and the landlord system in the former colonies: Enlarged edition), Ryūkei Shosha.

Asano, Toyomi, 2008, *Teikoku Nippon no Shokuminchi Hōsei* (The colonial legal system of imperial Japan), Nagoya Daigaku Shuppankai.

Asao, Naohiro, et al. (eds.), 1994, *Chiiki Shi Kenkyū no Genjō to Kadai (Iwanami Kōza Nihon Tsūshi Bekkan 2)* (Conditions and issues in studies of regional history: Iwanami overview of Japanese history vol. 2), Iwanami Shoten.

Awaya, Kentarō and Kawashima Takane (eds.), 1994, *Kokusai Kensatsukyoku Ōshū Jūyō Bunsho 1: Haisenji Zenkoku Chian Jōhō* (Important documents seized by the International Prosecution Section series 1: Post-defeat public security information), 1 and 6, Nihon Tosho Center.

Azuma, Eiichiro, 2005, *Between Two Empires: Race, History, and Transnationalism in Japanese America*, New York: Oxford University Press.

Bates, Diane C. and Thomas K. Rudel, 2004, 'Climbing the "Agricultural Ladder": Social Mobility and Motivation for Migration in an Ecuadorian Colonist Community', *Rural Sociology*, 69(1).

Benhabib, Seyla, 2004, *The Rights of Others: Aliens, Residents, and Citizens*, Cambridge: Cambridge University Press.

Bhabha, Homi, 1994, *The Location of Culture*, London: Routledge.

Bix, Herbert P., 2005, '"Shōchō kunshusei" e no koromogae (Changing into symbolic monarchy)' in Nakamura Masanori, Amakawa Akira, Yoon Geoncha and Igarashi Takeshi (eds.), *Sengo Minshu Shugi (Sengo Nihon: Senryō to Sengo Kaikaku 4)* (Postwar democracy (Postwar Japan: Occupation and reform 4)), Iwanami Shoten.

Chan, Sucheng, 1991, *Asian Americans: An Interpretive History*, Boston: Twayne.

Chen, Zhengxiong, 2004, 'Kyoto no kakyō (Chinese in Kyoto)', in Kōbe Kakyō Kajin Kenkyūkai, *Kōbe to Kakyō: Kono 150-nen no Ayumi* (Kobe and the Chinese: The 150-year history), Kōbe Shinbun Sōgō Shuppan Sentā.

Chifuri Kaitaku 60 shūnen Kinen Jigyō Iinkai, 2006, *Chifuri Kaitaku Rokujūnen no Ayumi* (The 60-year history of the Chifuri settlement), Chifuri Kaitaku 60 shūnen Kinen Jigyō Iinkai.

Chōsen Sōtokufu (ed.), 1924, *Chōsen ni okeru Shinajin* (Chinese in Korea), Chōsen Sōtokufu.

Chu, Soku, 2002, *Zainichi to shite Hibakusha to shite* (As a *Zainichi* Korean and as an atomic bomb survivor), Chu Soku Sensei 'Jibunshi' Henshū Iinaki.

De Bary, William Theodore et al. (eds.), *Sources of Japanese Tradition, 2nd edition pt. 2*, New York: Columbia University Press.

Dore, Ronald, 1959, *Land Reform in Japan*, London: Oxford University Press.

Dower, John, 2000, *Embracing Defeat: Japan in the Wake of World War II*, New York: W. W. Norton & Company.

Dusinberre, Martin, 2012, *Hard Times in the Hometown*, Honolulu: University of Hawaii Press.

Embree, John F., 1972, *Suye Mura: a Japanese Village*, Chicago: The University of Chicago Press.

Fanon, Frantz, 1967, *The Wretched of the Earth*, Harmondsworth: Penguin Books.
Federico, Giovanni, 2009, *An Economic History of the Silk Industry, 1830–1930*, Cambridge: Cambridge University Press.
Foucault, Michel, 2007, *Security, Territory, Population: Collège de France lecture 1977–78*, trans. Graham Burchell, New York: Picador.
Fujino, Yutaka, 2012, *Sengo Nihon no Jinshin Baibai* (Human trafficking in postwar Japan), Ōtsuki Shoten.
Fujita, Shōzō, 1958, 'Jikkan no imi (The meaning of concrete feelings)', in *Kōza Gendai Geijutsu* (Modern arts lectures), 5, Keisō Shobō.
Fujihara, Tatsushi, 2007, 'Gaku ni kizamareta Manshū no kioku: Sugino Tadao no "nōgyō takushokugaku" (Memories of Manchuria inscribed in study: Tadao Sugino's "agricultural development studies")', in Yamamoto, Yūzō, *Manshū Kioku to Rekishi* (Manchuria: recollections and history), Kyōto Daigaku Gakujutsu Shuppankai.
Fuke, Takahiro, 2013, 'Kyoto Minshu Sensen no ichi shiron (An essay on the Kyoto Democratic Front)', *Jinbun Gakuhō* (Journal of humanities), 104.
Fukumoto, Yoshio (ed.), 1979, *Haneda Ichirō Ikōshū* (Collected posthumous works of Ichirō Haneda), Haneda Ichirō Ikōshū Kankō Iinkai.
Fukuoka Chihō Shokugyō Shōkai Jimusho, 1928, *Nōgyō oyobi Saisekigyō Naisenjin Rōdō Jijō* (Conditions of Japanese and Koreans in agriculture and quarrying), pamphlet.
Fukushima-ken Nōchi Kaitakuka (ed.), 1973, *Fukushima-ken Sengo Kaitakushi* (The postwar history of agricultural settlement in Fukushima Prefecture), Fukushima-ken.
Futamatsu, Hiroki, 2005, *Sakareta Daichi* (Torn earth), Kyoto Shinbun Shuppan Sentā.
Gaimushō (ed.), 1966, *Komura Gaikōshi* (History of the Komura diplomacy), Hara Shobō.
Gaimushō Kanrikyoku Keizaika, 1949, *Nihonjin Imin ni kansuru Shōrai no Shomondai* (Various future problems relating to the migration of Japanese people), Gaimushō Kanrikyoku Keizaika.
Gaishi Iinkai Jimukyoku, 1952, 'Gaishi dōnyū no kaiko to tenbō (jō) (ge) (Review and outlook of the introduction of foreign capital (parts 1 & 2)', *Gaikoku Kawase* (Foreign exchange journal), 41 and 42.
Gotō, Kōji, 1991, 'Kyoto ni okeru Zainichi Chōsenjin o meguru jōkyō: 1930-nendai (Situation surrounding *Zainichi* Koreans in Kyoto: 1930s)', *Zainichi Chōsenjinshi Kenkyū* (Research on the history of *Zainichi* Koreans), 21.
Gotō, Renichi, 1966, *Kaigai Ijū Fushin no Senzaiteki Yōin ni Kansuru Kōsatsu* (A study of the potential factors contributing to low overseas migration trends), Nōgyō Takushoku Kyōkai.
Habermas, Jürgen, 2004, *Tasha no Juyō* (The inclusion of the other), trans. Takano, Masayuki, Hōsei Daigaku Shuppankyoku.
Hall, Robert K. (ed.), 1974, *Kokutai No Hongi: Cardinal Principals of the National Entity in Japan*, trans. John Owen Gauntlett, Newton: Crofton Publishing.
Hara, Takeshi, 2005, 'Junkō (Imperial tour)', *Tennō, Kōshitsu Jiten* (Iwanami dictionary of the Emperor and the Imperial House), Iwanami Shoten.

———, 2008, *Shōwa Tennō* (Emperor Shōwa), Iwanami Shoten.

Hashimoto, Denzaemon, 1939, 'Kōreichi kaihatsu no mondai (Problems in the development of cold highlands)', in *Nōgyō to Keizai* (Agriculture and economics), 6 (9).

Hata, Ikuhiko, 1981, *Senzenki Nihon Kanryōsei no Seido, Soshiki, Jinji* (Institution, organization and human resources of the prewar Japanese bureaucracy), Tokyo Daigaku Shuppankai.

Henshūbu, 1946, 'Hikiagesha Gakkō Senkyo Jiken no Shinsō (The truth about repatriates' school occupation incident)', *Shinsō* (Truth), 6.

Higashimura, Takeshi, 2006, *Sengoki Ainu Minzoku: Wajin Kankeishi Josetsu* (Ainu–Japanese historical relation in postwar periods), Sangensha.

Higuchi, Yūichi, 1998, *Senjika Chōsen no Nōmin Seikatsushi* (History of the wartime livelihoods of Korean peasants), Shakai Hyōronsha.

———, 2009, 'Kyōwakai kara Kōseikai taisei e no tenkan to haisengo e no ikō (Transition from Kyōwakai to Kōseikai and the shift to the post-defeat period)', *Kaikyō* (Strait), 23.

———, 2010, 'Shokuminchi makki no Chōsen nōmin to shoku (Korean farmers and food in the final period of colonial rule), *Rekishigaku Kenkyū* (Journal of historical studies), 867.

Hisama, Kenichi, 1943, *Chōsen Nōsei no Kadai* (Challenges of agricultural policy in Korea), Seibidō.

Hirabayashi, Taiko, 1979, *Hirabayashi Taiko Zenshū* (The collected works of Taiko Hirabayashi), 12, Ushio Shuppan.

Hirakawa, Mamoru, 1989, 'Tanigakikun to no omoide (Memories of Mr. Tanigaki)', in Takahashi Shigezō and Tanigaki Osami (eds.), *Tanigaki Senichi o Omou* (Remembering Senichi Tanigaki), Tanigaki Senichi Tsuiokuroku Kankō Iinkai.

Hirose, Shurei, 1934, *Zaibei Kōshūjin Funtō Gojū Nenshi* (50th anniversary of the fighting people from Yamanashi Prefecture in North America), Nanka Yamanashi Kaigai Kyōkai, reprinted in Okuizumi, Eizaburō (supervising ed.), 2003, *Shoki Zai Hokubei Nihonjin no Kiroku (Hokubeihen)* (Publications of early Japanese in North America (Continental North American edition)), 21, Bunsei Shoin.

Hirotani, Yutaka, 1947, 'Hikiagesha mondai no kakushin (The crux of the repatriate issue)', *Jiron* (On current affairs), 2(2).

Hiyoshi Chōshi Hensan Iinkai, 1987, *Hiyoshi Chōshi* (History of Hiyoshi Town), 1, Hiyoshichō.

Hizen, Eiichi, 2003, 'Yakusha kaidai: Makkusu Wēbā no Higashi Erube, Doitsu nōgyō rōdōsha chōsa hōkoku ni tsuite (Translator's Note: Regarding Max Weber's report on the study of farm labor in Eastern Elbe, Germany)', in Max Weber, 2003, *Higashi Erube, Doitsu ni okeru Nōgyō Rōdōsha no Jōtai*, trans. Hizen Eiichi, Miraisha. Originally published as: Max Weber, 1892, *Die Lage der Landarbeiter im ostelbischen Deutschland*, Leipzig: Verlag von Duncker & Humbolt.

Ho, I-Lin 1999, 'Taiwan Chishikijin no tainichikan: Shā Nankō to Ō Hakuen o chūshin to shite (Taiwanese intellectuals' view of Japan: With special focus on Shieh Nanguang and Wang Baiyuan)', *Tankō Shigaku* (Tamkang history review), 10.

Hōmufu, 1950, *Shōwa Nijūyonendo Hōmu Sōsai Iken Nenpō* (Head of the Legal Affairs Bureau annual report of opinions for the 1949 fiscal year), Hōmufu.

Hōmushō Nyūkoku Kanrikyoku (ed.), 1981, *Shutsunyūkoku Kanri no Kaiko to Tenbō* (Review and outlook on border control), Hōmushō Nyūkoku Kanrikyoku.

Hong, Jongpil, 1987, *'Manshū' (Chūgoku Tōhokubu) ni okeru Chōsenjin Nōgyō Imin no Shiteki Kenkyu: 1910nen–1930nen o Chūshin ni* (Historical study on Korean agricultural immigrants in 'Manchuria' (Northeast China): Focusing on 1910–1930), PhD Thesis, Graduate School of Agriculture, Kyoto University.

Hyōgo-ken Minseibu Engoka and Hyōgo-ken Rusu Kazoku Renmei (ed.), 1964, *Sakebi: Hyōgo-ken Mikikansha Hikiage Undōshi* (Crying: History of movement to bring back non-repatriated persons in Hyogo Prefecture), Hyōgo-ken Minseibu Engoka.

Ibaraki Shiyakusho Keizaika, 1965, *Nōgyō Kōzō Kaizen Shiryō (Nōka no Ikō Chōsa)* (References for agricultural structural improvement (opinion surveys of farming households)), Ibaraki-shi.

Iguchi, Kazuki, 1988, 'Kyoto-fuka ni okeru Manmō Kaitaku Seishōnen Giyūgun ni tsuite (On the the Manchurian Youth Corps Brigade in Kyoto Prefecture)', *Katsuragawa Ryūiki Gakujutsu Chōsa Hōkoku* (The scientific reports of the Katsura River basin), Kyoto Furitsu Daigaku and Kyoto Furitsu Daigaku Joshi Tanki Daigakubu.

Iida-shi Kyōiku Iinkai (ed.), 1976, *Ushinawareta Sanson no Seikatsu: Nagano-ken Iida-shi Matsukawairi* (Lost livelihood of mountain villages: Matsukawairi, Iida City of Nagano Prefecture), Iida-shi Kyōiku Iinkai.

Iino, Masako, 2006, '"LARA" kyūen busshi to Hokubei no Nikkeijin (LARA relief supplies and Japanese in North America)', in Lane Ryo Hirabayashi et al. (eds.), *Nikkeijin to Gurōbarizēshon: Hokubei, Nanbei, Nihon* (New worlds, new lives: Globalization and people of Japanese descent in the Americas and from Latin America in Japan), Jinbun Shoin.

Imai, Ryōichi, 2007, *'Manshū' Nōgyō Imin no Keiei to Seikatsu ni Kansuru Jisshōteki Kenkyū: Kyōdō Keiei no Kaitai to Jinushika no Ronri* (Empirical studies on the business management and livelihoods of 'Manchurian' agricultural immigrants: Logic of the cessation of cooperative management and becoming landlords), PhD Thesis, Graduate School of Agriculture, Kyoto University.

Ishihara, Haruyoshi, 1949, *Nōji Kunren to Tai Soshiki ni yoru Shokuryō Zōsan* (Increasing food production through gricultural training and the organization of units), Nōgyō Gijutsu Kyōkai.

Itō, Atsushi, 2006, 'Sengo kaitaku ni okeru Katō Kanji no einō shidō (Kanji Katō's guidance on agricultural management in postwar settlement)', *Sonraku Shakai Kenkyū* (Journal of rural studies), 13(1).

―――――, 2013, *Nihon Nōmin Seisakushiron: Kaitaku, Imin, Kyōiku Kunren* (Japan's peasant policy in the wartime and postwar periods: Reclamation, immigration and education and training), Kyoto Daigaku Gakujutsu Shuppankai.

Itō, Jun, 2007, 'Teikō to hōkai, shoshite kasukana shokō e no katei: Shōwa toiu jidai ni ikita sakka Kishi Yamaji ten, hoi (Resistance, collapse and the process towards a gleam of hope: Collection and supplements of writer Yamaji Kishi who lived in the Shōwa era)', *Tokushima Kenritsu Bungaku Shodōkan Kiyō: Suimyaku* (Tokushima Prefectural Museum of Literature and calligraphy bulletin: Currents), 6.

Itō, Jun (ed.), 2006, *Kishi Yamaji Shōsetsu Shū: Tanba Ariran* (Collected novels of Yamaji Kishi: Tanba Arirang), privately printed.

Itō, Sei, 1983, *Taiheiyō Senshō Nikki (San)* (The Pacific War diaries (3)), Shinchōsha.

Itō, Takeo (ed.), 1959, *Murata Shōzō Tsuisōroku* (Recollections of Shōzō Murata), Osaka Shōsen Kabushikigaisha.

Iwagami, Junichi, 1946, 'Shin-Nihon Bungakukai sōritsu taikai no hōkoku (Report from the New Japan Literary Association inaugural conference)', *Shin Nihon Bungaku* (nuovo japana literaturo), 1.

Iwamura, Toshio, 1972, *Zainichi Chōsenjin to Nihon Rōdōsha Kaikyū* (Zainichi Koreans and the Japanese working classes), Azekura Shobō.

Jang, Boksun, 1999, *Omoni no Okurimono* (Gift from mother), Ushio Shuppansha.

Jeong, Cheonjeong, 1984, *On to Han to Kokoku to: Wagako ni Tsuzuru Zainichi Chōsenjin no Kiroku* ('On' and 'han' and motherland: Record of Zainichi Koreans for my children), Nihon Editā Sukūru Shuppanbu.

Jeong, Huijeong, 1984, *Nikkan no Hazama ni Ikiru* (Living in between Japan and Korea), Futami Kikaku.

Jeong, Seungbak, 2001, 'Kurisu Shichirō den (Tale of Shichirō Kurisu)', *Suihei no Hito* (Person of the horizon), Mizunowa Shuppan.

Jinkō Mondai Kenkyūkai, 1941, *Jinkō, Minzoku, Kokudo* (Population, ethnos and the national land), Jinkō Mondai Kenkyūkai.

Jōyō-shishi Hensan Kenkyūkai (ed.), 1977, *Jōyō-shishi Nenpyō* (Chronology of Joyo City), Jōyō-shi.

Kaga, Kōji, 1947, 'Inoshishi no higai (Damage by wild pigs)', *Nōsei Hyōron* (Agricultural policy review), 1(12).

Kagoshima-ken, 1954, *Kagoshima-ken Nōchi Kaikakushi* (History of agrarian reform in Kagoshima Prefecture), Kagoshima-ken.

Kanazawa, Yoshio, 1953, 'Jisakunō Sōsetsu Tokubetsu Sochihō ni yoru tochi no shobun ni kansuru oboegaki (sennihyakukyū) (Memorandum on the disposal of land under the Special Measures Law for the Establishment of Owner Farmers (1209))', *Kikan Kanri Hōrei Kenkyū* (Japan occupation law review), 35.

Kase, Kazutoshi, 1997, *Shūdan Shūshoku no Jidai: Kōdo seichō no ninaite tachi* (Job selection and mass employment of farmers' children 1955–1965), Aoki Shoten.

Katō, Kiyofumi (ed.), 2001, *Kaigai Hikiage Kankei Shiryō Shūsei (Kokunaihen)* (Compilation of sources on overseas repatriation (domestic edition)), 8, Yumani Shobō.

———, 2001, *Kaigai Hikiage Kankei Shiryō Shūsei (Kokunaihen)* (Compilation of historical records on overseas repatriation (domestic edition)), 14, Yumani Shobō.

———, 2005, *Kaigai Hikiage Kankei Shiryō Shūsei (Kokunaihen)*

(Compilation of sources on overseas repatriation (domestic edition)), 17, Yumani Shobō.
Katō, Kiyofumi, 2012, 'Dai Nippon Teikoku no hōkai to zanryū Nihonjin hikiage mondai (Collapse of the Empire of Japan and war-displaced Japanese and the issue of repatriation)' in Masuda, Hiroshi (ed.), *Dai Nippon Teikoku no Hōkai to Hikiage, Fukuin* (Collapse of the Empire of Japan, repatriation and demobilization), Keiō Gijuku Daigaku Shuppankai.
Katō, Shinichi (ed.), 1961, *Beikoku Nikkeijin Hyakunenshi* (The hundred-year history of Japanese Americans), Shin Nichibei Shinbunsha.
Katō, Yōko, 2005, *Sensō no Ronri: Nichiro sensō kara Taiheiyō sensō made* (The logic of war: from the Russo-Japanese War to the Pacific War), Keisō Shobō.
Kawaguchi, Tomoko, 2014, *Tatemono Sokai to Toshi Bōkū* (Building evacuations and urban air defense), Kyoto Daigaku Gakujutsu Shuppankai.
Kawai, Tsuneo, 1952, 'Konnichi no kaigai imin ni tsuite (On overseas emigration today)', *Nōgyō to Keizai* (Agriculture and economics), 18(3).
Kawamura, Wakaji, 1929, *Naichi Nōgyō Keiei ni Arawaretaru Chōsenjin Rōdōsha no Kenkyū* (Studies into Korean laborers in agricultural operations on the homeland), graduation thesis, Agriculture and Forestry Economics Division, Faculty of Agriculture, Kyoto Imperial University.
Kawano, Shigetō, 1940a, 'Sennō no naichi teichaku: Shōnō kikō kaikaku no mondai to kanrenshite (Establishment of Korean farmers on the homeland: In relation to reform of the system for small farmers)', *Teikoku Daigaku Shinbun* (Imperial University News), 30 March, 806.
―――, 1940b, 'Yamaguchi-kenka ni okeru Sennō no teichaku katei (The settlement process of Korean farmers in Yamaguchi Prefecture)', *Nōgyō Keizai Kenkyū* (Journal of rural economics), 16(1).
Kikakuin Sangyōbu, 1938, *Nisshi Jihenka Nōsangyoson Seisanryoku Jittai Chōsa Hōkoku* (Report of a factual investigation into conditions in rural districts under the Second Sino-Japanese War), pamphlet.
Kikuchi, Keiichi and Ōmura, Ryō (eds.), 1964, *Anohito wa Kaette Konakatta* (He never did come back), Iwanami Shoten.
Kim, Chanmo, 1991, *Fūsetsu Shichijū-nen no Kaisō* (Recollections of 70 years of wind and snow), Ikuei Shuppansha.
Kim, Taegi, 1997, *Sengo Nihon Seiji to Zainichi Chōsenjin Mondai* (Postwar politics in Japan and the problem of Zainichi Koreans), Keisō Shobō.
Kim, Yeongcheol, 2012, *'Manshūkoku'-ki ni okeru Chōsenjin Manshū Imin Seisaku* (Policy of migration to Manchuria for Koreans in the 'Manchukuo' period), Shōwadō.
Kimura, Kenji, 2005, 'Hikiagesha engo jigyō no suii (Trends in repatriate assistance operations)', *Nenpō Nihon Gendaishi* (Modern Japanese history annual), 10.
―――, 2006, 'Senzenki Yamaguchi-ken ni okeru Chōsenjin no teijūka to Shimonoseki Shōwakan (Settlement of Koreans in Yamaguchi Prefecture during the prewar period and the Shōwa House)', *Shigaku Kenkyū* (A review of historical studies), 256.

Kinoshita, Risoji, 1939, 'Naisen ittai kyōwa jigyō zakkan (Miscellaneous thoughts on concordia enterprise for Japan and Korea as one entity)' in *Shakai Jihō* (Social news), 1939, 9(8); reprinted in Mizuno (ed.), 1997.

―――, 1940, Kinrō hōshi o kaerimite (Reflecting upon volunteer labor service)' in Chūō Kyōwakai (ed.), 1940, *Kyōwa Jigyō* (Concordia enterprise), 2(4); reprinted in Park, 1982.

Kishi, Yamaji, 1934a, 'Chiihō no hatten to sakka no tachiba (Peace Preservation Law and the position of writers)', *Yomiuri Shinbun*, 10–14 May.

―――, 1934b,'Bungakusha ni tsuite (yon): Bungakusha no kaikyūteki tachiba (Concerning writers (4): Writers' class position)', *Tōkyō Asahi Shinbun*, 5 December.

―――, 1945?, 'Kashū: Hitori (Collection of poems: Alone)', author's personal note.

―――, 1947, 'Kaitakuchi zakki (Miscellaneous records of reclaimed land)', *Nōson Bunka* (Rural village culture), 26(9), Nōsan Gyoson Bunka Kyōkai.

―――, n.d., 'Zetsubō Keikaku nōto (Notes on Project Despair)'.

―――, 1949, 'Sogan (Petition)', *Chijō* (Good earth), 3(6).

―――, 1951?, 'Kaitaku Jidai: Sōsaku Nōto 1951.9 (Settlement times: Creative notes 9/1951)'.

―――, 1952, 'Nōchi wa kōshite kaihō sareta (This is how farming land was opened up)', *Chijō* (Good earth), 6(6).

―――, 1955, 'Tanba ariran (Tanba arirang)', *Nōmin Bungaku* (Peasant literature), 1, reprinted in Jun Itō (ed.), 2006.

―――, [1934] 2009, 'Shindankai ni okeru konpon hōshin to bunsanteki keitai e no hōkō tenkan (Fundamental principles in the new phase and a change of direction towards a dispersed form)', in Jun Itō, *Ritsumeikan Bungaku* (Journal of cultural sciences), 614.

Kitagawa, Kenzō, 1997, 'Seinendan ni okeru sengo no shuppatsu: Shimoina Chihō Seinendan no undō o jirei toshite (The postwar departure of youth groups: A case study on the Shimoina District Youth Group)', *Shakaikagaku Tōkyū* (Social sciences review), 42(3).

―――, 2000, *Sengo no Shuppatsu: Bunka undō, seinendan, sensō mibōjin* (The start of the postwar: cultural movements, youth group and war widows), Aoki Shoten.

Kitasaki, Kōnosuke, 2009, *Sengo Kaitakuchi to Katō Kanji: Jizoku kanō na nōgyō no genryū* (Reclaimed land and Kanji Kato: The origin of sustainable agriculture), Nōrin Tōkei Shuppan.

Kiyotani, Masuji, 1985, *Tōi Hibi no Koto* (Those stories from long ago), privately printed.

Kobayashi, Mitsue, 1975, 'Nōchi kaikaku to gyōsei katei (Agrarian reform and administrative processes)', in Tōkyō Daigaku Shakaikagaku Kenkyūjo Sengo Kaikaku Kenkyūkai, *Nōchi Kaikaku (Sengo Kaikaku 6)* (Agrarian reform (Postwar reform 6)), Tōkyō Daigaku Shuppankai.

Kokusai Kyōryoku Jigyōdan, 1992, *Kaigai Ijū Tōkei* (Emigration Statistics), Kokusai Kyōryoku Jigyōdan.

Koizumi, Yuzuru, 1946, 'Kaigai hikiagesha dantai undō no genjō to sono hihan (The current situation of the overseas returnee organization movements and their critics)', *Shinzenbi* (The truth good beauty), 1(9).

Komagome, Takeshi, 2005, '"Teikoku no hazama" kara kangaeru (Thinking from the "threshold of empire")', *Nenpō Nihon Gendai shi* (Modern Japanese history annual), 10.
Kōno, Shion, 2007, 'Zasshi "Jitsuroku Bungaku" shōkai: Geijutsu taishūka ronsō kara Ōgai rekishi shōsetsu juyō e (Introduction to the magazine "Jitsuroku Bungaku": From the debate over the popularization of art to the reception of Ōgai's historical novels)', *Nihon Kindai Bungakukan Nenshi: Shiryō Tansaku* (The museum of modern Japanese literature annual magazine: Exploring collections), 3.
Koseki, Shōichi, 1977, *Kichi Hyakuri: Kaitaku Nōmin to Hyakuri Kichi Tōsō* (Hyakuri base: Settler-farmers and the Hyakuri base struggle), Chōbunsha.
Koshōji, Toshiyasu, 2010, 'Tsuruta Tomoya to sengo nōgyō mondai: Rakunō, kaitaku, kyōdōkeiei, nōminbungaku (Tomoya Tsuruta and postwar agricultural issues: Dairy farming, settlement, cooperative management and farmer literature)', *Shakai Bungaku* (Social Literature), 32.
Kumagai, Sonoko, 2004, 'Nijūisseiki sonraku kenkyū no shiten (Twenty-first century view of village studies)', *Sonraku Shakai Kenkyū* (Journal of rural studies), 39.
Kumei, Teruko, 2008, '"Imonhin ureshiku ukete" ("Happily receiving comfort articles")', *JICA Yokohama Kaigai Ijū Shiryōkan Kenkyū Kiyō* (Journal of the Japanese Overseas Migration Museum, JICA Yokohama), 2.
Kurata, Jun, 1938, 'Jūgo nōson shisatsu hōkoku (A report on visits to farming villages on the home front)', *Nōgyō Keizai Kenkyū* (Journal of rural economics), 14(3).
Kurihara, Hakuju, 1943, *Nihon Nōgyō no Kiso Kōzō* (The basic structure of Japanese agriculture), Chūō Kōronsha; 1979, *Shōwa Zenki Nōsei Keizai Meichoshū* (Collection of masterworks on agricultural politics and economy from the early Showa period), 7, Nōsan Gyoson Bunka Kyōkai.
Kurokawa, Midori, 2006, 'Chiiki, sokai, haikyū: "Toshi to nōson" saikō (Regions, evacuation and rationing: Rethinking 'urban and rural')', in *Nichijō Seikatsu no Naka no Sōryokusen (Iwanami Kōza Ajia Taiheiyō Sensō 6)* (Total war within everyday life (Iwanami lectures on the Asia-Pacific War 6)), Iwanami Shoten.
Kuroda, Toshio, 1977, 'Atarashii chiikishi no tame ni (For a new regional history)', *Nihonshi Kenkyū* (Journal of Japanese history), 183.
Kuwahara, Masanobu (ed.), 1976, *Tsuchi ni Ikiru: Nōgyō Boki to Tomoni Yonjūnen* (Living on the land: Forty years with agricultural book-keeping), Meibun Shobō.
Kyōchōkai, 1939, *Jihenka no Nōson Shomondai* (Issues of agricultural villages in the times of crisis), Kyōchōkai.
Kyoto Chiku Gakusei Dōmei no Kiroku Henshū Iinkai (ed.), 1996, *Zaigai Fukei, Dōhō Kyūshutsu Gakusei Dōmei Katsudōshi* (Information digest of the Student Alliance to Rescue Orphans and Fellow Compatriots Left Overseas), privately printed.
Kyoto Fugikaishi Hensan Iinkai, 1983, *Kyoto Fugikai Rekidai Giinroku* (Historical register of the members of Kyoto prefectural assembly), Kyoto Fugikai.

Kyoto Fujin no Ayumi Kenkyūkai (ed.), 1976, *Kyoto Fujin no Ayumi: Kyoto Sengo Fujin Undō Shōshi* (The progress of women in Kyoto: A short history of postwar women's movement), Kyoto Fujin no Ayumi Kenkyūkai.

Kyoto Furitsu Sōgō Shiryōkan, 1970, *Kyoto-fu Tōkei Shiryōshū: Hyakunen no Tōkei 2 (Nōrin Suisan, Shōkō)* (Collection of Kyoto prefectural statistics: One hundred years of statistics 2 (agriculture, fishery, commerce and industry)), Kyoto-fu.

Kyoto Teikoku Daigaku Gakusei Undōshi Kankōkai, 1984, *Kyoto Teikoku Daigaku Gakusei Undōshi* (History of the student movement at Kyoto Imperial University), Shōwadō.

Kyoto Teikoku Daigaku Nōrin Keizaigaku Kyōshitsu, 2006, *Nōka Keizai Chōsabo* (Farm household economic survey records), DVD edition, Fuji Shuppan.

Kyoto-fu, 1955, *Kyoto-fu Hikiagesharyō, Kaku Shisetsu Gaiyō* (Overview of Repatriates' dormitory and other facilities, 1953–1955), Kyoto-fu.

Kyoto-fu, 1973, *Kaitaku no Ayumi* (History of settlement), Kyoto-fu.

Kyoto-fu Manshū Kaitaku Seinen Giyūtai Renraku Kyōgikai 'Giyūtai Damashī' Henshū Iinkai (ed.), 1970, *Giyūtai Damashī: Manshū Kaitaku Kyoto Chūtai no Rekishi* (Spirit of the volunteer army: History of the Kyoto company of pioneering Manchuria), Kyoto-fu Manshū Kaitaku Seinen Giyūtai Renraku Kyōgikai.

Kyoto-fu Minsei Rōdōbu Engoka, 1950, *Shōwa Nijūgo-nendo Minsei Antei Seigyō Shikin Ikken* (Documents relating to the fund for operating business for livelihood stabilization in the 1950 financial year), Kyoto-fu.

Kyoto-fu Nōchi Kaikakushi Hensan Iinkai (ed.), 1980, *Kyoto-fu Nōchi Kaikakushi* (History of agrarian reform in Kyoto Prefecture), Kyoto-fu Nōgyō Kaigi.

Kyoto-fu Nōchibu Nōchi Kaitakuka, 1953, *Nōchi Kaitaku no Genkyō* (Current agricultural land reclamation situation), Kyoto-fu Nōgyō Kakigi.

Kyoto-fu Nōgyō Kyōdō Kumiai Chūōkai (ed.), 1968, *Kyotofu Nōgyōkaishi* (History of agricultural associations in Kyoto Prefecture), Kyoto-fu Nōgyō Kyōdō Kumiai Chūōkai.

Kyoto-fu Rusu Kazoku Dōmei Hikiage Undō no Kiroku Henshū Iinkai (ed.), 1962, *Kyoto-fu Rusu Kazoku Dōmei Hikiage Undō no Kiroku* (Record of repatriate movements by the Kyoto Alliance of the Families Left Behind), Kyoto-fu Rusu Kazoku Dōmei Hikiage Undō no Kiroku Henshū Iinkai.

Kyoto-fu, 1955, *Kyoto-fu Hikiagesharyō Kaku Shisetsu Gaiyō Shōwa 28–30-nen* (Overview of dormitories and facilities for returnees in Kyoto Prefecture 1953–1955).

Laclau, Ernesto, 2007, *On Populist Reason*, London: Verso.

Lee, Jeonghui, 2012, *Chōsen Kakyō to Kindai Higashi Ajia* (Chinese in Korea and modern East Asia), Kyoto Daigaku Gakujutsu Shuppankai.

Lee, Silgeun, 2006, *Pride: Kyōsei e no Michi Watashi to Hiroshima* (Pride: Road to co-existence, Hiroshima and I), Chōbunsha.

Maeda, Kazuo, 1991, 'Gakudō sokai shi kenkyū nōto (Research notes on the history of the evacuation of schoolchildren)', *Rikkyō Daigaku Kyōiku*

Gakka Kenkyū Nenpō (Annual report of the Department of Education, Rikkyo University), 35.
Mainichi Shinbun Jinkō Mondai Chōsakai (ed.), 1968, *Sekai no Jinkō 2* (World population 2), Mainichi Shinbun Jinkō Mondai Chōsakai.
Manmō Shiryō Kyōkai, 1989, *Manshū Jinmei Jiten Chū* (Biographical dictionary of Manchuria: Volume 2), Nihon Tosho Sentā.
Manshū Ijū Kyōkai, 1941, *Tairiku Kinō Kaitakumin* (Return to agriculture continental emigration), pamphlet.
Manshū Kaitaku Osaka no Rekishi Hensan Iinkai, 1995, *Manshū Kaitaku Osaka no Rekishi* (Osaka's history of Manchurian settlement)', Osaka Jikōkai.
Manshū Kaitakushi Kankōkai, 1966, *Manshū Kaitakushi* (History of Manchurian settlement), Manshū Kaitakushi Kankōkai.
Maruyama, Masao, 1969, 'Nationalism in Japan', *Thought and Behavior in Modern Japanese Politics, expanded edition*, New York: Oxford University Press.
Masterson, Daniel M. and Sayaka Funada, 2003, 'The Japanese in Peru and Brazil: a comparative perspective', in Samuel L. Baily and Eduardo Jose Miguez, *Mass Migration to Modern Latin America*, Wilmington: Scholarly Resources Inc.
Matsumoto, Motomitsu, 1929, *Kashū Jinbutsu Taikan: Nanka no Maki* (Japanese who's who in California: Grand Japanese who's who in America. Part of Southern California), reprinted in Eizaburō Okuizumi (supervising ed.), 2003, *Shoki Zai Hokubei Nihonjin no Kiroku (Hokubeihen)* (Publications of early Japanese in North America (Continental North American edition)), 10, Bunsei Shoin.
Matsuo, Takayoshi, 2002, *Sengo Nihon e no Shuppatsu* (Starting point of postwar Japan), Iwanami Shoten.
Michiba, Chikanobu, 2002, 'Atarashii nanmin: Sengo kaitaku to nōmin tōsō (New refugees: Postwar settlement and farmers' struggle)', *Gendai Shisō* (La revue de la pensée d'aujourd'hui), 30(13).
———, 2008, '"Sengo kaitaku" saikō (Rethinking "postwar settlement")', *Rekishigaku Kenkyū* (Journal of historical studies), 846.
Minakami, Tsutomu, 1977, 'Tanba Shūzan', *Minakami Tsutomu Zenshū 20-kan* (Collected works of Minakami Tsutomu, vol. 20), Chūō Kōronsha.
Minamikawa, Fuminori, 2007, *'Nikkei Amerikajin' no Rekishi Shakaigaku* (The historical sociology of 'Japanese Americans'), Sairyūsha.
———, 2011, 'Sedai no kotoba de esunishitī o kataru: Nikkei imin wa ikani "Nikkei Amerikajin" ni nattanoka (Speaking of ethnicity using generational language: How did Japanese migrants become "Japanese Americans")', in Nihon Imin Gakkai (ed.).
Miyamoto, Tsuneichi, 2006, 'Yūryō jikkō kumiai katsudō jōkyō shisatsu hōkoku (Report on the inspection of the state of activities of eminent practice associations), *Miyamoto Tsuneichi Chosakushū 46: Shinnōson e no Teigen I* (Collection of works by Miyamoto Tsuneichi 46: Proposals for new rural villages I), Miraisha.
Miyanishi, Naoki, 1982, 'Kishi Yamaji no gyōseki to jinmin sensen (Kishi Yamaji's achievements and the popular front)', *Osaka Rōdō Undōshi Kenkyū* (Research on the history of the labor movement in Osaka), 7.

Miyata, Noboru, 1986, 'Nikkei imin no "kuni" ishiki (Japanese emigrants' consciousness of their native country)', *Gendai to Minzoku (Nihon Minzoku Bunka Taikei 12)* (Modern times and folklore (Compendium of Japanese folkloristics 12)), Shōgakukan.
Miyoshi, Akira, 1959, 'Hinkon kaisō to shite no hikiagesha no engo ni tsuite (On relief for repatriates as the poor)', *Meiji Gakuin Ronsō* (The Meiji-Gakuin review), 52(1).
Miyoshi, Yutaka, 2008, *Kōreichi Rakunō no Sōchi Keisei Katei to Rekishi* (A historical study on the formation processes of grassland in dairy farming in highlands), Nōrin Tōkei Kyōkai.
Mizoguchi, Saburō, 1943, 'Kōkoku nōson kakuritsu to tochi kairyō (Establishment of Imperial farming villages and land improvement)', *Nōsei* (Agricultural policy), 5(10).
Mizuno, Naoki (ed.), 1997, *Kyoto ni okeru Chōsenjin no Rekishi, Shiryōshū (Daiissatsu)* (Collection of resources on the history of Koreans in Kyoto (Part 1)), Sekai Jinken Mondai Kenkyū Sentā.
Mizushima, Haruo and Miyake, Katsuo, 1942, 'Nai-Sen konketsu mondai (Japanese-Korean mixed-blood problem), in Nakayama, Yoshio (ed.), *Jinkō Seisaku to Kokudo Keikaku* (Population policy and national land planning), Jinkō Mondai Kenkyūkai.
Mizuta, Naomasa, (ed.), 1976, *Shiryō Senshū, Tōyō Takushoku Gaisha (Yūhō Shirīzu 21)* (Selection of documents: Oriental Development Company (Yūhō series 21)), Yūhō Kyōkai.
Momose, Takeshi, 1987, 'Naichi kaitaku de katsuyaku shita Mantakujin gunzō ((Portraits of Manchurian settlers who played an active role in the reclamation of mainland Japan)', in Mantakukai, *Zero Kara no Saishuppatsu* (Starting again from zero), Mantakukai.
Mori, Hatsuya, 1945, *Naichi Zaijū Hantōjin Mondai: Nōkō Tenkan Keikō to no Kanren ni tsuite* (The problem of Koreans living on the homeland: links with changing agricultural trends), graduation thesis, Division of Agriculture and Forestry Economics, Faculty of Agriculture, Kyoto Imperial University.
Mori, Takemaro, 2005, 'Sōryokusen, fashizumu, sengo kaikaku (Total war, fascism and postwar reform)', *Naze Ima Ajia Taiheiyō Sensō ka (Iwanami Kōza Ajia Taiheiyō Sensō 1)* (Why now the Asia Pacific War? (Iwanami lectures on the Asia-Pacific War 6)), Iwanami Shoten.
Morita, Akira, 2005, 'Sengo no jisannan mondai (The problem of second and third sons in the postwar period)', in Tabata, Tamotsu and Ōuchi, Masatoshi (eds.), *Nōson Shakaishi (Sengo Nihon no Shokuryō, Nōgyō, Nōson 11)* (History of agricultural villages (Food, agriculture, and rural villages in postwar Japan)), Nōrin Tōkei Kyōkai.
Morita, Yoshio, 1955, *Zainichi Chōsenjin Shogū no Suii to Genjō* (Changes in the treatment of Zainichi Koreans and the current situation), Hōmu Kensyūjo.
Morris-Suzuki, Tessa, 2007, *Exodus to North Korea: Shadows from Japan's Cold War*, Plymouth: Rowman & Littlefield.
Mouffe, Chantal, 2005, *On the Political*, New York: Routledge.
Murakami, Yoshikazu, and Hashimoto, Seiichi (eds.), 1997, *Kindai Gaikokujin*

Kankei Hōrei Nenpyō (Chronological table of contemporary laws and regulations related to foreigners), Akashi Shoten.
Murakawa, Yōko, 2007, *Kyōkaisenjō no Shiminken* (Citizenship on the boundaries), Ochanomizu Shobō.
Nagae, Masakazu, 2001, 'Sengo kyōdō keiei to kyōdō shugi (Cooperative farm management in the postwar period and cooperativism)', *Rekishigaku Kenkyū* (Journal of historical studies), 755.
Nagano-ken (ed.), 1988, *Nagano-kenshi Kindai Siryō Hen* (Nagano Prefectural History: Modern History Sources), 4.
Naikaku Seido Hyakunenshi Hensan Iinkai (ed.), 1985, *Naikaku Seido Hyakunenshi (ge)* (One hundred-year history of the Cabinet system (2nd volume)), Naikaku Kanbō.
Nakai, Hisao, 2011, *Saigai ga Hontō ni Osotta toki* (When the disaster really hit), Misuzu Shobō.
Nakai, Seijirō, 1943, *Ten Haigyōsha no Shinro* (The path of people who had ceased working or changed occupation), Yōbunsha.
Nakamura, Kōjirō, 1973, *Genya ni Ikiru* (Living a wild life), Kaitakushi Kankōkai.
Nakamura, Satoru, 1991, *Kindai Sekaishizō no Saikōsei: Higashi Ajia no Shiten Kara* (Reconstruction of the image of modern world history: From the perspective of East Asia), Aoki Shoten.
Nakano, Shigeharu, 1998, 'Sokai shita bungakusha e, sokai sakka no iru tochi no hitobito e (For the literati who evacuated and for the people of the places to which writers evacuated)', *Teihonban Nakano Shigeharu Zenshū* (Collected works of Nakano Shigeharu standard edition), 27, Chikuma Shobō. First published in January 1946, in Shin-Nihon Bungaku Sōkan Junbi Iinkai, *Shin-Nihon Bungaku sōkan junbigō* (Inaugural preparatory issue of nova japana lieraturo).
Namiki, Masayoshi, 1959, 'Sangyō rōdōsha no keisei to nōka jinkō (Formation of industrial workers and agricultural population)', in Tōbata, Seiichi and Uno, Kōzō (eds.), *Nihon Shihon Shugi to Nōgyō* (The peasant farmer and capitalism), Iwanami Shoten.
Narita, Ryūichi, 2003, '"Hikiage" ni kansuru joshō (Introduction to "repatriation")', *Shisō* (Thought), 955.
Ngai, Mae. M, 2004, *Impossible Subject*, Princeton: Princeton University Press.
Nichibei Jiji, 1949, *Kikan Fukkōshi Narabi Jūshoroku* (Evacuation resettlement report and 1948 Japanese directory), Nichibei Jiji.
Nichibei Shinbunsha, 1922, *Zaibei Nihonjin Jinmei Jiten* (Japanese who's who in America), reprinted as (1995) *Nikkei Imin Jinmei Jiten (Hokubei Hen)* (Dictionary of names of Japanese migrants (North America edition)), 1, Nihon Tosho Sentā.
Nihon Dobokushi Hensan Iinkai (ed.), 1973, *Nihon Dobokushi: Shōwa 16-nen—Shōwa 40-nen* (History of civil engineering in Japan, 1941–1965), Doboku Gakkai.
Nihon Imin Gakkai (ed.), 2011, *Imin Kenkyū to Tabunka Kyōsei* (Migration studies and multicultural symbiosis), Ochanomizu Shobō.
Nihon Kaigai Kyōkai Rengōkai, 1957, *Shōwa Sanjūni-nendo Nōgyō Ijūsha*

Kōshūkai Jisshi Hōkokusho (Report of the 1957 information session for agricultural emigrants), brochure.
Nishida, Yoshiaki and Kase, Kazutoshi (eds.), 2000, *Kōdo Seichōki no Nōgyō Mondai* (Agricultural issues in the high growth period), Nihon Keizai Hyōronsha.
Nōchi Kaikaku Kiroku Iinkai, 1951, *Nōchi Kaikaku Tenmatsu Gaiyō* (Summary account of agrarian reform), Nōsei Chōsa Kai.
Nōchi Kaikaku Shiryō Hensan Iinkai (ed.), 1976, 1978, 1981 and 1982 *Nōchi Kaikaku Shiryō Shūsei* (Compilation of sources on agrarian reform), 4, 9, 15 and 16, Nōsei Chōsa Kai.
Nōchi Seido Shiryō Shūsei Hensan Iinkai (ed.),1972, *Senji Nōchi Rippō ni Kansuru Shiryō (Nōchi Seido Shiryō Shūsei 10)* (Resources regarding wartime agricultural land legislation (Compilation of sources on agricultural systems 10), Ochanomizu Shobō.
Noda, Kimio, 1989, *Senkanki Nōgyō Mondai no Kiso Kōzō* (Basic structure of agricultural issues in the interwar period), Bunrikaku.
———, 2006, 'Sekai nōgyō ruikei to Nihon nōgyō (Types of world agriculture and Japanese agriculture)', *at*, 6.
———, 2008, 'Nihon shōnōron no aporia (The aporia in small farmer arguments)' in Imanishi, Hajime (ed.), *Sekai Shisutemu to Higashi Ajia* (The world system and East Asia), Nihon Keizai Hyōronsha.
———, 2012, *Nihon Nōgyō no Hatten Ronri (Meicho ni Manabu Chiiki no Kosei 5)* (The logic of the development of Japanese agriculture (Individual characters of different regions learnt from classics)), Nōsan Gyoson Bunka Kyōkai.
Noda, Kimio (ed.), 2003, *Senji Taiseiki (Sengo Nihon no Shokuryō, Nōgyō, Nōson 1)* (The wartime regime period (Food supply, agriculture and villages in postwar Japan I)), Nōrin Tōkei Kyōkai.
Nōgyō Takushoku Kyōkai, 1964, *Nōka Keiei no Jittai kara mita Kaigai Nōgyō Takushoku no Hitsuyōsei* (The need for overseas agricultural settlement from the perspective of the actual condition of farm management), Nōgyō Takushoku Kyōkai.
———, 5, *Iwate-ken Okunakayama Kaitakusha no Shūdan Nanbei Nōgyō Ijū* (Group agricultural emigration to South America of settlers in Okunakayama of Iwate Prefecture), brochure.
———, 1966, *Sanson Nōka no Jittai kara mita Nōgyō Takushoku no Jūyōsei* (The importance of agricultural settlement from the perspective of the actual condition of village farmers), brochure.
———, 1968, *Kaigai Nōgyō Ijūsha Sōshutsu Nōson Jittai Chōsa Hōkokusho Dai 1-sshū* (Report of a factual investigation into villages that sent off overseas agricultural emigrants volume 1), brochure.
Nōgyō Takushoku Kyōkai (ed.), 1965, *Sengo Kaigai Nōgyō Ijū no Shokan to Kikō* (The jurisdiction and organization of postwar overseas agricultural emigration), Nōgyō Takushoku Kyōkai.
Nojiri, Shigeo, 1947, 'Shitsugyō jinkō no kinō to nōson kajō rōdōryoku no seikaku (Return to farming by the unemployed population and the nature of the surplus agricultural labor force in farming villages)', *Nōsei Hyōron* (Agricultural Administration Critique), 1(3) and (4).

Nōrin Daijin Kanbō Sōmuka, 1957 and 1972, *Nōrin Gyōseishi* (History of agricultural administration), 1 and 6, Nōrin Kyōkai.
Nōrin Suisanshō Hyakunenshi Hensan Iinkai (ed.), 1981, *Nōrin Suisanshō Hyakunenshi* (The one hundred-year history of the Ministry of Agriculture, Forestry and Fisheries), supplementary volume, Nōrin Suisanshō Hyakunenshi Kanko Iinkai.
Nōrinshō Daijin Kanbō Kōhōka (ed.), 1950, *Nōrin Suisan Nenkan* (Statistical agriculture, forestry and fishery yearbook), Nihon Nōson Chōsa Kai.
Nōrinshō Kōchika, 1941, 'Kōgenchi no kaihatsu (Development of high plains),' *Shūhō* (Weekly bulletin), 245, 18 June.
Nōrinshō Kyoto Nōchi Jimukyoku, 1949, *Shōwa Nijūyonen Nōka Keizai Chōsa Hōkokusho: Kyoto-fu Goma Kaitaku Chiku* (The 1949 report of the economic investigation of agricultural households: Kyoto Prefecture Goma settlement area), Nōsangyoson Bunka Kyokai Toshokan, Kondō Yasuo Bunko.
Nōrinshō Nōseikyoku, 1943, *Saikin ni okeru Naichi Zaijū Hantōjin no Nōkō e no Tenkan Keikō* (An outline of the recent trend for Koreans living on the homeland to convert to farming).
Nōrinshō Sōmukyoku Tōkeika, 1946, 'Sengo ni okeru waga kuni nōka oyobi nōka jinkō: Nōka jinkō chōsa gaihō (Farming households and farming population in Japan in the postwar periods: A preliminary report on the farming household population)', *Nōrin Tōkei Geppō* (Monthly statistical report on agriculture and forestry), 91.
Nōrinshō Tōkei Chōsabu, 1949, *Ittan Miman Nōka no Gaikyō: 22.8.1 Rinji Nōgyō Sensasu* (The general condition of farming households with less than 1 tan: The special agricultural census of 1 August 1947), Nōrin Tōkei Kyōkai.
Nōseikyoku Nōson Sōmushitsu, 1944a, *Fukuoka-kenka ni okeru Chōsenjin Nōgyōsha no Gaikyō* (Overview of the Korean farmers in Fukuoka Prefecture), October, brochure.
———, 1944b, *Yamaguchi-kenka ni okeru Chōsenjin Nōgyōsha no Gaikyō* (Overview of Korean farmers in Yamaguchi Prefecture), October, brochure.
Nozoe, Kenji, 1976, *Kaitaku Nōmin no Kiroku* (A record of settler-farmers), NHK Books.
O Gisun-san Tsuitō Bunshū Kankō Iinkai (ed.), 1980, *Asa o Miru Koto Naku* (Without seeing the dawn) O Gisun-san Tsuitō Bunshū Kankō Iinkai.
Oh, Gyusang, 2009, *Dokyumento Chōsenjin Renmei: 1945–1949* (Documents on the Alliance of Koreans Living in Japan: 1945–1949), Iwanami Shoten.
Ochi, Dōjun, 1957, *Minami Kashū Nihonjinshi Kōhen* (History of Japanese in Southern California: Part 2), Nanka Nikkeijin Shōgyō Kaigisho.
Oguma, Eiji and Kang, Sangjung (eds.), 2008, *Zainichi Issei no Kioku* (Memories of first generation Zainichi Koreans), Shūeisha Shinsho.
Ōishi, Kaichirō (ed.), 1985, *Kindai Nihon ni okeru Jinushi Keiei no Tenkai* (The development of rural landlords' management in modern Japan), Ochanomizu Shobō.
Ōkado, Masakatsu and Yanagisawa, Asobu, 1996, 'Senji rōdōryoku no kyūgen

to dōin (Supply source and mobilization of labor during wartime)', *Tochi Seido Shigaku* (Journal of agrarian history), 151.

Ōkado, Masakatsu, 2008, *Rekishi e no Toi/Genzai e no Toi* (Questions about history/questions about the present), Azekura Shobō.

Ōkōchi, Kazuo, 1946, 'Kokumin seikatsu no furōka ni tsuite (On the prevalence of homelessness in the lives of people)', *Sekai* (World), 2.

Ōkubo, Yuri, 1996, 'Senjika no Fukuoka-ken Yame Chihō ni okeru Zainichi Chōsenjin: Nōchi Kaihatsu Eidan jigyō o chūshin ni (Zainichi Koreans in the Yame Region of Fukuoka Prefecture during the wartime: Focusing on Agricultural Land Development Corporation projects)', *Zainichi Chōsenjinshi Kenkyū* (Research on the history of Zainichi Koreans), 26.

Osa, Shizue, 2013, *Senryōki, Senryō Kūkan to Sensō no Kioku* (Occupation period, occupation space and war memory), Yūshisha.

Osaka-fu Naimubu, 1927, *Nōgyō Keiei Kaizen Shitei Nōjō Seisekisho* (Performance report on farms designated for improvement of agricultural management), Osaka-fu.

Osaka-fu Nōchibu Nōchika, 1952, *Osaka-fu Nōchi Kaikakushi* (History of agrarian reform in Osaka Prefecture), Osaka-fu.

Osaka-shi Jinken Hakubutsukan and Osaka Kokusai Rikai Kyōiku Kenkyū Sentā, 1999, *Kikigaki Zainichi Korian no Seikatsushi* (Listening and writing: History of Zainichi Koreans), Osaka-shi Jinken Hakubutsukan and Osaka Kokusai Rikai Kyōiku Kenkyū Sentā.

Ōshima, Kiyoshi, 1975, '"Nōgyō Kōryō (Kōryō Iinkai Sōan)" ni Tsuite (On the "Agricultural mission statement (drafted by the Mission Statement Committee)")', *Hōsei Daigaku Ōhara Shakai Mondai Kenkyūjo: Shiryōshitsuhō* (Hosei University Ohara Institute for Social Research: Resource centre report), 217.

Ōtsuki, Masao, 1939, *Kokka Seikatsu to Nōgyō* (National life and agriculture), Iwanami Shoten.

———, 1941, *Nōgyō Rōdōron* (On agricultural labor), Nishigahara Kankōkai.

Ōya, Kazuto (ed.), 2007, *Gunsei (Nanbā MG) Repōto Dai 7-kan Kansai* (Military government (number MG) report Kansai volume 7), Gendai Shiryō Shuppan.

Ozawa, Tomoko, 2009, 'Nisei interpreters/translators of the U. S. military', *Kaigai Ijū Shiryōkan Kenkyū Kiyō* (Journal of the Japanese overseas migration museum), 3.

Park, Chaeil 1957, *Zainichi Chōsenjin ni Kansuru Sōgō Chōsa Kenkyū* (Comprehensive research on Zainichi Koreans), Shinkigensha.

Park, Hyunok, 2005, *Two Dreams in One Bed*, Durham: Duke University Press.

Park, Heonhaeng, 1990, *Kiseki: Aru Zainichi Issei no Hiari to Kage* (The path: Light and dark of one first-generation Korean in Japan), Hihyōsha.

Park, Gyeongsik, 1981, *Zainichi Chōsenjin: Watashi no Seishun* (Zainichi Koreans: My adolescence), San-Ichi Shobō.

Park, Gyeongsik (ed.), 1975, *Zainichi Chōsenjin Kankei Shiryō Shūsei* (Compilation of sources on Zainichi Koreans), 1, San-Ichi Shobō.

———, 2000, *Zainichi Chōsenjin Kankei Shiryō Shūsei (Sengohen)* (Compilation of sources on Zainichi Koreans (Postwar edition)), 1–2, Fuji Shuppan.

―――, 1982, *Chōsen Mondai Shiryō Sōsho* (Series on the materials on Korean problems), 4, San-Ichi Shobō.

Park, Yeongseok, 1981, *Manpōzan Jiken Kenkyū: Nihon Teikoku Shugi no Tairiku Shinryaku Seisaku no Ikkan toshite* (Analysis of the Wanpaoshan Incident: As part of Japanese imperialist continental invasion policy), Daiichi Shobō.

Rakuhoku Kaitaku Jigyō Kyōdō Kumiai et al. (ed.), 1968, *Kaitakushi* (Settlement Chronicle), privately printed.

Rakuhoku Kaitaku Nōgyō Kyōdō Kumiai, 1990, *Takukon: Nyūshoku 40-shūnen Kinen Kaitakushi* (Settler spirit: Commemorative settlers' publication for the 40-year anniversary of settlement), Rakuhoku Kaitaku Nōgyō Kyōdō Kumiai.

Ringhofer, Manfred, 1981, 'Sōaikai: Chōsenjin dōka dantai no ayumi (Mutual Friendship Society: The history of Korean assimilation organizations), *Zainichi Chōsenjinshi Kenkyū* (Research on the history of Zainichi Koreans), 9.

Rōdō Seisaku Kenkyū-Kenshū Kikō, 2007 and 2010, *Dēta Bukku Kokusai Rōdō Hikaku* (Statistical summary of international labor comparisons), Rōdō Seisaku Kekyū-Kenshū Kikō.

Rusu Kazoku Dantai Zenkoku Kyōgikai (ed.), 1959, *Ubawareshi Ai to Jiyū o: Hikiage Sokushin Undō Jūyonen no Kiroku* (Stolen love and freedom: A record of around ten years of the repatriation promotion movement), Kōwadō.

Sagawa, Kazuo (ed.), 1974, *Kyoto Chiji Senkyo: Mae to Ato* (Kyoto prefecture gubernatorial election: Before and after), Shinseiki Seikei Shiryō Bunpukai.

Saitama-ken Heiwa Shiryōkan, 2001, *Kikakuten 'Saitama e Sokai Shita Bunkajintachi'* (Exhibition: 'People of culture who evacuated to Saitama'), pamphlet.

Saitō, Hitoshi, 1989, *Nōgyō Mondai no Tenkai to Jichi Sonraku* (The development of the agricultural problem and autonomous villages), Nihon Keizai Hyōronsha.

―――, 1999, *Nōgyō Mondai no Ronri* (The logic of the agricultural problem), Nihon Keizai Hyōronsha.

Sakaguchi, Mitsuhiro, 2001, *Nihonjin Amerika Iminshi* (History of immigration of Japanese to America), Fujishuppan.

―――, 2012, 'Shutsuimin kenkyū no kadai to hōhō (Themes and methods in emigration studies)', *Kyoto Joshi Daigaku Daigakuin Bungaku Kenkyūka Kenkyū Kiyō Shigakuhen*, 11.

Sakane, Yoshihiro, 2002, 'Nihon ni okeru senjiki nōchi, nōchi seisaku kankei shiryō (2) (Materials related to agricultural land and agricultural land policies in wartime Japan (2))', *Hiroshima Daigaku Keizai Ronsō* (The Hiroshima economic review), 26(1) and (2).

―――, 2011, *Nihon Dentō Shakai to Keizai Hatten (Meicho ni Manabu Chiiki no Kosei 3)*, (Traditional Japanese society and economic development (Learning about the individuality of the regions from great works)), Nōsangyoson Bunka Kyōkai.

Sakata, Yasuo (ed.), 1994, *Nikkei Imin Shiryōshū Dai 1-ki Hokubeihen*

(Compilation of sources on Japanese migrants: Volume 1, North America Edition), Nihon Tosho Center, 15.
Sano, Shinichi, 2012, 'Anpon: Son Masayoshi Den (Anpon: biography of Masayoshi Son)', Shōgakukan.
Sasayama, Shigetarō, 1939, 'Gunjuhin kyūgenchi to shite no nōson (Agricultural villages as the supply source of munitions)', *Nōsei* (Agricultural policy), 1(1).
———, 1978, *Hakuun Kyorai* (White clouds coming and going), Rakuyū Shobō.
Satō, Takumi, 2005, *Hachigatsu Jūgonichi no Shinwa* (The myth of the 15th August), Chikuma Shinsho.
Scholte, Jan Aart and Roland Robertson (eds.), 2007, *Encyclopedia of Globalization*, New York: Routledge.
Sebata, Hajime, 2010, 'Shōwa Tennō "sengo junkō" no saikentō (Reexamination of Emperor Shōwa's "postwar imperial tours")', *Nihonshi Kenkyū* (Japanese historical research), 573.
Sekiguchi, Tetsuya, 2003, 'Shūsen shori katei ni okeru kaku shōkan giron no tenkai (Development of ministerial discussions on postwar processes)', *Hisutoria* (Historia: journal of Osaka Historical Association), 184.
Senda, Shōsaku, 1971, *Nōgyō Koyō Rōdō no Kenkyū* (Research on agricultural employment and labor), Tokyo Daigaku Shuppankai.
Sengo Kaitakushi Hensan Iinkai (ed.), 1967, *Sengo Kaitakushi* (Postwar history of reclamation), Zenkoku Kaitaku Nōgyō Kyōdō Kumiai Rengōkai.
———, 1968, *Sengo Kaitakushi (Shiryōhen)* (Postwar history of reclamation (Sources edition)), Zenkoku Kaitaku Nōgyō Kyōdō Kumiai.
Shibano, Kei, 2010, 'Tengyō kaitakudan no Manshū taiken: "Kashiwazakimura" kaitakudan kankeisha no katari kara (Experiences of the 'tengyo'-settlement in Manchuria: Based on the narratives of ex-emigrants in Kashiwazaki settlement)', *Nōgyōshi Kenkyū* (Journal of agricultural history), 44.
Shimada, Katsuhiko, 2001, 'Senkyūhyaku nijū–sanjū-nendai no toshi ni okeru rōmu kyōkyū ukeoi gyōsha (Labor supply contractors in cities in the 1920–1930s)', *Hisutoria* (Historia), 175.
Shimaki, Kensaku, 1947, *Ōgigayastu Nikki* (Ōgigayatsu Diary), Bunka Hyōronsha.
Shimizu, Ikutarō, 1953, 'Senryō ka no Tennō (Emperor under occupation)' *Shisō* (Thought), 348.
Shimizu, Kaoru, 1967, 'Watashi no ayunda hosomichi (sono jūhachi) (Narrow road I took (vol. 18))', *Gendaijin* (Modern people), 15(11).
Shin, Giwook, 1996, *Peasant Protest and Social Change in Colonial Korea*, Seattle: University of Washington Press.
Shiode, Hiroyuki, 2015, *Ekkyōsha no Seijishi* (A political history of people who cross borders), Nagoya Daigaku Shuppankai.
Shiraishi, Kenji, 1997, *Guwatapara Ijū Jigyō* (Guatapara immigration project), Nihon Tosho Kankōkai.
———, 2001, *Chūnanbei Ijū Jigyō Henreki* (The journey of the Central and South America immigration project), Bungeisha.

Shōji, Shunsaku, 1999, *Nihon Nōchi Kaikakushi Kenkyū* (Studies on the agrarian reform in Japan), Ochanomizu Shobō.
Sonoda, Kōyū, 2008, 'Terada kaikyūki (Memoir of Terada)', in Sankō Kinenshitsu (ed.), *Senchū, Sengo Sankō Shōshi* (The short history of Third High in the wartime and postwar period), Sankō Jishōkai.
Strauss, Anselm L., 1954, 'Strain and harmony in American-Japanese warbride marriages, *Marriage and Family Living*, 16(2), May.
Suenaga, Ryūichi, 1954, 'Sanson ni nobiru rakunō: Kyoto-fu Funai-gun Gomagō-mura (Expansion of dairy farming into mountain villages: Kyoto Prefecture Funai District Gomagō Village)', in Sekisetsu Kanrei Chitai Chijikai (ed.), *Nōson Shinkō no Ayumi* (History of the promotion of the development of rural villages), Nōrin Kyōkai.
Sugihara, Tōru, 1998, *Ekkyōsuru Tami* (People crossing borders), Shinkansha.
———, 2002, *Chūgokujin Kyōsei Renkō* (Forced immigration of Chinese), Iwanami Shoten.
Sugimoto, Hiroyuki, 2015, *Kindai Nihon no Toshi Shakai Seisaku to mainoriti* (Urban social policy and minorities in modern Japan), Shibunkaku.
Sugiura, Minpei, 1954, '*Kichi Roppyakugogō* (Base no. 605)', Kōdansha.
Suzuki, Kumi, 2006, 'Zainichi Chōsenjin no kikan engo jigyō no suii: Shimonoseki, Senzaki no jirei kara (The development of projects to assist repatriation of Zainichi Koreans: Case studies of Shimonoseki and Senzaki)', *Zainichi Chōsenjinshi Kenkyū* (Research on the history of Zainichi Koreans), 36.
Tadekura, Sanroku, 1967, *Shiragiku Ichirin Ōkiku Niou: Ikeda Shikan Den* (A single highly-scented white chrysanthemum: The story of Shikan Ikeda), Shinkōsha.
Takahashi, Kamekichi, 1926, *Meiji Taishō Nōson Keizai no Hensen* (Meiji Taishō: Long-term changes in the economy of agricultural villages), Tōyō Keizai Shinpōsha.
Takano, Akio, 2009, *Kindai Toshi no Keisei to Zainichi Chōsenjin* (Formation of modern cities and Zainichi Koreans), Jinbun Shoin.
Takeda, Junichi, 1929, *Zaibei Hiroshima Kenjinshi* (History of the development of the people from Hiroshima Prefecture), Zaibei Hiroshima Kenjinshi Hakkōjo.
Takemae, Eiji, 1977, 'Nihon senryō no kagi o nigiru otoko: John Aiso kaikenki (A man who holds the key to the occupation of Japan: Interview with John Aiso)', *Chūō Kōron* (The central review), 92(12).
Takemae, Eiji and Nakamura, Takafusa (supervising eds.), 1996, *Jinkō (GHQ Nihon Senryōshi 4)* (The population (History of the non-military activities of the occupation of Japan 4)), trans. Toshio Kuroda and Michiko Ōbayashi, Nihon Tosho Center.
Takemae, Eiji and Nakamura, Takafusa (supervising eds.), 1997, *Nōchi Kaikaku (GHQ Nihon Senryōshi 33)* (The rural land reform (History of the non-military activities of the occupation of Japan 33)), trans. Gōda Kimikazu, Nihon Tosho Center.
Takenaka, Tatsunori, 2007, 'Kyoto Shihan Gakkō Fuzoku Shōgakkō ni okeru Eigo kyōiku (English education in Kyoto Normal School-affiliated Elementary School)', *Nihon Eigo Kyōikushi Kenkyū* (Research into the history of English education in Japan), 22.

Tanaka, Sadamu, 1978, 'Sagaken Nōgyōron (Agricultural arguments in Saga Prefecture)', first published in 1939, *Keizaigaku Kenkyū* (Kyūshū Teikoku Daigaku Keizai Gakkai) (Economics Research (Kyushu Imperial University Economics Society)), 9(3) and (4).
Tanaka, Toyotoshi, 1976, *Ikiteiru Nōkyōshi* (The living history of agricultural cooperatives), Ie no Hikari Kyōkai.
Taniguchi, Zentarō, 1972, *Tsuri no Dekinu Tsurishi* (Fishermen who can't fish), Shin Nihon Shuppansha.
Tatara, Toshio, 1999, *Kyūen Busshi wa Taiheiyō o Koete* (Relief supplies over the Pacific Ocean), Hoken Fukushi Kōhō Kyōkai.
Terayama, Yoshio, 1973, 'Nōgyō Imin Seisaku to Hirakawa Mamoru-shi (Agricultural migration policies and Mr. Mamoru Hirakawa)', *aff: Nōrinshō Kōhō* (aff: Ministry of Agriculture and Forestry PR magazine), 4(9).
——, 1974, 'Shūsenji no nōheitai to Tanigaki Senichi-shi (Farmers' armies at the end of the war and Senichi Tanigaki)', *aff: Nōrinshō Kōhō* (aff: Ministry of Agriculture and Forestry PR magazine), 5(1).
Teruoka, Shūzō (ed.), 2008, *Agriculture in the Modernization of Japan 1850-2000*, trans. Sarah Ham Akamine, New Delhi: Manohar.
Tōa Nōgyō Kenkyūjo, 1942a, *Nōgyō Shinsoshiki Kensetsu ni Kansuru Kyōgikai* (Conference on the establishment of a new agricultural organization), pamphlet.
——, 1942b, *Nōgyō Shinsoshiki ni Kansuru Kyōgikai Keika (Sono-ni)* (Proceedings of the conference on a new agricultural organization (Part 2)), pamphlet.
——, 1943, *Saga Nōgyō no Kenkyū* (Studies of agriculture in Saga), Tōa Nōgyō Kenkyūjo.
Toba, Kōji, 2010, *1950-nendai: Kiroku no Jidai* (The 1950s: The age of reportage), Kawade Shobō Shinsha.
Tobe, Hideaki, 2008, 'Posutokoroniarizumu to teikokushi kenkyū (Studies of post-colonial imperial history), in Nihon Shokuminchi Kenkyūkai (ed.), *Nihon Shokuminchi Kenkyū no Genjō to Kadai* (The present condition of and themes in Japanese studies of colonialism), Atenesha.
Tōda, Shinji, 1967, 'Hikiage to kaitaku no omoide (Memories of settlement and repatriation)', Sengo Kaitakushi Hensan Iinkai (ed.), *Sengo Kaitakushi* (Postwar history of reclamation), Zenkoku Kaitaku Nōgyō Kyōdō Kumiai Rengōkai.
Tokunaga, Mitsutoshi, 1997, *Nihon Nōhōshi Kenkyū* (Studies on Japanese farming practices), Nōsan Gyoson Bunka Kyōkai.
Tōkyō Daikūshū, Sensaishi Henshū Iinkai (ed.), 1973, *Tōkyō Daikūshū, Sensaishi* (Magazine on the history of the Great Tokyo Air Raid and war damage)', 3, Tōkyō Kūshū o Kirokusuru Kai.
Tominaga Bunichi, 1944, 'Kōkoku nōmindō no kakuritsu (Establishment of the Imperial farmers' way)', *Chōsen Nōkaihō* (Korean Agricultural Association bulletin), 18(1).
Tomiyama, Ichirō, 2002, *Bōryoku no Yokan* (Presentiments of violence), Iwanami Shoten.
Tonomura, Masaru, 2004, *Zainichi Chōsenjin Shakai no Rekishigakuteki*

Kenkyū (Historical studies on the Zainichi Korean communities), Ryokuin Shobō.

———, 2006, '"Nihon naichi" zaijū Chōsenjin dansei no kazoku keisei (The family formation of Korean men living on the "Japanese homeland")', in Tsunehisa Abe et al. (eds.), *Modanizumu kara Sōryokusen e (Danseishi 2)* (Modernism to total war (Men's history 2)), Nihon Keizai Hyōronsha.

———, 2012, *Chōsenjin Kyōsei Renkō* (Koreans for Forced Labor), Iwanami Shoten.

Tonooka, Kazuo, 1941, 'Teito jinkō kyūyō no anzen ni shisuru kokudokeikaku no hitsuyō to sono ichian (The need for national land planning that contributes to the safety of a population supply for the Imperial capital, one proposal)', in Jinkō Mondai Kenkyūkai (ed.), *Jinkō, Minzoku, Kokudo* (Population, ethnicity and the national land), Jinkō Mondai Kenkyūkai.

Tsukasaki, Masayuki, 2004, 'Chōsenjin chōhei seido no jittai: Buki o ataerarenakatta "heishi" tachi (Actual conditions of the conscription of Koreans: "Soldiers" who were not provided with weapons)', *Zainichi Chōsenjinshi Kenkyū* (Research on the history of Zainichi Koreans), 34.

Ueno, Terumasa, 1978, 'Sengo Kyoto ni okeru bunka undō to chishikijin (Cultural movement and intellectuals in postwar Kyoto)', *Kōbe Joshi Yakka Daigaku Jinbun Kenkyū Bessatsu* (Kobe Women's College of Pharmacy studies in humanities special issue), 5.

Uesugi, Shinobu, 1998, *Kōminken Undō e no Michi* (Road to the civil rights movement), Iwanami Shoten.

United States Department of Agriculture, 1920, *Census of Agriculture*, USDA Census of Agriculture Historical Archive, Albert R. Mann Library, Cornell University.

Uranishi, Kazuhiko, 2001–2003, 'Kishi Yamaji "nikki" (The "diary" of Yamaji Kishi)', *Kokubungaku* (National literature), Kansai Daigaku Kokubungakkai, 81, 82, 85 and 86.

———, 2009, 'Kishi Yamaji to "Bungaku Annai" (Yamaji Kishi and "Introduction to Literature")', *Chojutsu to Shoshi Dai 2-kan: Gendai Bungaku Kenkyū no Kitei* (Work and bibliography 2: The basis of modern literature research), Izumi Shoin. First published in 2005 in *Bungaku Annai Kaidai, Sōmokuji, Sakuin* (Bibliographical introduction, cumulative contents and indexes of Bungaku Annai), Fuji Shuppan

Ureshino, Masuo, 1980, '"Jiron": Taigadō', in Tamura, Yukio (ed.), *Aru Ikizama no Kiseki* (A trajectory of one way of life), privately printed.

Wakatsuki, Yasuo and Suzuki, Jōji, 1975, *Kaigai Ijū Seisakushiron* (Historical survey of emigration policies), Fukumura Shuppan.

Wakatsuki, Yasuo, 2001, *Gaimushō ga Keshita Nihonjin* (Japanese people who were erased by the Ministry of Foreign Affairs), Mainichi Shinbunsha.

Watanabe, Takashi and Gomi, Fumihiko (eds.), 2002, *Tochi Shoyūshi (Shintaikei Nihonshi 3)* (The history of land ownership (New comprehensive history of Japan 3)), Yamakawa Shuppansha.

Watanabe, Tōru, 1959, *Kyoto Chihō Rōdō Undōshi* (History of labor movement in the Kyoto region), Kyoto Chihō Rōdō Undōshi Hensankai.

Watt, Lori, 2009, *When Empire Comes Home*, Harvard University Asia Center, Cambridge: Harvard University Press.
Welshman, John, 2010, *Churchill's Children*, New York: Oxford University Press.
Wilson, Norman J., 2005, *History in Crisis?* 2*nd* edition, Upper Saddle River: Pearson Prentice Hall.
Yamada, Moritarō, 1949, 'Nōchi kaikaku no rekishiteki igi (Historical significance of the agrarian reform)', in Tadao Yanaihara (ed.), *Sengo Nihon Keizai no Sho Mondai* (Various issues surrounding the postwar Japanese economy), Yūhikaku.
Yamada, Seiichi (ed.), 1948, *Shūsengo no Nōson ni okeru Beisaku Chitai to Tokushu Chitai no Keizai Jōtai no Sai* (Difference between the economic condition of rice-producing areas and special areas in agricultural villages in the postwar periods), Nihon Ginkō.
Yamada, Shōji (ed.), 1978, *Manshū Imin (Kindai Minshū no Kiroku 6)* (Emigration to Manchuria (The record of the masses in the modern era 6)), Shin Jinbutsu Ōraisha.
Yamada, Shōji, Koshō, Tadashi and Higuchi, Yūichi, 2005, *Chōsenjin Senji Rōdō Dōin* (Wartime mobilization of Koreans for labor), Iwanami Shoten.
Yamada, Shinichi, 2011, *Kindai Hokkaidō to Ainu Minzoku* (Modern Hokkaido and Ainu people), Hokkaidō Daigaku Shuppankai.
Yamaguchi, Yaichirō, 1942, 'Yakihata kōsaku ni taisuru hansei to kōgenchi kaihatsu (Reflection on slash-and-burn cultivation and development of high plains)', *Shakai Seisaku Jihō* (Social reform), 256.
Yamanaka, Tokuji, 1941, 'Shokugyō kunren to tairiku kinō (Job training, continental emigration and returning to agriculture)', *Umi o Koete* (Across the sea), July.
Yamashita, Toshirō, 1948, *Senjika ni Okeru Nōgyō Rōdōryoku Taisaku* (Agricultural workforce measures during wartime), 1 and 2, Nōgyō Gijutsu Kyōkai.
Yamawaki, Keizō, 1994, *Kindai Nihon to Gaikokujin Rōdōsha* (Modern Japan and foreign workers), Akashi Shoten.
Yamazaki, Shirō, 2004, 'Senji chū shōkōgyō seibi no tenkai to Kokumin Kōsei Kinko (The progressive wartime curtailment of small and medium-sized commercial and industrial operations and the National Reconstruction Bank)', in Hara, Akira and Yamazaki, Shirō (eds.), *Senji Chūshō Kigyō Seibi Shiryō* (The resources on the small and medium-sized business readjustment), 1, Gendai Shiryō Shuppan.
Yasuoka, Kenichi, 2013, 'Kichi hantai tōsō no seiji (Politics of the anti-base struggle)', in Kimio Noda (ed.), *Nōrin Shigen Kaihatsushiron I* (Discussion on the history of development of agricultural resources I), Kyoto Daigaku Gakujutsu Shuppankai.
———, 2014, 'Bunson no sengo shi (Postwar history of "Branch Villages")' *Shinano*,66 (10).
Yokoyama, Gennosuke, [1899] 1985, *Nihon no Kasō Shakai* (Japan's lower classes), Iwanami Bunko.
Yoneyama, Hiroshi, 2000, '"Nikkei Amerikajin" no sōzō (Creation of

"Japanese Americans")', in Nagao Nishikawa et al. (eds.), *20-seiki o Ikani Koeru ka* (How do we overcome the 20th century?), Heibonsha.

Yoon, Geoncha, 1989, 'Sengo rekishigaku ni okeru tasha ninshiki (Awareness of others in the postwar study of Japanese history)', *Rekishigaku Kenkyū* (Journal of historical studies).

Yoshizawa, Kayoko, 2003, 'Naichi haken Chōsen Nōgyō Hōkokutai: Hakensaki naichi o chūshin ni (Korean Agricultural Patriotic Service dispatched to mainland Japan: Focusing on the dispatch destination), in Kan Dokusan Sensei Koki Taishoku Kinen Ronbunshū Kankō Iinkai (ed.), *Nicchō Kankeishi Ronshū* (Essay collection on the history of Japan-Korea relations), Shinkansha.

Young, Louise, 1998, *Japan's Total Empire*, Berkeley: University of California Press.

Zadankai, 1949, 'Kaitaku sanshūnen kinen zadankai kiji (Proceedings of the third anniversary of reclamation commemorative discussions)', *Kaitaku Kenkyū* (Reclamation Studies), 2(3).

Zadankai, 1978, 'Tasūha no undō to sono jidai (The movement of the majority and its time)', *Undōshi Kenkyū* (Research on the history of movements), 1.

Zai Man Nihon Taishikan, 1935, *Shōwa Jūnen Zaiman Chōsenjin Gaikyō* (The general condition of Koreans in Manchuria in 1935).

Zainihon Daikanminkoku Kyoryū Mindan Osaka-fu Chihō Honbu, 1980, *Mindan Osaka 30-nenshi* (The 30-year history of Mindan Osaka), Zainihon Daikanminkoku Kyoryū Mindan Osaka-fu Chihō Honbu.

Zenkoku Shakai Fukushi Kyōgikai (ed.), 1964, *Minsei Iin Seido Yonjūnenshi* (40 years of the Welfare Commissioners' system), Zenkoku Shakai Fukushi Kyōgikai.

Zenkoku Takushoku Nōgyō Kyōdō Kumiai Rengōkai, 1958, *Nōgyō Ijūsha Sōshutsuson Jittai Chōsa Hōkoku* (Report of a factual investigation into villages that sent agricultural migrants).

———, 1961, *Kaigai Nōgyō Ijū* (Overseas agricultural migration), Zenkoku Takushoku Nōgyō Kyōdō Kumiai Rengōkai.

Zennō Seinenbu Osakafuren, 1931, 'Nōgyō rōdōsha soshiki ni tsuite (Regarding farm worker organizations)', *Nōmin Tōsō* (Peasants' struggle), 14.

Periodicals in Japanese

Asahi Shinbun; *Ehime Shinbun*; *Osaka Asahi Shinbun*; *Osaka Shinbun*; *Kaigai Ijū Tōkei* (Emigration statistics); *Kaitaku Nōmin Shinbun* (Settler-farmer news); *Kaihō Shinbun* (Liberation news); *Kyoto Shinbun*; *Kyoto no Hata*; *Kyoto Hinode Shinbun*; *Kyoto-fu Kaitaku Nyūsu* (Kyoto Prefecture reclamation news); *Kyoto-fu Kōhō* (Gazette of Kyoto Prefecture); *Kyoto Nichinichi Shinbun*; *Kyōren Renrakuhō* (Newsletter of the Kyoto Federation) [by Kyoto-fu Kaigai Hikiage Dōhō Renmei]; *Kokusai Shinbun*; *Kokusei Chōsa Hōkoku* (National census report); *Sangyō Kōzō Kihon Chōsa* [by Sōri-fu Tōkeikyoku]; *Zairyū Gaikokujin Tōkei* (Statistics of foreign residents); *Shiga-ken*

Nōkaihō (Report of the Shiga Prefecture Agricultural Association); *Shisō Geppō* (Monthly report on thought); *Shinano Mainichi Shinbun*; *Junkan Tairiku Dōhō* (Thrice-monthly continental compatriots); *Shakai Undō no Jōkyō* [by Naimushō Keihokyoku (Police Bureau, Ministry of Home Affair)]; *Shashin Shūhō* (Weekly photographic journal); *Shōwa Jūgo-nen Kokusei Chōsa Hōkoku Genpyō* (Original statistical tables of the 1940 national census); *Taishū Shinbun*; *Chōsen Nōkaihō* (Korean Agricultural Association bulletin); *Joseon eui Byul* (Stars of Korea) [by Nihon Kyōsantō Kantō Chihō Iinkai]; *Dōmei Jihō* (Alliance reviews) [by Zaigai Fukei Kyūshutsu Gakusei Dōmei]; *Tōkyō Asahi Shinbun*; *Tokushima Shinbun*; *Teikoku Nōkaihō* (Imperial Agricultural Association bulletin); *Tokkō Geppō* (Special Higher Police monthly bulletin); *Tokkō Gaiji Geppō* (Special Higher Police monthly bulletin of external affairs); *Nanshin*; *Niigata Nippō*; *Nichibei Jiji* (Nichi bei times); *New Canadian*; *Nakagyō Nyūsu* [by Kyoto-fu Kaigai Hikiage Dōhō Renmei Nakagyō Shibu]; *Nihon Nōgyō Nenkan* (Japan agricultural yearbook); *Nōgyō Oyobi Engei* (Agriculture and horticulture); *Nōgyō Chōsa Kekka Hōkokusho* (Report on Agricultural survey results) [by Nōrinshō Nōrin Keizaikyoku Tōkeichōsabu]; *Nōgyō Dōtai Chōsa Zenkoku Kekka Gaiyō* (Outline of national results of the agricultural surveys); *Nōchi Kaikaku Shitsumu Sankō* (Administrative references for agrarian reform work); *Nōrinshō Tōkei Hyō* (Ministry of Agriculture and Fisheries statistical tables); *Hawai Hōchi*; *Hōmu Sōsai Iken Nenpō* (Attorney General annual report of opinions fiscal year); *Minsei Shinbun* (People's Welfare Newspaper) [by Kyoto-fu Kaigai Hikiage Dōhō Renmei]; *Murazukuri* (Village-making); *Yamaguchi-ken Nōkaihō* (Report of the Yamaguchi Prefecture Agricultural Association); *Yūkan Kyoto*; *Yomiuri Shinbun*; *Yomiuri Hōchi*; *Rakunan Taimusu*; *Rafu Shinpō*.

Periodicals in Korean

Haeban Shinmun (Kaihō Shinbun); Daejung Shinmun (*Taishū Shinbun*).

Administrative documents

Diplomatic Archives of the Ministry of Foreign Affairs of Japan
Administrative documents of Kyoto Prefecture [Kyoto Prefectural Library and Archives]
National Institute for Defense Studies Military Archives
Administrative documents of Ibaraki Prefecture [Ibaraki Prefectural Museum of History]
Terada Village documents and the Farm Land and Agricultural Committees documents [Joyo City Folk Heritage Museum]
Administrative documents of Tottori Prefecture [Tottori Prefectural Library and Archives]

Administrative documents of Osaka Prefecture [Osaka Prefecture Archives]
Documents of Tatsuoka Office [Iida City Institute of Historical Research]
Administrative documents of Hiroshima Prefecture [Hiroshima Prefectural Archives]

Documents preserved by relevant organizations

Osaka-fu Kaitakumin Jikōkai Bunsho (Documents of the Osaka Prefectural Settlers' Self-support Association), Osaka-fu Jikōkai.
Noda Tetsugorō Papers, Zenkoku Kaitaku Shinkō Kyōkai.
Mōri Hideoto Papers, National Diet Library Modern Japanese Political History Materials Room (Kensei-shiryōshitsu).
Shimosaka Masahide Papers, the Ohara Institute for Social Research

Internet

Densho, The Japanese American Legacy Project (https://densho.org/)
Kishi Yamaji net Siryokan (Kishi yamaji online archive) (http://www.kisiyamaji.com/)
Kokkai Kaigiroku (Proceedings of the National Diet of Japan)
Japan Center for Asian Historical Records
Marxists Internet Archive
National Archives of Japan Digital Archive
Teikoku Gikai Kaigiroku (Database System for the Minutes of the Imperial Diet)

Interview participants

Arakawa Sueo, Itō Jun, Ōishi Masami, Kuroda Masao, Sagawa Kimiya, Sōi Michio, Tamura Hisae, Tokuyasu Hirotoshi, Hata Shūzō, Hanashiro Takeo, Hayashi Makoto, Hirano Tsuyako, Maehara Hidehiko, Murata Shinkichi, and members of the Association of Families Concerned with the Kyoto Byōrei Village Reclamation Group (Byōrei Kyōto Kaitakudan Kazoku no Kai)

Name Index

Aiso, John 207, 313
Akazawa, Shirō 13
Amemiya, Shōichi 12
Asahara, Rokurō 113

Baldwin, Roger 203
Benhabib, Seyla 14

Eguchi, Kan 100

Fujita, Shōzō 12

Hashimoto, Denzaemon 151
Hirakawa, Mamoru 235, 251, 270, 288, 297
Hirano, James 204, 210
Hirooka, Shinichi 205–207

Ikoma, Takatsune 151
Ishiguro, Tadaatsu 18–19, 52–54, 270, 277–278, 288
Ishii, Einosuke 52, 270

Jeong, Seunbak 18, 275

Katō, Kanji 246
Kawano, Shigetō 63, 278
Kimata, Shūsui 166–167, 172, 301
Kishi, Yamaji (real name Itō Kōichi) 16–17, 94–95, 97–105, 108, 112–114, 117, 120–126, 128–140, 177, 255, 264, 287
Kishida, Kunio 94
Kitagawa, Kenzō 13
Kiyotani, Masuji 220
Kobayashi, Takiji 135
Kodaira, Gonichi 151, 237–238
Kohiyama, Naoto 155
Komagome, Takeshi 10
Kōno, Ichirō 235
Kurahara, Korehito 122, 287
Kurihara, Hakuju 8

Maehara, Sekisaburō 175–176, 178, 184, 296
Maruyama, Masao 146
Maruyama, Yoshiji 102, 294
Masaoka, Mike 216
Minakami, Tsutomu 282
Miyamoto, Tsuneichi 282
Mizoguchi, Saburō 107, 277
Mori, Takemaro 11
Morishige, Tateo 151
Morita, Sōhei 94
Mukaeda, Katsuma 204, 209

Nakamura, Kōjirō 152, 242
Nakamura, Satoru 26
Nakano, Shigeharu 90, 100, 122
Namiki, Masayoshi 231, 233

Nasu, Shiroshi 238, 270
Ninagawa, Torazō 137, 302
Nishida, Yoshiaki 7
Noda, Kimio 10, 192–193
Noda, Ritsuta 100
Nosaka, Sanzō 173
Nozoe, Kenji 295

Oh, Gisun 78
Ōkado, Masakatsu 13
Ōtsuki, Masao 9, 26, 270

Putnam, Emilie 169

Sagawa, Kazuo 166–167, 301
Saitō, Hitoshi 8
Sakaguchi, Mitsuhiro 9, 212
Sasayama, Shigetarō 119, 128, 148

Shimaki, Kensaku 92
Shimizu, Ikutarō 145
Shōriki, Matsutarō 102
Sō, Mitsuhiko 151, 176
Sugino, Tadao 227

Takayama, Gizō 166, 302
Tanaka, Sadamu 8, 35–36
Taneya, Seizō 237
Taniguchi, Zentarō 97, 114, 117, 121, 126, 140
Teruoka, Shūzō 7

Waguri, Hiroshi 148, 150, 236
Wakatsuki, Yasuo 226, 239, 251

Yamazoe, Risaku 82, 311
Yoon, Geoncha 5
Yoshikawa, Eiji 102

Subject Index

Administration Bureau,
  Ministry of Foreign
  Affairs 148–149, 150–151,
  188, 236, 297
agrarian racism 278
Agricultural Administration
  Bureau, Ministry
  of Agriculture and
  Forestry 52, 54–55, 64, 82,
  106–107, 119, 198–199, 278,
  310–311, 313
Agricultural Association 49,
  119, 150, 294
Agricultural Basic Act 233
Agricultural Co-operatives
  Act 295
Agricultural Economics Society
  of Japan 54
Agricultural Land
  Committee 79, 84–85, 95,
  97, 121, 128, 130, 168,
  198–199, 209, 215, 221–222,
Agricultural Land Development
  Corporation 106, 111–112,
  114–115, 117–119, 121, 123,
  141, 255, 279, 292, 294, 297
Agricultural Land Development
  Law 106, 130
Agricultural Patriotic Service
  Youth Corps 51
Ainu 14, 263
Alien Land Law 209, 213–214,
  218

Alien Registration
  Ordinance 81
All-Japan Settlers' League 121,
  126, 135, 152, 321
All-Kyoto Democratic
  Front Unification
  Conference 137, 167
American Civil Liberties
  Union 203
Association for International
  Collaboration of
  Farmers 151, 226, 238
autonomous villages 8

bereaved families 160, 170,
  175, 308
Association of Bereaved
  Families 13
birth control 231, 247, 252, 265
black market 79, 136, 284
bunson (branch village) 245,
  248, 251
bunson imin (emigrating in
  groups to establish a
  branch village) 17, 177,
  183, 243

Cabinet Legislation
  Bureau 244
Cabinet Planning Board 48,
  87, 288
California Alien Land
  Law 194, 202, 312

353

ceased working 108, 289–290
Central Federation of Repatriate
   Groups (*Hikiagesha Dantai
   Chūō Rengō Kai*) 300
Central Union of Agricultural
   Cooperatives (*Zenchū*) 243,
   245
Civil Property Custodian
   (CPC) 198, 210, 215
Civil Rights Defense
   Union 202–204
Colonization Division, Ministry
   of Agriculture and
   Forestry 234, 240
Committee for Compatriots
   Living in Enemy
   Countries 217
common people 266–267, 270
Compatriots' Relief
   Association 175, 294
concrete feeling (*jikkan*) 12
construction camps 37, 44
Cotia Youth Migration 243
Council for Overseas
   Emigration 237, 239
Curtailment of Business
   Operations Ordinance 104

depopulation 228, 234
discrimination 168, 171, 174,
   180, 188, 202, 229, 260,
   265, 278–279, 284, 308, 316,
   321

economic revitalization 235,
   241
 economic revitalization
   movement 236, 243, 251
Economic Revitalization
   Section, All Japan

Federation of Youth
   Groups 317
Emergency Measures
   Controlling Movement into
   Urban Areas 134
Emigrants Protection Act 240
Emigration Bureau, Ministry of
   Foreign Affairs 240
equal sharing of war
   sacrifices 156, 165
evacuation (*sokai*) 90, 92–95,
   98, 105, 109, 112–113, 131,
   139–140, 286
evacuees 15

family registers (*koseki*) 164
farmhand 273 *see* '*sakuotoko*'
Federation of Agricultural
   Cooperatives for
   Colonization 235, 243–248
Federation of Japan Overseas
   Associations 237
Federation of Kyoto
   Prefecture Repatriates'
   Cooperatives 167
feminization of the
   workforce 50, 234, 259
Foreign Investment
   Committee 84

gaichi (external territories) 92
Greater East Asia Ministry 148,
   188, 236, 247
Hanshin Educational
   Struggle 83, 293, 295
Heian Village Settlement
   Group 116, 292
homeland 9–10, 15–16, 19, 22,
   25, 50, 53, 92, 108–110, 141,
   158, 256, 260, 263–264

Subject Index

Honolulu Chamber of
    Commerce 199
human trafficking 2, 231, 268

imperial tours 143–146,
    172–175, 177–178, 190
imperial villages 10, 261
Implementation Outline for
    Urban Evacuation 91, 110
'in group' 220
Information Board 104
Īrin Yamashiro Settlement
    Group 181, 183–184

'Japan and Korea as one body
    see 'Naisen Ittai'
Japan Communist Party 48,
    83, 96–97, 100, 122, 137,
    141, 155, 164, 166, 276,
    284, 287
Japan Emigration Service 239
Japan Farmers' Union 83,
    124–125, 130, 135
Japan Proletarian Writers'
    League (Writers'
    League) 96, 99, 101, 104,
    275, 287
Japan Reclamation
    Association 128
Japan Settler-farmers'
    League 126, 136
Japan Socialist Party 164, 166,
    302
Japanese American Citizens'
    League (JACL) 203–204,
    213–214
Japanese Literature Patriotic
    Association 104
Japanese Refugees' Relief
    Committee 199

Japanese Students' Overseas
    Emigration League 227
Jōnan Plant 78, 179–182, 184,
    306

Kokutai no Hongi
    (Fundamentals of Our
    National Polity) 4
Kōminka (imperialization) 278
Korea Agricultural Patriotic
    Service Youth Corps 19
Korean War 264
Kyoto Association of Taiwan
    Repatriates 157, 163, 166
Kyoto Branch of the National
    Salvation League for
    Democracy 166
Kyoto Byōrei Village
    Reclamation Group 116,
    181, 292
Kyoto Democratic Party
    166–167
Kyoto Military
    Government 165
Kyoto Prefectural Settler-
    farmers' Cooperative
    176–177
Kyoto Prefecture Confederation
    of Fellow Overseas
    Repatriates 163–164
Kyoto Prefecture Federation
    of Fellow Overseas
    Repatriates 157, 163, 300
Kyoto Repatriates' Political
    Alliance 164, 166–168
Kyoto Prefectural Settler-
    farmers' Unions 128,
    136–137, 167
Kyoto Settlers' Self-support
    Association 175

Kyōwakai (Concordia Society) 62, 72–73, 76, 88, 280–281

landlord 15, 17, 26, 41, 48, 50, 62, 64–65, 72–73, 81–82, 129, 182, 192, 276–277, 309, 314
landlord system 7, 77, 89, 254, 261, 269
Absentee landlords 4, 17, 82, 193, 195–196, 198–200, 202–209, 211–214, 216–220, 241, 262, 286, 312–314, 316
Absentee Landlords Rally 204
repatriated landlord 214, 309
small landlord 130
land-owner 18
Law Concerning Special Measures for the Establishment of Owner-farmers 84, 196, 198, 201
League of Koreans Residing in Japan 80–83, 281, 283–284
Liberal Party of Japan 164, 166
Licensed Agencies for Relief in Asia (LARA) 195

Manchukuo Repatriates' Relief Association 150
Manchuria 17, 29–30, 53, 87, 108, 116, 129, 133, 142–144, 146, 148, 155, 182–183, 188, 235–236, 241, 247–249, 256, 315

Manchuria and Mongolia Compatriots' Relief Association 150–151, 155
Manchuria Colonization Bureau 148, 235
Manchurian Development Corporation 119, 151–152, 242, 298
Manchurian Immigration Council 151, 289
Manchurian Youth Corps Brigade 149, 175, 177–179, 183–184, 282, 304–305
mechanization 48, 233
mixed marriage 278
mixed residence 24
Movement to Establish Imperial Farming Villages 51, 88, 277

Naisen Ittai (Japan and Korea as one body) 53, 76
National Agricultural Associations 151, 153
National Farmers' Union 46, 48, 72, 275, 280
National Federation of Overseas Repatriates 156
National Federation of Repatriate Groups 300
National General Mobilization Law 107, 116
National Salvation League for Democracy 167
National Settlers Self-support Association 151–152, 176–177
nationalist Japanese (*Nihonshugi*) 48

Subject Index

nation-state 1–2, 4, 14–15, 22, 143
Natural Resource Section, GHQ 128, 135–136, 198, 203
neighborhood association 77, 168–169, 290
New Japan Literary Society 97
Newspaper Industry Ordinance 103
Nichinō see 'Japan Farmers' Union'
*n*ōhonshugi (the idea that agriculture should form the basis of Japan's economic and social life) 4–5, 259

Okinawans 14
'On the Matter of the Acquisition of Property by Foreigners' 84
Oriental Development Company 87, 119
others 4–6, 9, 14, 65, 86, 95, 141, 190–191, 195, 227, 254, 257, 263, 267
'out group' 220
Outline for the Acceleration of General Evacuation 110
Outline for the Implementation of Emergency Land Reclamation 119, 142, 147, 188, 196
Outline for the Implementation of Settlement Operations 135, 153
Outline of Emergency Measures for the Decisive Battle 104, 110
Outline of Emergency Measures Regarding the Employment of City Evacuees in Farming 111, 188
Overseas Emigration Colloquium 237

Patriotic Agricultural Association 19, 53
Peace Preservation Law 96, 98–99, 275, 307
Peace Treaty 81, 304, 306
Personnel Office, Ministry of Agriculture and Commerce 106, 119, 148
Plan for Establishing Population Measures 51–52
Police Affairs Bureau, Ministry of Home Affairs 24, 31, 49
population 2, 51–53, 62, 87, 143, 221, 228–229, 231, 250, 259, 268, 289
  ageing population 234, 250, 260, 317
  surplus population 30, 78, 88, 226, 241, 243, 247
population problem 233–234, 247, 250, 252, 265
Potsdam Declaration 120
Promotion Bureau, Ministry of Agriculture and Forestry 245
'prospects' 266
Public Assistance Act 157, 168, 170, 299
Pumasi (traditional Korean agricultural labor exchange practice) 76

(putting down) roots 29, 63, 140, 146, 156, 159, 253, 255

Rakuhoku Settlers' Agricultural Cooperative Union 176, 184–186
rearmament 264, 306
Reclamation Bureau, Ministry of Agriculture and Forestry 106–107, 119, 128, 136, 142, 147–148, 152, 188, 235–236, 297
red repatriates 296
Repatriate Relief Authority 149, 283, 300
Repatriated Manchurian Settlers' Remedial Treatment Plan 149–150, 153
Repatriates' Political Alliance 166–168
Repatriation Relief Authority 283
Resolution Regarding the Population Problem 231
return to farming 17, 88, 93, 95, 105–109, 111–113, 116–117, 120, 292, 134, 139
  Head Office of Return to Farming 106, 111, 119–120
Rice Riots 27
sakuotoko (male farmhand) 26, 30–31, 33, 255
second and third sons 226, 253
semi–repatriates 164
Senki (Battle Flag) 102, 275
Settlement Division, Ministry of Agriculture and Forestry 238

Settlement Research Institute 152
Settlers Division, Ministry of Foreign Affairs 150
Settlers' Relief Association 151–152, 179
Settlers' Self-support Association 178, 184, 236
Mutual Friendship Society 274
source of the nation 4, 52, 53, 255, 260
South Manchuria Railway 155
Special Higher Police Unit 65, 70
spiritual demobilization 146
structural improvement policies 233
Student Alliance to Rescue Orphans and Fellow Compatriots Left Overseas 159, 171

Taishō Democracy 72, 193
Taiwan Development Corporation 119
Tanba Ariran (Tanba Arirang) 115, 141
tenant dispute 25, 37
Tōjō cabinet 12–13, 104, 119, 155
toshiyatoi (laborers hired by the year, or servants) 26
trainee 276
  agricultural trainee 41, 49
  trainee system 87

war victims 12–13, 92, 95, 123–124, 128–129, 133–134, 137, 141, 153, 155–160, 165–166, 168, 170, 174–175,

178, 181–182, 190, 299, 304, 306
war widows 13
Wartime Damages Protection Act 157, 180
welfare commissioner 157, 168–170, 282, 298, 303
Writers' League *see* 'Japan Proletarian Writers' League'

yosomono (stranger) 5 *see* 'others', 'out group'

Zainichi Koreans 14, 19–20, 31, 77–78, 81–82, 84–85, 171, 219, 229, 277, 279
Zenkoku Nōmin Kumiai (*Zennō*) *see* 'National Farmers' Union'
Zenkoku Takushoku Nōgyō Kyōdō Kumiai Rengōkai (*Zentakuren*) *see* 'Federation of Agricultural Cooperatives for Colonization'

www.ingramcontent.com/pod-product-compliance
Lightning Source LLC
Chambersburg PA
CBHW060939230426
43665CB00015B/1998